PENGUIN BOOKS

# MANHATTAN MEMOIR

A former magazine editor and longtime member of *The New York Times* editorial board, Mary Cantwell lived in Greenwich Village.

# MANHATTAN MEMOIR

*American Girl*

*Manhattan, When I Was Young*

*Speaking with Strangers*

# MARY CANTWELL

PENGUIN BOOKS

PENGUIN BOOKS
Published by the Penguin Group
Penguin Putnam Inc., 375 Hudson Street, New York, New York 10014, U.S.A.
Penguin Books Ltd, 27 Wrights Lane, London W8 5TZ, England
Penguin Books Australia Ltd, Ringwood, Victoria, Australia
Penguin Books Canada Ltd, 10 Alcorn Avenue, Toronto, Ontario, Canada M4V 3B2
Penguin Books (N.Z.) Ltd, 182–190 Wairau Road, Auckland 10, New Zealand

Penguin Books Ltd, Registered Offices:
Harmondsworth, Middlesex, England

This volume first published in Penguin Books 2000

1 3 5 7 9 10 8 6 4 2

*American Girl* first published in the United States of America by
Random House, Inc., 1992
Reprinted by arrangement with Random House, Inc.
Published in Penguin Books 1993
Copyright © Mary Cantwell, 1992
All rights reserved

*Manhattan, When I Was Young* first published in the United States of America by
Houghton Mifflin Company 1995
Reprinted by arrangement with Houghton Mifflin Company
Published in Penguin Books 1996
Copyright © Mary Cantwell, 1995
All rights reserved

*Speaking with Strangers* first published in the United States of America by
Houghton Mifflin Company 1998
Reprinted by arrangement with Houghton Mifflin Company
Published in Penguin Books 1999
Copyright © Mary Cantwell, 1998
All rights reserved

LIBRARY OF CONGRESS CATALOGING-IN-PUBLICATION DATA
Cantwell, Mary.
Manhattan memoir / Mary Cantwell.
p.   cm.
First work originally published: New York : Random House, 1992. 2nd work
originally published: Boston : Houghton Mifflin, 1995. 3rd work originally
published: Boston : Houghton Mifflin, 1998.
Contents: American girl—Manhattan, when I was young—Speaking with
strangers.
ISBN 0 14 02.9190 3
1. Cantwell, Mary. 2. Manhattan (New York, N.Y.)—Biography. 3 New York
(N.Y.)—Biography. 4. Cantwell, Mary—Childhood and youth. 5. Bristol
(R.I.: Town)—Biography. 6. Bristol (R.I. : Town)—Social life and customs.
7. Cantwell, Mary—Journeys. 8. Voyages and travels. I. Title.
F128.54.C36.A3     2000     974.5'5042'092—dc21            99-052553

Printed in the United States of America
Set in Sabon
Designed by Cathryn Aison

# ❖ CONTENTS ❖

# AMERICAN GIRL:

*Scenes from a Small-Town Childhood*

FOR THE FAMILY
THAT LIVED AT 232 HOPE STREET

◈ **P R E F A C E** ◈

*I* STARTED TELLING THE STORIES a long time ago because they gave color and shape to someone who, for a while, was invisible to herself. She was a young woman who lived in New York and was married to a young man who looked a lot like Montgomery Clift. But the young woman couldn't locate herself either in New York City or in her marriage. It was only when she talked about the town in which she grew up that she could find her place on the map.

Every morning this young woman got out of bed, dressed and walked a few blocks with her husband to a corner where they waited for the Madison Avenue bus. Before she took the elevator to her office (she was a secretary on a fashion magazine) she waited on line in the coffee shop downstairs for a blueberry muffin and black coffee. The muffin stuck to the roof of her mouth and she would never really like coffee, but breakfast at one's desk seemed to her a New York thing. She wanted very much to do the New York thing.

At noon she wandered through stores like Bloomingdale's and B. Altman for white sale sheets and blankets, and at night she stopped at a grocery store for Kraft's Seven-Minute Macaroni Dinner and the occasional veal scallopini. She had no idea how to cook except from a book her husband had given her called *Quick and Easy Meals for Two*. But he liked everything she turned out:

He was serious about domesticity. She was not serious about any-thing because no one thing struck her as any more important than any other.

When they went to bed she took off her wedding ring before turning off the lamp and pulling up the sheets. That way she could forget that she had committed herself to a lifetime under the body that, like clockwork, turned to hers the minute the light was out. In the morning her husband looked at her from eyes in which hurt and trust were inextricably and permanently mixed, and she sees them now as sharply as she did then.

But all that is another tale, and one that's too painful to tell. In any case it comes down to just one sentence: In marrying that par-ticular young man that young woman had traveled too far from home.

That was, as I said, a long time ago. But I go on telling the sto-ries, though now I tell them only to myself. A silly habit, I suppose, but there it is. On insomniac nights my lips move and a soundless voice says "One day Ganny and I were walking toward the dry-goods store when . . ."

## One

AROUND SIX O'CLOCK of a Friday afternoon, three or four weekends a year, I travel the subway from Times Square to Penn Station. If it is summer, and it usually is, the stairs down to the hole in the ground are ripe with the stench of urine. I clutch the railing hard and stiffen my shoulders, prepared for the shove in the back, the grab at the purse, and my eyes are everywhere and nowhere. It isn't wise to be caught looking at anybody in Times Square, and even less wise not to be looking at everybody. Sooner or later in New York one learns the trick of the blind, all-seeing gaze.

The subway is jammed and so is the lower level of Penn Station, where the commuters are flowing toward the stripped-down, sliding-door trains that will take them to Long Island and backyard cookouts. The upper level, with its long curve of ticket windows and big waiting room, is jammed too, but not necessarily with travelers. Some people are simply waiting out the day, and night, their backs to the signboard. But I'm watching it, watching for The Merchants Limited  Track  13  On Time  and the dispatcher's sonorous "Stopping at Rye, Stamford, Bridgeport, New Haven, New London, Kingston, Providence, Route 128, and South Station, Boston."

When the train is announced I move with the speed of long practice and zigzag down the dingy iron stairs to the platform. Within minutes I find a seat, shove my bag into the overhead rack, put on my reading glasses (I have only just acquired them) and bury myself in a book. I have traveled a great deal, and almost always alone, so I am adept at settling in, getting comfortable.

Oblivious to the tunnel and fleeting Westchester and the frequenters of the lavatories and the café car who lurch up and down the aisles, I read until New Haven, where the train halts while it goes from diesel to electric. Or is it from electric to diesel? The lights go out then, and there is nothing to do but stare out the window at the posters for Broadway shows and try to picture where those who are getting off are going.

I might have lived in New Haven: When I was nineteen I had a boyfriend there. He had fair hair and a camel's-hair polo coat, a heavyweight's shoulders and a hound's thirst, and when he danced his feet skimmed the floor. My children can't believe that a woman, a girl, like me, could ever have liked a man, a boy, like him. He doesn't seem, could never have been, their bookish mother's type. But, then, they never saw the width of his shoulders in his camel's-hair coat, or the lazy stretch of his long gray-flannel legs.

We have been traveling about an hour and a half now, and as far as I'm concerned the trip—though it isn't literally so—is halfway over. Because once we leave New Haven we will be entering my country.

Except in June, when wild red roses reach toward the tracks, my country is somber when seen from the windows of a train. The landscape is sepia-toned and the water that laps the occasional stretch of lonely beach is a dull, dense blue. The houses are small and sober. Those near the beaches are standing on stilts and those in the hollows have above-ground pools. Those nearest the tracks have roller shades at the windows, and limp curtains. Where there are trees they are up to their shins in ferns, and where there are reeds it is muddy, and there are waterfowl.

The traffic in the aisles is a trickle now. Many of the passengers are dozing, their heads wedged into odd and impossible corners. But I am wide awake, straining to see beyond the glass, beyond the night. Ah, the train is moving again, the lights are on, a few people have returned to their books. Not I. This is where I start to count milestones.

Here's Old Saybrook and its long, low bridge—I sailed under

that bridge once—and here's New London. "Look," I would say if
I had anyone to say it to, "look up there to the left. See that tall
smokestack? That's where I went to college." In an oatmeal-
colored tweed suit with silver buttons, from Best & Company.

The trains were nicer in those days, and had dining cars with
slick starched tablecloths and bud vases. Their tiny kitchens served
what everybody said was the best broiled scrod you could get anywhere, and ice cubes clinked in the sweaty silver pitchers. This
train has no dining car, no glassed-off sections in which businessmen and secretaries off on a toot can drink old-fashioneds and
smoke till the air is blue. Now all anybody drinks is diet soda and
New York State wine in screw-top bottles, and there's a crumpled
potato-chip bag in every other seat pocket.

The train is picking up speed, or maybe it is I who am picking
up speed, and the stations are becoming blurs. Here's Westerly—
there used to be a good ice-cream place in Westerly—and South
Kingston, where my sister went to school, and Wickford, which is
rich and boaty. Here's the Gorham Silver plant, and a huge, flat-
roofed store called Ann and Hope, and here's the scattering of
gawky multi-family clapboards that is New England's way of announcing urban sprawl. Another hour or so and I will be in what
mothers from time immemorial have called "your own little bed."

The train is slowing down, the conductor has pinned back the
doors between cars, and a few of the passengers, half-asleep, are
taking down their Samsonites and duffels and garment bags. It's
time to disembark, time to walk down a long steep hill in a city that
is always choked with damp to a bus shelter that stands lighted and
lonely in front of City Hall. It's late, and I will be on the last bus of
the evening.

Sometimes kids are sitting in the back of the bus drinking from
beer cans stashed in paper bags, hilarious after a night on the town.
But for the most part the passengers are regulars heading home at
the end of the late shift, who greet the driver familiarly and stare
sleepily through the window as the bus swings out of the station.
One by one they are dropped off at corners and gas stations and
bus shelters in the middle of nowhere. " 'Night," they call back to
him as they step off into the dark. " 'Night," he calls out after
them.

We have traveled about seventeen miles, through flat fields and solitary houses and sudden spreads of water, when, at last, we cross a kind of causeway. On the right a harbor is glinting darkly; on the left a pond is silver as a coin. The trees close in and hide the harbor, and after several blocks of houses, Victorian mostly, a white marble school building and a mansion behind a long, wrought-iron fence, we enter a small business district. There are no lights in any of the stores, no passersby, and few cars. A blink, and we're out of it, and the trees have closed in on us again.

It's near midnight now and the bus is almost empty. Wait! There's my stop, that corner, beside the brick wall. I pull the cord, collect my bag and walk to the front of the bus, fearful the driver will go right past it. The brakes shudder, the door whumps, and I step off into air that smells like the air coming off the Hudson. Only this air is ten times saltier and has a green top note.

Across the street a light is burning over a doorway reached by a tall flight of stairs. The house, too, is tall, and white, and riding peacefully at anchor. Downstairs is dark: My aunt, who is serene in the belief that I am sure to get there, wherever "there" may be, has been asleep for hours. Upstairs, however, is blazing from stem to stern. My mother, who has no such certainty, is thumbing through a magazine, ears pricked for the sound of the bus as it hurtles toward Newport, and the abrupt wheeze that tells her it's stopped to let somebody off.

Behind me the harbor is whispering softly, and above me the trees are rattling in a light breeze. I look cautiously to the left and to the right—at this hour there's little traffic, but you never know—and as I do I feel my body growing lighter by many years, many pounds. The breeze is lifting them off and carrying them out over the water—out past Hog Island and Prudence Island and all the way to Narragansett Bay. I sling my bag over my shoulder, breathe deeply of the brine and cross the street. No longer am I the middle-aged woman who descended those subway steps 200 miles ago. I am Mary Lee Cantwell, and I am the child of this house.

# *Two*

<br>

IN MY PARENTS' WEDDING PHOTOGRAPH my mother is smiling toothily from underneath an enormous horsehair hat and her bouquet is dripping stephanotis and small bows. Her sister, Esther, is also wearing a big hat and carrying a big bouquet. My father and his best man, a boyhood friend named George Driscoll, are wearing striped trousers; a grape arbor is directly behind them. Milling about somewhere outside the frame are the bride's parents, whom I will call Ganny and Gampa, the groom's mother, whom I will never know, his brothers and sisters, and assorted guests. Before this day is over one of the guests will suffer the splash of a pear on his head.

I have seen that picture many times, but never as clearly as I see one that exists only in my mind. It is of Leo Cantwell and Mary Lonergan at one o'clock of a weekday afternoon, standing on the town common of Bristol, Rhode Island. Leo is on his lunch hour from the U.S. Rubber Company; Mary is on her lunch hour from the Walley School, where she teaches third grade; and they are courting.

They were introduced, at Leo's request (he had seen Mary at a Yacht Club dance) by Esther, who also works at the rubber factory. Marriage is inevitable. She, after all, is a pretty Catholic girl and he is an up-and-coming Catholic boy. Actually, they are not kids—he is twenty-five and she twenty-six when they marry—but never mind. Both are innocent.

They are also very different from each other. Mary is shy and self-contained and high-strung. She grew up in a place where to be Irish is to be second-class, and she trusts the designation. Leo will have none of that. He is the son of a Glasgow man, a soldier in the Scots Guards, and a tall Irishwoman with snapping black eyes, and he has no awe of such as Mayflower descendants. "Imagine!" I will hear him say, "just because that bird's great-great-grandfather had a livery stable in Bristol in 1818 he thinks he's royalty. Hah!" And when, knowing children whose ancestors' names are in my history books, I ask whom I'm descended from, he will say "You're descended from me, and don't you forget it."

But that is later, many years later, and Mary and Leo are still standing on the dusty, dun-colored Common. I can see the gold chain that swags his stomach and the blue-and-gold enamel watch, a Christmas present from him, that hangs on the chain around her neck, but I can only guess at their conversation. Perhaps he is telling her about how some of the gay blades who live at the Belvedere Hotel—young men like him, from out of town, moving up the executive ladder at U.S. Rubber—went down to the kitchen last night to take potshots at the rats. Maybe he's inviting her to the movies, or maybe Esther has found a new speak. "Every time they raided a blind pig," he will tell me one day, "they found your Aunt Esther sitting in the middle of it." Not that Esther is a tosspot, oh no, but she is lively, so lively that soon she will travel to New York for Rudolph Valentino's wake.

Or perhaps it is all settled between them, and they have exhausted the Yacht Club dances and the picnics at Colt Farm and the shore dinners at Rocky Point and are talking about a dining-room table. Perhaps they are deciding on the mahogany bedroom set from Cherry & Webb and whether the silver should be Gorham, as is everyone else's, because the company's in Rhode Island. (And, yes, it will be Gorham. Fairfax, to be exact.)

Anyway, one hot August morning they are married, in the basement of St. Mary's Church because its Gothic superstructure isn't finished yet. Gampa, tall, skinny, not as shrewd as his brothers and sisters but the only one of them, Papa says, who has a heart, gives the bride away. The groom is taking her to New York for their honeymoon, on the old Fall River Line. It is Prohibition so I don't know about the liquid refreshments, but since one of Gampa's brothers owns a hotel and Gampa himself once owned a bar, I suspect there is alcohol present. If there is, no drop will pass Ganny's lips.

The photographer summons the bride and groom. Leo, Mary, Esther, and George line up. A breeze stirs the lawn in front of the grape arbor. The August sun is like a hammer. Behind the bridal party, on one of the two trees beyond the arbor, a pear—a pear about which my parents will tell me and I will tell my children and my children will tell theirs because it stamps this day into the family memory more surely than a photograph—is poised for the drop.

ON THE NIGHT BEFORE the May morning I was born, my father sat on the front steps of our house on Bradford Street, smoking a Fatima and watching the sun set into Bristol Harbor.

Bristol Harbor is enclosed by two claws—a big claw, which is the town itself, and a little claw called Poppasquash Point—and sailboats dance on it in summer. Lobster boats plow through it all year round and so does the dumpy Prudence Island ferry.

There are two islands in the harbor, Hog and Prudence, and people live on them when the weather's warm, in rackety houses with outdoor plumbing. Once past Prudence, which is the biggest and the farthest out, the harbor sweeps into Narragansett Bay. So, pouring from the east side of the big claw, does Mount Hope Bay, which separates us from Massachusetts. Bristol people tend to be long-lived. Some say it's the brine that keeps them.

While Papa smoked and studied the sunset, my mother and her widowed Aunt Annie were on the telephone, turning the town upside down to find him. Neither thought to look out the window. Finally he finished his Fatima, stood up, stretched and walked inside. "Leo," my mother said. "You'd better call Horse Lanoue."

Horse Lanoue. Never was there such a town for nicknames as Bristol. Among my parents' contemporaries are Bink, Fruit Face,

Skeet, Kitty Eyes, Bumper, Twister, Punk, Poop, Crackers, Peanuts, Pinhead, Funnybird, Beanie, Silent Sid, and Hungry Frank. Among mine will be Zip, Fat, Tweet, Eppie, Nutsy, and Gut.

Mother got into Horse's car—Papa didn't have one—and Papa followed, slinging her small suitcase into the front seat. Off they went, up to the corner of High and Bradford streets, where Horse made a left. Meanwhile, Aunt Annie, who was lame, limped her way toward 232 Hope Street, where Ganny and Gampa had given her the hall bedroom, with the news. And I, eyes closed, limbs flailing, still cozy in the amniotic sac, began my tour of what was to become my territory. My country.

High Street is broad and leafy, and goes from ship-owner's Federal at its south end to millhand's three-decker at the north. The big gray Congregational Church, outside which I will wait to eye the bride and her bridesmaids on Saturday afternoons, is on High Street, along with the sober stone mansion that is its parish house. So, until some nitwit tore it down a few years ago, was a curious triangular building that had housed some of Lafayette's troops and been sledged across the ice from Poppasquash Point after the Revolution. One learns about history early in Bristol, simply by looking around.

A left, then a right, and the travelers were on Hope Street, passing Guiteras Junior High—the gift of the descendants of a rich Cuban planter and my future alma mater—and heading for the Neck. That's the name for the north end of town. They passed Fort Hill, where Lafayette set up his command post and where the Cantwell girls will go sledding, and Collins Pond, where they will ice skate, and Colt Farm, through which the elder, along with Ruthie and Joan and Jeanne and Anne (none of them here yet but all of them in progress), will take long Sunday afternoon walks.

They passed a house that was built in 1680 (Bristol's first church services were held here), a rambling red clapboard in which Lafayette spent a night, a two-room school, dairy farms, a few bungalows, a house ordered from a Sears, Roebuck catalogue, and the estate of a woman who was born America's richest baby. And they drove, as one does everywhere in Bristol, under a canopy of oak, horse chestnut, maple and, until the Dutch disease got them, elm trees.

Was my mother nervous? Of course. This was her first confine-
ment. Was my father excited? He wanted six children, all of them
female. What about Horse? He was saying things like "Won't be
much longer, Mary," and "Nothing to worry about, Leo."

Over the town line they went and into Warren, where my
mother's father came from; through Barrington, at whose annual
Thanksgiving Day football game with Colt Memorial High School
their daughters will suffer chills and muddy feet; through dreary
Riverside and into Providence with its stinking river and its steep
hills. A few hours later I will be born, at Lying-In Hospital, and in
a few years I will not forgive my parents this journey. Their bringing me to Providence to be born means that, unlike my mother and
grandmother and great-grandmother, I am not, strictly speaking, a
Bristolian.

IT'S PROBABLY DIFFERENT NOW. Probably everyone who
moves to town these days thinks it's okay to call himself a
Bristolian. But once only those born right on the spot could claim
the title.

My great-grandmother was a native. Her parents, too, for all I
know. My knowledge of my own genealogy doesn't extend past the
rough wooden box that's shoved well under the eaves of 232 Hope
Street. My grandmother called it "the Irish trunk."

The Irish trunk held—I assume—blankets or a change of
clothes or a crucifix or whatever it is you take when you're running
from a famine. Or maybe my ancestors beat it out of Ireland before
the potatoes failed; maybe they just had itchy feet. All I'm certain
of is that by 1852 there were 300 Irish in Bristol, one of whom or
perhaps it was several of whom, had lugged that chest across the
Atlantic.

The town they came to was undergoing a slump. It had been
rich, thanks to privateering and the slave trade, and it would be
middling rich again, once it acquired a rubber mill. But at the moment every other mansion was a boardinghouse, and the poor
camped out on the meadows back of town.

Ganny's family, which was large and handsome, married half
the town, which is why she had both Catholics and Protestants

among her relatives. One of them was a descendant of the man to whom Philip, King of the Wampanoags and son of Massasoit, sold 100 acres near Mount Hope. Mount Hope is a sprawl of mills and swamp and scrub and stagnant ponds and poison ivy on Mount Hope Bay. Philip had his longhouse on Mount Hope, and the quartz throne on which he donned his wampum stole and scarlet cloak overlooks the bay. For centuries Bristol's children risked poison ivy to sit on Philip's throne, but none but Boy Scouts out hiking go there anymore.

In 1676 there was a great battle on Mount Hope; and Philip, who was now trying to oust the settlers from his land, was shot dead. His oracles had told him no Englishman would get him, which was true. Philip's killer was an Indian named Alderman, whose brother he had tomahawked.

Alderman's commander, Benjamin Church, was rewarded with Philip's regalia and Alderman with his hand, which he carried about in a bucket of rum. Four Boston investors acquired the land, laid it out in a grid—four streets by nine—and five years later, at a town meeting, it was christened Bristol. Two hundred years later four Bristol schools were christened after them: the Messrs. Byfield, Walley, Oliver, and Burton.

The first Bristolians attended Congregational services, raised geese and onions, and were legendarily peculiar. But in the mid-eighteenth century a Bristolian named Simeon Potter made a fortune in privateering at about the same time the Church of England sent a missionary. From then on Bristol was more Cavalier than Puritan.

In 1775 the town was bombarded by British warships, and in 1778 British troops burned thirty houses, which is why Bristol's best bear no date earlier than 1784. Lafayette arrived the same year, to set up a line of defense across the Neck, but left when the weather turned chilly. In 1781 George Washington paraded down Hope Street on a carpet of evergreens and pussy willow strewn for the occasion.

Then came the rich years; these were followed by the poor years, and, eventually, the inflation of a modest rubber works owned by one Augustus Bourn into the United States Rubber Company.

By the turn of the century half of Bristol's residents were foreign born, come to work in the rubber mill. Most of them were émigrés from southern Italy, lured—or so the story goes—to Bristol by Terence McCarty, the factory manager and Ganny's uncle. When Terence dropped wages to a dollar a day the employees struck, and he, as cagey as any skinflint Yankee, had handbills touting the Promised Land distributed in Scafati, a town near Salerno.

The Portuguese came too, most of them white, from the Azores. A few of them, *bravas* the color of coffee ice cream, came from Cape Verde. French Canadians arrived, along with a few Jews, a family of Swedes, and a veritable tribe of Syrians.

By the time I began my journey toward Lying-In Hospital the town had Congregationalists, Episcopalians High and Low, Baptists, three varieties of Catholics, Holy Rollers, a flock of Benjamin Church descendants, rich and poor and in between, summer people and locals, teetotalers and drunks and peculiars and—oh Lord!—what *wasn't* there among the 11,000 folk who made up Bristol!

# *Three*

FOR MANY YEARS I have carried in my wallet a photograph of a plump dark-haired man in ice-cream pants standing in front of a tall rosebush and holding a plump dark-haired baby. There is no telling me that I was too young to remember that picture being taken. I am adamant in my recollection of warmth, bees, and the bliss of being in my father's arms.

The rosebush is red, and its tip has been trained to ramble across the wire stretched between it and its twin, a pink rosebush whose tip has also been trained to ramble. Red and pink meet in the middle. Beyond the roses there's a long rectangular plot, nestled next to the sagging blue fence that divides ours from the Tingleys' lawn, planted with phlox and pansies and sweet william; a hydrangea and, behind it, another rectangle, planted with peonies; a flowering quince; a circle of tulips centered by a sundial; a square of more tulips; a grape arbor and, beside it, two pear trees. Along the back fence are lilacs, hollyhocks, and, in early spring, violets.

Soon my sandbox will be built beside the grape arbor, and my swing hung from its roof. But we aren't yet living at 232 Hope Street, and the arbor still looks as it did when my parents' wedding reception was held in the backyard.

This is my first birthday, and my picture is being taken by our next-door neighbor, Miss Emilie Connery, whose stockings are always wrinkled around her spindled legs and who wears a tailored suit and a felt hat winter and summer. Miss Emilie has a box camera and records such occasions for a small fee. Daughter to Sam and Honey, sister to Miss Aida, who's soprano soloist at St. Michael's Episcopal Church, Miss Emilie is one of the Protestant Connerys.

Another Protestant, Mrs. Emma Rounds, has supplied my birthday cake, angel food with white icing and my name in pink, also for a small fee. Emma is my grandmother's first cousin, one of the Protestant McCartys, and the organist at St. Michael's. Emma is as famous for her angel food cake as Miss Emilie is for her photography. It won't be long before I am famous, too, for being "a good reader."

WHEN, EIGHT MONTHS LATER, my mother, father, and infant sister, Diana, and I move to Ganny and Gampa's house the sidewalk in front is gravel. (Soon the WPA will come and lay cement.) Two blocks further on the gravel peters out and one walks on matted grass. This marks the end of the town proper. Beyond it lies the Ferry, meadows mostly, the estates of the summer people, Narragansett Bay, and soaring over it, the Mount Hope Bridge, which connects Bristol to Newport. The ferry itself, which the bridge replaced, is long gone. Even so, anyone heading south is heading "down the Ferry."

The harbor is on the other side of Hope Street, and we tell the weather by it. "Red sky at night, sailor's delight," Papa chants when the sun drops blazing into the waves; "Red sky in the morning, sailor take warning," when a gray dawn obscures Poppasquash Point. "Whitecaps today," Mother says some mornings. "It's going to squall."

In a town of beautiful houses, 232 Hope Street is among the ugliest. Not that its builders weren't ambitious. Two flights of steps, one granite, one wood, lead to the glass-paneled front door, and their intersection is marked by a pair of geranium-bearing stone urns. Over the door there's a balcony. To the right of the door there's a two-story bulge of bay windows. Around the corner there's a pair of porches, one on top of the other. Seen head-on the house is narrow, pinched; seen from the side, especially at night when every window is lit, it looks like the *Titanic*. But what supports 232 Hope Street is not the ocean swell but centuries of Indians piled higgledy-piggledy beneath its red-brick cellar. Whenever, barefoot, I prance about the lawn, my toes probe for bones.

The front hall is tall and dark, and at the foot of the curving staircase that leads to our second floor (Ganny, Gampa, and Esther are on the first) is a bronze lady, bare-breasted and barefoot, whose upraised hands hold a lamp. My, but she is lovely, so lovely I trail through the hall dressed in my mother's wedding dress, which has been dyed red, singing holy, wordless songs for her. They are like the vocal exercises I have heard Miss Aida Connery trilling on the Saturday night before the Sunday morning performance, and once my mother says "You're a good girl, Mary Lee, to be singing on Good Friday."

But I am always a good girl and so is Diana. When I ride my tricycle along the cement path next to the windows through which the coal rumbles down the chutes and into the bins, Gampa says "A regular Billy Be-damned." When Diana waddles into the living room dressed in her underpants, Papa announces "The great John L.," and Diana strikes a fighting pose, fists up, fanny out. When we bathe, Gampa and Esther come to watch; when Papa lures us to bed with "Button, button, who's got the button?" they applaud. Only Ganny, too stout and stiff to climb the stairs, stays away. She is in her rocker, reading the *Providence Evening Bulletin* through her magnifying glass.

The *Bulletin* arrives at about four o'clock, hurled to the front steps by a boy on a bicycle, and that means the best part of the day is beginning. In an hour or so, after the five-o'clock whistle blows, Papa and Esther will come home from the rubber factory, "the shop." The gate to the front steps, one of three in our long green fence, will creak open; Judy, Gampa's cocker spaniel, will bark; and there they'll be, Papa in a three-piece suit and a felt hat, and Esther in a print dress and pumps that show off her pretty legs.

There's always news from the shop and I run up and down the stairs between the messengers, giddy with the bustle they have brought into the house. Downstairs Gampa is in his morris chair smoking his pipe and Esther is saying she's got to rinse out a few things, and Ganny is in the kitchen making supper. Or maybe Esther is upstairs, visiting us, which means that Ganny's going to bang on the riser with a spoon. "Supper's ready, Esther," Di and I chorus, and we race downstairs to see what she's getting. Often we beg to stay.

Downstairs food and upstairs food are different. Downstairs tends toward baked beans, clam chowder, codfish cakes, johnny-cake and apple pie. Upstairs is usually a roast, a green vegetable, a yellow vegetable, a starch, and no dessert. Downstairs and upstairs look different, too.

Downstairs, but for the tick of the clock on the fireplace mantel and the drip of the kitchen faucet, is very quiet. It is also very plain. The pictures on the walls of the two parlors are steel engravings and the furniture is hard. Next to the tiled fireplace, which is sealed with a polished brass shield, is a small radio, turned on only for Ganny's daily listen to *Vic and Sade* and Gampa's nightly installment of *Ace 'n' Andy.* "*Amos 'n' Andy,*" I tell him, but he won't obey. There are no magazines, but lots of old-fashioned books, thick, with gilt letters on their maroon covers, in a mahogany bookcase.

Esther's room is plain, too, but her closet—Ganny calls it a clothespress—is so big Di and I can walk around it, inspecting her dresses, which are many, and her shoes, which are even more. When we clop into the parlor wearing her high heels, Esther says "Look at those two, would you?" and we clop back, excited, to pick out others.

But the kitchen is the best place downstairs, not at night when it's cold and its corners are dark, but in the morning when it's sunny and Ganny's baking. The kitchen has two stoves, one gas and one coal, and Esther keeps saying "Ma, don't you think it's time you got rid of that old thing?" Ganny won't listen. She puts her bread to rise on top of the coal stove and bakes her beans in its oven. She polishes it weekly with stove blacking and keeps a little poker to stir up the coals, and she claims there's nothing like it for a good, even heat. She has two iceboxes, too, the electric one in the kitchen, and the other in the back entry, which gets a new block of ice twice a week and has a drip pan, which it is my job to empty outside the back door after the iceman leaves. Esther says that while she's at it she ought to throw out that old thing, too, but Ganny says you never know when the lines will come down. That's why she keeps a row of kerosene lamps in the pots-and-pans closet.

Upstairs, Diana and I have our own little maple beds, pushed together because she is forever falling out of hers, our own little blue dining table, and our own little chairs. We also have our own little playroom, off the hall, and our own little silver cups, which make our milk taste thin and steely.

Ganny's bay window has a rocker in it so she can sit and watch the passing scene. Upstairs, though, there's a rope-legged mahogany table on which is a row of books bracketed by leather bookends, a crystal cigarette box monogrammed with Papa's initials, a lamp made from a ginger jar, and a silver-framed portrait of my mother and myself. I, barefoot in white lawn, am on her lap. She, lovely in polka-dotted silk, is smiling like Irene Dunne.

The chairs and couches are fat and squashy, and the dining-room closets crammed with cups and plates and platters. Mother doesn't like to entertain, but people say she sets a beautiful table, and Papa, who does like to entertain, has a glass for every kind of cocktail. "Have a snort?" he asks when somebody drops in after church, and gets out the sugar cubes, the Angostura bitters, and the bourbon. His old-fashioneds are famous, he boasts, for miles around.

My mother calls her parlors living rooms, and fusses because we are impossible. "You will put me in the nut-house!" she cries. Diana can't keep her feet off the furniture and I can't remember to pick the funny pages up off the floor, and Papa leaves his books lying around. Each of us has a favorite place in which to flop, but my mother can't seem to light anywhere. I look like her, and Diana looks like Papa, but both of us have his brown eyes and his blarney and teeth so crooked they seem to dance. We are also to inherit his passion for reading and in a few years the three of us, without lifting our eyes from our books, will sound a simultaneous "Shhh!" whenever Mother comes into the living room. Sometimes she studies us with puzzled eyes, a saluki among spaniels.

The wallpaper in our bedroom has robins on it, and when we take our nap I pretend they are cheeping us to sleep. Naps are after lunch, after a morning out in all weather. We are always outdoors, in the side yard, and I hate that because I want to be indoors, listening to Ganny talk, or lying on the floor upstairs with the funny pages. But I can't come in, my mother says, until there are roses in my cheeks. So I say to Di again and again, "Diana, do you see any roses yet?" Diana loves to be outdoors, and she is never without roses.

But if Esther or Gampa is with us, I'll stay outdoors forever. On summer mornings when she's home Esther takes us across the street to the water for a dip. Gampa comes, too, so strong a swimmer he can ride us on his back. My mother's afraid of the water and sits on the sea wall crying "Don't go out too far. . . . You're turning blue. . . . You're over your heads. . . . Time to come in now." Papa's not afraid, but he can't swim.

He wants us to learn to swim, though; he wants us to learn to do everything. On winter nights when there's snow on the ground and ice slicking the trees, he takes us to Union Street, which rises in a slow hill to High. Then he stands at its foot, to watch out for the traffic on Hope. When he waves, Di and I go down the hill on short, stubby skis toward the dark harbor. It is so cold, so still, and the only sound is a long *s-l-i-i-i-sh*.

Snow, it seems to snow all the time, and once the harbor freezes in thick yellow curls. The white roses on Ganny's porch snow as well, and dusty purple grapes fall on the seat of our swing. The pears fall, too, and the sand in our sandbox, which is shaded by a green-and-orange striped awning, is warm to bare feet. Papa, not Miss Emilie because this is not a great occasion, takes a picture of Esther and me sitting on the little ledge that runs around it. I am skinny and pretty, and so is she, and I am holding a flower to her nose.

# Four

WHENEVER I SPEAK OF HIM, even now, my eyes fill and my nose gets pink, and I pray the listener won't notice the sudden thickening of my voice. For years after I came to New York, I would watch little girls standing next to their fathers and staring in toyshop windows, or leaning against their shoulders while the subway careened around the curves. I was jealous of those little girls. I envied them the big hands they were holding and the scratch of the tweed or flannel or raincoat poplin against their cheeks. I might have been one of those little girls. Hadn't my father loved New York? Hadn't he spoken of taking me to the shows some day, and buying me a sherry at the Astor Bar? "Oh God," he used to say, "I love that town."

But Ganny! When I talk about Ganny my mouth curls at its corners, and if my eyes are wet it's because they're apt to get runny when I laugh. I am full of stories about Ganny, like the one about the time she lambasted a telephone answering machine for its rudeness. "Now just you slow down," she said. "Just you mind your manners." When we told her that was a recording she was talking to her face flushed. "Dang thing made a fool out of me!"

Let me see her now, in a starched washdress under an apron that didn't come off unless she had callers. Under the dress there's a pink corset so stiff with stays that, folded, it looks like a venetian blind, a pink rayon vest, drawers, and slip. Her stockings stop just short of her knees, where they are rolled into a knot, but no flesh shows because her skirt stops just short of her ankles. Her shoes are black lace-ups, and if I had a dime for every time I tied them—Ganny cannot bend—I would be a rich young lady.

Ganny's eyes are green and somewhat slanted, and her white hair is coiled into a bun. When she goes to bed she takes out the pins and braids it into a long, loose tail. She has never worn makeup, although she likes what she calls a good strong scent, and her face is as unlined as a child's. She also likes thunderstorms, and when they are brewing goes out to the porch, lets her false teeth drop to her tongue, sticks it out, and dares the lightning with her choppers.

Finished with breakfast, I have trudged downstairs for my first morning call, and walked in on the usual scene. Esther is having a fit because once more Ganny has thrown some of her underwear in the incinerator. "Ma," she is screeching, "that was a brand-new slip."

"How was I to know?" Ganny asks, all innocence. "I thought it was just some old thing you wanted to be rid of, the way you left it lying around on that chair." Esther leaves for work fuming. Ganny trundles out to the kitchen, ordering "that dang hound," Judy, to get out from underfoot as she goes.

In the kitchen is the jug-eared boy from the next town she married when she was eighteen and he twenty, the eldest son of a prosperous grain merchant with a walrus mustache and his handsome wife, who had a bosom you could rest plates on. He is eating his breakfast egg, crumbling his toast into the yolk and waiting for his orders. There is no question about who rules the roost at 232 Hope Street. It is Ganny. Gampa does as he is told, Esther mutinies only occasionally, my mother sticks to her own territory—painting tole, crocheting bedspreads, and arranging flowers—and Papa, though he calls Gampa "Tom," addresses his mother-in-law as "Mrs. Lonergan." I, to whom she is as inevitable as sunrise and sunset, shadow her from morning till night while she makes beds, bakes bread, beats carpets. Short, stout, Ganny is strong as a navvy.

Labor ceases after the luncheon dishes are washed and draining by the side of the sink and the day is settled into somnolence. Afternoons are for strolls—to Eisenstadt's Dry Goods or the five-

and-ten or the foot of Union Street, which has a fine view of the harbor—and for callers.

The callers are Miss Munro, a small, thin woman with violet eyes and skin like wrinkled linen, who lives next door; Mrs. Horton, who wears big hats and has a deep, dark voice that keeps telling me not to be sassy; and Mame Lannon, a walleyed widow whose only child is dead. There is a fourth caller, Hope, but she stays only long enough to give Ganny a small, stitched packet. Hope is the local numbers runner, and secretary of the D.A.R.

Ganny has gambler's blood in her, thanks to her scamp of a father, who went out West and stayed for years, leaving behind two daughters, a son and a wife, the former Bridget McCarty, who died at twenty-eight. "I never liked him," Ganny says, as coolly as if she were dismissing vegetables, which she also doesn't like. When he finally came back East, to three motherless children who'd been passed from hand to hand among their aunts and uncles, he bought a little farm in Massachusetts. "But I never visited," Ganny says. "I wouldn't have given him the sweat off an ice pitcher."

My grandmother loves bingo, the numbers, and, above all, the horses. Every morning she takes the *Boston Daily Record* to her sitting room just off the second parlor, plumps herself into a rocker, and scans the racing pages through her magnifying glass until she finds the horse that owes her money. Then, rocking back and forth to gain momentum, she propels herself from the chair and calls her bookie, a cousin who runs a small variety store. "George," she whispers, "you know who this is. Put fifty cents on Jackie's Girl for me in the fifth." Ganny never gives her name. Maybe the police are listening, she says, and she'll end up in the hoosegow.

When the callers arrive, I lie on the rug pretending to look at the pictures in the big maroon books but of course I am eavesdropping. "Little pitchers have big ears," Mrs. Horton warns the ladies. But then they forget that I am there and rumble into talk.

The best talker is Mame Lannon, who lives on the very edge of mortality. With no family of her own left to bury Mame likes to help bury everybody else's. While the family is at the funeral she is the neighbor who stays behind to sweep the floor clean of the flowers knocked off the wreaths the undertaker's men have taken to the grave, and put the furniture back into place, and set out the ham and the macaroni salad and the cakes in the dining room and tell the returning mourners of how the deceased had given a little cough, or a little sigh, and just turned his head to the wallpaper. When, still a baby, I tried to get out of Ganny's kitchen and into the parlor where her younger sister, Annie, lay, sunk into the satin of a casket from the Protestant funeral parlor and flanked by guardian gladioli, it was Mame who blocked the door. (Bristol has four funeral parlors, one for the Italians, one for the Portuguese, one for the Irish and assorted converts, and one, Wilbur's by name, for Protestants. My family, by virtue of long residence, become Instant Yankees on dying and are buried by Wilbur's.)

I like these tales of illness and madness and death—there is no small talk in my grandmother's parlor—but I like even more the afternoons when there are no strolls and no callers and Ganny is sitting in the bay window, paring apples and hemming sheets. "Tell me a story," I beg. But not a made-up story. Made-up stories are not for me, and besides, Ganny doesn't know any.

Once she told me of Cromwell's siege of Ireland, an eyewitness account as I recall, and surely those were not the words of her father's Canadian ancestors. No, they came straight from the bog, through generations cursed with big, blue, distant eyes—harbingers, according to McCarty legend, of an early death. Mostly, though, she speaks of Bristol, of the massacred Indians and the cranky old Yanks and the ships that once filled the harbor, and of how the Bridies and Nellies and Maggies, servants all of them, sent back to Ireland pictures of a mansion called Linden Place and claimed it for their own. She speaks of Swamp Yankees, who are what the South calls Rednecks, and Black Yankees, who are religious bigots, and of how she wouldn't give either of them house room. Gleefully, she tells the tale of how an uncle of hers chased a Black Yankee named Simmons up a tree, and how that old man Simmons never dared plague him again.

Most of all, she speaks of Bristolians, of the people passing by the bay window and the people buried in the desk, memorialized by sepia photographs on deeper sepia cardboard. To me, the latter—the girls in white lawn and the babies in plaid dresses and the men in shapeless suits and round-crowned hats—are all dead, whether they are or not, and I mourn them as deeply as I do the child who is really gone. On the other hand, they are all alive as well, because when you live in a house that has been a home to so many you always see more people than there are in the room.

Aunt Margaret's doll, wearing my christening dress, stares from a small chair in Ganny's bedroom. The book she won in fifth grade, a satin-bound copy of the poems of Thomas Moore whose flyleaf reads "To Margaret Lonergan, for Excellence in Spelling," is in Ganny's bureau, and her big, blue, distant eyes watch her survivors from a gilt-framed photograph in Ganny's sitting room. The German shepherd who kept her company during the long nights when, for her health, she slept alone in a tent in the backyard, is buried near the rosebushes. Margaret, the second of Ganny's four children, died when she was eleven. Of pneumonia, Ganny says, but she is lying. She died of tuberculosis, caught from Aunt Annie's husband, and Ganny cannot bear to say the word. Nor can Mame Lannon and Mrs. Horton and Miss Munro. Often I hear them whispering about someone who's "gone up to Saranac" and am puzzled. What and where is Saranac?

"Margaret used to play up to Annie's all the time—oh, they were crazy about Margaret—and Frank was supposed to be over his pneumonia. But she got so thin and so tired, and the doctors around here didn't seem to know anything. So I took her to Providence, and when the doctor came out of the examining room he had tears in his eyes. 'Mrs. Lonergan,' he said, 'if only you had brought her sooner.' "

"You're a good-looking girl, Mary Lee," Ralph Kinder, the florist, said one day when I was sitting on his counter listening to him and Gampa talk about the wreath-and-bouquet count at a big Bristol funeral, "but you're not a patch on your mother. And your mother's not a patch on what her sister Margaret was."

"When your Aunt Margaret was sick," Mame Lannon told me, "young Hezzie Church brought her a little plant. And when she died"—she paused, and fixed me with her round fish-eyes— "the plant died."

All the good ones are dead—Mame Lannon says it's the finest blooms that are nipped in the bud—and their survivors aren't half of what they would have been. Here's Lawrence A., for instance, come to rake Miss Munro's yard. He is very tall and somehow loose, and his face looks like someone went over it with an eraser. Lawrence, who is backward, had a normal twin brother, "but when they were only a few months old he died and his mother was left with Lawrence." Ganny sighs, and together we contemplate God's vagaries.

Here's Mr. C., whose mother jumped off a roof with his baby brother in her arms. Now they're nestled in one coffin up to North Burial Ground, and the air is sweet above their tombstone.

Here's Aunt Annie Clark, the last of Ganny's McCarty aunts and uncles, and the oldest woman in Bristol. Aunt Annie had a sister, Winifred, who married an architect with a famous New England name and went to live with him in Boston. She died young. "Of what, Ganny?" I ask. "Of Boston," she replies.

Here's Ganny's cousin, invisible except to us, in a long gingham dress and high-topped shoes. When she played the game that children played at birthday parties—whoever pulled out the lump of dirt buried in a box of sand would be the first to die—it was her hand that closed about the damp intruder. She had the McCarty eyes.

Down Hope Street they march, the quick and the dead, and we see the one as clearly as we see the other. Swee' Walla Bullock, the thick-tongued seller of spring water; Indians in single file; the old lady who was poisoned by her relatives; onion farmers and clam diggers; Harold S., whose father spread the Turkey carpet with papers before he put a bullet in his head; Ganny's grandmother, who smoked a pipe; and the demented children of women who, embarrassed by pregnancy, pulled their stays too tight. Meanwhile shadows are eating up the corners of the room, and Nora Bayes is wailing "You left me like a broken da-ha-hahl" on the old wind-up Victrola.

"What are you two doing sitting in the dark?" My mother's in the room, pulling the chain on the table lamp. It's time to fill Judy's bowl, time for *Jack Armstrong, The All-American Boy,* time for Diana to come in from the yard and for Papa and Esther to come from the shop and for Gampa to come down the street from Ralph Kinder's, where he's been chewing the fat all afternoon. Banging the doors, calling out, running up and down the stairs, they'll rouse the house out of the past and into the present. But they are here too late for me. I have come down with the Bristol Complaint.

People who have the Bristol Complaint can never leave town. The elm trees snag them. So do the harbor and the wild roses and the history. Some people say the Vikings were here: there's a rock with funny letters on it at Mount Hope, near the throne where Philip, King of the Wampanoags, donned his regalia. Bristol isn't far from Plymouth. On Thanksgiving Day we breathe the Pilgrims' wet, gray air.

Ganny has packed my head with stories, so many I can scarcely close the lid. Every chink is taken up with women tumbling from rooftops and youngsters gathered around a sand-filled box and little girls in white lawn coughing out their lungs. I have never really seen Bristol. I have scarcely stepped beyond our long green fence. Never mind. I see it anyway.

# Five

*T*HE FIRST TIME I saw Diana she was wedged into the corner of a wing chair, wearing an undershirt, a diaper, and a belly band over her healing umbilicus. Her fair hair was little more than fuzz, and her scalp was an angry red. But, then, all of Diana was an angry red. She was screaming, her mouth wide open over toothless gums. Perhaps I'd pinched her.

Emilie Connery came around the corner and through the gate many times, box camera in hand, to photograph the Cantwell girls. Each picture is a testament to mayhem. Sometimes Diana is in her playpen, still in a diaper and undershirt and still screaming. I am standing alongside, in what look like lounging pajamas, and my eyebrows are in one long, mean line. Later there are photographs of us with our tricycle. In some of them Diana hoists a plump, triumphant leg over the seat and grins for the camera while I glower. In others I lay a proprietary hand on the handlebars and stare insolently into space. Beside me Diana is screaming.

Our parents dressed us alike, in little smocked dresses and little black patent-leather shoes for Sundays and little overalls and little brown oxfords for weekdays. Both of us had Papa's brown eyes so we looked a bit alike, but my hair was dark and her hair was light. This made me mad because it meant that I was the evil Rose Red and she was the good Snow White.

Snow White she was, too, dimpled and plump and amiable.

But I had thinned out and was all cheekbones and crooked teeth and knees. Esther said that holding me was like holding a bag of bones, and Mother said I'd get into trouble with those hands of mine one day. They were forever after Diana, poking and pushing and, once, going toward her throat until my mother yelled and yanked me away.

Somehow I must have known that once I had no peers, that for eighteen months I had reigned alone. The only time Diana and I were peaceful, when I wasn't shrieking "She did it, she did it!" or "Not fair!" was in bed, in the dark, when I changed her name to Jane and mine to Marie and we conversed. Of what I can scarcely imagine. But I suppose I said things like "Would you like more ice cream, Jane?" and she answered "That would be very nice, Marie."

Other times I tapped out tunes on the maple headboard of my bed. "Baa, baa, black sheep!" Diana would guess, and "Lazy Mary, will you get up!" I liked her then. Even more I liked not being alone in the dark. I liked the sound of her breathing—she was always asleep before I was—and the companionable creak of the mattress when she tossed and turned.

Diana was a tomboy, tearing her clothes on brambles and suffering scraped knees and playing "Run, sheepie, run" with the Tingley boys until it was too dark to see where anyone was hiding. So it was strange when she started getting the stomachaches, strange because it was I who complained of cramps in my legs and tingles in my fingers and believed that I breathed through a hole in my throat. I could feel it, truly, the cold air going in and out of the invisible puncture; and for several months, until I came up with a new peculiarity, I had my mother believing it too.

But this was Diana who woke up crying and clutching her belly, so the pain had to be real. Papa and Mother started whispering to each other. Then Mother whispered to Ganny and Ganny whispered to Esther, but nobody whispered to Gampa because he couldn't be trusted not to be tearful around Diana, who was his pet and his treasure. Once, when Diana had fallen asleep on the couch, I had watched while he picked her up to put her to bed, and his face was blurry with love.

The doctor who lived up the street bustled into the house often, bringing with him peace and sanity and the reassuring scents of ether and rubbing alcohol, but then he, too, started whispering. Papa, he said, would have to call in somebody from Providence.

The somebody from Providence came down, burly in his top-coat and exuding bonhomie, and said Diana would have to have her appendix out. She cried, fat tears tumbling down fat cheeks, and none of us, not even I, could bear the sight.

Let Papa or Mother even mention the hospital and how she'd have fun and get presents, and tears would well up in those big brown eyes and spill down the cheeks that always had roses in them. "My stomach doesn't really hurt," she'd sob.

The whispering began again, more terrifying than any shout, and I stalked the house with my ears laid flat against my head. Nobody was safe from my ears: Esther said I could hear the grass growing. "We'll tell her we have to take her to Providence for X-rays," Papa whispered to Mother, "and that she'll just have to stay in the hospital overnight. It's the only way we'll ever get that appendix out."

Diana crowed. Neither of us had ever been to Providence, and now she was getting a ride all by herself. Should I tell her what I had overheard? I should not. But now she, in her innocence, was even more of a Snow White; and I, in my knowledge, was even more of a wicked Rose Red.

It was still light on the evening they left for Providence, and Diana, sitting alone in the back seat, her blond pigtails sticking out from under a brown beanie, peered out the rear window at me, who was standing in the roadway. She waved, trustingly and triumphantly, then turned back, safe and happy, to our parents. The car made a left on Union Street, and she was gone.

Two weeks later Diana was home again, with a wonderful scar on her stomach and a wonderful wormlike souvenir floating in a jar of alcohol. It stood on the table between our twin beds and every day it looked a little worse than it had the day before. Bits and pieces of the worm broke off and the alcohol turned gray and turgid, and every morning I woke up to this disgusting reminder of my necessary crime. But I never begged her to throw it out. Guilt wouldn't let me, guilt and that passion to protect which sooner or later is the curse of the oldest child. Those blond pigtails still recede in the distance, and little wisps of hair still disturb our mother's careful central part.

A FEW MONTHS LATER I awoke with a neck so stiff I was pinioned to the pillow. My head ached too, so badly it seemed a manacle was crushing my skull. Mother and Papa hovered over my bed, and a doctor hovered with them. I remember astonishment and pleasure—finally, I had an ailment that couldn't be treated with a "Mary Lee, you have too much imagination"—and after that I remember nothing.

When I awoke again I was facing a faraway ceiling strung with bright white lights. Slowly, painfully, I turned my head, still pinioned to a pillow, to the left and saw a young black man, the first black person I'd ever seen, lying only a few inches away. His eyes were closed and I willed him to open them, to tell me where we were, but he kept on sleeping. A few days later, listening to the chatter of the nurses who were making up my bed, I heard that he had died.

We had polio, he and I and all the others who were lying on cots in the corridor of this hospital for contagious diseases. There weren't enough rooms to go around. There weren't enough doctors, either. It was a nervous intern who stuck a syringe into my spine and when, many years later, I had a second spinal tap I was astonished to have the first recalled so vividly. I recognized it instantly: that sense that the very marrow is being sucked out of one's back.

When I woke for the third time, I was alone in a great big room. Sometimes a nurse came in, but no one else. Mother and Papa were confined to the doorway, from which they smiled and wiggled their fingers and held up package after package, each wrapped like a birthday present and bristling with bows.

The manacle loosed its grip, my neck relaxed, and I got to sit up in bed and open my presents. Coloring books and paper dolls and picture books, all of which had to be burned before I left the hospital. They'd be covered with polio germs, the nurses said, so I couldn't take them home. Meanwhile I could have a good time.

I did have a good time. I colored in the books and cut out the paper dolls and called out to the little boys across the hall; and when Papa told me that the Bristol public schools were postponing their opening because of the polio epidemic, happiness had me swelling like a toad. I, Mary Lee Cantwell, had single-handedly stayed the school bells, shut the schoolhouse doors, given the schoolchildren (how grateful they should be to me, to me) another week of summer vacation.

Nor was I ever frightened, not even at night, when the windows seemed sad without curtains and the only light was that which seeped under the door. I could hear the nurses' footfalls as they went up and down the corridor, and once in a while the crackle of a uniform when one of them bent over my bed. Fear came later, when I went home.

I was in my own little bed, my little maple bed, nesting and unnesting the *matryoshka* doll Miss Emilie Connery had sent me, and eavesdropping on Papa and Ralph Kinder out in the living room. I was never one for repeating what I heard, and half the time I forgot it anyway. It's just that I loved voices, and language, and that my ears pricked to whispers.

"When they told me an intern had to do the spinal tap," Papa was saying, "all I could think was 'What if the needle slips? What if he misses?' And when I heard she had polio . . . well, Ralph, to tell you the truth I just sat in that waiting room and cried."

Papa cry? Papa lower that big head of his into his big hands and let his shoulders shake and icicles run from his big Roman nose? If my father could cry, than where was safety? If it was not with him, it wasn't anywhere.

A few minutes later I heard him laugh and say it looked like the sun was over the yardarm, so how about a snort? I breathed easier, and felt the fine hairs on my arms—they had risen like a cat's, I swear—lie flat again.

Except for our journeys to the Jane Brown Hospital (that was my sister's) and the Charles V. Chapin Hospital for Contagious Diseases (that was mine), Diana and I had never been outside the country of the blue-eyed. But oh my God, how far I'd traveled.

# Six

$\mathcal{I}$ CALL IT THE COUNTRY of the blue-eyed because of something a friend from New York said during a weekend in Bristol. When she looked around the restaurant to which we'd gone for dinner, the restaurant at which my parents had eaten many a lobster thermidor, she said, "Do you realize we're the only people here with brown eyes?"

She was speaking in metaphor, although what she said was also literally true. She is Jewish and I am an Irish Catholic, however well-hidden my roots, and we will never really be at home with a certain kind of Protestant—Episcopalian, usually, with the careless arrogance that can still bring waiters and salesladies to their knees. But as a little girl I lived in their country, and the drawers of my mother's desk are stuffed with mementos of my stay.

This clipping from *The Bristol Phoenix*, for instance: "Little Miss Nancy Church Mossop, daughter of Mrs. Wallace Mossop of this town, was hostess Saturday afternoon at her Poppasquash home to fifteen of her little friends. . . . She was the recipient of many lovely gifts, including a Colonial bouquet which was presented to her in a charming manner by young Bobby Kinder. The time was pleasantly spent playing games and enjoying refreshments in the service of which Mrs. Mossop was assisted by the mothers present." The mothers present (mine was the prettiest) stood behind their children's chairs, poised to intercept the fall of the fork, the dribble of the ice cream. A few months later, at my own birthday party, young Bobby Kinder presented me with a Colonial bouquet in a charming manner.

There's a rosette dangling a faded blue ribbon stamped with gilt letters that reads "First Prize." It commemorates my entry—nasturtiums Mother helped me cram into a white jug—in the junior division of the Bristol Garden Club's annual show. A ticket stub from my first evening at the theater, in the Colt Memorial High School auditorium, when students from the Lee School, which was where the parents from the country of the blue-eyed sent their children, whirled like dervishes under spinning colored lights. A snapshot of a group of little girls standing next to the horse that was the centerpiece of somebody's birthday party. All of us wore smocked dresses, and might have been cousins to England's little princesses.

I remember Newman's Grocers, where the men wore white aprons and the butcher a straw hat, and all the eyes blazed blue. And my mother's bridge afternoons, and the guests forking up meringues buried under strawberries and whipped cream. I remember pale, freckled forearms hung with little purses, and the scent of 4711 cologne, and long, skinny Yankee feet in long, skinny T-strapped shoes. I remember skinny voices too, dry as dust.

Sometimes I heard fatter voices—"Hey, Cheech!" and "Wallyo!" they shouted—coming up from the foot of Union Street on summer afternoons. But I was not to meet their owners for several years yet. My parents, like the people with whom Mother played bridge and Papa played golf, had enrolled their child in the Lee School.


THE LEE SCHOOL, a white clapboard house filigreed with gingerbread, was run by a Mrs. Dunbar and her daughter, Miss Fritzi. They lived on the first floor of the house; the second floor was divided into two classrooms. The big kids sat at desks in the room in front. The little kids sat around tables in the room in back. Almost nobody stayed past fifth grade, although the Dunbars were prepared to soldier on through eighth. Only one student stayed that long, a plain, plump girl with a famous name and a nervous disposition that Ganny blamed on the famous name. Whatever you were, Ganny figured, you were from the beginning. If you were born to a pair of crazy old Yanks you were bound to be a crazy young Yank.

Miss Fritzi, whose real name was Frederica, had bangs and a little crown of braids and was sweet as simple syrup. She smiled, she smiled all the time. She smiled when Billy G. wet his pants and she smiled when Jackie S. threw up, and when she realized that the only way that I could add was by penciling marks on scrap paper and totting them up, she just raised her eyes toward heaven and smiled.

But it was agony to me to be so stupid. The more Miss Fritzi tried to show me how to translate the marks into symbols, the more cotton seemed to be stuffing the corners of my head. The cotton seemed even thicker on the nights Papa sat beside me at the desk in the living room, pencil points breaking under his fierce attack. I snuffled and shook and his voice took on a steel edge, and when at last my mother shyly volunteered, the suffering eyes we turned on her were identical.

For several nights she sat at the desk beside this daughter whose eyes had been fixed on her father since the day she was born, and summoned up her old schoolteacher's skills. Sniffling at her left, I bent over a scratch pad watching while her small, shapely hand (a hand that could trace a line of gold leaf as fine as a hair) traced swoops and curlicues. Suddenly they assembled themselves into sense and the cotton fled my head, leaving it as clear and clean as a tide-rinsed seashell. Mother preened, for once sure of herself among these brown-eyed talkative Cantwells, and I knew a triumph second only to that I'd known on the morning I finally succeeded in tying my shoelaces into bows. I could add! I could subtract! But never as easily as I could read.

While the other first-graders—tears in their eyes, spittle wetting their lips—stood beside the tables stuttering out their A's and B's I was busy at the bookcase, diving and dipping in and out of words as freely as a dolphin frisks through water. *Red Feather, The Story of an Indian Boy* was my favorite book: I couldn't get enough of it. The cover was blue and the lettering red, and since my blue beret had a red feather woven into its label, I never ceased to thrill at the coincidence. "Look, Miss Fritzi," I'd command, waving book and beret. She'd smile.

At the Lee School the girls learned to curtsy like duchesses and the boys to bow like dukes, and we all learned "Alouette" and "Sur le pont d'Avignon." In midmorning the boys fell over themselves in the Dunbars' backyard and the girls gathered on the round porch to chatter. We turned our faces to the thin New England sun and sniffed the salty air and watched as Bristol Harbor, just across the street, capered in the light. D.D., who would grow up to be chic, had a big hat that tied under her chin and Ray, who was very tall, had her clothes washed by a laundress, and Nancy, who had red hair, said her mother squeezed oranges for her every morning. I wanted a hat like D.D.'s and long legs and a laundress like Ray's, and wished that my mother would give me orange juice every morning so that I, too, would have hair that flamed like a marigold. Still, D.D. and Ray and Nancy weren't as lucky as I was. They didn't have my father. My father was king of the Lee School's annual Field Day.

Jacket tossed to the ground, shirtsleeves rolled to the elbows of his milk-skinned Irish arms, black hair mussed by the wind, it was end man Leo Cantwell, all 224 pounds of him, who pulled the losing tug-of-war team across the line. It was Leo Cantwell who got slapped on the back, whose face reddened to the cheers and whose mouth split into a smile that was an entertainment in itself. "Who's the handsomest man in the world next to Ronald Colman?" he'd ask when we came home.

"You are!" Di and I would shout.

"Now," he'd say as he tucked us into bed, "you're as snug as bugs in a rug."

And so we were, all the time.

There came a chilly winter morning, though, when Miss Fritzi herded us little kids into the room where the big kids sat and lined us up on chairs facing the blackboard. Then Mrs. Dunbar, short and stout in dusty-rose crepe, told us a story.

The story was about how the king of England—I didn't catch his name—had had to give up his throne because he wanted to marry an American named Simpson. This Mrs. Simpson could never be a queen because she'd been divorced. English kings weren't allowed to marry divorced women, nor, Mrs. Dunbar added, could they marry Catholics.

Not marry Catholics! I had never heard of divorce, so that proscription passed right over my head. But hadn't Nancy once pointed out, her blue eyes fixed speculatively on my face, that I was the sole Catholic at the Lee School? Was it possible that I, the best speller and reader in the whole place, was the only girl ineligible to sit upon the English throne? What else was I *already* ineligible for, I wondered, and felt a cold, wet finger trace my spine.

I HAD SUSPECTED that Catholics came out of the second drawer ever since I had overheard Gampa complaining about a neighbor who'd refused to sell him a small parcel of land adjoining ours for a garage. "I suppose he thought a Catholic had a hell of a nerve," he said in a cold sour voice.

Another time I asked him why the shallow rise that separated the backyard from the front yard had two stone steps inserted in its center. "Because Protestants lived here," he said in the same sour tone, "and they love airs and graces."

Besides, why else was St. Mary's Church way up in the back of town, close to the rubber factory and a string of low, mean houses and dark, dank stores? Up there the air was yellow and stank of rubber, and there was no harbor breeze to take the heat off a summer day.

Sunday morning, gloved and hatted, we would leave 232 Hope Street, turn right at Constitution, left on High, and walk to the corner of Church. There we'd make another right and start the hike across Bristol Common. What little grass had ever grown on the Common had been beaten down by generations of softball players and schoolchildren, and the Fourth of July visits of traveling carnivals. The elms were lofty, so lofty they brushed the sky, but they were few, and in summer there was no shelter from the sun. In winter there was no shelter from the wind that swept across the Common as if it were the tundra.

St. Mary's Church sheered, rawboned Gothic, out of a steep flight of granite steps, with never a leaf to hide its nakedness. Our pew—our p.u., I thought, using the worst word I knew—was next to a stained-glass window of Jesus and a lamb. Two blocks to the south and west of this chilly sepulcher, my Lee School classmates were filing into ivy-covered St. Michael's for another turn on the social round. But I had been sentenced to Purgatory, forbidden to move, forbidden to whisper, eyes nailed to a faraway figure who bowed and whirled and occasionally extended his arms in our direction. On the rare Sundays when we went to High Mass, incense clouded the aisles and pricked my nose. "P.u.," I'd mutter to myself. Everything was p.u. at St. Mary's Church.

Walking home we moved from yellow to blue, from rubber to salt. The funny papers lay ahead; so did leg of lamb, carrots, lima beans, and a baked potato, vanillaicecreamwithchocolate-saucemarshmallowandwetnuts (always asked for in one breath) at Buffington's Drugstore and, after the sun set and the lamps were turned on, *The Shadow* and Jack Benny. Having traversed Purgatory, I was in Heaven.

Church had imposed an orderly start on what otherwise might have been a shapeless day, and I hated shapeless days. Too, in standing, sitting, kneeling, and bowing on command for an hour, I had achieved that sweet smugness that comes from abnegation. On Sunday, trembling to do good and knowing no beggar with whom to share a cloak and no child to carry across a river, I would instead arrange the dining-room chairs with mathematical exactness, and eat my leg of lamb with all the airs and graces of the blackest Protestant.

THE SOUL WAS LIKE A SHEET OF PAPER, and mine was still unsmirched. Once I reached the age of reason, however, it would be crisscrossed with thin lines if my crimes were small, and thick, terrible strokes if they were big. Thin line, venial sin. Thick stroke, mortal sin. All the marks were erased when one partook of the Blessed Sacrament. Those leaving the altar rail with a mouthful of wafer were walking up the aisle with a just-sponged soul.

This, as I understood it, was why I had to begin Religious Instructions at St. Mary's Parochial School, a brown wooden fire-trap of a building near the church. I was nearly seven, thus close to the age of reason, and the warranty that was my baptism was running out. Making my First Communion, it looked like, was a way to renew the insurance.

The class in Religious Instructions met once a week, and although I knew the way to St. Mary's School I was afraid to travel so far outside the country of the blue-eyed by myself. So every Tuesday afternoon, after the Lee School let out, I left salt air for rubber stink to lean against a telephone pole outside the Walley School and wait for the 3:30 bell and Ruthie. If the windows were open I could hear the drone of recitations and the teacher's "Now, class, let's turn to page . . ." and sometimes the slap of erasers. Then the bell tolled and out they'd pour, girls from the door to the left, boys from the door to the right, most of them dark and all of them strangers. All but Ruthie, honey-haired, myopic, and my savior.

Ruthie lived on Union Street with her Boston bull terrier, Brownie, her parents, and her appendix, which, like Diana, she kept in a bottle by her bed. (Eventually everyone I knew had their appendix in a bottle by their bed, everyone but me, who still worries if the pain—from too much wine, too many shrimp—is on the right.) Our parents weren't friends, they were scarcely acquaintances, but I think my mother had called her mother to ask if Ruthie could be my guide to St. Mary's. I trailed her as trustingly as I would have trailed Leatherstocking, and in a sense I trail her still.

We sat in a tan classroom strung with pictures of the Crown of Thorns, the Light of the World, and the Sacred Heart, holding small tan catechisms and facing an apple-faced nun, mysterious in her floating black, responding in rote:

"Who made the world?"

"God made the world."

"Who is God?"

"God is the creator of heaven and earth and of all things visible and invisible."

Were the nuns bald? Like every child who's ever faced those high calm foreheads, we wondered if they extended to the nape of the neck. What was the nuns' underwear like? Surely they couldn't wear corsets and pink drawers like Ganny. They must wear muslin, and it must scratch. One nun, Sister Edwina, said that she loved

Saint Peter most of all the saints because he had sinned. So Ruthie and I also loved Saint Peter best, mostly because we liked Sister Edwina and partly because (as we realized many years thereafter) we were more comfortable with sinners. All the nuns, when asked to explain the inexplicable, answered with a sibilant "But that, my child, is a mysssstery."

On these Tuesday afternoons the questions for which there were no answers, only cloture, mounted in a tall, dusty pile and the air grew thick enough for stirring. When—and oh, God, how the clock stalled in its paces—it was five o'clock and we filed out of the classroom and down the wooden steps I was as frantic as if I'd been sewn into a shroud.

By that hour the Common was almost dark and usually empty, and I would urge Ruthie to a race along the sidewalk that bisected it from northeast to southwest. It puzzled Ruthie, this wild run across the Common, and sometimes she slid opaque glances in my direction. No matter. Once we were on High Street we were out of the grave, and fresh air was lifting my hair and brushing my cheeks again.

At home I waited for the mysssstery to reveal itself. I hungered for the arrow that would pierce my body and make me a child of Christ. I begged God to appear in our bedroom some night after Diana had drifted off to sleep so I could see Him, and when He didn't I climbed to the attic and prayed to Aunt Margaret. The attic was that much closer to Heaven and surely she, who was bound to be there—if indeed there was a there—would bend her sad blue eyes in my direction and smile.

"Please, dear Jesus, give me a sign," I'd whisper, and finger the rosary I'd stolen from Ganny's bureau drawer, ashamed not just of theft but of ascribing magic to a string of little beads. The attic was very cold and musty, and the old trunks and stripped-down bedsteads looked lonely in the dark. The Irish trunk stood derelict under the eaves, and chamber pots that had held the piddle of people long gone were stacked on a closet floor. A hand-tinted photograph of my mother, taken when she was about two years old and blonde as an angel, swung crooked from a nail. I waited. The silence was absolute. There was nothing and no one to be heard up here.

On a Sunday morning in May I made my First Communion, fearful of the absentminded sip of water that would break the fast and of the accidental rip of the teeth that would torture the Host. Esther took my picture in the backyard that afternoon. My veil was drooping, my long white stockings, dependent from my first garter belt, were drooping, and so was I.

# Seven

$\mathcal{I}$T IS AN AUTUMN EVENING one year later, and Gampa's garden has been put to bed for the winter. I am sitting on a chair in the kitchen, directly under the ceiling light, and a towel is draped about my shoulders. My hair has been drenched with something that smells like kerosene and my mother is parting it into inch-wide sections, then riffling through them with a fine-toothed comb. Every once in a while she says "Gotcha!" and shakes the comb over a wastebasket. Like everyone who has ever shared a classroom with a member of the notorious V—— family, I have cooties.

Obviously I (and Diana, who is next in line for the kitchen chair) am no longer at the Lee School. No louse has ever crossed its threshold. Our parents have taken us out of there and enrolled us in public school. We go quietly, disappointed only that they wouldn't let us skip a grade. Given a mother who used to teach school and a father on the School Committee, we're a year ahead of ourselves. No, they said, you're too young. So here we are at the Walley School, Di in the second grade, I in the third grade, and both of us with lice.

Papa believes in the public schools as fervently as he believes in the Holy Ghost, the Holy Catholic Church, the Communion of Saints, the Resurrection of the Body and Life Everlasting, amen. Parochial schools will narrow our minds and our prospects. Private schools are all right if they're in Switzerland, which is where the

richest man in Bristol sent his children, because there one has all
the advantages of Europe. Otherwise they represent the most ar-
rant form of snobbery. Why, when he was a boy in Fall River the
daughters of textile tycoons sat side by side with the sons of mill-
hands, and that's the way America's supposed to be. So off we trotted, in eyelet-edged underwear and sashed gingham dresses from
Gladding's, Providence's nicest department store, and carrying
elaborate plaid schoolbags.

My first day at the Walley set the tone for all the years to follow. Still as timid about leaving the country of the blue-eyed as I
had been when I was taking catechism lessons, I tagged after
Ruthie. She ushered me through the squirming crowd at the entrance marked "Girls" and through the dreary corridors and up to
the big square classroom. But once in my seat—last one in the first
row—I was on my own. And the first thing I did was insult the
teacher.

I corrected her spelling. "It's not p-s-l-a-m, Miss P——," I said
of the word she'd written on the blackboard. "It's p-s-a-l-m.
You've spelled it puh-slam." I giggled, thinking she'd see the joke.
Miss Fritzi would have. "Don't you be so smart, Mary Lee
Cantwell," Miss P—— snapped, and her eyes were a basilisk's.

An hour or so later the music teacher, a barrel of a woman with
a chin you could wrap your hand around, bustled into the room.
She chalked some notes on the black-board with short, vicious
strokes, then went around the room, asking each student to read
aloud those she jabbed at with her pointer. When she got to me I
rose from my desk and said "I'm sorry, Mrs. D——, but I haven't
been taught how to read music." "I'm sorry, Mrs. D——," she
replied in perfect mimicry, "but I haven't been taught how to read
music." I sat down, my eyes hot and my stomach melting. Till then
I had believed that all rooms would brighten because I entered
them. As we walked home after school, Ruthie was silent and her
eyes were opaque behind her plastic-rimmed glasses.

For a few weeks I was a novelty. The girls gathered around me
at recess and lifted my skirt to see my French pants, which they admired, and touched my hair ribbon, which they said was "so-o-o-o
pretty." Years later I saw Gypsy children behave like that, stroking
and soothing and cooing like doves while we tourists moved down

a Yugoslav street, fearful lest those little brown fingers slip inside our purses. But now I was flattered and showed off a little, and offered my Smith Brothers Cough Drops to the crowd.

Except for Ruthie and a handful of others, my classmates were the children and grandchildren of immigrants, and they lived near the rubber factory. Their grandmothers wore shawls and stumbled over English, if they spoke it at all, and on feast days their fathers, stocky men in dark, shiny suits, bent their backs to wooden platforms from which plaster saints bestowed frozen blessings on the crowd. They and their families had changed the face of Bristol from blue-eyed to brown, from fair-skinned to olive, and their names were slippery and suspect to the northern tongue.

Down on the Yacht Club dock on summer Saturdays a legion of ladies, summer people and Ferry residents in Best & Company shirtdresses, were barking "Well *done!*" as the winning Herreshoff bull's-eye crossed the finish line, while up on the Common men in shirtsleeves were playing boccie. Meanwhile the last Yankees roamed their enclaves—the Neck and the southern ends of Hope and High streets—the blue veins under their thin skins knotted across their knuckles and their shinbones. Not only were they dying, they were dying out.

Public school, though, was in another country. Give an Italian the eye and he, or she, would give you the finger. And a shove and a fist and, once, a curse. When Papa insisted that a tubercular teacher leave her job for treatment, her relatives telephoned 232 Hope Street and told him they hoped his daughters would die of the same disease.

The novelty wore off, my innocence seemed arrogance which, in a way, I suppose it was, and now the crowd of girls who circled me at recess shouted "show-off!" and "stuck-up!" and "School Committeeman's daughter!" When I erred and revealed my report card they added "teacher's pet."

The hits that knocked me out of the ring during dodge ball were hard enough to leave a bruise, and I was always the last to be chosen for a team, any team. Often at recess I wet my pants from fear and nervousness, and spent the rest of the day sitting on one haunch so the moisture wouldn't seep through my dress. At night I rinsed out my underwear so my mother wouldn't see it, and during the day I sucked up to my tormentors, and distributed my cough drops with an ever more lavish hand. Once I brought a girl home to play after school, and when she said of the root beer my mother poured her "Oh, I've never had such a big glass before," I felt her well-aimed shiv between my ribs.

To be part of the gang I was willing to strip myself of my gingham dresses and my little red topper, my twenty-five cents a week and my giant box of Crayolas. What I couldn't discard was a home in the country of the blue-eyed, to which most of the kids at the Walley had been only for afternoons at the foot of Union Street, and I seldom made it to the blackboard without feeling the sting of a ruler on the back of my legs. When a girl with a pinched face turned out to be consumptive and became the toast of the school for the week before she left for a sanitarium, I envied her, so much so that every time I brushed my teeth I studied the spit, hoping for the bloody threads that would bring me, too, the love and admiration of my classmates. Then a new girl arrived, and for a blessed while nobody paid attention to me.

She sat for a few tortured months in the back row, her gray eyes anxious in her pudding face and her fat red hands knotted around one another. Every morning she traveled across the harbor on the Prudence Island ferry, and she reeked of fish and unwashed underwear. When we went outside at recess she stood alone, isolated by her terrible odor, while the V—— family, monuments to impetigo and perpetually painted with gentian violet, swarmed the Common, little boys fought to see little girls' underpants, and I, in the majority for once and desperate to remain there, smiled the smile of Uriah Heep and turned away my face.

The teachers at the Walley, like most of those in town, were Irish and Italian and Yankee spinsters, graduates of the Rhode Island Normal School. The only one (besides Miss P——) who sticks in my mind is the one who got married, and that only because everybody stared at her when she came back from her honeymoon, to see if she walked differently. Rumor had it that she would, though why wasn't specified, and I thought I detected a certain looseness through the thighs.

Every morning we pledged allegiance " 'a the flag of the United States of America," sat down, bowed our heads, and said the

Lord's Prayer. How it ended depended on whether the teacher was a Catholic or a Protestant. If she was the former her mouth snapped shut after "and deliver us from evil, amen," while the few Protestants among us continued with a loud and confident "For thine is the kingdom and the power and the glory. . . ." If the teacher was a Protestant her voice was loudest of all.

What did I learn, aside from two into six goes three and mis-sis-sippi spells Mississippi and how to convert my private-school printing into Palmer Method script? I learned how democracy works. Like this: Different-sized pegs are hammered into holes until they are all exactly the same height.

"Fair's fair, democracy wins," the kids yelled about everything from choosing sides for softball to class projects. So did Miss P——. Democracy lost, for instance, the day Papa gave me a dime-store bridge to span the pocket-mirror pond that was the center-piece of my Japanese garden. (We were making pie-tin landscapes.) "That's not fair to the others, Mary Lee," she said, "because not everybody's got a father who can afford to buy them bridges." I blushed, ashamed of myself and my garden and even of my father, who was so eager to help his children and so ignorant of the rules. When the teacher asked which of us wanted to bring home notices of the PTA meetings, I waved my hand and said I was sure my parents would want them. But my parents never went to the PTA meetings; I doubt anybody's parents went to the PTA meetings. Our world of dusty erasers and basement toilets and desks and chairs bolted to the floor was ours alone.

By early afternoon the sun slammed the windowpanes and the exhalations from forty squirming bodies slammed the ceiling. One of the big boys was summoned to let in fresh air with the long pole kept in the corner. Up he stretched, his shirttail going up with him, making pass after pass at the hole in the top of the window. Finally, the pole's metal hook caught, he tugged, the windows shimmied down an inch or so and in rushed the scent of rubber and dust and trampled grass. We lifted our noses, some of them blocked with boogers. We trembled, like horses in full whinny.

One morning during recess a wind came up and blew the dirt about as if it were tumbleweed. The grit freckled my bare legs, and the sky was a sick yellow. Some of the teachers, Diana's among them, sent their classes home. Miss P—— delayed—she thought the wind would die—and by the time she realized it would not, trees were falling without a whisper. I, stranded alone on High Street among toppled elms and hissing electric lines and a sound like a cow lowing, was more interested than scared. Being caught outdoors in a hurricane struck me as part and parcel of being in the third grade at the Walley School.


RUTHIE, MY MOTHER SAID, had "personality." Her parents came from out of town, which was enough to make her a foreigner in Bristol; that her father was a Swedish Lutheran and her mother a Polish Catholic only compounded her otherness. But I think it was that otherness, and the attendant wariness, that allowed her to navigate the public schools so successfully. Ruthie, as I could see by the crowd of kids that trailed her out the schoolhouse door, was a political genius. With Ruthie one was protected. Hanging around her was a lot like hanging a scapular around your neck.

After the Walley let out for the day we sometimes stayed up on the Common, playing tag or marbles—squatting in the dust and aiming aggies at the hole dug by twisting one's heel into the dry soil—until the sun sank and the wind chilled and the lights came on in the little High Street houses. Other days we scuffled through the leaves that carpeted Wood Street, all the way down to Tanyard Lane, where skunk cabbage perfumed the air in spring and the tree growing out of the roof of a crypt in an old family graveyard—"Its roots are in his skull," we'd shriek—made us shiver. There were no houses down here, only tall grasses and soughing trees and the occasional cow strayed from the meadows down the Ferry, and our eyes were eager for Indians, miraculously resurrected and padding noiselessly across the swampy ground.

More often, though, I trusted to my own company, mine and Ganny's, to get me through the hours till Papa and Esther came home with the news from the shop. Like Judy, I was forever underfoot. "You might as well come up street to the Bluebird Shoppe," or "I suppose you want me to take you to the five-and-ten," Ganny would sigh, and trundle into her bedroom for her hat.

Ganny's hats were brimmed, bowed, and often fruited, sat

square on her head and announced she was going places. The only
time she went out without one was when she was just crossing the
street to look at the harbor. Then her white hair escaped its pins
and flew around her face and turned her into a short, plump mae-
nad. Whenever, now, I hear the term "Wild Irish," I think of my
grandmother at the foot of Union Street, the water dancing and her
hair streaming and her green eyes glinting like beach glass.

THE BLUEBIRD SHOPPE was owned by Miss Norah Sullivan, a
tall, stout, sternly buttressed women who was privy to every female
bump and bulge in our part of town. Entering the Bluebird's deep
amber gloom was like entering a church. Voices were as hushed as
they were at St. Mary's, the customers leaning toward Miss
Sullivan much as they would toward the grille of a confessional
and murmuring into her bottomless ears. If I concentrated I could
catch a word or two—"garment . . . support . . . bust"—and once,
from Ganny, a sibilant, sinister "truss."

Silently the long thin boxes slid in and out of the shelves, and
the tissue paper rustled discreetly when it opened to reveal corsets
whose laces were longer than those that tied my shoes and garters
that dangled obscenely when Miss Sullivan pulled the "garment"
out of its virginal wrap. Together Ganny and Miss Sullivan whispered while Ganny ran a small, fat hand over her stomach and I,
half-thrilled, half-mortified, shivered at what it meant to be female.
Ganny disappeared behind a curtain. Miss Sullivan followed.

"Watch out for my hairpins." Miss Sullivan was pulling
Ganny's dress over her head. "I could take it a little tighter." Miss
Sullivan was lacing. "Here, just under the bust, it . . ." I felt sick.

I always took a deep breath when we left the Bluebird, driving
out the sweetness of dusting powder and sachet with the punch of
salt and privet. "Now," I'd command, "the five-and-ten," and off
we'd go, slowly because of Ganny's rheumatism, to the true up
street. "Anybody want anything from up street?" the grownups
said whenever they left the house for the drugstore or the five-and-
ten, and my mind would reel with possibilities.

At the five-and-ten, which smelled of the Spanish peanuts
roasting in the big machine by the entrance, I studied the paper

dolls and Ganny poked among the spectacles, looking for something that might replace her magnifying glass, and there one day she lost her underpants. The elastic gave way; they puddled, pink and voluminous, to the floor; she scooped them up with the end of her rubber-tipped cane and walked on, imperturbable. "No sense in being embarrassed," she said, seeing the skin around my eyes turn red, and stuck the underpants in her handbag.

From the five-and-ten, where we seldom bought anything and marveled over everything, we ambled down to Eisenstadt's Dry Goods, Ganny how-doing from side to side as we went. While she bought muslin for her nightgowns—V-necked, long-sleeved, and plain as sheets—I wandered the aisles, giddy among the bolts of fabric and tumbles of yarn and the sharp, clean scent of sizing. Then, past Buffington's and the jewelry store and the Y.M.C.A. and Alger's Newsstand and the ever-open, beer-haunted door of the Belvedere Hotel, we strolled toward home.

After Constitution Street the salt breeze got stronger and the trees moved with it. In the distance the bay windows of 232 Hope Street gleamed like a lighthouse lantern, and behind them Gampa watched as his short, stout Mag, leaning on her cane, came slowly into view. Tonight Ganny might take me to bingo up over G.A.R. Hall, and tomorrow she might take me up to Milk Street and let me watch while Miss Brelsford measures her for her nightgowns, and the next day she might let me go with her while she calls on Mrs. Horton, and never will she let me know that she knows that nobody at school likes me.

Instead she will infuse me with her delight in the ordinary. The one time I played bingo as an adult, on a Cunard liner crossing the Atlantic, my fingers were joyful on the old familiar markers. The day I wriggled into my first girdle and felt the garters bounce against my thighs I was returned to the Bluebird Shoppe and possessed of all its delicious, illicit, secretive femaleness. And whenever I smell starch or Spanish peanuts my veins fill with something that fizzes like ginger ale. Up, up, up it goes, to the top of my head, which has never worn, and probably never will wear, a bowed, brimmed, and fruited hat.

# Eight

_I_F ONLY MY MEMORY were more merciful. But let me climb the steps to 232 Hope Street and I remember the day a boy who was inarticulate with rage and perhaps love threw a stone at my receding back and broke one of the door's engraved glass panels. The glass that replaced it was frosted, with no curlicues, and stares at me now, ugly as a cataract.

Let me go down to the foot of Church Street to buy lobsters off the wharf, and I see a muscular girl named Teresa wrestling me to the ground, her dress riding up over her underwear and her socks sliding ever deeper into her shoes while her seconds, a gang from the back of town, cheer her on. I can see myself, too, struggling to stay upright and conspicuously short of adrenaline. This, I was thinking, is _dumb_.

Let me run a hand along the back of my head and my fingers probe for a scar that disappeared decades ago: souvenir of the day that Ruthie and I found a lost puppy.

It was shivering near the entranceway to Miss Hill's house. Miss Hill was principal of the Byfield School, where we were now fourth-graders, and traveled its halls like a miniature tank. We were very respectful of Miss Hill. To be otherwise was to sit, silent and seemingly forgotten, on the straight chair outside her office door until she looked up from her desk and said the punishment period was over and don't you ever do it again.

I suspect it was to get into her good graces, to show ourselves good citizens, that Ruthie and I thought of asking Miss Hill, and not our mothers, what we should do about the puppy. But as we stood hesitating over which of us should ring her bell, a boy who lived near the rubber factory, the same boy who had thrown the stone that broke the glass panel in the front door, came along and said, "Give it to me."

"Why should I?"

"Because I said," he answered, and tried to pull the puppy from my arms. When I hung on to it, he pushed me down on the cement sidewalk, splitting my scalp. The blood pooled around my head and he, frightened, ran for home. For weeks thereafter my skull was swathed in gauze and adhesive tape and I wore my bandages as arrogantly as if I were sporting the stigmata.

Even so, the boy had scared me. I thought he was crazy then and I think he is crazy now, and on the rare times when I see him—an unremarkable adult with a head that has lost its hair and a chest that had slid into his stomach—I pass without speaking. I can take care of myself, but the skinny, chattering girl I was could not, and I'm still touchy on her behalf.

There are others in Bristol, housewives and plumbers and electricians now, whom I might pass without speaking if I were certain that they had been among the crowd that followed me home from school one winter afternoon. But I'm not certain, because my eyes were fixed on the feet, shod in oxblood-colored cordovan with bright yellow laces, that were slowly and stubbornly taking me home.

My fifth-grade teacher at the Reynolds School, not realizing how unpolitic her choice, had chosen me as my home room's entrant in the school's annual talent show. In truth I had little talent, only a thin soprano that reached a lot of perilous notes. But I thought it was wonderful to be able to sing so high, and, turning the playroom into my rehearsal studio, practiced my entry every day. "Now 'neath the silver moon," I piped, and thrilled to my baroque "Sa-a-a-nta Lu-ci-i-a, Santa Lu-cia!"

On the night of the talent show we, as usual, left the house in a body: Ganny and Gampa walking very slowly up front, followed by Papa, Mother, and Esther, with Diana and me bringing up the rear. Into the Reynolds Auditorium we walked, a familiar place because it was the site of Bristol's Town Meetings, and my family solemnly took their places on the folding chairs. I joined the others onstage and, when the lights went down, strained to see them in the dark, sitting breathless lest I forgot the words.

The principal called my name. I stepped forward and stared blindly at the invisible audience. And I sang it! I sang "Santa Lucia" all the way through, without forgetting a word, and waited for the applause. But there was none, because when I stopped the piano went on. The accompanist was expecting me to sing the second verse. I didn't know it.

Later on I wished I'd pretended to faint, but I doubt it would have helped. If the bandages I'd worn around my head in fourth grade hadn't brought me love, lying supposedly unconscious on the stage of the Reynolds auditorium wouldn't bring it either. Instead I said to the accompanist, a friend of my mother's, "Mrs. Sturdevent, I didn't learn the second verse."

"Well, then, Mary Lee," she said, "why don't you sing the first verse over again?" So I did.

I was sitting with the residents of 232 Hope Street, all of them sad and quiet, when the judges announced that Mary Lee Cantwell had won first prize, a subscription to *American Girl* magazine, for her homeroom. Ruthie, who was sitting in the row in back of us, leaned over. "I think you'd better walk to school with me tomorrow," she whispered.

For now, though, there was the walk home along the sleeping streets and Gampa saying "Mary Lee, you did fine," and Papa saying "It's okay, Lulubelle. All famous actresses forget their lines once in a while," and Diana on the verge of tears because it is embarrassing to be my sister. And I? I was locked in a misery that has lasted me all my life. Let me hear "Santa Lucia"—and it seems to me I hear it all the time—and I am, for a moment, humiliated.

The next morning Ruthie was waiting for me at the corner of Constitution Street. We didn't speak while we trudged along High Street, and my back was damp with cold sweat. No one would come after me while I was with her, they wouldn't dare, but what would happen at lunch-time? Ruthie carried sandwiches to school because her mother was a nurse at the rubber factory, and I would have to go home alone.

At noon the mob settled quietly into place behind me, like birds settling on a telephone wire. At first they were silent, until somebody shouted "School committeeman's daughter!" Then all of them took it up. "School committeeman's daughter! School committeeman's daughter!"

My eyes stayed on my shoes, my shoes and the passing squares of pavement that told me that slowly, slowly I was nearing Constitution Street. Once I got there I would be entering the country of the blue-eyed, and the mob would stop at the border.

Constitution Street was less than a block away when a stone hit my arm, Another hit my back, and a third my leg and then they came in torrents, stones and pebbles and handfuls of dirt. On I plodded, turning left and up the steps of a small grocery store. "Mr. McCaw," I said to the owner, "could you please call my house?"

"Tom," he said when Gampa answered, "I think you'd better come up here and get Mary Lee."

When Gampa arrived, I was standing on the little porch of McCaw's Grocery and the mob was standing a few yards away, watching me with quick, curious eyes. Gampa didn't look at them, nor did he say a word to me. He simply extended his long, liver-spotted hand and escorted his grandchild across Constitution Street. I was over the border now, and safe.

# *Nine*

———◆———

$\mathscr{N}$EVER MIND. I had friends. Slowly, very slowly, we found one another. We recognized our tribal markings. We heard them in our speech—"ahsk" instead of "ox," for instance—and we spotted them in the the long white cards with the black printing on top that marked our membership in the Rogers Free Library. We all had mothers who wouldn't let us out of the house without a clean handkerchief in our schoolbags, and our shoes—sober oxfords— came from the same sober Providence shoe store. Four of us took piano lessons and I took watercolor lessons and except for Jeanne, who had three siblings and countless aunts, we came from small families. Ruthie, of course, and Jeanne, Joanie, Anne, and I. We didn't so much meet as coalesce, and we stayed together until the night we graduated from Colt Memorial High School. Two of us were Catholic and two of us were Protestant and one of us was half and half, and for all of us our strongest spiritual bond was with the Girl Scouts.

THE COLUMBINES met as often in winter and spring as they did in autumn, but in my mind the afternoons are always golden and the leaves are always turning as we Scouts file in the door of the Burton School and hang our coats on its old hooks.

The Burton, which was up on High Street, smelled of chalk and oiled floors and we smelled of wool and jujubes. The room (there were only two) in which we met to master the skills that earned us merit badges was bare and yellow in the western sun, and its radiators were forever thunking. I loved it there, the warmth and the coziness and the going to the bathroom in pairs, one of us pretending nonchalance while the other piddled into the toilet. We were fascinated by our bodies, and pretended to be casual about them by peeing in company, just as one day we would broadcast our menstrual periods. "Oh," we'd moan in years to come, "I'm like the Mississippi at flood tide."

We pretended to be casual about boys' bodies too, but a purloined copy of *The Boy Scout Handbook* was continually passing from hand to hand and falling open, automatically, to the chapter titled "Containment." It was erotic, unbearably so, with its talk about "nocturnal emissions" and the wisdom of sitting in a cold hip bath for fifteen minutes before bedtime and of seeking advice from "wise, clean, strong men." Powerful, too. "Keep control of yourself in sex matters," the handbook thundered. "It's important for your life, your happiness, your efficiency, and the whole human race." No wonder we never saw the boys of Troop Five, our brother troop, on parade without thinking of their silent, superior struggle and of the volcanoes concealed by their rolled-up (to signify they were veterans of Camp Yawgoog) khaki shorts.

About those skills we mastered: We tied knots, I know that, and one night we went to the home of the wife of the local optometrist for a lesson in spaghetti sauce and washing one's hands between bathroom and kitchen. For this exercise we were awarded the hostess badge. I had other badges too, plastering the left sleeve of my silvery-green uniform, but for what I no longer remember. Fire-making probably, and tree identification for sure. I can still tell an elm from an oak, and a birch from a maple.

I can recall the marching, though, around and around the patch of grass in front of the Burton, practicing for the Memorial and Armistice Day parades. Once, as I was counting a *sotto voce* "one-two, one-two," a fly flew in my mouth and was promptly swallowed. "I'm not surprised," my mother said. "Your mouth is always hanging open." She said I talked too much. Papa said I had the gift of the gab.

But all that practicing paid off. When we marched up Hope Street on parade mornings, I with the end of the staff that flew the Girl Scout flag nestled next to my belly button, we were a sight. The Goldenrods and the Marigolds weren't in it with us. When we passed 232 Hope Street, stepping smartly, my family clapped and Gampa raised his hat—felt on Armistice Day, straw on Memorial—for the Stars and Stripes. When we stood near the flag-markered graves in North Burial Ground and the bugler played "Taps," I threw back my shoulders and presented a brave face to the west. And when, on the evening of Armistice Day, Ruthie and I walked along High Street after the service at the Train of Artillery Hall, through the rustling trees and the dry leaves and the damp air, after the speeches and "My Buddy" and "There's a Long, Long Trail a-Winding," we were too blissfully sorrowful to speak. How lovely it was to feel the tears flowing down your cheeks and know that no adult could tell you to stop that sniffling, because you were weeping in a good cause.

Every spring I roamed the neighborhood, pad in hand, taking orders for Girl Scout cookies. A talker but shy, I never knocked on a stranger's door. Instead I called on Mrs. Connery, mother to Miss Aida and Miss Emilie, and Mrs. Tingley, who lived on the other side of the blue fence, and Ganny's friend Miss Munro, nosing around their back entries and sniffing at the smells from kitchens other than my own. On the day the cookies arrived at the Burton School I trotted out of 232 Hope Street after supper, my arms hooked around the boxes, feeling as if I were digging my heels into Bristol, that I was as much a part of its fabric as the iceman or the coalman. "Hope you enjoy them!" I'd say to Mrs. Connery, Mrs. Tingley, and Miss Munro, all of them flushed from cooking and fishing in their change purses. I sounded exactly like the man on the Arnold's Bakery truck.

Mrs. Connery, Mrs. Tingley, Miss Munro, Miss Aida, and Miss Emilie were looking out their windows the night I walked up Union Street for the Girl Scout dance. I know this not because I saw their faces or the twitch of their curtains but because in Bristol watching somebody leave the house for her first dance and the Junior Prom and her high school graduation was a way of telling time.

I had thought long and hard about what to wear, and finally settled on a yellow cotton blouse, a teal-blue wool skirt with a brown leather belt, beige knee socks and brown oxfords. What I hadn't thought about was not knowing how to dance. Perhaps I believed it would just come to me, or that simply being there, under a ceiling crisscrossed with crepe paper and surrounded by Pennsylvania Six Five Oh Oh Oh would be enough. Perhaps it would have been, too, except that Albert, Joanie's brother and a member of Troop Five, led me away from the rest of the Columbines and onto the floor. "No, Mary Lee," he said when I extended my right arm toward his shoulder. "Put your left hand on my shoulder and let me hold the other one." I did as I was told and then, staring intently at my feet, tried to make them follow his. They did!

Tall, blond, three or four years older than I, Albert never shared a dance, or even a dance floor, with me again. Still, he was the first male whose movements I had ever tried to mirror: and those slow, flat-footed steps of mine were, I realize now, as irrevocable as those with which, a baby, I had tumbled into my parents' waiting arms.

USUALLY I GRABBED EVERY OPPORTUNITY to put on my Girl Scout uniform and proclaim to the world my membership in a club, but not on the Fourth of July. Bristol's parade was the oldest in the country, and maybe the biggest, and I wouldn't have dreamed of marching in it. Miss the floats, the governor of Rhode Island, the drum-and-bugle corps from all over New England, the Fourth of July Committee with their ice-cream pants, boutonnières, and malacca canes, the antique cars and the fire engines and the servicemen from Newport and Jamestown and points north? Miss the balloon men and the eggnog Papa put in the punch bowl in the front hall and the thrill when some of the marchers—the governor, even—flourished their hats to his applause? They knew him! Leo Cantwell, member of the Bristol School Committee and defeated candidate for the Bristol Town Council. But only because it was a bad year for the Democrats.

EARLY IN THE MORNING when the sky is still gray we can hear the dull boom of the Fourth of July cannon. "Get up," my mother pleads. "Get up, get up, get up." Time to get out the old blankets and the folding chairs and spread them over the banking in front of 232 Hope Street because if you don't make it clear that this strip of grass is yours, all yours, people from out of town will come and park their carcasses right in front of you.

The Barrington crowd, friends of Papa and Mother, are up early, too, because if they aren't, strangers will take their parking places. Barrington is about ten miles from Bristol, a pretty place, more suburb than town, with the highest number of blonds per capita in Rhode Island. The Barrington crowd plays a lot of golf.

"We're going to have an army in here," my mother says, shooing Di and me out of the kitchen, out of the bathroom, out of the house. "Don't dirty those towels, don't use those glasses, put those books away this minute." Downstairs Papa is mixing the eggnog in Ganny's big punch bowl. "My theory," he says as he dribbles in the brandy, "is that everyone will have gotten here too early to have had breakfast. And here we have eggs and cream. . . ."

Esther, still buzzing from the night before the Fourth at the Belvedere—all Bristol meets there on the evening of July 3 to hoist a few—and dressed in red, white, and blue, is knocking ice cubes out of a tray. It's only nine o'clock in the morning, mind you, but she, like a lot of Bristolians, will spend the day with a glass in her hand. Gampa, having crawled out the window in the playroom, is on the balcony over the front door hanging out the American flag. Judy, her little backside wriggling, is barking at his heels. Meanwhile Ganny, to whom this is all foolishness, has taken herself to the porch.

Out on the sidewalks the crowds are gathering, neighbors and tourists and old Bristolians back in town for the Glorious Fourth, and some of them are breaking away from the pack to open the garden gate. They're friends and acquaintances come to stand beneath the porch and chat with Ganny. None will call her Margaret.

She is Mrs. Lonergan to everyone, just as her friends are Miss and Mrs. to her. That's how they go through life, fenced from one another by mutual formality, and although they're walking in the same direction, their shoulders never touch.

Gampa, off the balcony now and pulling out his pipe on the front steps, is Tom to everybody. But he, too, keeps his distance, his only true cronies being Old Man Connery, Old Man Connors (I will never know their first names) and Ralph Kinder, the florist, for whom he enjoys doing odd jobs. Gampa would like to have some eggnog, but he knows better. Once some Thames Street—that's the street that runs along the waterfront—tosspots lured him into the Hurricane Bar, and he had to be escorted home. Diana and I watched from the window while they hauled him stumbling up the front steps, and he went to bed in disgrace. Ganny walked around with thinned lips; Mother, always nervous of what people might think, was cold and dismissive: and Diana, who thought it was funny, called him "Hurricane" for weeks.

Drums are pounding in the distance, and cops on motorcycles are coming around the corner of Summer Street. Here they are: the Fourth of July Committee, swinging their canes and doffing their hats, the Colt Memorial High School Band (one day Ruthie will be drum major) in their spanking green and white, Bristol's own bugle-and-drum corps, straight-backed, small-buttocked, bugles high and blatting.

Fife-and-drum corps in colonial outfits. Two men and a boy in tatters and bandages portraying the Spirit of '76. The *Quarante et Huit,* World War I veterans packed into a boxcar, plump and cheering. Shriners looking silly in their silks and fezzes. (One of the Barrington crowd is wearing his fez and three-fingers a conspiratorial salute.) Cesar B., Bristol's richest *brava,* his brass-colored skin tarnished in the cold northern light, prancing on his palomino. Over all, the flag with the anchor that says "Hope" and the flag with the severed snake that says "Don't tread on me."

A wail, many wails, and the fire engines are bringing up the rear, with the boys of Bristol hanging from them like monkeys do from trees. Now Di and I can brush the grass off our shorts and hazard the bathrooms which, on Mother's order, have been the exclusive property of the Barrington crowd, not one of whom, she says, can hold it. Above us balloons have tangled themselves in the trees or drifted upward to push against the sky until they're out of sight, and their temporary custodians are sobbing into the lawn.

The afternoon is as flat as if someone has put a lid on it. Papa and Mother are at the chief marshal's reception; Esther is off somewhere with one of the girls from the shop; Ganny is in her rocker, scouring the *Providence Journal;* and Gampa is on the Connerys' back steps talking to Old Man Connery. There is nothing for Di and me to do but sit in the playroom, packing and unpacking the trunks of our Dy-Dee dolls, reading our Judy Morton books, and coloring our entries to the Dixie Dugan dress-design contest. Until Gampa decides, that is, that the air has cooled and the sun is low enough for us to go up to the Common and the carnival.

Summer's heat has settled on the Common and the yellow dust rises up to meet it, sifting through our sandals and our socks and lodging between our toes. Gampa buys us cotton candy, which sticks to our faces, and orange soda, which stains our mouths, and stands between our mounts on the merry-go-round. We are really too old for the merry-go-round, but he is not, and he is grinning as what he calls the dobby horses plunge up and down and the Common spins around us.

The games are shaded by a square of canvas tethered to four poles and we stand in the umber light with the rest of Bristol's gamblers, tossing pennies into numbered squares and rings around milk bottles. Next we try to fool the man who guesses weights by puffing our cheeks, and get our fortunes told by a battered automaton in a windowed box. A tall dark man is in my future. We peer into the trailers housing what all Bristol believes to be Gypsies, and we jump—Gampa, too—if any of their inhabitants glance in our direction. Certainly they look like Gypsies, these dark-haired, sallow people who run the carnival, and we shiver in the face of the footloose. "They leave signs, y'know, when they travel on," Gampa says, "but only another Gypsy can read them."

The Ferris wheel is the centerpiece of the carnival, and we save it for last, settling into the gently swaying seats with a sigh. Our feet are sore and our eyes runny and we have breathed too long of dust and cotton candy and motor oil. Up here, though, up here on the top of the Ferris wheel, our faces are brushed by the salt-laced wind that is fingering the tops of the elms. With Gampa, whose arms enclose us, we survey our domain. Bristol lies before us, as neat and tidy as it would appear on an aerial map.

If we look to the left we can see the greasy-pole contest and the water fight between the fire battalions and, behind them, lowering over Wood Street, St. Mary's Church, its rectory, and the convent for the parochial school nuns. Down on the corner is the old town cemetery, its worn gravestones half-swallowed by tall, coarse grass. "How many people are dead in there?" Papa likes to sing out as we walk toward church on Sunday. "All of them!" we chorus.

We can see the bandstand in the center of the Common, and the men setting up the folding chairs for the concert to be given by the Portuguese Independent Band. Our Lady of Mount Carmel, the Italian church, is to the right, and beyond it we can see the spires of St. Elizabeth's, the Portuguese church.

The Walley School is straight ahead, windows closed, shades drawn, silent as a clam. A strip of grass separates it from the Baptist church, and a broader strip runs between the church and the old courthouse. At the corner the Byfield School stares at the Reynolds School across the street, each of them as shuttered and as secret as the Walley. If we could peer through the trees that fringe the Common—but no, the leaves are too thick in summer—we could see Bristol Harbor, and sailboats on their last tack.

The sun is setting, and the men of the Portuguese Independent Band have taken their seats in the bandstand. A drum roll, and "Lady of Spain" crashes through the still, hot air. Fireworks star the sky and Roman candles shoot up from the backyards on Wood Street.

It's time to walk home, past porches from which we can hear low voices and the squeak of gliders, and see cigarettes glowing in the dark. Soon we'll be on our own porch, spooning up coffee ice cream from Buffington's and listening to the boom of fireworks from over Poppasquash way.

With the sun gone, the air is damp as a used towel, and the scent of low tide is drifting up from the foot of Union Street. The cars have all gone back to Providence and Taunton and maybe even as far as Boston, and the cleaning trucks have already swept through town. Di and I are perched on the porch railing, and

Ganny and Gampa are settled in their wicker chairs; and the coffee ice cream is puddling in Ganny's little glass bowls. "Isn't this a nice party?" Gampa says, happy because he wants no more at this moment than this wife, these grandchildren, and this house. "Please," Diana begs, "please, please do 'O, dem golden slippers.' "

Tall, thin Gampa hoists short, fat Ganny out of her chair and bang! goes the screen door as we trail inside. We take our seats and Gampa positions himself in front of the fireplace. Then, his feet sliding and scuffling through imaginary sand, he half-sings, half-whispers "O, dem golden slippers, O, dem golden slippers . . ." and sketches out a softshoe. Di and I applaud, Ganny's mouth curls at the corners. "Slapjack!" Diana commands, and we move into the dining room, to sit around the golden oak table, enclosed in the light from the amber-shaded chandelier, with a pack of tired cards. Screams, and flattened palms smacking the piles of cards and finally, after Ganny finishes rinsing the ice cream dishes, a foursome of whist.

A clatter at the front door. Mother and Papa are home after a lobster dinner with the Barrington crowd, and Esther is due any minute from God knows where. We look up, startled, and a little sad. Our club, the finest to which I will ever belong, is breaking up for the night.

# Ten

On the day that John Fitzgerald Kennedy was assassinated I heard the news while standing in line at a bank in Grand Central Terminal. The day after Francis Gary Powers drifted into Soviet air space I was on a Greenwich Village street, pushing my firstborn child in her plaid baby carriage and praying. "Dear God," I pleaded, "she's only had six weeks."

On the day that Franklin Delano Roosevelt died I was frightened, because he had been my president for about as long as Papa had been my father, and, with God, together they made up my own Holy Trinity. But about that first big day in my lifetime, the day the Japanese bombed Pearl Harbor, I'm uncertain.

Sometimes I can see my parents at the radio and hear the announcer's excited stutter. But did I really? After all, I can see the Hindenberg hovering over the foot of Union Street too, while Diana, the Tingley boys, and I stare breathless at the sky. It hung there like a big black cigar. But maybe not. Maybe I had only seen a photograph. No matter. If I can claim to have seen the Hindenberg, then I can claim that on Pearl Harbor Day I was taking my usual Sunday afternoon walk. And in truth I was so faithful to ritual—the season's first horse chestnut in my pocket to ward off rheumatism, the same five prayers recited every night—I probably was.

In my story, then, I'm heading south, the harbor at my right

and a horse chestnut in my coat pocket. As soon as I get to where
Wood Street, still wild and overgrown at its southern end, runs into
Hope Street and both become Ferry Road I will turn and start back
for *The Shadow* and supper in the kitchen. Now, however, I'm
passing Union Street, where some men in a skiff are taking up eels
with what look like long forks. I'm passing the Lee School, which
is banked in Sunday silence, and Burton Street, where the cement
sidewalk turns into a narrow gravel path; and the Herreshoff boat-
yards, where two America's Cup Defenders, stripped of their masts
and swaddled in tarps, present their sterns to the passersby.

Just beyond the Lobster Pot, the restaurant Mother and Papa
go to with the Barrington crowd on Friday nights, I pause to lean
on a cement-surfaced stone wall, another of the WPA's gifts to
Bristol, and look at the harbor. I am always looking at the harbor
and someday I want to be buried beside it, at the foot of Walley
Street, in the brilliant green grass that precedes the drop to a small
shingle. There I'll be toe to toe with Indian bones, and gazing out
at Poppasquash.

The harbor is naked today of all but the Prudence Island ferry,
and the sun is an orange ball falling slowly behind Hog Island.
Below me the water is washing over barnacled rocks and speckled
pebbles and rubbery strands of seaweed. Several seagulls are circling over the ruins of a breakwater and look! There's a rat slipping
into a crack in the wall.

I walk on, and spongy grass takes over for gravel. The harbor
disappears as the coastline moves westward, the trees thicken and
the air goes from salt to something damp, moldy and ineffably sad.
Wet leaves are sticking to the soles of my shoes now, so I cross the
street to higher, drier ground, face north, and slowly amble home.
Did I get to hear *The Shadow,* or was the radio tuned to the news?
I know only that the streets of Bristol weren't that empty again for
a long, long time. And that I was about to commence my education
in sex and reproduction.

It was the sailors. They were stationed in Newport, twelve
miles away, and looking for something to do. "Here's a nickel,
honey," they'd sing out to kids, myself among them, as they
hopped off the Shoreline bus, bold and bandy-legged and bent on
the Belvedere. "Call me up in five years."

Bristol basked in the grandeur of being a possible target for any bombers and a landing point for any submarines that might manage to slither across the Atlantic. We were prepared. Each night we drew the curtains and pulled the cords on the venetian blinds and Gampa stepped forth on patrol, a tin hat on his head, a flashlight in his hand, a whistle clenched between his false teeth. Let just one streak of light escape a blind and Gampa would shriek the careless householder into shame.

Uncle John, the youngest of Ganny and Gampa's children, was with the Navy in the South Pacific, a great relief to his parents because this was the first time in years they'd been sure of his whereabouts. There was little of Uncle John at 232 Hope Street, only a few pictures of a sharp dresser with a pipe in his mouth, some old phonograph records—Kid Ory and His Creole Jazz, Red Nichols and His Five Copper Pennies—and a big polished shell that said "Pitcairn Islands." Whenever I asked Mother and Esther about my dashing young uncle, known to one and all as "Red" because of his russet hair, their faces snapped shut like purses.

Diana and I had dogtags in case of evacuation, but Ganny figured we could sit out anything. To her, war was the equivalent of the lines coming down, and she was ready for it. Let a bomb strike the Narragansett Electric Light Company, and she'd bring out the kerosene lamps, put the milk and butter in the ice box in the back entry and fire up the coal stove. Let the water mains collapse and it would be necessary only to pry up the slab that had sealed Miss Munro's well for these past fifty years and lo! there was water enough to flush our toilets into the next century.

When I think of us as we were then, every image that surfaces seems straight out of *Life* and *The Saturday Evening Post*. We are clichés, all of us.

There's me marching to the front of the classroom every week to deposit a dollar in my Defense Bond account. Papa coming home from trips to New York for U.S. Rubber with tales of standing room only so he had to sit on his suitcase all the way to Grand Central, and no rooms at the Biltmore so he had to stay in some fleabag on the other side of town. Ganny puzzling out the ration books through her magnifying glass. Diana, who had memorized a book on airplane identification, crouched in the bushes that hid the

red-brick foundation of 232 Hope Street and scanned the skies for
the Luftwaffe. Gampa leaving home in helmet and raincoat for his
evening patrol. Mother making a face as she crushed the orangy-
yellow pellet into the lardy oleo to make it look like butter.

One afternoon she saw a little boy walk past the house with a
brick of real butter in his hand. He'd taken off the paper wrapper
and was licking it like an ice cream cone. If I could not still hear her
voice telling the story—"Oh, I tell you, he made me laugh," she
says—I would think him a figment of Norman Rockwell's imagination. Such homely images, however, don't account for the change
in the weather, my sense that we were always on the verge of an
electrical storm. It was as if those sailors swarming through town
charged the air.

Whenever I walked up street now, my ears were pricked for the
whispered invitation—"How's about you and me stepping around
the corner for a beer?" If it had come, I'd have turned it down. I'd
have drawn back affronted. I would have fixed that sailor with a
cold stare, I would, and smiled inside my skin. But I was safe, and
I knew it. I was young, too young to attract, too young to be guilty
of being sexy.

I saw them going down to Newport for dinner at the Officers'
Club, the nice Bristol girls with the pageboys and the Peck & Peck
sweaters and the flat cigarette cases. An officer's uniform constituted a social bona fide, so the cocktail parties down the Ferry were
thronged with young men in spotless white uniforms and gold-
braided caps, and there was always what my mother called "a
good-looking crowd" at the bar of the Lobster Pot. Even Esther, in
her thirties now and feigning horror when Diana and I stuck her
with the Old Maid card, stained her bare legs brown and painted
her mouth with Germaine Monteil's Beauty Red and shared man-
hattans and lobster Newburgs with a balding lieutenant named
Stoner.

But the sailors! Who knew who they were, in their funny little
bell-bottoms with their funny little fronts that let down like trap-
doors to reveal the reason they were hopping from buses and packing the Thames Street bars? Sailors had to make do with Bugeyes
and Margie.

Bugeyes, whose legs bowed and whose eyes bulged, was new to

Bristol. But we knew Margie. Everybody knew Margie. Margie was terrifying.

Margie's mother, Gladys, was a cleaning lady. Ganny said she'd been with the circus, but Ganny had a way of providing people with backdrops. Because her father came from Canada, for instance, she liked to claim he was an Eskimo. That Gladys was small and wiry and hennaed her hair and buttered her mouth with magenta lipstick was cause enough for Ganny to put her in spangles. But then again, maybe she was with the circus. Nobody knew where she came from, only that her husband slid, drunk probably, in front of a car and that Margie was their only child.

The pear trees in our backyard were prodigious bearers, and in August, when they sagged with fruit, passing children asked to pick it. When she was small, Margie was among them. Agile as a monkey, she flew from branch to branch, plucking the pears and tossing them to the grass beneath. Seeing her up there against the sky one could indeed believe her mother had swung on a trapeze and spanned the ceiling of the big tent. On the ground, though, she was a foul-mouthed fireplug of a girl with hair the color of dingy brass. Margie and Gladys looked like the people who worked the carnival booths—sallow, stringy, and dusty—and although they lived in a house on Constitution Street they seemed more suited to a trailer.

Margie had a temper. She pounded on Bristol as if it were a cage, and no one was safe from that terrible anger. One afternoon after school let out she growled Ruthie and me, who had stayed up on the Common to shoot marbles, up the steps of the bandstand and into a corner. "Don't you ever look at me again, you little bitches," she screamed. When she walked away her heels struck sparks off the pavement and her anger stained the air.

So of course Margie grew up to prance down Hope Street with a sailor on her arm, trapped-up and high-stepping as a circus pony. "Don't you dare look at me," her fierce eyes said, and nobody did. Blindness overtook Bristol whenever Margie strutted through downtown: To glance was to risk a scolding from that boiling tongue.

What she did, she did for seats at the Pastime or beers at the Belvedere or to rattle the bars of the cage, and she did it constantly, brazenly, ferociously. "Guess what I saw this afternoon?" Diana

whispered from her bed one night. She had seen Margie dive off the
Coast Guard dock and swim the twenty or so yards to where a
boat and some sailors were waiting, cheering, to haul her aboard.

We knew what Margie did. We knew what our parents did too,
although we refused to believe it. Once, poking about in Papa's top
drawer, I found a package of something called Trojans, recognized
them for the rubbers I had heard some boys talking about, and felt
a strange, slow tearing down my chest. Not my father. No!

Another time, while I was on one of my secret, silent prowls of
the house, prowls in which I opened purses and thumbed through
my mother's lingerie and plundered the desk for traces of the life
my parents lived without my knowing it, I climbed upon a chair
and ran my criminal fingers along a shelf in their bedroom closet.
Van de Velde's *Ideal Marriage* was up there, hidden behind a set of
hatboxes. Only a few minutes elapsed before I heard Mother coming up from downstairs, but they were long enough for me to read
about the Mound—or was it the Mount?—of Venus and how the
pubic hair of women in obscure parts of the world sometimes grew
to enormous length. When, a few months later, tiny circles of
brown hair began appearing on my pubis, I lay in bed at night, my
hand on the forbidden place, and stubbornly, painfully pulled
them out.

One morning I found my underpants stiff with rusty, iron-
smelling blood, and cried that I had lost my innocence. Mother and
Esther rigged me a sanitary belt out of a torn-up old sheet and two
safety pins, and said it meant I was turning into a big girl. Esther
said she'd run up to the five-and-ten and get me a box of Modess.
"I always ask for a box of candy," she said, "and the salesgirl
knows what I mean." Mother said "whatchamaycallit" lasted for
four or five days.

For a long time I sat on the toilet, not trusting that torn-up
sheet, and watched the water in the bowl turn red. I wasn't safe
anymore. I was the same as Margie now. Both of us wore pads between our thighs, both of us sported the same curly patch. We were
similarly disgusting.

Eventually the worst thing that could happen to anybody happened to Margie. I heard about it the way I heard about everything,
by lurking unobserved next to the sliding doors that separated

Ganny's two parlors. "Guess who's expecting?" Esther said to her when she came home from the shop one autumn night. "And guess what Gladys is telling everybody? She says it's just that Margie drank some canned grapefruit juice that had gone bad, and that it made her swell up."

A few days later Ganny sent me to Buffington's for corn plasters. Just to the left of the entrance was the toiletries display, chaste rows of Elizabeth Arden creams and face powders, my mother's favorites and as evocative of her as Germaine Monteil's thick satiny lipsticks were of Esther. My mother even looked like the woman in the ads, the woman with the marble skin and the mummy wrappings around her head. The door opened and let in a gust of Juicy Fruit gum, laundry soap, and Bourjoie's Evening in Paris, familiar to me because it was sold, in tasseled blue vials, at the five-and-ten. Margie. I could see her reflection in the glass.

She walked to the prescription counter in the rear of the store and stood with her back to me. If I turned my head just a little bit I could see the bulge, the telltale swell of sin. No, too dangerous. Breathless, I stared at that evocation of order and austerity that was Elizabeth Arden cosmetics until a slam of the door announced that chaos had left the store.

Margie and Gladys were never seen in Buffington's, or anywhere else in Bristol, again. Esther heard they'd left town on the early bus, and I pictured them in the wet gray dawn, Margie's bulge buttoned into that big coat and their luggage bumping against their legs. I pictured them, too, on bleak city streets and in theatrical boardinghouses and dragging themselves, down at the heels, through dreary railroad stations: the stuff of countless Saturday afternoons at the Pastime Theater.

Margie was gone and Bugeyes dissolved back into wherever it was she came from, but the sailors were still there, still bounding off the bus and keeping an eye open for a girl who might split a beer and take them off the streets they were so hopelessly strolling. One late afternoon one of them approached Diana.

Tall for her age, she was up on the Common, poking along on her long, bird legs, when he asked her how she'd like a tumble. She came home crying. What was there about her that made him think she'd do something like that? "It's your own fault," I said. "You never look like you know where you're going. You should walk faster, and quit drifting about the way you do."

"I'll try," she sobbed, and thus I shifted the blame for an insult from a randy sailor to a child's blameless but unmistakably female back.

# *Eleven*

<hr/>

$\mathcal{I}$T IS STILL THERE, the Pastime Theater, only now it's called the Bristol Cinema and is divided into two narrow screening rooms. Tickets are very cheap and the shows change twice a week. Even so the Bristol Cinema is always up for sale, always rumored to be closing. Nobody, except for the very old and a few little kids, goes to the movies anymore. There was a time, though, when Bristolians attended the Pastime as regularly as they attended church. It was, in fact, the only place in town where Protestants and Catholics didn't feel the one was getting an edge on the other.

My parents said it was really Joanie's aunt who ran the Pastime, that the man who owned it couldn't have managed without her. She sold the tickets and, trotting across the tiny lobby, sold the candy, and on Saturday afternoons walked the aisles after the curtain went up, flashing a light on whoever was tossing spitballs or whistling through his fingers or squabbling with the kids in the next row. I was a regular at the Saturday matinee, bouncing on the cracked leather seats, gumming up my teeth with jujubes and dodging the flashlight, drunk on the darkness and the big screen and the pervasive salt/grease smell of Spanish peanuts. I loved the serial, the cartoon, the newsreel, the Fitzgerald travelogue, the Pete Smith specialty, the feature, and whatever served as dessert—the Three Stooges usually, but once a short of black men sitting in a row, knees pressed together, singing "Dem bones, dem bones, dem dry bones," that had me chanting "The thigh bone connecka to the knee bones and the knee bones connecka to the . . ." for weeks thereafter.

When the fast-talking daughter of the fat lady who lived on Byfield Street eloped with the sailor she'd picked up in Providence, her mother proclaimed that all was forgiven by appearing with them at the Friday night movies. When a couple started going together they announced it by their presence at the Friday night movies. When people recovered from illness or came out of mourning, the first place they went was the Friday night movies.

In summertime the Ferry crowd showed up, Shetland sweaters looped over their spanking white shirts, Sperry Topsiders lending a bounce to their walk. The big cheeses from Colt Memorial High—football players and cheerleaders and honor-roll students whose names were always in *The Bristol Phoenix*—jammed the aisles, and the kids who lived up the Neck arrived in a body. If the feature starred Bette Davis the grownups from the country of the blue-eyed came, too, and so, finally, did Di and I, graduated at last from the Saturday matinee but escorted by Gampa.

To Gampa, Diana and I were as dear as his cocker spaniel, Judy, and he looked at the three of us with the same loving eyes. Many were the nights we found him sitting in his morris chair sucking on his pipe while Judy gnawed blissfully at the hand he'd let dangle over the side. "You know how to tell when Gampa's talking to Ganny and when he's talking to Judy," we teased. "Judy's the one he calls 'darling.' "

When Joanie's aunt handed him the tickets, Gampa said "Thank you kindly" and ushered us to a row midway down the aisle. We sat on either side of him, and all three of us were smiling—he because he was going to see the picture show and Di and I because we were excited by the hustle and the bustle and the smack of the wadded-up candy wrapper in the back of the neck that announced that somewhere in this theater was somebody who had a crush on one of us. (One night I looked down our row past Gampa and saw a boy with eyes as blue as bachelor buttons. He returned my look, laughing, and I knew for the first time—as did he, I learned a few years later—what it is to feel your heart dissolve.) Then the lights dimmed, the red velvet curtain went up, Movietone

News sounded its salute and we were lifted out of our seats and deposited, gently, in heaven. Betty Grable flashed her flawless knees; Dan Dailey grinned his loopy grin. "That Dan Dailey," Gampa whispered. "He's a hummer!"

By the time the Pastime let out it was nearly eleven and the streets were deserted. Most of the houses were dark and sleeping, and the few cars that sped along Hope Street were, we figured, rushing the sick to the hospital in Providence or rushing for the last train out of Rhode Island. Why else would anyone be driving so long after sundown? Buffington's, however, was open and crowded.

The high school kids were lined up at the marble counter calling for lemon Cokes and Dusty Roads, and the air was thick with the whir of mixers, the squawk of the soda pull, and the thuds of the covers on the ice cream cases. Invariably, Gampa paused out front and asked if we wanted cones. We blushed at the picture he'd make in there—an old man in a three-piece suit among the gods—and worried lest somebody looked out the door and saw us, two young girls and their grandfather, peering in at Olympus. Someday, I knew, I'd be in there too, sipping a Coke and tossing back my pageboy. But not now, not yet. Comfortable in my chrysalis, I pulled at Gampa's hand and we walked on, toward the light that Ganny had left burning over the front door and the sleep that would bring me one day closer to my blooming.

MY BLOOMING, my blooming. In just a few more years I would be part of the Friday night crowd at Buffington's Drugstore and of the great mass that moved slowly down High Street after the football games at Guiteras Field. My breasts would bud and my hair turn under at the ends, and the faint scattering of pimples across my forehead would have succumbed forever to Acnomel. All that was to come, and it *would* come some day, some day when I was older: when I, like Ruthie, had personality; when I, like my mother before me, entered Colt Memorial High School. For now, though, there was hearing the factory whistle blow at noon and the town clock peal the hours and knowing how to translate the fire alarm's telltale honks. There was Alger's Newsstand and the penny-candy store next to the firehouse and the Rogers Free Library, where I studied the shelves for Gene Stratton Porter and Rafael Sabatini and sat at its golden oak tables turning the pages of *Life*. But above all there was my father. When I walked uptown with him on a Saturday morning, through the buzz and the busyness and the slams of car doors and shouts of "Ay paysan!" from workmen he knew at the shop, I was as shaken by joy as if it held me in its teeth.

He was born in North Brookfield, Massachusetts, but grew up in Fall River, a city so dingy its very name was a pejorative. "When we were kids," my mother would say, "and somebody said something dirty we'd say 'Oh, that's Fall River!' " But Papa could turn dross into gold, the merely dreary into Hell. When he sat on the toybox at night, talking Diana and me to sleep, we clamored for Fall River as we would have for ghost stories.

"In the mills, the floors were so slippery with cottonseed oil that all the boys worked barefoot. The men were mostly English, with bad teeth, and all of them had redheaded wives. I swear! I can see them now, those redheads, coming down the hills with their husbands' tin lunch pails when the noon whistle blew."

Yes, Fall River has hundreds of redheaded women who descended its hills like brushfires, not to mention a remarkable boulder that an Ice-Age glacier deposited there on its trek down the Atlantic seaboard. But, then, everything in Fall River is remarkable. A woman whom Papa knew as a child had a terrible disease that turned her to stone; that's the kind of place Fall River is. His father's cousin, Dr. Kelly's wife, lived next door to the Borden family and was the last person to see Andrew Jackson Borden alive. A crime like that—well, that's Fall River for you. Rich textile tycoons lived washed in cool breezes atop Fall River's seven hills, while the poor sweltered in the heat below and the air hummed day and night with the sound of spinning. When you crossed the bridge from Somerset and entered the city, a cloud descended and wrapped you in its folds. Fall River! The heart sinks.

"Tell us about the policeman who used to chase you," we'd ask, wriggling deeper into our pillows.

"Martin Quigley. He was tough. You see, I was bad, *really* bad. After school I'd hang around under the street lamp with a bunch from the neighborhood. We'd stay out way past our bedtime, and run and hide when our mothers called us in. Then Martin Quigley would come and chase us home."

Delighted that our father had been bad, we'd squirm. (I can still feel that squirm, that small joyous spasm, because I still squirm when I'm happy, when someone—a writer, say, or Fred Astaire—does something and does it dead-on.) "Did your mother think you'd been bad?"

"Ahhhh," and his voice would grow suddenly, atavistically Irish. "I wish you'd known her. She was six feet tall and had snapping black eyes. They were all tall, both sides. My father's mother, also six feet tall, ran around Glasgow on Orangeman's Day tearing down the orange flags. She was a Catholic, and she didn't like those damn Presbyterians."

More joy than we could handle. We were the descendants of heroes. We slept as if couched on zephyrs.

"Of course, I'm a carpetbagger in Bristol," Papa told me more than once, "not like your mother's family. And I'll always be a carpetbagger. Like that Joe who applied for the janitor's job at the Reynolds. Did I ever tell you what happened to Joe?

"His application came up before the School Committee and it looked to me as if he was as suitable as anybody else. Hell, all he had to do was push a broom. But somebody said, 'No, I think we ought to give the job to a native.'

"So I said, 'I thought Joe was a native.' Not by their standards! 'Leo,' they said, 'Joe didn't come to Bristol until he was three months old.'

"Can you beat it, Mary Lee?" he said, his outflung arm taking in St. Michael's Church and the clapboard houses and the old soaks hanging around the entrance to the Belvedere Hotel as we strolled up Hope Street. "Can you beat this town for craziness?"

Taking a walk with Papa was like looking out the bay window with Ganny. Because of them I, too, saw my fellow Bristolians as participants in an enormous parade that marched daily, and for my benefit.

"There is little more beautiful in this world, Mary Lee, than the sun sinking into Bristol Harbor. You and your sister are very fortunate to live in a place like this. Why, people go on vacation to places like this." Papa waves his arm again.

In places like this the main street is one big living room. Here they come, for instance, the old maids of Bristol, all of them converging on the Rogers Free Library where they will exchange a Frances Parkinson Keyes for a Mazo de la Roche, or a Mazo de la Roche for a Frances Parkinson Keyes. Louise DeWolf, a high school classmate of my mother's, is here, shod as usual in sneakers that call attention to the fact that her legs appear to have been put on upside down. So is Miss Alice Morgan, who has sojourned in Istanbul, wrapped in a long flowing cape; and Miss Bourn, who had been engaged to a German nobleman until her father lost his little rubber works, with her mesh evening purse over her arm; and our neighbor, Miss Belle Bosworth, her hair in a pouf, her dress to her ankles, her late father's watch on a chain around her neck, and her long ivory hand twirling a parasol. One block to the south, Miss Evvie Bache, descendant of Benjamin Franklin and terrible housekeeper, is picking her way through the stacks of old newspapers and mounds of cat vomit that litter her eighteenth-century house. (I know, because I was sent there once to borrow costumes—I was Martha Washington in a Bache ancestor's ancient sprigged dimity—for the fifth-grade history pageant and threw up upon leaving.) "Mary Lee," Papa says, "I hope to God you marry when you grow up."

Now we are in the library, and Papa is asking for the best-seller the librarians have hidden under the counter for him. They are two of Joanie's aunts: Swedish, blond, and spinsters all. A third aunt is the wonder that runs the Pastime Theater and a fourth aunt keeps a firm hand on the second grade up at the Walley School. That makes the area bounded by State, Bradford, Hope, and High streets, Papa says, the Kingdom of the Osterbergs.

One of the Miss Osterbergs slips him the new A. J. Cronin. "They say it's very good," she whispers. Conversations at the library never rise above funeral-home level: The Osterberg sisters are fast with a "shhhh" and an upraised index finger. They are also so neat and clean—"Swedes always look like that," my mother claims—I think they polish themselves with a chamois before they leave the house in the morning.

"They" who pronounce on books are Ralph Kinder, the superintendent of schools, and the minister of St. Michael's Church who,

along with Papa, are the library's best readers. Some of Papa's
glory rubs off on his children. The Osterbergs deem certain books
unsuitable for certain age groups, but they allow me a little leeway.
For instance I am permitted Kathleen Winsor and Thomas B.
Costain, since the sisters figure I'm reading them for the history.
Anybody else my age would be looking for the dirty parts.

Miss Osterberg stamps Papa's card, and motions him closer.
"I'm getting in the new O'Hara next week." Papa beams. "Mary
Lee, I'm a lucky guy."

Papa's kingdom is on Wood Street. It's the U.S. Rubber
Company, where he is production manager. He cannot stay away
from the shop, even on Saturdays when only the factory workers
are on hand. To go there we stroll east on Bradford Street, past
Colt Memorial High School and the house he and Mother lived in
when they were first married.

"It was on those steps that I was sitting on the night you were
born and your mother and your great-aunt Annie were turning the
town upside down looking for me. Wouldn't you think one of them
would have had the sense to stick her head out the window?" He
laughs fondly and I laugh with him, smug in the knowledge that I
am a true Cantwell, and that the family into which he married and
to which I am related is—however handsome—feckless, absent-
minded, and no real part of us. A Cantwell would have had the
sense to look out the window.

The entrance to the U.S. Rubber Company is spanned by a red-
brick arch, and a watchman sits in at little tower at its right. Papa
waves a grand, seigneurial wave and steers me past a time clock
and row after row of little yellow cards and up a broad staircase to
a big, empty room. While he's in his office checking out the production sheets, I stay in the clerks' bull pen, delirious among the
pads and pencils and typewriters and comptometers and ditto machines, the last of which I can work because he showed me how. I
love the very smell of them, the effluvium—sharp and very clean—
that rises from paper and ink and metal type. In fifth grade I
printed a homeroom newspaper on one of the ditto machines, but
it only lasted one issue. "If we're going to have a newspaper," the
teacher said, "we've got to do it properly and elect an editor in
chief." I wasn't elected. I wasn't even nominated, and the person

who was never produced a follow-up. "Never mind," Papa said when I cried so hard I was sick. "Someday you'll live in a place where there are lots of people like you."

Papa is finished with the production sheets. "C'mon, Lulubelle," he calls. "Let's go see what the factory's doing."

The factory is doing war work, so the men are battening on overtime. The spinners are whirring and the extruders are squeezing out long, fat rubber worms and we are above it all, up on the catwalks looking down on Papa's kingdom. "Ay Leo! Ay coompah!" somebody yells up to him. Papa waves, and inhales the stink of rubber as joyously as another man would sniff a rose.

Better get home. He's got a golf game this afternoon, and then he and Mother are going to a dinner dance at the Rhode Island Country Club with the Barrington crowd. They're stopping at our house first, though, for a few of Papa's famous old-fashioneds. I, who am a nuisance, will hang around to watch him—tall and plump in a dark Brooks Brothers suit ("Put me in tweed," he says, "and I look like a racetrack tout"), a gold watch chain swagging his stomach. His hazel eyes, which are roofed with thick, black brows, will be fixed on the sugar cubes he is crushing, and when it comes time to shake in the Angostura he'll be as careful as a chemist. "*Nosdorovya!*" he'll say when he extends the glasses. "Bottoms up!"

We cross the Common, hand in hand. I am really too old to hold a parent's hand, but I cannot bear to give his up. When I was a baby, he—natty in a navy-blue jacket and ice-cream pants—flourished me for Miss Emilie Connery's camera, and even now I feel that I am still riding his shoulder. "Hurry up there, Lulubelle." I double my footsteps to match his stride. "They'll be wondering if we ran away."

# Twelve

WHEN THE TIDE CAME IN at Union Street it gobbled up the Popsicle sticks and greasy paper bags and soda bottles the afternoon crowd had left behind and carted them out to Narragansett Bay. I was like that tide, gobbling up Bristol street by street. Summer was when I was hungriest, during the long light days when the world asked nothing more of me than that I be home in time for dinner.

Summer, everybody said, was when Bristol couldn't be beat. On Back Road the air was stiff and sullen, and uptown the sun had baked the sidewalks. But once you crossed Court Street you were strolling through green tunnels. By the time you reached Constitution a salt breeze had sprung up, and by the time you neared Union you could hear the screams of swimmers. Sailboats bucked and winged around the harbor, and if the yacht club was holding a regatta, the deep blue water was thick with Herreshoff bull's-eyes and snipes and catamarans, bowing and curvetting and tugged by urgent spinnakers.

Sometimes it was enough to spend the morning at Union Street, and the afternoon sprawled on the porch glider with a book balanced on my chest. More often, though, I was wandering the streets, peering into windows and trying to see into backyards. When anyone moved in or out of a house I was among the group on the sidewalk watching the furniture go by. It was as if Bristol were a book I couldn't put down.

If Bristol's population was small, the town itself was big. There was much of it I hadn't seen, still haven't seen for that matter. So when I heard about a farm up on the Back Road that hired kids to pick raspberries during the season, I begged to go. The Back Road, miles from our house and the harbor and everything I knew, would be a new chapter.

On a map the stretch of two-lane highway that connected Warren to the Mount Hope Bridge bore King Philip's Indian name, Metacom. But only a stranger would have called it Metacom Avenue. To everyone else it was the Back Road.

At its Warren end the Back Road was a squeeze of shabby houses, gas stations, and greenhouses. But as the road ran south toward Newport it opened into fields. Beyond the fields, a mile or so from the road, ran an inlet known as the Narrows and a pebbly beach lined with modest vacation cottages. Their owners showed up at St. Mary's Church on summer Sundays along with the cooks and maids from the big houses down the Ferry, most of whose employers were bowing their heads a few blocks away at St. Michael's.

The Old Soldiers' Home was on the Back Road, as was the estate of a Providence beer baron and the shipshape white clapboard of a retired rear admiral. But the only part of that long, lonely blacktop that I can claim to know is an acre or so of raspberry bushes.

A picture postcard, one of a group of old cards I found at Alger's Newsstand and saved, shows a whale's jawbone framing the entrance to the farm. I never saw it, what with always having to keep my eyes on the raspberries I was trying to yank from their canes, but it signified social status more surely than money ever could. The farm's owner, a homely red-haired woman descended from one of Bristol's first settlers, had whalers among her ancestors. In southern New England that beat out a Rockefeller any day.

She was married to the Portuguese field hand she'd put through college, and their four daughters took after him. They were handsome, like he was, and rumored to be foolish about men. When they rode their horses in the Fourth of July parade they topped their chignoned heads with flat-brimmed sombreros, and their mounts jingled silver trappings. If Bristol had had a café society they'd have been in it.

The pickers, none of them besides myself from the country of the blue-eyed, met near St. Mary's soon after daybreak, crawled into the back of a pick-up truck and were deposited ten minutes later at a stone wall by which a dark-haired woman in halter and shorts was waiting. The couple's second daughter, she slapped a riding crop against her bare legs and stalked the rows with the zeal with which her ancestors, who were also in the slave trade, had stalked their ships.

For each basket filled we were to be paid five cents, she said, and each of us could take one home. But if somebody driving by, somebody, she implied, from out of town, were to offer to buy our berries, we had to say no. Not only would we be depriving our families of their supper treat, but we would be depriving her family of business that they would have had but for their generosity in allowing us to take a pint of berries. We nodded solemnly, we bent our backs, the sun slapped us on the shoulders.

While his daughter prowled the rows, her father, magnificent in a mustache, white suit, and Panama hat, stood smiling broadly, a gold tooth glinting in the sun, and waited for us to bring him our baskets to be counted. Sometimes, a fellow picker whispered, he gave the prettiest girls a feel. It was an honor. "He's my uncle," the Portuguese kids said, or "He's my father's cousin . . . my mother's brother-in-law's relation." He was a big man among the Portuguese, famous for his good looks and his dashing daughters and his flourishing farm. I halfway hoped he'd give me a feel, but I never even got a glance. Maybe I'm not pretty enough, I told myself, but I knew I was. More likely he trailed his long elegant fingers, if he trailed them at all, only over those who shared his blood.

It was another world up there on the Back Road, so far from the harbor and the breeze and the persistent scent of salt. The air shuddered in the heat, and working so close to the ground I could smell nothing but dirt and berries. The other kids scrambled through the rows, serious about their picking, and soon I was serious, too. Here, as everywhere, I wanted to be part of the gang, even of a gang whose names I seldom caught and with whom, given the rigid tracking of Bristol's public schools, I would never share a classroom. We seldom spoke, only tugged at those resistant raspberries and exchanged sheepish smiles when we caught sight of one another through the bushes.

Walking the three miles home through the drowsy afternoon, sunburned and scratched and sweaty, I was as happy as I had ever been. This suited me, this silent companionship and the wallowing in the dust before a dip in the harbor, a dip that would wash away the dirt and iodize the scraches and leave me with the face all Bristol children sported in summer: red-eyed, with a nose that dripped salt water. That fresh air was all that separated the Portuguese kids who were so happy to be working for a kinsman in a spotless white suit from the children who ran barefoot over the oil-slicked floors of the Fall River mills never entered my mind.

FERRY ROAD WAS ONLY A STROLL from 232 Hope Street, but in a way it was as inaccessible as the Back Road. More so, really. Its residents were barely glimpsed figures on Raleigh bicycles with hand brakes and, at cruising speed, a purr like a cat's; or passengers in wooden-sided beach wagons with the names of their houses discreetly stenciled on the driver's door; or among the guests at weddings at St. Michael's. Ruthie and I loved weddings, especially those at St. Michael's, with its solemnly tolling bell and tall trees and the crumbling old gravestones in its churchyard, and were sorry that we couldn't be married there. Not only did St. Mary's not have a clock, but you had to climb a mile of steps to get to the front door, and when you came out all you saw was that grubby Common and all you smelled was the rubber factory. But the bridal couples at St. Michael's emerged to a sidewalk dappled with shade and air that was scented with salt, and cars slowed and seemed to tip their hats as they passed the limousines lined up out front.

In winter the summer people lived in Providence and showed up regularly in the Sunday society section of *The Providence Journal,* which I had taken to reading because of the bridal pictures. Down at the Ferry they stuck pretty close to home, playing tennis and sunning themselves at the foot of Monkeywrench Lane, and the most conspicuous evidence of their presence were the cooks and maids in the back rows of St. Mary's at eleven o'clock mass. In truth, there was another sign, but it was heard not seen: the moans of Bristol's grocers. The rich never paid their bills until after Labor Day.

Actually they didn't do anything, at least nothing that I could see. When my friend Jeanne, who had a baby-sitting job down the Ferry, got the grippe, I bicycled down Monkeywrench Lane every morning for a week, to a big house with grounds that spilled into Narragansett Bay. While I sat by the water with her babies, their mother drifted about the lawn and in and out of the house. Somebody was cleaning, somebody else was cooking, I was minding the children, and she was as vagrant as floss from a milkweed pod.

In the town proper every person was a filament in an enormous web. When one thread shook, the entire web shuddered. Our next-door neighbor Belle Bosworth walked uptown to meet Jessie Molasky, the junior high school librarian, to exchange her copy of the previous Sunday's *New York Times Book Review* with the latter's copy of the *Herald-Tribune Book Review*. Ganny phoned her bookie. The Misses Osterberg, commanding the Rogers Free Library, forbade Ruthie *Forever Amber*. Even at midnight, when all sober Bristolians were in bed, the web shivered. But here there was no web, only figures moving across a landscape that, however much they paid for it and however many years they made their annual visit, they couldn't possibly possess.

To me dailiness was nine-tenths of possession, and how could anyone own something she knew only in the summer? How could anyone know Bristol if she didn't know that in autumn half its backyards flaunted winter cherries? Or that the Congregationalists put on the best Christmas fairs? Or that in spring the linden trees in front of the high school had a scent so sweet and haunting it was enough to make you cry? I didn't envy the summer people, although I coveted their bikes and wished my parents had a beach wagon like those they nosed through town. But it was I, not they, who was a Bristolian—at least a Bristolian as they understood the term. If I had ever heard myself described as a "local," I would have assumed it was a compliment.

There was only one place in Bristol proper besides St. Michael's and, sometimes, the Pastime Theater, where the summer people could be found. That was the Bristol Yacht Club, a small and incongruous monument to International Style at the foot of Constitution Street.

The old yacht club, a shingled nondescript, was lifted off its perch by the Hurricane of '38 and shoveled into Bristol Harbor. The old flagpole survived, or did until the night the designer of the new yacht club, a middle-aged Bristolian with flat feet and a famous name, had one too many and chopped it down. Another night when he'd had another one too many, he called the exchange and told the operator who number-pleased him that he was going to bed but that she could continue to put his calls through. His dog, a dachshund whose low-bellied shuffle duplicated his, would answer.

The new yacht club smelled of teak, leather, and salt, which in coastal New England is the smell of money. Its members were teak-colored, leather-skinned, and salt-streaked, which in coastal New England is the look of money. For the most part they—men with high-bridged noses and long teeth and women whose freckled hands flashed big old-fashioned diamonds—were around only for the Saturday races. But during the week the yacht club belonged to their children, and to a few of the children from the country of the blue-eyed. Me, for instance, who was as eager to become a junior member of the Bristol Yacht Club as I had been to join the Girl Scouts.

We looked the same, we dressed the same, but we were not the same. I realized that the afternoon I was commandeered to pass the sandwiches at a yacht club tea. Not knowing I'd been positioned on the wrong side of the tea table, I was happy circulating my trays of egg-salad triangles and watching the S. sisters, cousins of the club's architect and famous tightwads, sliding theirs into their handbags. But after I boasted to Papa about how well I'd handled the trays he said, "Did ——— pass sandwiches?," naming the daughter of a pillar of St. Michael's. "Did ———?," naming another. When I answered no to both questions he said, "Then don't you ever do it again." He was furious, and I? I was as icy-spined as I was the day I found out I'd never be queen of England.

Once I'd propped my Schwinn in the gravel parking lot and entered that teak-smelling room, past the bulletin board with the announcement of regattas at Marblehead and race results, my antennae probed the air as cautiously as they had learned to probe the chalky fug of the Walley School. But the insults were subtler here: You could be snubbed and never know it.

Oil from the Coast Guard boats slicked the water near the dock, but none of us swimmers cared. I cannonballed off that dock a dozen times a day (my left leg still bears traces of the time the waves pushed me against a barnacle-crusted piling) and came up spitting gasoline. When the dock palled, Ruthie, whom I had talked into joining, and I would duck under the float at the side of the club, our heads just above the water and our hands grasping its wooden supports, to eavesdrop on the S. sisters, who were sunning themselves just above us.

They were pretty, the younger in particular, and they lounged on the float for hours, knitting intarsia sweaters and rubbing Skol into each other's backs. Neither had gone to college but, given their famous name, they couldn't be expected to work either, and suitable husbands weren't available in Bristol. So they drove around town in their little car and sat on the porch of their little house and knitted their little sweaters and waited. Perhaps their famous name didn't really reverberate outside Rhode Island, but all Bristolians believed it did, and when a Bristol girl married a New York millionaire there was talk that the S. girls might meet the proper suitors—rich men anxious to blue their bloodlines—at the reception. Alas, they did not, and went on waiting, round and luscious in their Skol-soaked skins.

They were moist and she was dry. Nonetheless, the S. sisters reminded me of Belle Bosworth, who skittered the streets of Bristol with her parasol and her books, her loneliness frosting the air around her. On hot nights, when she left her window open for what little breeze came from the north, I could hear her typing in the room she rented at Miss Munro's, a stone's throw from where I sat on the porch glider. She was said to write poetry, and what the residents of the country of the blue-eyed called "a good letter." I'd read one of them, sent to my mother when she'd had a hysterectomy. After telling her how she envied her the hospital and the doctors and the nurses who were there to wait upon her hand and foot, Miss Bosworth said, "I am cold and desolate as a clam, and all the winds of Rhode Island and Providence Plantations are pressing against my window."

"That Belle Bosworth is a character, all right," my mother said, and slid the letter into her desk. It was embarrassing, she told me, but too good to throw away.

Yes, a character. All the old Yanks were characters, Ganny said. They couldn't help it. One Halloween night, when Ruthie and I were out looking for STOP signs to tip over, we saw Miss Bosworth butterflying down Hope Street, wearing a mask and trying to disappear into a crowd of roaming children. On summer afternoons, when the crowd down at Union Street had left for supper, she'd pick her way through the broken glass and the greasy bags to sit among the rocks and read till the sun went down. Once Diana saw a rat vault her lap. She didn't notice.

Her books were novels mostly, from the Rogers Free Library, but a few were schoolbooks. She was teaching herself the Romance languages and often, if I'd wandered down to watch the sun set, she'd ask me if I'd hold the book while she reeled off what she had memorized that day.

While she conjugated French verbs or counted one through ten in Italian, I'd check the text. "That's a devilish word," she'd say when corrected. "I hope I never have to use it." In me Miss Bosworth felt she'd found a kindred soul. I felt so too, and feared for my future.

But there were years to go before I might end up a spinster with skin as thin as crepe paper and dessicated veins, so I gave myself over to the long, green summer and the green light under the float, to the gentle slap of the water against the pilings and the click of the S. sisters' knitting needles and their murmured "Could you do my back?" and "Ooh, that sun is hot." And when Ruthie and I finally emerged, prune-skinned, there was the sleepy afternoon to look forward to, and the sight of Joseph Cotten coming in the door.

That is to say, he looked like Joseph Cotten. He was one of the summer people and soon to inherit $7,000,000—from the poor side of the family. Their house on Monkeywrench Lane had a swimming pool, the only one in Bristol, and people said that when you swam underwater you could see the name of the estate spelled out in light bulbs.

His hair was fair and ridged like Joseph Cotten's, his eyes were blue like Joseph Cotten's, and his voice was the voice of Joseph Cotten, only flattened by St. Paul's and Yale. Ruthie stuck a recording of "I'll See You in My Dreams" on the old Victrola every time he entered the yacht club, but I doubt he noticed. I doubt he noticed much besides Linda.

Linda was the prettiest girl in Bristol. Her hair was long and dark, and so were her eyes, and in summer she toasted to the burnished brown of a coffee bean. If she could only get in with the right crowd, everybody said, Linda would marry well. That was why her parents were sending her to a junior college in Boston in the fall. Meanwhile she was spending the summer on the yacht club dock, rotating as regularly as a bird on a spit and looking at a glorious future out of her long sloe eyes.

Along about three o'clock she'd get up, shrug a long shirt over her two-piece swimsuit and saunter barefoot into the big downstairs room. "Anybody seen Teddy?" she'd drawl, the first words she'd said all day. Then she'd curl up in one of the big leather chairs, pull out an English Oval whose smoke she'd let curl up into her narrow nostrils, and stare at the doorway.

When Teddy/Joseph Cotten entered she'd leave as if to go to the ladies' room, then sneak upstairs to a small room that opened onto a large deck. The door was always locked—there was a cupboard bar up there—except for parties, but Joseph Cotten had acquired a key somehow. A few minutes later he followed.

For summer afternoon after summer afternoon the room was his and Linda's, and I longed for some adult to step out on deck, see the drawn curtains, and say "What's going on in there?" I'd never gotten away with anything, from telling lies to stealing change from my mother's purse, and I didn't want anybody else to, either.

Finally, on an afternoon when Ruthie and I were playing Ping-Pong and wondering, as usual, about what was going on upstairs and how far Linda was willing to go to get Teddy, high heels sounded in the club's foyer. In she came, an answered prayer. Linda's mother.

"Where's Linda?" she asked. "Upstairs with Teddy," I replied, keeping a straight face but waiting, as was Ruthie and everyone else in the room, for her to rush upstairs.

"Oh," she said and turning—click-click-click-click—left the yacht club.

My mother didn't believe me when I told her how Linda's mother, her old high school classmate, had deliberately left her daughter in a locked room with a boy. I must have misunderstood, or, rather, Linda's mother must have misunderstood me. "Don't you go around spreading stories like that, Mary Lee Cantwell," she said. "You've got too big an imagination."

But I didn't have too big an imagination. I'm not sure if I've ever had much of an imagination. I had eyes.

On the afternoon I handed round the egg-salad triangles I had seen the attention Bristol's locals paid each pearl that dropped from the Ferry crowd's lips. I had seen, too, the magnetic field that enclosed the rich as if it were a fence, and that I was able to pierce it only because I was carrying a tray. Linda could no more hope to open the gate and carry off one of those boys with the flattened *a*'s and the impenetrable courtesy than she could hope to climb Everest.

And neither, my antennae told me, could I.

# Thirteen

---

IF THE FRONT DOOR of Guiteras Junior High School was ever opened, I do not know it. Its façade, which was grand and Grecian, faced a small pond called Silver Creek and the mansions on Poppasquash Point, but it presented a plain backside to the tarred parking lot and football field behind it. That's where we went in and out, boys through the door to the left, girls through the door to the right, and all of us monitored by the principal, who took no guff. Once he wiped the forbidden lipstick off a girl's mouth with his handkerchief; another time I saw him wrestle a boy to the ground. Nobody ever took offense, the boys in particular being flattered by the implication that we were all wild beasts.

Here we were neither little kids nor big kids. Guiteras was Limbo, a way station between elementary school, which was remembered as fun, and high school, which was assumed to be glorious. Guiteras was neither in nor out of town. Instead it was at the beginning of the Neck, a breezy, barren stretch where the oldest house in Bristol, the place the Congregationalists held their first meetings, was dying of neglect.

If I'd lived just a few blocks farther down toward the Ferry, I'd have been eligible for the school bus and its noisy camaraderie. As it was, I bicycled back and forth at least four miles a day, grateful for the solitude. There were two of me by now, or perhaps there always had been, the one who watched and the one who did, and we talked to each other constantly. "Wonder what Ralph Kinder's doing up-town at this time of day," I'd say as we biked past the post office. "Maybe he's got a package," the other Mary Lee would reply. It was a family trait, of course, this continual monitoring of other peoples' endlessly interesting lives. Our gossip never went beyond 232 Hope Street, but its rooms hummed with "Why do you suppose that light's on so late over at the Connerys?" and "Just saw a car turning into the Howes' driveway. Funny hour to have company, don't you think?"

Guiteras was the sieve in which future stenographers, domestics, and factory workers were separated out from future dentists and dermatologists. Now friendships were based not on the same neighborhood or the same church but on our parents' aspirations. Those of us who were slated for college or, at least, a genteel high school education—Ruthie, Joan, Jeanne, Anne, and I, for instance, and the best-mannered boys—took Ancient History and Latin, and littered our conversation with *"amo"* and *"cum"* and *"habemus."* Clearly, we would edit the Colt Memorial High School yearbook someday, and have our positions on the honor rolls proclaimed in *The Bristol Phoenix,* and be the big cheeses at the Pastime on Friday nights. We knew it, too. We swaggered.

Suddenly our teachers became infinitely amusing to us, part of the scrapbooks we were unconsciously accumulating about our school days. Now we were old enough to have pasts, old enough to begin our sentences with "Do you remember when . . ." My favorite teacher was a small, round Italian who taught Latin and Ancient History. He found us infinitely amusing, too. His tongue was literally (he explored his lower right molars all day long) and figuratively forever in his cheek.

That I will go to my grave knowing that Hannibal crossed the Alps with elephants is because he once had the smallest boy in the class ride the back of the fattest boy down a row of desks masquerading as mountains. While Ruthie intoned Plato, he had me mime the shrewish Xanthippe turning a cold shoulder on the dying Socrates as the latter lay draped across a desk. Spurred by his invention, Ruthie, Joanie, and I formed a trio we called the three Neroinas and, wrapped in sheets and wearing our mothers' chenille bedroom slippers, sang a song we'd composed about why

Rome fell. But despite this joyous introduction to the ancient world I remained dubious about anyone or anything that had come out of the Mediterranean. The day our Latin teacher said idly, "You know, you are all descendants of Roman soldiers," I raised my hand and claimed an exemption. "Most of my ancestors came from Ireland," I told him, "and I never heard tell of any Roman invasion there."

In grade school, physical education had consisted of standing next to one's desk touching fingers to toes while a teacher snapped "One-two! One-two!" At Guiteras we had a real gym instructor, a tall, terrifying woman in a bloomer suit and black support stockings, who strode through the shower room after class pulling back the curtains and peering into the cubicles to make sure that everyone was getting wet. "Under the shower, under the shower," she'd bark, while the girls from the back of town, for whom public nakedness was torture, cowered and covered their groins. One year everybody got plantar warts from the communal foot bath through which she insisted on herding us, and at lunchtime the tarred parking lot was thick with girls on crutches.

We played volleyball and girls' basketball, dullest of all games, in a dark and dreary gym lighted by high dirty windows. In warm weather we went outside and played softball on the football field. I lazed in left field, praying that nothing would come my way, mystified that anyone would care about hitting or catching that dumb ball. The sun burned my face, the grass made me sneeze, boredom had me dizzy.

At recess, where once we had played tag and marbles on the Common, we now stood on the parking lot in whispering clumps, eyeing the boys. Occasionally one of them would dart into our territory and grab a hat or a scarf. We'd scream.

Words like "cherry" floated over from their side to our side, and boasts that had the boys jittering like monkeys. "Had a date with Fat Teresa last night" was the most frequent.

Fat Teresa. I never saw Fat Teresa, but I didn't have to. I could imagine her. Her hair was black and oily, and her cheeks rose in mounds on either side of a button nose. Her hands were short and puffy and her breasts like elongated gourds, and her skirt was strained across a massive rump. The skin on her round, thick legs was stretched so they looked like sausages about to pop, and her feet were snuggled into little white socks and black A. S. Beck loafers. She was all I feared about sex incarnate, and I shivered at the picture my mind had made. When recess was over I bounded for the door, happy to be enclosed again in the safe, sinless scents of chalk and floor polish and old books.

Guiteras Junior High. Finally my teachers had taken on faces and I had taken on friends. But in my memory the years dissolve into one another and all that surfaces are film clips. They are always sepia-toned.

I see Diana, for instance, bouncing a small rubber ball at recess. She is wearing my tan coat, and her wrists and knees are rubbed raw by a November wind. Our coats were always alike, and when I outgrew mine it was automatically handed down to her. But Diana has gained inches on me without our parents' noticing, and my old coat is far too small for her.

She looks like the orphans in the movies, chilly, chapped, in ill-fitting clothes, and suddenly my heart feels fat in my chest. Because I see Diana day after day I don't see her at all. Now she is visible: fair-haired, with Papa's thick, dark eyebrows, and ankles like a bird's. Oblivious to the weather and to the sight she makes in that coat, she keeps on bouncing her ball, as blessedly unselfconscious as she was when she was a little girl poking out her fanny and raising her fists to "the great John L."

I see Ruthie and me on Poppasquash Point after school, pushing our bikes down a dirt road past a sign that reads, NO TRESPASSERS. We are furtive because we fear arrest, and resentful that any part of Bristol should be off-limits. I can respect a neighbor's lawn and am proud that Papa drove a man from the Watchtower Society off ours—"I don't like what you people say about my church," he thundered—but I am furious that so few can prohibit entry to so many. The estates on Ferry Road don't faze me: They are simply houses with bigger than usual backyards. But Poppasquash has woods and deer and ponds that I will never see, and I cannot bear the proscription.

We don't go very far, only to Hey Bonnie Hall, the last but one of the great nineteenth-century mansions and soon to burn to the ground. No one enters it now but children looking for a mirror to break or a place on which to carve an initial, and peeking through a broken shutter on a tall French window we glimpse books scattered on a mahogany floor. The house was grand once, and lovely, and it pains me that no ancestor of mine has ever lived in this place. I am jealous of those whose claim on Bristol is stronger than my own.

But it is an afternoon in a second-floor classroom that faces west toward Silver Creek and Poppasquash Point that I see most clearly. I remember the dialogue, too, and the slight choke of the little polka-dotted bow tie under the collar of my white blouse. We have art with a teacher named Miss Nerone once a week, and today I am the model, standing stiff and trying not to squint because the sun is low and shining in my eyes.

"Mary Lee," she says, "has a bony face, which means it has highlights and deep shadows. That makes it easy and interesting to draw. In fact, real artists often look for faces like Mary Lee's."

I am stunned, not because Miss Nerone says I am easy to draw—I know that already, having practiced self-portraits in front of the bedroom mirror—but because of her allusion to faces like mine. She has taken my cheekbones and the hollows beneath them out of Bristol and placed them elsewhere.

I know there is an elsewhere. Even so, elsewhere is not a place in which I have ever really imagined myself. But because Miss Nerone has set my kind of face in other parts of the world she has, somehow or other, set me there too. I look out at the sun, which is dipping its fingers into Bristol Harbor, and I am so excited I can hardly hold the pose.

"WHITE LACE. I think. Mary Lee." Miss Nerone was visualizing the dress I would wear the day I went down the aisle of St. Mary's Church to marry—whom? Someone, Miss Nerone said, I have yet to meet, but whom I will meet, as I will meet so many other exciting people once I get out of Bristol. Miss Nerone loves Bristol. There is no town like Bristol. But it is not the *world*. Peggy Nerone,

Margaret Frances Nerone, art supervisor for the public schools of Bristol, Rhode Island, spoke in italics.

Miss Nerone's eyes were big and green and slightly popped (after her sister saw *Now Voyager* she said, "Bette Davis was the dead spit of Peggy. I've never seen her look so bad"), and one front tooth curtsied across the other. She was said to be New Yorkish, what with getting her clothes there and being the only person in town who dared a Kelly-green coat and a hat with a feather that stabbed the sky, and thought nothing of running up to Boston for a show. She was always running, one way or another, and the freckles on the back of her legs made them look perpetually mud-splashed. "Ompen the window!" she'd say huskily when she entered a classroom. "Hand me an ampron!" when she bustled about her tiny kitchen. Besides not looking like anybody else in Bristol, she didn't sound like anybody else either.

Miss Nerone lived on Church Street, nestled under the caves of a tall, thin house. The ceilings of her apartment slanted and those windows that weren't close to the floor were set in dormers. All of them wore wooden shutters instead of curtains. Where the light wasn't green it was amber, and together they cast what I now recognize as a Pre-Raphaelite shimmer over the Victorian furniture, the crammed bookcases, the funny old prints, and the framed autograph of Eamon de Valera. "Welcome to my garret," she said to those who made the three-flight climb up the back stairs. "Mind the door!"

Years of students made that climb and had their futures prophesied by Peggy Nerone. "If you'll just get out of Bristol you can be . . . you can be . . . you can be." Few of them ever did, and then she said "if only . . . if only . . . if only." The abilities she saw in us, realized or not, she saw forever. None of Miss Nerone's pets were ever failures. It was just that they'd postponed success.

Peggy Nerone, whom I was never to call by her first name, and Papa were pals. Sometimes they walked uptown together, talking about New York and Graham Greene and William Butler Yeats and the new movies, both of them starved for a certain kind of conversation that Papa called "smart talk." He was pleased when, on a spring evening during my last term at Guiteras Junior High, I made the climb to the garret for the first time. Miss Nerone had invited me for dinner, and here, maybe, was the world in which I'd like to live someday.

I was fussy about clothes by now, and tortured my hair with bobby pins and kid curlers and rag rollers, and more than once my father had chastised me for looking too long into the mirror. That's why I remember so well what I was wearing: a flowered rayon jumper, all greens and yellows with a splash of magenta, over a long-sleeved white blouse. I was also wearing my retainer, a semicircle of wire attached to a pink plastic plate over which I was supposed to position my lower jaw. It was the last stage in seven years of nonstop orthodontia.

We had sherry before the consommé, the candles flickered in the May night, and I recall being pleased at how well I was doing: my back straight, my left forearm invisible and my soup spoon skimming away from, not toward, me. Miss Nerone told me to be sure to read James Stephens's *Crock of Gold,* and that I must, I really must, ask Papa to take me to the Gardner Museum and to the Ballet Russe de Monte Carlo when it came to Boston. The world was expanding as she spoke, and so was I.

Then it happened. After the roast chicken and the peas and the vanilla ice cream, I looked for the plastic retainer presumably hidden in my lap. It wasn't there. How could I face my parents, who had spent a fortune for this hardware? There was nothing for it but to ask Miss Nerone to help me look for the darn thing.

Together we crawled about the rug searching for the retainer which, out of my mouth, looked like an especially hideous set of dentures. Then I remembered. Before we'd sat down at the small walnut table I had palmed the retainer and slid it into my jumper pocket.

By now my eyes were wet and my face red and my back damp. "It's in my pocket," I said, still staring at the floor.

"Only Mary Lee Cantwell would have her hostess on her hands and knees," Miss Nerone crowed, and sent me home a queen.

That summer Miss Nerone roped Ruthie and me into the Bristol Community Theater. Bristol hadn't had a little theater since Aida Connery's glory days, when she'd been Butterfly in *H.M.S.*

*Pinafore* and Peg in *Peg O' My Heart*. Instead we had the Rotary Club Minstrel, for which Ganny's cousin, Emma Rounds, played the piano and Miss Nerone did the makeup. But Bristol had what my mother described—in a lemon-juice voice—as "an arty crowd" and it clamored for something more than blackface and straw hats. That was why Ruthie and I who, hanging on her every word, walked Miss Nerone home whenever she taught at Guiteras, found ourselves one night sitting timidly in a corner of a smoke-filled room above the Y.M.C.A.

Some of the arty crowd were new to Bristol and some were what my mother called sissy, but all of them were people I'd seen traipsing about town and in and out of the Pastime behaving just like everybody else. Here, though, they were transformed.

They perched on tables, rather than on the Y's folding chairs, swinging their legs (if they weren't crossed) and taking deep drags on their cigarettes. They talked fast, too, more often out of the side than out of the center of their mouths, and their consonants rang like steel. Ruthie and I didn't catch their references, nor did we get their jokes, but I was certain we were listening to smart talk.

*Kitty Foyle* was to be the first production, and having found a Kitty (the prettiest girl in the senior class at Colt Memorial High School) the arty crowd was looking around for a Veronica Gladwyn, the rich boy's snooty fiancée. "There she is, right over there!" the smartest talker—a man whose hands waved like palm fronds—exclaimed, and pointed at me, bony-faced beyond my fourteen years.

On the evening of the performance, in the same dirty-windowed gymnasium in which I'd played girls' basketball, Miss Nerone sank my cheeks with rouge, dimmed my skin with powder and painted my lips into Katharine Hepburn's downturn. My costume was a broad-shouldered black crepe dress loaned by my stage mother, and black suede pumps loaned by my real mother, and when I stood waiting in the wings with the rest of the cast, all of us in paint and powder and borrowed clothes and sheepish smiles, I felt myself one of a company of players, their age and their peer. Then the house lights dimmed and Eddy Duchin's recording of "Love Walked In" troubled the hush—sad and sonorous and the smartest talk I'd ever heard.

It sounded like New York, the New York that Miss Nerone talked about when she came home from her summers working in Saks Fifth Avenue's handbag department. A place where you could see Ginger Rogers tapping an impatient toe at a glove counter (Miss Nerone had) and skyscrapers pierced clouds and something called a shuttle burrowed between Times Square, where the lights were, and Grand Central, where the *Yankee Clipper* pulled in puffing.

But no matter how Miss Nerone's green eyes glowed in the telling, nobody at 232 Hope Street, except for Papa, would have dreamed of living in a world where laundry dripped into bathtubs instead of grass, and one slept on sheets that had never known sun.

My mother had gone to New York several times, and kept in the desk a photograph, framed in fake red plush, of her and Papa sitting at a table in Billy Rose's Diamond Horseshoe. Beside Esther's bed was a picture of herself and Agnes, one of the girls from the shop, at the World's Fair. And, of course, there was that other trip, when she, along with all the other fans, pushed and shoved to see Rudy in his coffin. Gampa, too, had been to New York, on its outskirts anyway, when he and Ralph Kinder would zoom along the Merritt Parkway to see how fast they could get from Bristol to there and back. Still, no amount of shows, nightclubs, neon signs, and puffing camels could make up for the crowds, the dirt, and the heat. "You don't get a breeze like this in New York," Bristol said when the harbor flashed little white ruffles. "They say the prices in New York are something terrible. . . ." "I bet you don't get lobster like this in New York."

Eddy Duchin went on picking out the melody, each note clean and firm and somber. The music sounded like what you got out of Bristol for, but what that was I couldn't have said. New York was as good a term as any, if by it you meant something that was more an idea than a place.

Papa, Gampa, Ganny, Esther, and Diana were out front, along with Mother, who was just sliding into her seat. A few minutes earlier she'd sneaked backstage to see how I looked in the black crepe dress and the high-heeled shoes. Side by side we stood, staring into the full-length mirror propped against a wall, and for once there were no proscriptions about admiring oneself.

My eyes were brown to her blue; my head topped hers by a good three inches. But we had the same broad cheekbones and the same broad shoulders. I would never be as pretty as my mother, but I had inherited enough of her to be handsome. "Boy!" I thought to myself. "I look like New York."

# Fourteen

*A* FEW YEARS AGO, sitting in a cab that was going up Madison Avenue and staring through the rain at the umbrellas and puddles and the shops that sold French bags and Italian shoes and English chintzes, it suddenly occurred to me that I was happy. But why? It was the way the cab smelled.

The previous passenger had been wearing shaving lotion, something ordinary like Old Spice or Aramis, and to sniff that scent was to be in the glider on the second-floor porch of 232 Hope Street, with a boy whose shirt smelled of starch and fresh air and whose young, flushed face smelled of his older brother's after-shave. He was the boy I had seen at the Pastime Theater when I was eleven or so, and for all the time I was in that cab he was in it too.

He had dark wiry hair and a thin wide mouth, and all that was even slightly exceptional about him were his eyes, which were very blue. His eyes were what I noticed the night I looked along the row at the Pastime. I don't know what it was he noticed about me.

Who was he? I had never seen him at the Pastime before, nor at Buffington's Drugstore, nor at church. I was pretty sure he wasn't one of the summer people because it was in winter that I had seen him; and he didn't go to St. Mary's, the Congregational Church (I asked Joanie) or St. Michael's (I asked Anne).

I looked for him at Alger's Newsstand and at the library, and on Friday nights when I went to the Pastime my eyes were searchlights sweeping the lobby and the aisles. But I didn't find him for over a year, and when I did it was in the tarred parking lot of Guiteras Junior High.

It was the first day of school and he was standing alone, sliding quick looks in my direction. He lived up the Neck, somebody said, miles away from 232 Hope Street, and had just graduated from St. Mary's Parochial School. No wonder he'd been invisible.

His name was Norman, and he was entering the ninth grade. I was just entering the seventh. When he left Guiteras I would be just moving into the eighth, whereas he would have gone on to the greater glory that was Colt Memorial High School. By the time I got there he'd have gone out with lots of girls, maybe even kissed a few. But at least I'd have a year during which we'd be passing each other in the hallways, hanging around the same parking lot, sharing the same auditorium.

It would have been enough to go on staring, to glimpse him as he traveled the corridors, to sit in the seat that had been his when he left for his next class. But he kept on sliding those quick looks, and the boys on the school bus howled and stroked their index fingers and chanted "Normie likes Mary Lee-ee! Normie likes Mary Lee-ee!" Still, we never spoke.

There was a little ritual we schoolkids practiced every June: mock terror when the report cards were handed out. Suppose we hadn't passed? But of course we passed. Only odd kids with streaming noses and wet lips weren't promoted. So I was stunned when the whispering began on the girls' side of the parking lot. Norman, cocky Norman, would have to repeat ninth grade.

For a minute I fell out of love, and then, laboriously, I fell back in. Norman was moody, unpredictable, untameable. He was, in fact, the lover for whom Ruthie and I cried at the foot of Union Street. "Heathcliff," we'd call into the wrinkling water and the setting sun. "Where are you, Heathcliff?" Heathcliff would not have given a fig for not passing ninth grade.

Another year with Norman: Ruthie said it was fate. The following fall he started drifting away from the boys with whom he stood at recess. Each day he drifted a little farther until, finally, he ended up on the girls' side. "Saw you up on the Common, Tuesday," he'd say, and "Bet you *live* at the library."

Standing so close to him made me nervous. "I didn't see *you,*" I'd reply, and "I do *not.*"

Ruthie, Joanie, Jeanne, and Anne would giggle, and back to the boys' side he'd saunter. The boys would cuff his arms or try to trip him; I'd turn away, pleasure spreading through me like warm milk.

Sometimes he walked me home, veering off to kick a horse chestnut or jump for a dangling leaf, then homing back to my side. We seldom talked. If we had, I might have said "What was it about me?" I might even have said "I think it was your eyes."

No, I wouldn't have. I would have chattered about anything in the world but love, and when, years later, he asked me to say the word—just say the word—the "*l*" stuck to my tongue.

Every Saturday afternoon I went to confession, kneeling in a golden oak box and scraping my mind for sins. "I got mad at my sister three times, Father, and twice I disobeyed my mother." Taking communion on Sunday meant being visible to everyone in church, and I wanted Norman to see me, pretty in my reefer and beret and transfigured by piety. He no longer went to the eleven o'clock mass with his family—that they went to that service was another reason I'd never seen him until that night at the Pastime— but took the bus downtown to sit alone across the aisle from us at the nine o'clock. When I left the communion rail, my mouth closed primly over the wafter, I'd sneak a glance toward his pew. If he was there, I sank to the kneeler and buried my face in my hands. In theory I was praying, but in fact I was smiling, and the heat from my cheeks was warming my fingers. "Forgive your sister," Papa would say when I snarled at Diana or refused her a game of slapjack. "She's in love."

"Did Hotlips walk you home from school today?" he'd ask over supper. Norman played the trumpet. I kept my own lips shut when Papa teased, but happiness curled them at the corners. Someday Norman was going to kiss them, the first boy who ever did, but I could wait. Because what I really wanted was to pass right into him.

I had never been lonely before, even when nobody at school

liked me. I had always had myself to talk to. But I wasn't enough for me anymore. Now when I walked down Union Street after an evening up at Ruthie's, the scent of salt and privet, which I had loved, made me desolate instead. I peered into the Tingleys' and Miss Munro's lighted windows and believed myself to be irrevocably outside, destined, like Belle Bosworth, to butterfly down Hope Street forever. Still, desolation was exciting. "Alone, alone," I chanted, and marveled at the sound the words made, like a bell tolling. Once in a while I kept on walking, right down to where the water lapped, black and oily in the dark. Rats whispered among the rocks, and the damp curled my hair. "She walks in beauty like the night," I breathed, and assigned the words to me.

Spring arrived, the last spring that Norman would be at Guiteras Junior High. He had passed. The horse chestnuts in front of 232 Hope Street were strung with candles; the linden trees in front of Colt Memorial loosed their scent; when the rain fell in late afternoon it felt like a sponge full of warm water was being squeezed over my head. And Norman, at last, picked up the family telephone and asked for four-six-one.

My mother washed my hair in the afternoon while I hung my head over the side of the bathtub, and gave it a chamomile rinse. I put on my best dress, a shadow-plaided pink-and-white cotton, white socks, and my Bass Weejuns, and replaced my silver barrette with a maroon grosgrain ribbon.

Breathless in my perfection I went downstairs so Ganny, Gampa, and Esther could look me over, then trotted back upstairs so Mother, Papa, and Diana could have their turn. "See he brings you straight home afterward," my mother said, and retied the bow in my hair. When the doorbell rang I was reluctant to answer; reluctant to leave this room and Diana in her long braids and Mother taking off her apron and Papa pushing up the knot on his loosened tie and all of them smiling at Mary Lee, who was about to cast off from the dock.

It was still daylight, which meant that everyone could see us when we walked uptown. So when we got to Court Street I made him walk ahead of me so that the guys who hung around the front of the Y.M.C.A. and had something to say about everyone who passed wouldn't realize we were together.

Once past the Y and across State Street Norman stopped and, turning, waited until I caught up. Then we linked hands for the first time, and walked under the linden trees up to Bradford Street. We were heading, of course, for the Friday night show at the Pastime Theater.

# Fifteen

$\mathcal{W}$HERE I LIVE NOW, close to the Hudson, the air smells of iodine, and seagulls dive into the piles of debris heaped beside the docks. By most people's standards it's a desolate area, but not by mine. The water and the gulls remind me of Bristol, and I am as at home here as I can ever be in New York. There's one thing that's bothersome, though. The traffic. I can never get away from the whine of traffic.

If I interrupt this narrative, it is because I want to celebrate a silence, a silence I can't find even in Bristol anymore. In my childhood, Bristol was noisy only with winds and birds and people's voices and lawn mowers and waves lapping and factory whistles hooting and pins scattering at the bowling alley. Except on Saturdays, when uptown was clogged with cars unloading passengers at the library or Buffington's or one of about twelve stores, ten cars heading south in five minutes were enough to make Ganny say "They're going to have a regular traffic jam down by the Mount Hope Bridge."

A car going through town late at night was reason to rush to the window. What, short of an emergency, could bring anyone out on the road after eleven o'clock? A car suddenly braking in front of the house had my mother saying "Must be one of those crazy New York drivers."

Families had cars, of course. They used them to go to

Providence, and if they lived up the Neck or down the Ferry they used them to go to church on Sundays. On the night of the Junior Prom or the Senior Reception at Colt Memorial High they lent them to their sons; and the sons of families that didn't have cars were frantic until they found a friend with whom to double-date, because one couldn't ask a girl to trail her evening gown through town. But most of the time Bristolians walked. Walking was economical; it was healthful; and, most important, it was virtuous. To ride when you could walk betrayed a kind of moral sloth.

On Thanksgiving Day when we were small Diana and I walked toward the Ferry with Esther, so as to work up an appetite for the turkey. Esther couldn't make anything but penuche, so nobody expected her in the kitchen, and setting the table was Gampa's job because he'd learned from his brother, the one who'd owned the Warren Hotel, how to fold napkins into fancy shapes. So Esther was free, as she was always free, to be our playmate. She was also free of ever having to be called "aunt." From the beginning Diana, myself, and Miss Hot-Cha, Miss Charleston (she taught us how, hands grasping the back of a chair), Miss-Five-Foot-Two-Eyes-of-Blue were the same age.

Off we'd go, scuffling through the leaves and taking deep breaths—Esther believed that salt air was good for the lungs and salt water good for the skin, which was why hives and rashes always had us standing neck-deep in Bristol Harbor—and exchanging good mornings with other Bristolians out to work up an appetite. Usually there were one or two boats tacking their way about the harbor, somebody out for a last sail before winter set in.

Our eyes on the harbor, Diana and I pretended not to notice when Esther scooted ahead of us to hide behind a tree. Dutifully we screamed when she leaped out, then on we'd go. When we got to the yellow caution light suspended above the intersection of Hope and Wood Street she'd say "Getting hungry, girls?" and not waiting for an answer turn back, the ritual complete.

Once past the caution light one was down the Ferry, and no longer on a walk but taking a hike. A hike meant continuing down the worn, leaf-carpeted path on the west side of Ferry Road (the right side was grassy and pathless and on higher ground) past a house with two porcelain cats on its roof, a Gothick cottage and, beyond a gatehouse, the rhododendron-screened summer residence of a rich Providence family, all of whom had long teeth and carrot-colored hair.

No matter how bright the sun or how warm the day the air was damp and cool at the beginning of the Ferry. Moisture dropped from the dense evergreens and the leaf mold smelled like melancholy. Squirrels made sudden darts up trees and down stone walls. There were no passersby, and the houses were still and secretive.

Stillest of all was a house called Blithewold, whose owners were seldom, if ever, there. Blithewold was separated from the path only by knee-high stone walls between whose posts swung long, loose chains. Even so, no intruder ever strolled its thirty-three acres or sheltered in the shade of its copper beech or its sequoia, the tallest for thousands of miles, or sat in its tiny gazebo. No guards were needed to keep the stranger off the grass; the house itself did that.

Sprawled insolently on the lawn, its white stucco shining in the sun, it turned blind windows on the world, and I, eating my hiker's apple on the low wall, trembled lest, sensing my presence, it told me to get up. Every once in a while in Bristol, money, old money, rose up and hit you in the face. Sometimes it was in the form of a sentence—"But everyone we *want* to know about it will be there," a friend from the yacht club said when I asked if her debut would be reported in the *Providence Journal*. Sometimes it was in the form of a locked and silent house.

Past Blithewold the trees thinned and hills rolled and crouched behind them, invisible from the road, were St. Joseph's Seminary, which sent St. Mary's its summer priests, and the Convent of St. Dorothy, home to an order of Portuguese nuns of whom nobody ever saw hide nor hair. Behind St. Joseph's a large crucifix reached by a long flight of stone steps brooded over the harbor. For several Good Fridays Ruthie and I knelt on those steps for the long hours from noon to three o'clock when the sky darkened and the heavens split and Jesus gave up his spirit. But I could summon no more religiosity there than I could in the attic during the days before my First Communion, when I waited among the chamber pots for God to send me a sign. There was no room in this spartan landscape for votive lights and chasubles and bleeding hearts. The very town looked Protestant.

As one neared the end of the Ferry the road forked, and Narragansett Bay blazed blue. To the right was the entrance to the Mount Hope Bridge; to the left a short stretch of road that ended in a rocky shore. Here old men fished for flounder while the occasional car sped overhead across the bridge, and the occasional suicide tumbled from the bridge railings. Usually they went over without a sound, but a woman from Barrington, who had traveled hell-for-leather down Hope Street to make the plunge, screamed when she hit the air. Everybody said she had probably changed her mind the minute her foot left the railing.

Beyond the shore, crumbling cliffs edged the meadows in which cows browsed and dropped the flops that had Ruthie and me uttering warning cries and, all too often, a disgusted "Ugh." We wandered the meadows every spring and fall looking for arrowheads and striking romantic poses; and once a friend spent the night in that lonely place. At least that is what we think she did the time she ran away from home. We never asked, afraid the answer might involve a boy and a precocity we perceived as dirty. Neither did her mother, who feared her daughter's flat blue eyes. So we all chose to imagine her in the meadows, sitting against a tree, shivering in the dark, while cows lowed and cars hummed on the bridge and Indians pussyfooted along the paths that would take them to Mount Hope and Philip's longhouse.

We never walked down the Ferry in winter. The meadows were sodden, and the wind that came off Narragansett Bay was wet and cold as an icicle. Instead we walked north, toward the Neck and, if it had snowed, Fort Hill, where Lafayette had stamped about and slept and ate and which he abandoned when the harbor froze and locked the town.

Snow must have fallen in Bristol by day as well as by night, but it is always in the dark that I see the flakes, whirling ghostlike around the streetlights or dropping past them straight as needles. Down into the front hall Diana and I would creep, to open the door and watch snow blanket the bushes and the lawn and the empty roadway, and listen to its curious hiss. In the morning we awoke to deep drifts and iced trees and the scrape of Gampa's shovel on the sidewalk.

Come afternoon, we bellyflopped down Fort Hill, me on the bottom because I was the older, one hand steering our Yankee Flyer, the other over my mouth so a spill wouldn't lay waste to years of orthodontia, the two of us diving straight into the western sun. It was low in the sky by three o'clock, and orange, and the shadows in the snow were blue. By the time we left the hill for the long walk home, everything around us was white or gray or black.

Because no Bristolian would dream of turning on the electricity while it was still light out, the houses were as desolate as the streaming gutters. The windows in some were chinked with newspaper and fogged with the torrid heat from kerosene stoves whose pipes had been tunneled into sealed fireplaces. Bristol was a hard place for the elderly to be in winter, less because it was cold than because the damp was cruel to old bones. Still, I never heard of anyone leaving town. Old bones stayed indoors with Ma Perkins and her handyman, Shuffle, and got their groceries delivered and didn't show their faces until the end of March, when the backyards were mud and the milk had stopped freezing and forcing the cream out of the tops of the bottles.

As I got older Fort Hill palled, and the Yankee Flyer became Diana's alone. Now Ruthie, Joanie, Jeanne, Anne, and I, our ice skates tied together and hanging around our necks, hiked every Saturday to Collins Pond, to skate with the boys we knew from birthday parties and Girl Scouts. But I, the first of us to have an official boyfriend, skated mostly with Norman. Sometimes he stuck his bare hand into my mitten, and our entangled fingers became slick with sweat. He couldn't quite look in my eyes then, nor I in his.

Collins Pond was in a hollow behind a two-room schoolhouse, and had narrow, reed-bordered tributaries that meandered eastward toward St. Mary's Cemetery, where Ganny's family slept row on row. One could travel the tributaries single file until they narrowed too much even for a blade, and whenever I skated into the reeds I felt as if I were slipping through centuries. But not into

Bristol's past. Miss Nerone had shown the class a print of Brueghel's *Woodchoppers,* and it was into that still, serene landscape I was skating.

Dressed in caps, scarves, mittens, peajackets, snow pants, and two or three pairs of socks apiece, we bumbled up and down the pond, stumbling over our own and everyone else's blades and frequently crashing to the ice. And just as the woodchoppers are fixed on canvas so we are fixed in my mind, to go on bumbling and stumbling and crashing until the projector shuts down.

Across the road from Collins Pond two bronze bulls, snorting and stamping on their marble pedestals, proclaimed the entrance to Colt Farm, Private Property, Public Welcome.

S. Pomeroy Colt, the man who inflated the rubber works, had had a good time with his money. He ran a road around the farm's perimeter, threw a bridge over an inlet called Mill Gut, and set facsimilies of the Venus de Milo and the Discus Thrower on its buttresses. The Jersey cows he named after his girlfriends were housed in a tile-roofed stone barn, and a big, shingled casino in which he gave glorious luncheons boasted a statue of Silenus holding a goatskin purse that spurted milk punch.

By the time I came along, S. Pomeroy, his girlfriends, his luncheon guests, and his cows were dead, the casino was in ruins and Silenus had disappeared. But the barn sat solid and substantial on a sea of grass, and the bronze dog S. Pomeroy had set on a pudding stone near a narrow beach still stared at Narragansett Bay.

The dog was death to the touch but so lifelike to look at that I half-believed it had watched the boats that ran along this pebbly shore during Prohibition. If it had, it might have seen my grandfather among the Bristolians who stood ankle-deep in the purling water, passing the cases from hand to hand while the moon sailed overhead. Or so I had heard. But I couldn't ask Gampa if the story was true, because he'd have been as embarrassed by the question as he was by his granddaughters having seen him the night he was escorted home from the Hurricane Bar. Nor could I ask Ganny, because any talk of liquor had her frowning, or my mother, because she'd say "Where did you ever hear such a thing?" and be cross at suppertime. But I believed it. Even when he was walking Judy uptown on the end of her clothesline leash, with his shirt open at the neck and his pants flapping about his skinny legs, Gampa had the air of a Dapper Dan. I could see him in that purling water, oh yes, with the moon shining on his white hair and a cigarette in the corner of his mouth.

Before there had been any Colts or cows or bronze bulls or bootleggers, however, there had been the poorhouse. It was still up there, white as a skull, with three rows of hollow eyes that stared at North Burial Ground. To explore it one had to hazard a deceptively grass-filled ditch and a barrier of nettles, but they weren't what kept the poorhouse unviolated. Bleached and bare and bony, it evoked what lay beneath the burying ground's old slate markers and the flags that waved cheerily on veterans' graves.

"I shall end up in the poorhouse," Ganny would say whenever she looked into her change purse, and meant it. She remembered when people really did: old Yanks and a few old Irish, some of them dirty and some of them clean, some of them well-mannered and some of them know-nothings, and all of them with faded blue eyes.

Beyond the poorhouse a long straight road arrowed through a double file of maple trees under which the Portuguese and Italian families who lived in the three-deckers off Wood Street picnicked in summer while their children swam off the flat gray shingle known as the Town Beach. The children shrieked and the parents shouted, but the cars parked on the grass slumbered until it was time to pack up the kids and the coolers and the leftover *chourice* and go home.

Sunday afternoon was our time at Colt Farm, when Ruthie, Joanie, Jeannie, and I walked the entire perimeter, stopping only to take snapshots of one another, our faces turned to the wind so we could display our profiles and our skirts plastered against our lean thighs.

We walked through air that was as silver as the bay, following the road that led us past the poorhouse and through the file of trees and over the bridge to the head of the harbor.

We passed the little hill on which my mother had sat with a beau for a photograph, toothy and pretty, her arms curved around her silk-stockinged legs and her feet long and narrow in her T-strapped shoes. Uncle John had posed for a picture here, too, handsome and a bit flashy in his two-toned wingtips, and companioned by a girl in a cloche hat and skimpy jersey dress.

We passed S. Pomeroy's stone barn, and families clamming in the shallow, polluted water and, in the last stretch, a peculiar building called the Castle, stuccoed and turreted and ugly. And when, abruptly, we were out on Hope Street again we saw Guiteras Junior High just down the road and moaned.

We walked, no matter how late the hour or how long the distance from here to there. We walked down the Ferry and up the Neck, along the Back Road and across the Common, down Thames Street, where spinning mills thrummed and spilled their dyes into the harbor, and up Tanyard Lane where in spring some funny, fleshy plants poked what look like penises out of pale-green leaves and made us blush and titter.

We walked along Wood Street, past U.S. Rubber with its red-brick archway, past cobblers' shops and dimly lit stores that sold bacalao and olive oil, past St. Mary's Parochial School and St. Mary's Church and the convent for the Sisters of Mercy and the old town graveyard, and past the dingy bar in whose backroom a rich, high-nosed parishioner of St. Michael's held court among the town layabouts every Sunday after church.

We walked through salt air and burnt-rubber air, under skies that were clotted with clouds or gray as pewter or as hard and blue as Canton ware. We walked at night when there wasn't another soul on the street and the trees sighed and dipped their heads and the bushes shuddered in the dark. We walked if it rained and we walked if it snowed and we walked if whitecaps presaged a squall. When a hurricane came up, and seventeen miles of flooded roads and downed trees lay between the Tingley boys' father and home, he did what any Bristolian would have done. He walked.

# Sixteen

---

FINALLY IT HAD ARRIVED: my first day at Colt Memorial High School. My blooming.

I would go to football and basketball games, no longer a shy spectator unsure of my place in the crowd but an acquaintance of the guys on the team, a friend of the cheerleaders. I would see my name in *The Bristol Phoenix* when I made the honor roll, and on Friday nights I would swagger down the aisle of the Pastime Theater because this was my territory now. And when the crowds gathered on a May night to watch the Tonys in their white dinner jackets and the Annas in pastel tulle arriving for the Junior Prom, they would see me too. Mary Lee Cantwell, the dead spit (I thought) of Gene Tierney.

When I was six or so Diana and I—she in a checked cotton dress that hugged her cheerful plumpness and I in an eyelet-edged gingham that hung off my bony shoulders—stood on the marble steps of the high school, along with thirty other females of assorted sizes and shapes. We were participants in a pageant celebrating 300 years of Rhode Island, and all the costumes, all but the two Puritan get-ups, came from Bristol attics.

A photographer from the *Phoenix* took our picture, and Papa ordered two copies: one for me and one for Di for when we grew up. I love to look at it, not simply because I know so many of the faces—Miss Nerone is there, and Miss Hill, two of the four beau-

tiful sisters who used to ride their horses in the Fourth of July parade, and the leader of my Girl Scout Mariners troop—but because
it shows so clearly the astonishment that was Colt Memorial High.

Colt Memorial High School was S. Pomeroy Colt's tribute to
his mother, Theodora, and he had brought to it the same passion
for the ancient world that had informed his improvements to Colt
Farm. In the first place, the school was a veritable temple of learning, being completely faced with marble, its windows set in bronze.

On either side of the marble walkway stood a bronze boy and
a bronze girl. He wore a few odds and ends of drapery; she wore a
chiton and was holding a book. Hair bound in a fillet, her nose
straight as a die, she looked like my mother, who might have mod-
eled for Praxiteles.

The walkway led to marble steps that in turn led to a massive
mahogany front door framed by Corinthian columns and enor-
mous bronze lanterns. To the left of the entrance was a big block of
marble supporting beasts and men in bloody combat; Rodin's
*Naked Eve* would have graced the front lawn had not the School
Committee of 1909 demurred. To walk in the front door of Colt
Memorial High School was, in theory if not in fact, to set foot on
Parnassus.

So here I am, on a warm day in early September, coming down
the steps of 232 Hope Street in the blue-and-white striped dress
that, outgrown or not, is my lucky charm for every first day of
school. The horse chestnuts are just beginning to litter the sidewalk, and I—sniffing the air, tossing my pageboy—am in full
gallop.

On this as on every schoolday for the next three years a flat
blue purse that closes with two red Bakelite stars is balanced on top
of the notebooks cradled in my left arm. All it will ever hold is a
comb, a handkerchief, small change, and a tube of Chen Yu lipstick, but to go out without it is inconceivable. Ruthie, Joanie,
Jeanne, and Anne also carry such purses, shielding their contents
from the boys when they lift the flaps, implying that they cache female secrets. Sanitary napkins, say, and the attendant safety pins.

Behind me, Mother is sitting down for her second cup of coffee, an English Oval in her left hand and relief written all over her

face. We are out of the house, all of us, and the silence is settling over her shoulders as lightly as a swan's-down cloak. We wear her out, we Cantwells.

Downstairs Ganny is punching pillows and yanking sheets, and if she can talk Gampa into hauling it out to the clothesline for her, she'll probably go out to the backyard and beat Esther's bedroom rug. It is wonderful to see Ganny at work. Unable to bend, she washes the kitchen floor by pushing the rag around with her foot. When she is making a pie she tosses the pastry as if it were pizza dough. "Get that hound out from underfoot," she calls to Gampa as she perambulates the house. "Tom, why don't you take that dang dog out for a walk?" Meanwhile he, bored and restless, is skimming the newspaper or dipping into the only book he ever reads. It is Mary Lasswell's *Suds in Your Eye,* picked up once or twice a week, and makes him laugh till his nose runs.

Ahead of me, uptown is shaking itself out of sleep. Newman's Grocery is gone, but the grumpy old man from whom I used to buy foreign stamps for my album, ten per glassine envelope, is sweeping the sidewalk in front of his variety store. I bob my head in his direction, a queen in a glass coach, but he is sour and saurian as ever. Miss Norah Sullivan of The Bluebird Shoppe is sweeping her sidewalk, too, the secrets of every female bulge, sag, and varicosity in the country of the blue-eyed safe beneath her massive corset.

Across the street from the Bluebird, Ralph Kinder, the florist, is wiring the stems for the roses in today's first coffin blanket. If Ganny succeeds in getting Gampa out of the house, he'll be sitting at Kinder's in an hour or so, slapping his knee while Ralph skewers the passersby. If anyone comes in the shop, he'll show them Judy's gallstones, which he keeps in a pocket of his vest. "Did I ever show you what my little dog had in her?" he'll ask. He probably has, but the person will look anyway. That Gampa is crazy about Judy is well known in our part of town.

Next to Kinder Florists, the woman who runs the beauty parlor where Mother gets her semiannual permanent has the front door open to let the air in; but the Women's Exchange will stay shut until noon. The tarnished spoons and brass candlesticks and dusty Limoges in its window are testament to a hundred Bristol weddings. Its proprietor, a pillar of St. Michael's Church, is testament to Bristol's years in the slave trade, being both black and a member of the town's most prominent family.

Beyond the Solders' and Sailors' Monument and the police station, Alger's Newsstand is doing a brisk trade in *The Providence Journal* and *The Bristol Phoenix,* and the latter's editor is dashing into the post office for the first mail. A small, skinny man with a toothbrush mustache, he is always dashing—scooping up the news, I suppose—and I am proud when he stops to tip his hat and croon "Goo-oo-ood morning, Mary Lee!"

The regulars for morning coffee at Buffington's have taken their places at the marble counter, but the awnings aren't yet down at Eisenstadt's Dry Goods. Thank heaven the sidewalk in front of the Y is still free of the boys who'll be there later, cracking wise.

Once across State Street I am part of the crowd converging on Colt High. If Bristol were still the town I have created out of Ganny's stories, the students would look like George Gibb and Emily Webb or, closer to home, my mother in her youth. The actuality, however, is Dolores Canario and Anthony Guglielmo. How can I see the Bristol I want to see, the Bristol where Indians stalked Mount Hope and George Washington paraded down Hope Street and Ganny, in her best dress and high-topped shoes, stood weeping at her mother's grave, when the town has taken on so Neapolitan an air?

And yet I can, because by now I have double vision. I have listened so long to Ganny's stories and spent so many hours studying the pictures in her copy of *The 1903 Pictorial Supplement to The Bristol Phoenix* that when I walk around town I can see both what is there and what preceded it. One of Bristol's first houses, for instance, a clapboard whose walls were stuffed with eelgrass for warmth, stayed on its foundations long enough for a photographer to record it around the turn of the century. It's more vivid to me than its replacement, an asbestos-sided cottage with a wavy aluminum awning over the front door.

First stop, the auditorium. It's white-walled and high-windowed, with portraits of S. Pomeroy and Theodora on either side of its shallow stage, and the seats are green leather with the Colt crest stamped in gilt on the back. The principal walks onstage. We rise. (Years later, at my first college assembly, I am startled when nobody rises as the president enters.) He greets us on this, the opening day. A bell rings. We're off!

*Bzzzz.* The buzzer is sounding and Ruthie, Joanie, Jeanne, Anne, and I are in our English class, where we will drowse over *Gammer Gurton's Needle.* Our teacher, a third-grade classmate of my dead Aunt Margaret (in their class photograph they are side by side, my aunt thin and watchful and my teacher with thick hair and a mouth like a rosebud), is the quintessential Yankee, dry to the touch. She is rumored to hand out A's as reluctantly as a miser hands out money. Eventually, however, she will hand them out to me, and even laughs a rare laugh when I give her a story about a rabbit who puts her ears in rollers for Easter.

*Bzzz,* and we travel the olivewood-paneled corridors to history class, where we flinch from the room's stench. The teacher's legs are ulcerated, and she has spread newspapers around her desk to catch the drip. Soon, though, we will take the stench and the drip and the newspapers for granted, just as we will soon take for granted her slow, halting walk to school and back. We are thoughtless, but perhaps that is a kindness.

*Bzzz,* and I pause for water from a marble bubbler over which is a marble plaque that reads "To thine own self be true." The only one of us to stay with the language after Guiteras Junior High, I am going alone to Latin class, to sit next to a window from which I can see Hope Street's hustle and bustle. "Look," somebody whispers as a descendant of S. Pomeroy Colt's emerges from Linden Place next door. "He's carrying his money bags over to the Industrial Trust." We believe it. Our notion of money has nothing to do with checks or stock certificates. As far as we're concerned those are dollar bills that S. Pomeroy's descendant is lugging across Hope Street in those two canvas bags, and maybe we're right. Ganny says the old Yanks still have the first dime they ever made.

The teacher usually stands by that window, her round face pinked by the morning sun and splitting into a gap-toothed grin. "Can you hear him?" she asks after reading us the Cicero that follows our ninth-grade Caesar. "Can you *hear* him?" We can. After we're settled into our seats there are no games or giggles in this room, no notes slipped from hand to hand. There is nothing here but Cicero speaking, and the sun ribboning our desks.

*Bzzz*, and I rejoin Ruthie, Joanie, Jeanne, and Anne for French class. The French teacher is lame, and lists when she walks. Miss C. is cherished, having taught so long that she is as much an institution as the Bristol/Barrington Thanksgiving Day football game and the Senior Reception. In fact, she was my mother's teacher too, and often the two of us meld in her mind's eye and she calls me by my mother's maiden name.

What little French she teaches is peculiar, but her conversation—and this is what our class is, one long conversation—is enthralling. When she isn't describing the Catholic ladies' college she attended a million years ago, she is talking about her great passion for France, a country which, *malheureusement!*, she will never see unless they build a bridge across the Atlantic Ocean because she is, *hélas!*, terrified of boats. Then she talks about us.

Thomas, the smartest boy in the whole school, is going to do remarkable things in science; and Anne has a genius for pronouncing French correctly; Ruthie is a born leader, and I? Miss C. puts a serious look on her small, pug-Irish face. "God has given Mary Lee," she says, "the gift of writing." When we leave her class we are twice as big as when we entered. But we have no French.

Forty minutes for lunch in the basement cafeteria! We buy the hot dish—our parents can afford the twenty-five cents it costs—but many of the Portuguese girls cannot. They are huddled uncertain in the girls' toilet, taking furtive bites of the sandwiches they have brought from home. How can they stand it, the constant flushing and the stink of disinfectant? My nose narrows. I reapply my Chen Yu lipstick; the peroxide streak I have put in my dark brown hair is canary yellow under the ceiling lights.

*Bzzz.* Time for chemistry lab and an hour in our rubber aprons, twiddling microscopes and duplicating aspirin and shuddering when the fumes from acid hitting acid spiral from our test tubes. We love chemistry class, the slumping on our stools and the casual walking around and no proscriptions on whoops and conversations. Above all we love the teacher, big and blond and forever frazzled. He is said to be witty, and God knows we will think him so. But how can one help but find hilarious a man who has been put on earth to keep a roomful of kids from setting themselves on fire with Bunsen burners?

*Bzzz.* Last class, up on the third floor in a room with a sloping roof, most of it a frosted-glass, chicken-wired skylight. We are in another of Miss Nerone's garrets, and she is whipping from easel to easel, cocking her head, squinting her eyes, framing the student's view of the bowl of fruit or the pitcher with the spray of bittersweet with a freckled hand. All the Italian boys draw very well—it's in their genes, she tells me—but I, being mostly Irish, will not be skilled in the visual arts. Never mind, she says, half-Irish herself. Nobody can talk or write like the Irish can.

*Bzzz.* It is two thirty, and school is over for the day.

We leave in a body, Ruthie, Joanie, Jeanne, Anne, and I. Our plaid skirts are switching over our rumps, and our white socks reach halfway to our knees. Textbooks have been added to the notebooks cradled in our left arms, and our ever-present purses are laid carefully over them. We are heading south for lemon Cokes at the Hope Drug, which is where we will go in the afternoon instead of Buffington's because the owner's son, Bobby, is in our class, and we are loyal. But before we step off the marble walkway, I reach out and pat the bronze girl who wears my mother's face.

TWO AFTERNOONS A WEEK, however, I don't head south with the rest of the gang. Instead I turn north, to the Bristol District Nurses Association and Miss Emilie Connery, who has called my house to ask if I would like a job helping her address envelopes for the infantile paralysis appeal. I am thrilled, but no more so than Papa. After supper on the night she called he sat me down in the living room and said "I'm proud of you, Lulubelle, to be earning your own money. You're going to be a scrapper, like your old man."

We go through the phone book, I reading out the Bristol names and addresses and Miss Emilie writing them down. Maybe there is an easier way to locate possible donors but we don't know one, and we are happy as the shoeboxes we keep on a table next to Miss Emilie fill up with the fruits of our labor. Some days Miss Emilie steps into the room across the way so the district nurse can give her a liver shot; and always, about half-past three, she sends me to Buffington's for a coffee cabinet, which is Rhode Island's name for a coffee milkshake. "See you get Mr. McCaw, and see you tell him it's for me. He knows how I like them."

At five o'clock we shut up shop. Miss Emilie puts on her fedora and I stack my books and together we stroll down Hope Street. We are pleased with our output, and Miss Emilie has been further fortified by her liver shot and her personalized coffee cabinet. But that isn't why we have a certain strut, a certain . . . amplitude perhaps, as we pass the darkened five-and-ten, and Eisenstadt's, where the awnings have been rolled up for the night, and the shuttered jewelry store and barber shop.

Miss Emilie's taste in cabinets is known to Mr. McCaw and her skinny flank is known to the district nurse, and I am known to Miss Emilie since the morning I was born. It is because of my sharp eyes and her Palmer Method script that hundreds of Bristolians are going to pony up money for the infantile paralysis appeal. Miss Emilie and I aren't just drifting alone on the stream of life. We've got a mooring here. We belong to this town, and it to us.

# Seventeen

———◆———

As BOYS, Ganny's brother George had been famous for his soft-ball game and her son John for having won a race swimming from the foot of Byfield Street to Hog Island and back, while the order he was supposed to be delivering for Newman's Grocery was spoiling in the sun. Ganny herself was famous for her baked beans, as famous as her cousin Emma was for her angel food cakes, and a neighbor, old Mrs. Church, was for not letting people enter her house by the front door until they were eighteen years old. Ralph Kinder was famous for having driven the Merritt Parkway to New York faster than anyone else in town, and his brother Joe was famous for once having landed his plane on Hope Street, up near Silver Creek.

Usually, however, fame was acquired in high school. Even so, it lasted a lifetime, although often it had more to do with potential than with realization. The girls' gym teacher, for instance, was famous for the fact that she would have been a tennis champion had she only had a proper coach and a proper court to play on. A former student of Miss Nerone's was famous for the fact that he would have been a great artist had he not died in World War II. A boy in my class was famous both for being a natural athlete and for being too lazy to live up to his gifts.

That Ruthie was going to be famous was obvious from the beginning of her career in the public schools of Bristol, Rhode Island. Ruthie would be famous for being popular. Not only was she voted into every office for which she ran, but the schools' musical director, the barrel-body who had made fun of me when I couldn't read notes in third grade, had chosen her to lead the Colt Memorial High School Band.

She was a glorious sight marching down Guiteras Field at halftime and up Hope Street on the Fourth of July, a long green jacket belted over her white skirt and a tall shako riding the rim of her glasses. The marshal's baton was heavy, and raised a callus between the base of her thumb and the base of her index finger, and she employed it as one would a plunger. Straight up, straight down, and never a toss above the head or a pass through an upraised leg.

"*Breeep!*" her whistle signaled. Down went the baton and off she'd go, trailed by ten or so band members, among them Norman, his lips flattened against the mouthpiece of his trumpet; Jeanne, her eyes close to crossed over her clarinet; and whoever was the fattest boy in school strapped to the big bass drum. Joanie was Ruthie's alternate, tall and poker-stiff and bending a stern Swedish gaze on her charges.

Anne had achieved fame, too, as a cheerleader. "Green and White fight/Green and White fight/Green fight/White fight/- Green and white fight," she'd urge, her bowling-pin legs bouncing her high into the air. The cheerleaders wore thick white sweaters and short green skirts, and when they flew up their skirts flew up with them and showed their neat little green cotton underpants.

The cheerleaders looked good all the time, but never better than on Friday nights in winter, basketball nights, when parents, students, and boosters crowded the Andrews Gym, big and bright and smelling, irremediably, of sweat. The Industrial Arts teacher was there, famous for his four-syllable name. "Mr. Agatiello, whatcha doin' tonight?" we'd sing to the tune of "In the Mood." "Mr. Agatiello, whatcha doin' tonight?"

The coach was there, famous for having guided the team to the Class C championship. A pin-headed man whose legs turned out curiously from his hipbones, he was married to a woman who painted her lips well outside their margin. What with his invitational legs and her knowing mouth we thought them sexy. We thought they knew a thing or two. The high school principal was there, famous automatically. And I was there, famous only for turning in a lot of book reports.

During the half, Anne and the rest of the girls would swoop across the court, little skirts flashing little pants, to greet the cheerleaders for the opposing team. Standing in a circle, they bent their heads and exchanged what appeared to be deep, intensely female secrets. Then, suddenly, like flowers unfolding, they'd break loose from one another and run back, flushed and pretty, to their own sides.

Once a year, one night in midwinter, I too was out on that floor, standing before hundreds of Bristolians in a blue bloomer suit and waving Indian clubs in unison with Ruthie, Joanie, Jeanne, and Anne. I wasn't agile enough for rope-climbing, the trapeze, or the horse, but at least I was on the team.

In autumn I played field hockey, left half, on the big field in back of Colt, shin protectors buckled to my legs, hockey stick blistering my hands, eyes fixed on the small white ball as it appeared and disappeared in the stubby grass, in a light that was as bronze as the trees. We played till our lips and hands and knees were blue, and by the time we walked home the light, too, was blue, and dense and chill as the harbor.

On Saturday afternoons in fall a crowd moved slowly down High Street after the football game at Guiteras Field, and I moved with it, feeling as if our legs were powered by the same piston. On Thanksgiving morning Esther walked toward the Ferry alone because Diana and I were standing, our feet nearly frozen to the rimed grass, at Victory Field in Barrington, cheering on the team. The Barrington kids were stuck-up, we said, and their songs, we knew, put ours in the shade. "Viva la viva la viva l'amour. Viva la viva la viva l'amour. Viva la Barrington," they choroused, their blond heads glinting in the pale November sun. Once I had wanted classmates who looked like them—blue-eyed and bound for Princeton, Wellesley, Smith. Not now. Now I looked at the motley crowd that was the student body of Colt Memorial High School and found myself thick with love.

I WOULD LIKE to have had them all well behind me, the catechism lessons and the rustle of nuns' robes and priests' cassocks and the hiss of "myss-sstery" and "sssym-bol." But there was one more sacrament to be achieved. I had never been confirmed.

When the bishop of Rhode Island made his previous quadrennial visit to Bristol, Ruthie and I had been a few months shy of twelve, and thus too young for confirmation. Now we were the oldest students in the class that met every Friday afternoon in the dark basement chapel of St. Mary's.

My parents had been married in that chapel and now, over twenty years later, I sat there shivering in the damp while a priest warned us of the hardships awaiting Catholics in a hostile world. "When the bishop slaps your cheek," he said, "that slap will symbolize the blows you will experience in the defense of your faith." "Snubs" he should have said, I thought. It would have made the message more contemporary.

Just as we had run across the Common after leaving our First Communion class nine years before, so Ruthie and I ran across the Common after our confirmation lessons. It was darkening now as it was then, and the empty bandstand looked lonely as ever. Only this time we were running back to school, and the Friday afternoon dance.

The green leather chairs were stacked in the corridor outside the auditorium, and Perry Como sang "Kiss me once and kiss me twice and kiss me once again," while the girls with no boyfriends watched at the sidelines, and the boys with no girlfriends nudged one another or, if they were shy, studied the floor. My having a boyfriend made me seem popular, so I got to dance, raised slightly on my toes as Papa had taught me and stiff-arming my partner. I tried to hold myself back a bit when I danced with boys, to leave a little space between my stomach and theirs, but sometimes I couldn't and felt against my thighs a worm stirring, then struggling to escape. That was torture, and never more so than when it was Norman with whom I was dancing, Norman who put out a shy hand to mine when we were at the Pastime and who put a hesitant arm over the back of the glider when we sat on the porch. Norman of the clean, clean shirts and his older brother's after-shave. My small breasts had done this to him, my breasts and the backside that started rounding only a few inches from where he placed his scrubbed, short-nailed hand.

On a Sunday evening at the end of November I was finally confirmed, in a white dress borrowed from Miss Nerone's niece, who went to a Catholic school in Providence and needed white dresses for processionals and Maytime crownings of the Virgin Mary. My old First Communion veil, white tulle pendant from a kind of bicycle clip, sat oddly on my head, and the dress, because the niece was shorter than I, barely covered my knees. Some of the girls, though, the ones who went to St. Mary's Parochial School, were as dressy and radiant as brides.

We were supposed to take for a middle name the name of a saint we admired. My mother mourned the day she'd chosen Gertrude and Esther said she didn't know what was on her mind when she'd picked Genevieve, so I stuck with my baptismal name and was confirmed "Mary Mary."

Then, while the organ thundered and the incense eddied, we children of the church walked up the aisle of St. Mary's Church and out the door into the lobby.

The outer door was open, too, and the Common stretched before us, desolate and curiously romantic in the darkness. I was pure, pure as the sacraments could make me, and white from my underwear out. And never again would I have to sit in a classroom or a chapel while somebody tried to stuff my head with something that couldn't be taught. The last building block was in place.

# Eighteen

*I* KEPT DIARIES. I cannot say I kept "a diary" because the term implies continuity. Instead I would write for a few weeks in a little spiral-bound notebook, misplace it, and start again a few months later with another spiral-bound notebook. Sooner or later I would misplace that one, too, and start all over again. Once I read an essay about socks, and how they seem as to give birth to one another. That's the way it is with my diaries. Whenever I am visiting 232 Hope Street, a corner of the attic or a drawer that hasn't been opened in years gives up another little spiral-bound notebook.

The girl who filled those notebooks with a curious hybrid of Palmer Method script and private school printing, was very fond of French words. "Who should meet me ce matin mais mon coeur?" she wrote about a boyfriend. She was worried about sex and concerned that she not receive a "rep," but safeguarded by her coldness. "Kissing doesn't bore me. It just doesn't affect me. Some parts of my emotions have yet to be uncovered, I can see." On the other hand, she wasn't really safe because she was determined to feel something. "I'm afraid I'm too curious. I want to see if anything will affect me, and it doesn't." Her determination, however, was somewhat sapped by her Puritanism. "I hope I never lose my head to the baser pleasures. Not that I'm not a base person—I am in many ways—but I hope I remain forever dead to these emotions. I may miss a lot. I don't know. I'm so confused."

Her relationship with Ruthie, Joanie, Jeanne, and Anne appears to be harmonious, although once she refers to "those harpies who call themselves my friends," and that with boys, tortured. "You know, Cantwell, you give me a big yack. In four weeks you have fallen for and away from three boys, and you all but threatened to commit suicide over one of them. Cantwell, don't be a boob. Don't believe a word they say. I mean it!"

Her most tortured relationship was with Norman. "I love him so, in spite of it all. It is no quick love of passion and glad moments. Instead my love brings misery and pain. It lies within not as warm and comfortable but as a stone upon my heart."

She went to the movies every Friday night, sometimes with Norman, but usually with Ruthie, Joanie, Jeanne, and Anne; and to dances at the Y.M.C.A., again with them. Having a boyfriend was not the same as having dates. The boyfriend part of it had to do with being walked home afterward. Dates, real dates, were only for the Junior Prom.

The linden trees in front of Colt High were in full, heartbreaking scent in May, in time for the Junior Prom, and on the great night the enormous lanterns outside the entrance were lighted. Friends and families of the Franks and Tonys and Sals ("Nobody can wear white jackets like the Italians can," Miss Nerone said) and Lucys and Theresas and Doloreses lined the marble entranceway to watch them promenading toward the massive mahogany door. It never rained, not once, and the air was like feathers.

My entrance—I always thought of it as an entrance, during which I would astonish with my glamor or, in the year I wore a pleated periwinkle blue crepe I thought Grecian, with my glorious austerity—was preceded by an afternoon at Mother's hairdresser, Mary Cappucilli. Blissful I was among the hiss of the shower sprays, the whine of the hairdryers, and the piles of *Photoplay* and *Modern Screen* while Mary rollered my straight hair and her helper, Angie, crimsoned my fingernails. Ganny and Gampa saw the hairdo first, then, head held stiffly so I wouldn't crack the glaze, I mounted the stairs to show Mother.

Supper was early and the bedroom still pink with sun when I put on my gown and Mother rummaged in her closet for her brocade evening wrap and in her top drawer for her beaded purse. At last I'd drift into the living-room and, spreading my skirts so they wouldn't wrinkle, sit. And sit and sit. No matter how well I knew my escort, usually someone with whom I'd had a Coke at the Hope Drug before my appointment with Mary Cappucilli, my knees were rubber and my palms wet.

The doorbell rang. We smiled—Papa, Mother, Di, and Esther shared the vigil—and the living room came back to life. The boy entered, a white box from Kinder's in his hand, and I would slide the corsage—gardenias, or, once, a raft of red roses that extended splintlike to my elbow—onto my wrist. Then down the stairs and out to somebody's father's car, and Ganny and Gampa peeking out the window.

A five-piece band blared from the auditorium stage; the girls smiled at one another over their partners' shoulders; the crepe paper hung in swags and balloons bobbed from the chandelier. This was the only time when it was okay to have a boy's arm around your waist, and to feel the length of him against the length of you. Sometimes the worm stirred, and then I'd extend my right arm slightly and try to back discreetly away.

By "Stardust" our skirts were crumpled, our feet were hurting in their unfamiliar heels and our cheeks were damp and reddened by hours of adhesion to our partners' cheeks. If our partner had a heavy beard, they were also somewhat chafed. My escort would help me into Mother's wrap, lifting my hair so it would clear the collar and sending, more surely than a kiss ever did, a tingle of sexuality along my spine. Shaken, I'd rustle into somebody's father's car and keep my eyes on the road and my hands in my lap as we headed for the Newport Creamery.

At the Creamery, Ruthie and Joanie and Jeanne and Anne and I spread our skirts along the booths and tossed our heads to display our mothers' earrings and anticipated the kiss, or kisses, that would end the evening. Norman kissed with flat, dry lips; Bobby, the boy whose father owned the Hope Drug, kissed wetter. J.B., who was older than the rest of us, had a mouth that smelled of tobacco. In three years at Colt High I was kissed by three boys.

One Junior Prom, however, ended differently from the others. The mother of one of the nicer boys (nicer meant somebody who lived on Hope or High Street and would go to college) gave a small party after the dance. She had been in my mother's class at Colt Memorial, just as her son was in mine, and was famous for her bridge luncheons and cocktail parties.

We wandered through her living room, suddenly strangers to one another, Ruthie in plaid taffeta and I in white tulle, and the boys in their white jackets. We sipped from little glass punch cups and plucked Vienna sausages from the "porcupine" Billy's mother had made by sticking them, on toothpicks, into an upended grapefruit half. If we sat it was only on the edge of the chair, and when we walked it was as gingerly as if we were treading ice. Our voices were soft and our laughter low, and I longed for a cigarette to punctuate my sentences. But of course I didn't smoke, none of the nicer kids smoked. This was going to be our world someday, this world of drinks and Vienna sausages and murmured conversations, and we swaggered a little bit, getting used to it.

That was the best evening, that and the night that again Ruthie wore her plaid taffeta and I wore the halter-necked white tulle that was my favorite evening gown to usher at the high school graduation. This night there were no worries about a doorbell not ringing or a boy dancing too close or of slipped shoulder straps and crushed skirts and smeared lipstick. Nor would I be crammed into a car, sitting on a boy's lap and miserable and guilty because I'd felt his penis swell beneath my thighs. Tonight Ruthie and I would come home as immaculate as we went forth.

After the graduation ceremony, when the last parent had left the auditorium, Ruthie and I hung around for a little while, watching the janitor pack up the folding chairs. By the time we started down Hope Street it was empty and a faint mist had come in off the harbor. When we got to St. Michael's Church Ruthie said "Shall we dance?" "*Mais oui!,*" I replied and dropped a curtsey. Nobody saw us as we dipped and swirled and flung our arms to the sky because all Bristol was in bed.

When we got to 232 Hope Street we kept on dancing, she with Rhett Butler and I with Heathcliff, and both of us as giddy as if we'd been drinking spiked punch. One or two cars drove past the house, the light was on over the front door, and the fallen petals from the white rose bush that climbed Ganny's porch were like candles in the grass.

# *Nineteen*

GAMPA'S BACHELOR BROTHERS, Uncle Johnny and Uncle Jimmy, have given me luggage. Blue. Aunt Mame, Gampa's rich sister, a watch she bought in Switzerland when she made the Grand Tour in 1929 and a ring set with three small diamonds—one from Uncle Johnny, one from Uncle Jimmy, and the third from the engagement ring left me by Aunt Annie. Papa and Mother have given me a Smith-Corona portable in a maroon leather case. Ganny and Gampa, a card with a handkerchief and a ten-dollar bill tucked inside. I also have cards from Miss Nerone, Miss Munro, Miss Bosworth, Miss Emilie, and Miss Aida Connery and several of the Barrington crowd. I am about to graduate from Colt Memorial High School.

Any longer at 232 Hope Street and my case of the Bristol Complaint will be fatal. The harbor and the air and the trees will have snared me so firmly that I will never be able to leave town. I will never be able to see the world. "When you get out of Bristol . . ." Papa says. "When you get out of Bristol . . ." Miss Nerone says. I will never get out of Bristol if I don't do it while I'm young.

I have always hated three o'clock in the afternoon. At three o'clock *Our Gal Sunday* and *The Romance of Helen Trent* are over and my mother comes into the bedroom with an eggnog and says "You have to nap now or you'll never get over that cold." At three o'clock the light turns a funny yellow and Ganny plumps herself into her rocker to doze a little, and the faucet is dripping in the kitchen, and the clock on the mantelpiece is ticking and the dishes are draining by the side of the sink. At three o'clock Alger's Newsstand is empty because the oldsters are napping and it's too early for the schoolkids, and the Misses Osterberg are enjoying the pause at the Rogers Free Library. The ticket booth at the Pastime is closed and there's not a soul on the Common. If I don't get out of Bristol it will always be three o'clock in the afternoon.

When Mother sends me down to the front hall to snap the lock for the night, I feel the dark and indeed all Bristol pressing against the door. Let me thumb down the button on the lock, though, and they can't get in. Nothing can get in. Years later, when so many of its rooms are empty and the warriors who thronged them are present only in the dent in a mattress or a chip in a plate, I will still think of this house as a fortress.

But Papa wants me out of the house and out of Bristol. We have such plans! First, he wants me to do well in college because, he says, "I've always wanted to wear a Phi Bete key." We chuckle at the picture he'll make: Papa with a Phi Bete key dangling from the gold chain that always swags his stomach.

My junior year I will spend abroad, preferably at Trinity in Dublin, where I will see *The Book of Kells* and the bullet holes in the Post Office walls and walk on St. Stephen's Green. "You should know your heritage, Mary Lee, it's something to be proud of."

After college we're not sure what path I should take, but we think probably graduate school. I will study some branch of English literature and get my Ph.D.—"Always wanted one of those in the family"—and along the way I should marry some nice guy. My first son I will name Donovan, which was Papa's mother's maiden name.

Details, details. In the end the details don't matter. What matters is that I am going to see the world. I cannot wait to see the back of this town!

Papa knows as well as I do what will happen if I stay in Bristol and sleep in my own little bed forever. I will be like the S. sisters, wasting my sweetness on the desert air. Then I will dry up and drift down Hope Street like a leaf on the wind. Eventually I will end up sitting among the rocks at Union Street and teaching myself French and Italian. Sooner or later I will be what Bristol calls a character. "Get out," Papa says, "get out."

I want to go to a women's college, the kind where the students roll hoops on May Day and wear gray flannel shorts with boys' letter sweaters turned inside out, and visit Yale and Princeton on the weekends. And both of us want me to be some place where nobody's ever heard of my Uncle John. I have yet to meet him, but once I eavesdropped on Gampa and Ralph Kinder when they were talking about "Red," and I think I heard the words "cell block seven." Papa is the only one in the house who ever talks about him out loud. "One day God picked up a rock," he told me, "and your Uncle John crawled out."

I want to go to the place my father promised, the place where there'd be lots of people like me. Above all I want to be queen of England.

I have never aspired to be part of the Ferry crowd, and I never will. But by now I am a monument to antennae, all of them waving fiercely when they discern a snub. The day a boy from down the Ferry, one of the summer people, was riding me home from the yacht club on the bar of his Raleigh, for instance.

We were nearing 232 Hope Street when Gampa came along, an old shirt tucked into his khaki trousers and his loafers—my father's cast offs—floppy on his skinny feet. Judy, her rump wiggling, was pulling on her clothesline leash.

"You be careful on that bicycle, Mary Lee," Gampa called out.

"My grandfather," I said to the boy, and waved.

"Is that *really* your grandfather?" he asked, and his eyes chilled to blue marbles.

He had long rabbit teeth, and I longed to push them down his throat. I would have, too, if Papa hadn't told me never to let people realize that they had gotten to me. My anger was our secret.

Today, on this Thursday morning in mid-June, Ruthie and I are heading toward Andrews Memorial for the graduation rehearsal. Andrews Memorial is a big red-brick building across the street from Colt, and it houses the gym, and the model home for the girls whose career will be housewifery and the machine shop for the boys who will work with their hands. Papa was on the building committee for Andrews, and I thrill when I see his name on the plaque in the entryway—no S. Pomeroy Colt perhaps, but enrolled in Bristol's history anyway.

Ruthie and I are wearing old sweaters, old skirts, and scarves over our hair, which is in curlers. The idea is to look as rotten as possible so as to make tonight's transformation from grub to butterfly all the more amazing. As we go by Kinder Florists, Ralph Kinder sticks his head out the door. "Congratulation, Mary Lee," he shouts across the street. Mr. McCaw, the druggist, says it, too, when we stop at Buffington's. Everybody's been saying it all week, and the yearbook picture of each and every member of the graduating class of Colt Memorial High School was in Tuesday's *Phoenix*.

The yearbook is lying on a table in the living room, autographed by most of my classmates and all of my teachers. Ruthie was *The Green and White*'s editor in chief; Jeanne would have been its business manager if she weren't out of town for a year with her parents; and Anne and I were the literary editors. Together we have chosen quotations from Papa's copy of *An Anthology of World Poetry* to introduce each section and to run under each student's photograph. "These are the days of our youth, the days of our dominion . . . all the rest is a dream of death, a doubtful thing. Joy of joys for an hour today, then away, farewell," it says at the beginning of the senior class section. My throat swells when I read it aloud, and I feel powerful, as if there were a scepter in my hand.

Ruthie and I have chosen "No coward soul is mine,/No trembler in the world's storm-troubled sphere" for Anne. Anne and I have chosen "A heart with which to reason and a head with which to contrive and a hand with which to execute" for Ruthie. (Ruthie doesn't look quite herself in the yearbook because the photographer made her take off her glasses.) My quotation, chosen by Ruthie and Anne, is from Louis Untermeyer: "A glow, a heartbeat, and a bright acceptance of all the rich exuberance of life." In the class will Ruthie has left a case of aspirin to her successor and I have bequeathed a girl in the junior class my leftover book reports. My passion for Norman is recorded for all time in the class prophecy: Anne, who wrote it, has me living in an old age home and knitting instrument covers for retired musicians.

It's been a busy year. Ruthie played the lead in the senior class play, *Don't Take My Penny,* about a stagestruck girl, Penny Pringle, who wants to play the role of Dimity West in a movie to be made of a best-seller called *Stars in Her Hair.* I was cast according to type, I guess: My character, Penny's stuffy older sister Mavis, was in the tradition of Veronica Gladwyn. The cast picture—we are assembled on the stage of Guiteras Junior High, site of my performance in *Kitty Foyle*—is in *The Green and White.*

So are two pictures, one of the principals and the other of the chorus, of the cast of *Marianne,* the senior class operetta, which was set in Alguarra, a fictitious country in South America. Ruthie, Anne, and I are standing together in the chorus, wearing the Alguarran national dress: off-the-shoulder blouses, dirndl skirts, white socks, and loafers. The martinet who was musical director for the public schools, the woman who made fun of me in the third grade and whom I will never, ever forgive, directed both the play and the operetta, and choreographed the latter as well. "Now girls," she barked, "link your arms. Now take two steps to the left and give a little low kick with your right foot. All right? Now, two steps to the right and a little low kick with the left. Now, move again to the left, kick, two steps back to the right, kick. Now, *two* to the right and kick and back and two to the left and kick and back. Got it? Okay!" At intermission one of the Alguarran caballeros played "Over the Waves" on his accordion, and at midnight the streets of Bristol rang with the Alguarran national anthem.

It's warm in Andrews this morning, and strange to be walking on the gym floor in regular shoes. This floor is precious as rubies, and unsneakered feet are allowed on it only on Graduation Day. It's noisy, too, because the custodians are setting up the folding wooden chairs and the martinet is nipping at our heels, trying to get her sheep in line for the processional. We will march in two by two in alphabetical order. Then those on the left will turn and mount the left-hand stairs to the stage, and those on the right will go up on the right-hand side. Seeing that my name begins with C, my seat is in the first row.

Up and back, up and back we march until our halting, flat-footed steps are absolutely on the beat of "Pomp and Circumstance." Then we practice, over and over again, our three musical offerings—"Vienna, City of My Dreams," "Panis Angelicus," and our finale, "The Battle Hymn of the Republic." We are singing "Panis Angelicus" because this year is the year for a Catholic hymn. Next year is the Protestants' turn, so the hymn will probably be "A Mighty Fortress Is Our God." At high school graduation the religious niceties are as rigorously observed as they were in grade school, when we preferred our alternate endings to the Lord's Prayer.

The light is the color of golden syrup, and the air is getting thick. It's time to amble home, time for an afternoon nap and a long soak in the tub and, finally, the putting on of the white organza dress that Papa bought me at Saks Fifth Avenue in New York. It is hanging on the closet door now, and is the last thing I'll see as I sink into sleep.

THE DRESS has a double Peter Pan collar, tiny covered buttons, long puffy sleeves, a white sash and a big full skirt, and it falls over me like a cloud. Under it I am wearing—drawn on as slowly and as punctiliously as a bullfighter draws on his suit of lights—a white cotton bra, white cotton underpants, a white cotton garter belt, a pair of my mother's nylons, a white cotton petticoat and gold sandals that we have bought at A.S. Beck, a rather low-class shoe store in Providence, because it doesn't do to spend good money on shoes you're only going to wear once or twice.

Mother gave me a bottle of Prince Matchiabelli's Wind Song cologne for Christmas, and I have worn it only to dances. Now I dab some behind my ears and on my wrists, and Papa, having read of this trick somewhere, suddenly asks Mother where she keeps the Vaseline. "It's supposed to make the eyes lustrous," he says, and slicks some on my lids.

The doorbell rings. It's Ruthie, come to get me for the ceremonial walk uptown. We look like brides, and along about State Street we join a host of other brides—and grooms—all of us converging on Andrews. As we walk through the entranceway we are handed our flowers—Colonial bouquets: tea roses and baby's breath furled into lacy paper doilies and twin to those young Bobby Kinder used to present to the birthday girls.

Just before the ceremony starts, as we are standing near the plaque that bears my father's name, my Uncle Johnny arrives with his handyman, Happy. They have driven down from Warren in Uncle Johnny's auto—a 1929 Chrysler Imperial because my relatives are no more inclined to throw out cars than they are to get rid of furniture—just so Johnny can rush in, red-faced and stocky, to shake his grandniece's hand. I am proud to have an uncle who thinks nothing of traveling four miles for a moment's meeting, and even prouder that mine is a family that exchanges gracious handshakes and not sloppy hugs.

The martinet nods from the doorway, and—at last!—I stare at her coldly. "Dah dah *dah dah dah* dah" sounds from the gymnasium and in we march, as slowly as if we are following a hearse, the boys in white jackets, the girls in white dresses, and the Colonial bouquets trembling in damp hands.

We go up the stairs as lightly as shadows, take our seats as gracefully as kings and queens take their coronation chairs. The class president will greet the audience of family and friends "to whom we owe so much." I have already heard the valedictorian's and salutatorian's speeches, because they had to recite them at rehearsal. Both boys, both good at math, they are going to college. The principal will hand out the athletic trophies, and Ruthie, we all know, is getting the school's highest honor, the Walsh Memorial Medal, for being "a leader in the better ideals among students, of sterling integrity and character, truthful and commanding respect." The superintendent of schools, at whose wedding Papa was an usher, will give us our diplomas. Till then, except when we're singing, I can relax.

Tomorrow night is the Senior Reception, to which I am going with Norman, who has my number now. A few weeks earlier he took me to Providence on the bus, to buy records, and I was thrilled because wandering around the city with a boy struck me as illicit. But we quarreled, we are always quarreling, and he said, "The trouble with you, Mary Lee Cantwell, is that nobody will ever measure up to your father."

To the Senior Reception I will wear, as custom dictates, my beautiful white graduation dress. The dance is for seniors and their escorts, faculty and parents only, and I am looking forward to seeing Papa in black tie and Mother in one of the little bellboy jackets *à la* Schiaparelli and long black crepe skirts she wears to dances at the country club in Barrington. Norman has no rhythm so I plan to dance a lot with Papa, partly because he is, as all heavy men are said to be, light on his feet, but mostly because bliss for me is now and ever shall be being in my father's arms.

But that is not for another twenty-four hours, and now I am trying to see beyond the footlights to where Ganny and Gampa, Esther, Mother, Papa, and Diana are sitting. Miss Nerone is out there as well, Miss Nerone, who has determined where I am to go to college. On the day that I got my acceptances—one for the school for which Papa and I had always planned, the other from a school to which I applied because I'd seen an article on it in *Life* and liked the way the girls dressed—I ran into her in front of Kinder's. "I hope you're going to ———," she said, naming the second. "It'll give you a little sophistication. You're enough of a bluestocking as it is." Then and there I settled on the school with the girls who wore sailors' middies, and thus do we make the great decisions in life.

Behind me several girls are crying, one of them because her white dress hides a tiny bulge and she has to get married next week. Some of the boys are red-eyed too, and honking loudly. On Monday they've got to start looking for jobs. "I forgive you," I say to myself. "I forgive you for pulling up my dress to look at my underwear and calling me 'Teacher's pet' and throwing stones and never choosing me for the softball team. Were it not for you, I would not be the person I am today." I can afford forgiveness; I am leaving town. I am giving Bristol the back of my hand.

The martinet raises her hands slightly, palms up. We stand, careful not to let our chair legs scrape the stage. "City of love and sparkling wine," we sing. "You're such a part of this heart of mine." Unbeknownst to me my heart bounds over the edge of the stage and rolls up the aisle, out the door and south on Hope Street until, finally, it comes to rest on the pebbly beach at the foot of Union Street. Where it will stay, as it turns out, forever.

A little later we follow it, Ganny and Gampa and Esther, Papa, Mother and Diana and I. We are walking slowly, in deference to Ganny's rheumatism, and Gampa looks very tall and thin beside her. He is wearing his best suit, brown with a thin stripe, and the tie Diana picked out for him. Ganny is wearing her best dress, purple crepe, with her jeweled-basket brooch pinned at its neck, and one of her bowed and fruited hats sits squarely on her head. Papa looks tall, too, and portly, in striped seersucker with a bachelor button bouttonière. Mother and Esther are on either side of him, exactly the same five-foot-two, eyes of blue in their pretty prints. Diana is wearing a cotton dress, and her long, heron's legs end in white socks and loafers.

In less than three years two of these people will have been folded into coffins, and Ralph Kinder will have woven a blanket made of red roses for each of them.

Tonight, though, we are all together, walking down Hope Street while a breeze sighs through the lindens, the maples, the elms, the oaks, and the horse chestnuts. Aunt Margaret is with us, too, and King Philip, and Ganny's cousin who stuck her hand into a box of sand and came out with a lump of dirt.

The houses are stiff and silent in the dark. My dress is softly brushing my stockinged legs, my garter belt is tugging at my hipbones. My ears are sharp as a fennec fox's and my eyes as large as a lemur's, I am launched!

# ◈ A F T E R W O R D ◈

*A* FEW YEARS AGO we seven met again, on an equally formal occasion. Gampa, wearing the brown suit he'd worn to my high school graduation, was under the grass, next to Papa, who was dressed in one of his Brooks Brothers pinstripes. Ganny was about to join them, in mulberry-colored crepe accessorized with a long stemmed pink rose. A little boy, Aunt Annie Clark's great-great-grandson, had put it in the box just before the undertaker fastened the lid.

Mother, Esther, Diana, and I were above the grass, standing by the brilliant emerald carpet—was it Astroturf?—that framed Ganny's grave, not far from a headstone that read MARGARET. It's the only marker in the entire family plot. My mother's family doesn't set much store by headstones, nor by ritual either. The puritanism of the old Yanks among whom they were raised rubbed off, I guess, and left them streaked with granite. Myself, I'm streaked with Irish moss, which is why Mother and Esther were keeping an eye on me. I can't be trusted not to cry.

At breakfast, before we left for the funeral parlor and a few prayers by Ganny's bier, Esther told her husband that it didn't matter who said the funeral mass, that it was the service alone that was important. He is a Congregationalist, acquired when she was fifty-seven and he sixty-six, and although we have never known him to go to church he thinks all things Protestant superior. Especially

Protestant funerals, which are, he claims, cozy and comforting. "You and your old Congregationalists," she barked. "Think you know everything."

But when a gigantic black man, a Nigerian who spoke in a singsong, strode out in front of the altar, Esther's jaw dropped. Who would have thought the rector of St. Mary's would have left the job of burying his oldest parishoner—Bristol's oldest resident, in fact—to a priest who was just passing through? Not only that, but Ganny's ancestors were St. Mary's first parishoners, part of the group that had to row across the harbor to hear mass before the church was built. Ganny never knew a black man in her life, except for the one who used to ride the Jewish ragman's truck, and now here she was in a stranger's hands. "The next time they pass the basket at St. Mary's," Esther whispered, "they can forget about getting anything from me."

"What can you expect?" she said later, forgiving the rector of St. Mary's and, indeed, the passage of time that was taking us all down into some soon-to-be-forgotten sump. "There's hardly a person in Bristol who can remember who anybody was now. And, besides, today it's the Portuguese that are running the town."

Our Portuguese grocery boy is buried in St. Mary's Cemetery, killed by trichinosis (he'd eaten homemade *chourice*) at fifteen. He had wild blue eyes that seemed to roll around the kitchen, and for weeks after he died I saw them skittering about the walls and ceiling. Diana's best friend is in St. Mary's, too, a little girl with banana curls and peach-colored skin who looked like wax fruit in her coffin. So is Miss Nerone, in green wool, with a rosary looped through her fingers.

I could walk up and down these rows pointing to a neighbor here, a teacher there. I could do it at North Burial Ground as well, where Miss Bosworth is lying with the watch that belonged to her father on a chain around her neck. And at Juniper Hill, where the older S. sister, who grew tired of waiting and lay down under her car next to the exhaust pipe, is now awaiting the Resurrection. All Bristol is an archaeological dig to me.

My stratum is not yet filled in. Once it is it will represent, I suppose, a kind of Mesozoic Era. The dinosaurs, the old Yanks, were dying out and the flowering plants, those sturdy Mediterranean and Lusitanian blooms, were starting to flourish. But my family's shards are puzzling. Neither old Yanks nor new émigrés, we're hard to classify.

When I am under this grass, toe to toe with Indian bones at last, I will finally have achieved my old goal, to be indissolubly a part of Bristol. But not the part of Bristol I'd prefer. Like my father, who disliked St. Mary's Cemetery, up near the Back Road and sweltering in the sun, I prefer North Burial Ground. Or if I had the money and connections, Juniper Hill, which is as beautiful a garden as there is in town. Oh well. Papa used to say that Protestants always did get the best seats in the house.

After the Nigerian intoned his last singsong and the bearers had tossed their gray gloves onto the top of Ganny's coffin, Diana made a beeline for the back seat of the limousine as determinedly as she used to make a beeline for our tricycle. "Diana," I said firmly, "since I am the older and thus Miss Cantwell, and you are the younger and thus Miss Diana, it stands to reason that you, and not I, should ride on the jump seat." "Oh Mary Lee," she sighed. "You never change!" Then she giggled, and Mother turned on us a deep blue frown.

When Gampa and Papa had their wakes, the baskets and bouquets went all the way from the front hall into Ganny's two parlors; and Mame Lannon had her hands full accepting the cakes and macaroni salads and baked hams that came in by the back door. Hundreds of visitors filed in, in a cloud of 4711 Cologne and dusting powder, past the receiving line that was Mother and Esther, Diana and me. Then they peeled off to talk to Ganny who, too old to stand that long, sat in her rocker, moved for the occasion from the bay window to her bedroom.

First it was Gampa who lay in the bay window, his long ivory-colored hands curled around his ivory-colored rosary. A night or two after he dropped dead—midway between his bed and the bathroom—I dreamed that he sat up in his coffin. "Gampa, I love you," I cried, but he lay down again before I could finish the sentence.

There was time to say it to Papa, though, or, rather, he said it for me. Six months later, when I was home from college between semesters, he took me out to Ganny's kitchen and made me watch while he sterilized a syringe and shot some morphine into his thigh.

He wanted me to see that he was in charge, that he could manage the cancer that would have him dead in May.

"I've had some bad luck, Mary Lee," he said, "so I'm not going to be around much longer." The ceiling light was bright on the white enamel table, I remember, and the water in which he'd boiled the needle was still giving off steam. I looked at my father's thin white thigh—I had never seen his legs before and now his bathrobe was askew—and began to cry. My father winced.

"Please, please don't do that. It makes it worse. Don't say anything. You don't have to. I know how you feel about me." That was all that had to be said, really, by either of us.

So, streaked with Irish moss though I may be, I didn't cry; and when I stood beside the pretty trench, all fake green grass and heaps of flowers, into which his coffin was about to be lowered I was as granitic as my relatives. Serene, too, because I believed that now I was cloaked in him, that now he would never leave me. In truth, as I found out, I was cloaked only in the curious peace that attends the visitor to the graveyard.

Ganny's funeral was different from Gampa's and Papa's. At one hundred and five she had outlived all of her own generation and most of her daughters', and there were few left who knew her well enough to say good-bye. That's why we buried her from the funeral parlor and not from home, and why the only time I saw her in her coffin was on the morning of her burial.

But I had seen her a few months earlier, up at the nursing home. The cheerful young nurses called her Mag, which only Gampa had ever dared do, and kept her clean and polished. She was reminiscent of a bird by then, her nose a little beak and her wisps of hair tied back in a twist of scarlet yarn, and all that was left to show she'd been plump were her fat little feet in white anklets from the five-and-ten. Ganny's mind never wandered, but she kept long silences. "Waiting to die," she told me, "is very tiring."

Still, even Ganny dreamed. "I had a hummer last night," she told me. "I dreamt I was back on Pearse Avenue with my uncles and my aunts. Oh I tell you, Mary Lee, I was digging like a good un'." I, too, dig like a good un'. Too much, perhaps.

Several of the neighbors came in for cold cuts and sherry and to murmur "Mrs. Lonergan was a wonderful old lady" and

"You'll miss her," but by the time Ruthie came to drive me up to Providence the house was as quiet as it was on the afternoons when Ganny and I sat in the bay window and watched the Hope Street parade. Downstairs hadn't changed at all. The late afternoon sun was striking the steel engravings, and dust motes were suspended in the beam. I was suspended, too, somewhere between mourning and memory. "If you don't get a hustle on, Mary Lee," my mother said, "you'll miss that train."

She didn't want me to leave. She never wants me to leave. But when I'm finally out the door, she's glad to see me go. It isn't very peaceful having me around. My husband used to say I had no serenity. She puts it more simply. She says I can't sit still. That I can't light anywhere, that I always have to be on the go. That's true. In my whole life I've never found a comfortable chair.

Ruthie took the route my parents took the night I was born: past Guiteras Junior High and Fort Hill and Collins Pond. Collins Pond is buried now, drained for a housing tract, and we hear the ranch houses and split-levels that replaced it have damp basements. Serves them right, we say. We miss Collins Pond and are sorry that nobody goes sledding on Fort Hill anymore, and would be sad to see the Pastime Theater, now the Bristol Cinema and desperate for customers, close its doors.

On the whole, however, Ruthie is not as nostalgic as I am. She doesn't have to be. She married one of the Catholic Connerys and never left town.

Did I? In my voice I can hear the voices of my family, my schoolteachers, the neighbors, all braided into one unmistakably Yankee tone. And once, when I was walking west with my then-young daughters, I sniffed that ummistakeable low-tide scent that comes off the Hudson and said, "Doesn't that smell like home!"

"Mother," my older daughter said, "this *is* home."

Ruthie and I talked while we waited for the train to pull in from Boston, but about what I don't know. Whenever we meet, even after months of separation, we just seem to pick up from wherever we left off. But we are both discreet, secretive even. Some people would say that's a loss, but I say it's a gain. We've been friends for so long that we have to use words only for the nonessentials. The rest we can say without ever having to open our mouths.

In a few hours I would be in the place my father promised, the place where there'd be lots of people like me. I have lived there a long time now, longer than I lived in Bristol, and for much of it I've been happy. But often when I'm out walking, when I find myself on, say, Fifth Avenue on a summer afternoon, I am puzzled. Then I ask that old friend with whom I am forever chatting, "What is Mary Lee Cantwell doing in this place?" The old friend doesn't answer.

I like this place. Sometimes I even love it, especially in early fall when the setting sun is poised midway between the old brick houses on either side of my street and that salty breeze has come up off the Hudson. I love it, too, when I take a cab through the Upper West Side late at night and those great old behemoths of buildings loom out of the dark like prehistoric monsters. Then New York is everything that Papa, for whom it was Ilium, said it would be.

Even so, it is not my country. My country is 200 miles away by Amtrak, and all it would take is the sale of an apartment and the packing up of some books and furniture for me to live there again. But if I did I suspect I'd be another Belle Bosworth butterflying my way around town.

I can see myself now, walking down Union Street toward 232 Hope after an evening at Ruthie's. The salt scent would be coming up off the harbor and the trees would be hanging heavy in the darkness. I'd move out toward the road as I passed the privet-hedged vacant lot next to the Tingleys' house because I've always feared that someone was lurking there. I'd reach out and touch Miss Munro's house as I always do because I know the brick came to Bristol as ballast and I like to imagine who touched it first. I'd hear the water lapping at the foot of Union Street and remember how I howled for Heathcliff. Then I'd look up toward the second floor of my house and see the lights still on: my mother up and worried because her child wasn't home.

There'd be no young man with hurt, trusting eyes. No daughters. No New York. No Mary, really, only Mary Lee. It would be as if nothing had ever happened, as if nothing had ever changed. Bristol, my Bristol, would blot out everything that came after it. No, the only way I can go forward—to where? I don't know—is to keep on running away from home.

# MANHATTAN,

# WHEN I WAS YOUNG

FOR KATIE AND MARGARET,
THE BEST PART OF THE JOURNEY

———◆———

"I think one remains the same person throughout, merely passing, as it were, in these lapses of
time from one room to another, but all in the
same house."

—J. M. BARRIE

## ❖ PROLOGUE ❖

*T*HERE IS A HOUSE I pass every night on my way home from work. It is nineteenth-century brick, with a fire escape that spoils its facade and Con-Tac paper in imitation of stained glass pasted in the fanlight. I lost a bloodstone ring in that house, and one of my younger daughter's red-ear turtles walked off into the darkness there. So I wonder sometimes if the present tenants have ever found that ring or, under a radiator perhaps, a dried turtle shell.

There is another house, on West Eleventh Street, whose windowboxes, crumbling now, were built by my husband's friend Jerry. And a third, on Perry Street, with a granite urn in the areaway in which I used to plant petunias. Because I am the kind who cannot escape a hotel room without leaving a toothbrush behind, I am sure that all three houses still hold, still hidden, some remnants of myself.

There is a fourth house, a big apartment building on the other side of town. I turn my head whenever I pass that one, because I remember the girl who lived there and she is painful to contemplate. One Saturday, shopping at a shabby Twenty-third Street A & P, she stuck her hand in the meat bin and, awakened suddenly by the sight of her long thin fingers poised over a rolled roast, said, "How did I get here?" I'm afraid that if I look at that apartment building I'll reenter it, put her on again, and go back to sleep.

I have a remarkable memory for objects. If I were to go into any one of those four houses, I could show you where the couch was, where I kept the pots, name the color of the walls. About the people who lived in them I cannot be so precise. Myself, for instance. I think I know her, but friends tell me I am wrong, that the person I describe lives solely in my head. Well, she does. But then, so do I.

But wait. There is a fifth house, which is in fact the first house and in which I left nothing behind. To begin with, I took to it only a wardrobe of unsuitable clothes, a few records, five or so anthologies of English literature, and a copy of *The Poems of Gerard Manley Hopkins*. The last was a kind of intellectual bona fide, a reminder that I had once contemplated graduate work and that Columbia University, though not the Yale at which I had imagined myself, was not yet out of the question.

This house has had its face lifted, its bricks steamed of their soot, and its windows refitted. There's new wiring and surely there's new plumbing—when I lived there the kitchen sink doubled as a bathroom sink, and four of us shared the toilet in the hall—and I doubt that water seeps under the back door and into the ground-floor rear apartment anymore when it rains. But it did, it did. Many were the dawns when I swung my feet off the studio couch and onto a damp floor.

I can see us now, me with my wet-soled feet on one side of the room and a college classmate named Allie with her wet-soled feet on the other. Both of us are wearing pajamas with fly fronts and rope ties, because the fashion in the women's college from which we have just graduated was to dress like a boy unless you were going away for a football weekend, in which case you packed a sheath so you could look like a vamp. Allie's hair is in pincurls, mine is in kidskin rollers, and there are a few dots of Acnomel on my chin.

In a few minutes I will struggle into my Sarong girdle—so named because of its sarong-like curves and seaming—which I don't need, because on my fattest day I weigh only 118 pounds. Then I will put on a sternly constructed cotton broadcloth bra, which I also don't need, a full-breasted nylon slip, and the pink Brooks Brothers shirt and black-and-white-checked gingham skirt that constitute my version of office garb. My shoes are black suede pumps, leftovers from my sheath days. But first I have to beat the men who share the room next door to the hall toilet and take a shower in the kitchen and toast an English muffin over our stove's very low flame and drink a cup of the coffee Allie has made in our five-and-ten percolator.

Allie is long and lean, with a deep voice and a way of dragging on a cigarette that is pure Lauren Bacall, who, come to think of it, she resembles. Allie is also the reason I take my coffee black. One morning of our junior year, while we were having breakfast in our dorm's dining room, she noticed the big glass of milk beside my plate.

"Funny," she said. "You look like the kind that drinks black coffee." The next morning I stood at the big urn, whose spigot I didn't even know how to operate, and poured myself a cup. It was the first coffee I had ever tasted. To this day I have no idea what coffee is like with cream and sugar. Even though I am now many years older and many pounds heavier, I like to think of myself as still looking like the type that takes her coffee black.

Allie has a certain mystery about her. Sometimes she drinks too much, not in the absent-minded way I'm apt to, but deliberately; and I know that on her mother's side, at least, she comes from a long line of the rich and scatty. I am always attracted to people who seem one way or another to be doomed, provided they carry their fate stylishly, and Allie reminds me of Temple Drake and Lady Brett Ashley. So she is right up my alley and I guess I am right up hers, although I don't know why. Both of us are prone to long silences, however, and we could listen to the cast recording of *Pal Joey* till the cows come home. "Take him," we sing along with Vivienne Segal, "I won't make a play for him. Take him, he's yours."

Washed, fed, and dressed, Allie and I pull on our short white cotton gloves, lock up, and travel a dimly lit corridor painted the dead amber of tobacco juice to a short flight of stairs. They lead to a shabby front hall with a big double door that opens onto a narrow street lined with tired brick houses like ours, a convent, and several small turn-of-the-century apartment houses, one of which has a Mexican restaurant in the basement. This is Waverly Place. Sixth Avenue is to our right, and Christopher Street starts a block or so to our left. We live in Greenwich Village because we had heard of it, and because the only other parts of New York City we know are the theater district, the Biltmore Hotel, and a Third Avenue beer hall called the G.A.

We're heading for the E train (the subway stop is at our corner), which will take us to Fifty-third and Fifth. There we'll wait in line for the escalator, because walking up that horrendous flight of stairs, Allie says, will give us legs like Cornell girls. Cornell girls, cursed with a hilly campus, are rumored to have bowling-pin calves. Once on the street, Allie will walk east toward Park Avenue and her secretarial job at an advertising agency. I will walk north to my secretarial job at a fashion magazine.

Behind us, our apartment—our one room plus kitchen/bath— is dark and silent. Little light penetrates the one ground-level window, and the garden, to which we have sole access, is a wasteland of weeds and broken glass. The furniture—two studio couches, a big table, a couple of hard chairs, and a pier glass leaning against the fireplace—belongs to the landlord. We have our reading lamps from college, though, and Allie's phonograph, an ironing board and iron from S. Klein's on Union Square, some pots and pans, a small bottle of vermouth, and a fifth of Dixie Belle gin.

We have, in short, everything we need. Everything I need, anyway. There are nights when, cross-legged on my studio couch, Vivaldi's *Four Seasons* on the phonograph and stray cats scrabbling in the weeds outside the kitchen window, I can feel joy exploding in my chest. Because from this house I emerge every morning into the place my father promised would be mine one day. The place where there'd be lots of people like me.

# *148 Waverly Place*

### ◈ 1 ◈

"*IT WAS A QUEER*, sultry summer, the summer they electrocuted the Rosenbergs. . . ." That's how Sylvia Plath started *The Bell Jar* and how I want to start this. Because that's the way I remember my first summer in New York, too. It was hot, and before we went to bed Allie and I would set our version of a burglar alarm along the threshold of the door that led to the garden so we could leave it open all night. Any intruder, we figured, would be deterred by that fearsome lineup of juice glasses and dented pots and pans from Woolworth's. Sometimes, soaked in sweat and sucking at the cottony air, I would wake and look toward the black rectangle that was the yawning doorway and wonder if we weren't being pretty stupid. But we would smother without that little breeze from the south, and besides, this was the Village! Afraid to take the subway, afraid of getting lost, afraid even to ask the women in the office where the ladies' room was (instead I used the one at Bonwit Teller), I felt peace whenever, after one of my long, lazy strolls down Fifth Avenue, I saw Washington Square Arch beckoning in the distance.

There was a newsstand near our subway stop, and every day the tabloids screamed the Rosenbergs' impending death. The headlines terrified me, because my boyfriend was Jewish. When my mother, back home in Rhode Island, met him for the first time, she asked him his religion, and he told her he was an atheist. She paused, and said in her nicest voice, "Does that mean you're a Communist?" He said no, but I knew his aunt and uncle had been, and the weekend we spent at their cabin in the Catskills smearing cream cheese on toast was torture, because they reminded me of the Rosenbergs and I thought we would all be arrested and that I, too, would die in the chair.

Somewhere I've read that the Lindbergh kidnapping marked a generation of children; that, knowing about the ladder propped against the second-story window and the empty crib, they had nightmares of being whisked away. Myself, I was marked by Bruno Hauptmann's execution. The radio must have been on the day he died—all I know of the 1930s, really, is what my ears picked up as I wandered around the living room during the six o'clock news— because I remember once asking an uncle what electrocution was. "It means," he said, "that somebody sets your hair on fire."

So I believed—a belief never wholly lost (and is the reality preferable?)—that one sat in the chair, the switch was pulled, the current streamed upward from the toes and erupted in a halo of flames around one's face, and *whoosh!* out brief candle. The chair. In childhood I thought about the chair, the slow climb and the fast flambé, all the time. And now, years later, I thought of Ethel Rosenberg's peanut face, which became mine. So when I neared the newsstand, I would turn my head and fix my eyes on the dirty stone steps that led down into the West Fourth Street station and the cars with the yellow straw seats that ripped your nylons if you didn't smooth your skirt along the back of your thighs before you sat down. But what I dodged during the day I met at night, in dreams, when I waddled down a long green corridor to the chair.

Sylvia Plath was already a familiar name. I was secretary to the press editor of *Mademoiselle,* where she'd been a guest editor just a month before, and my first task was to scour the newspapers for notices of her suicide attempt. "Smith Girl Missing," they read, fol- lowed by "Smith Girl Found," and I would cut and paste the clips for my boss's scrapbook of press notices, unclear whether all this publicity was good or bad for the magazine's forthcoming College Issue. In retrospect, I suspect it was good. Just as one studies the photograph of the parachutist before the fatal jump, so in the August *Mademoiselle* one could study the Smithie before the sleeping pills and the slide under the front porch. I studied her pictures myself. "What was she like, Mr. Graham?" I asked my boss. "Like all the others," he replied. "Eager."

Many years later I saw a television documentary on the life of Sylvia Plath, but all I recall of it now is a clip of seniors, black as crows in their graduation robes, in procession along a route lined by girls in white dresses who held an endless chain of daisies. The scene reminded me of my own long march into the Connecticut College Arboretum on Class Day. Our daisy chain was a laurel chain, but everything else was the same: the June day, the pageboy hairdos, the cloud of Arpège. Trust me on that last point. I was delicious then. We were all delicious, and we all smelled of Arpège.

THAT ALLIE WORKED for an advertising agency and I for a fashion magazine was improbable, but no more improbable than our being employed at all. Strictly speaking, we had no skills, and skills were very important in those days. In fact, some of our classmates had gone to Katie Gibbs to get them. Still, New York was full of girls like us—graduates of women's colleges with good looks and good manners and, though not in my case, money from home—and we were all working. Wearing the store-prescribed little black dress, we sold expensive glassware at Steuben. (Often we sold it to our friends, because everyone was getting married that first year after college, and a Steuben compote or a Georg Jensen bottle opener, the one with the acorn, was our wedding present of choice.) We were researchers and news-clippers at Time-Life, whose recruiters had made it very clear when they came to our schools that reporting was not in our future. A few of us had jobs in book publishing, mostly in the textbook departments, and in some of the smaller art galleries. A lot of us were, like Allie, in advertising, and the luckiest of us were on fashion magazines. True, we were poorly paid—it was assumed by our bosses, even out loud, that we had other income—but at least we weren't locked up in a back room with the out-of-town newspapers and a rip stick.

When I came to New York, on the same train that had taken me from Providence to New London for four years, I had $80 and the Smith-Corona portable my father had given me for my high school graduation. Allie, who had come up from her home in Maryland, had a bit more cash and a sterling silver brush, comb, and mirror given her by a great-aunt. Between us, we thought, we had enough. The funny thing is, we were right. I can't believe it now, that the city opened before us like some land of dreams, but it did.

Of course there were disappointments. We had assumed that the cute little houses in the Village would have cute little signs— APARTMENT FOR RENT—dangling beside their front doors, and that you just walked right in off the street and said to your friendly landlord, "I'll take it!" So it was a bit of a letdown when, after hours of walking, we finally had to call on a real estate agent. That the one-room apartment he showed us was the back half of a basement was also a bit of a letdown, but that we would have to share the toilet in the hall with the tenants of the front apartment was no problem whatsoever. After all, it had taken us only a day to find this place. And what was a toilet shared with two men compared to a multistalled bathroom shared with forty girls? We were used to communal living.

Finding jobs was easy, too. Allie had majored in art and thought she'd like to do "something" with it. But people who ran art departments wanted people who knew layout and paste-ups, and that kind of practical training was as foreign to our college as a course in typing would have been. I thought I'd like to do "something" with my English major, but what, besides teach, can one do with Chaucer? So instead we registered at a Seven Sisters outpost called the Alumnae Placement Agency, which sent Allie to the ad agency and me to the Metropolitan Museum and *Mademoiselle*.

The job at the Met—working on the museum bulletin, I think it was—was the one I wanted. There I would improve my mind, which the young man who was half the reason I was in New York was very anxious to have me do. "How can you read this stuff when you could be reading Virginia Woolf?" he would say when he saw me with yet another John Dickson Carr. "God! You haven't even read *Tristram Shandy*."

The job at *Mademoiselle*, however, was the one I got.

*Mademoiselle*'s famous College Issue was all I knew of the magazine. For four years I had wallowed in the photographs of that happy land where all the girls had shiny hair and long legs and all the boys had good jawlines. I wallowed in the text, too, about what was happening at Wellesley! At Skidmore! At Smith! I, too, was a student at one of those zippy schools, one of those girls in the Shetland sweaters and gray flannel Bermuda shorts, and this was our club bulletin. But work at *Mademoiselle*? That was no place for me, the aspiring . . . well, actually, I didn't know quite what I was aspiring to, but it had something to do with library stacks and a lonely but well-lighted carrel. My father had hoped I would be an English professor. When he died, when I was twenty, his authority was transferred to the young man who wanted me to improve my mind. Sometimes, even then, I thought of myself as the creation I know now was called Trilby. Only never having read the novel, I thought she was named Svengali.

Afraid the managing editor of *Mademoiselle* would reject me, I arrived at the interview prepared to reject her, and the entire fashion industry, first. Before she could shame me with her chic, I would shame her with my chill. I put on the pink Brooks Brothers shirt, the black-and-white gingham skirt, and entered 575 Madison Avenue determined to be *dégagé*. Now, when I visualize myself in that lobby, waiting for the elevator under what I believed was an Arp but wasn't, I am touched by the sight of me: my feet uncertain in high heels and my gloved hands clutching one of my mother's cast-off purses. But I, though dimly aware that suede was unsuitable in summer, probably thought I looked swell.

Cyrilly Abels, Sylvia Plath's Jay Cee, was a homely woman in her forties with a low smooth voice and a box of Kleenex carefully positioned next to the chair at the left of her desk. The Kleenex was not for her but for the younger members of the staff, who tended to cry in her presence. Miss Abels would give the box a little push, a tissue would be withdrawn, and the resultant honk would proclaim to the gang in the bullpen just outside her door that once again C.A. had drawn tears. Calling her C.A., though not to her face, was how they defended themselves against her implacable certainties.

Since only she and the editor-in-chief, Betsy Talbot Blackwell, were known by their initials, however, I figured "C.A." magnified rather than diminished. That is one of the reasons I never referred to her other than as Miss Abels. The second is that I needed no defense. Skilled as Miss Abels was at finding others' sore spots, she never made a serious search for mine. When, years later, a friend who had suffered dizzy spells and crying jags in C.A.'s employ asked why I was one of the few who had not, I laughed and said, "I wasn't sick enough to interest her." Half the office—the half that lived in Miss Abels's sphere—was, as everyone said then, "on the couch." Only the fashion editors were presumed immune from neurosis. They weren't thoughtful enough.

Even so, I was exactly the sort that Miss Abels liked to hire: a graduate of a women's college and obviously not a slave to fashion. She herself had gone to Radcliffe and every fall bought two simple wool crepe dresses, princess-line to show off a bosom of which she was rumored to be very proud, and an absolutely correct coordinating coat from Trigère. After a few minutes' conversation, during which I made it clear that I read a lot and she made it clear that she was a close personal friend of every writer worth knowing, she sent me to the promotion department, to meet the press editor. He, swayed by my plea not to put me through a typing test because I would die on the spot, said, "You kids!," laughed, and hired me anyway.

That afternoon I met the young man I was to marry, in Central Park. He was wearing the navy blue serge we called his Puerto Rican revolutionary suit, which he'd bought for job interviews, and carrying peanut-butter sandwiches, one for each of us. "I'm so proud of you," he said, and I, because there was no father to say that to me anymore, felt tears quickening behind my eyes.

We had met my junior year in college, in the living room of my dorm. He, just back from his junior year abroad, was lean and dark and had a copy of *Orlando* in the pocket of his beige raincoat. When, along with the girl who lived across the hall and a fraternity brother of his at Wesleyan, I wriggled into his old Plymouth, he studied my backside and said, "Guess we'll have to get you a girdle." Ten minutes into our acquaintance and he had taken over. I couldn't have been more grateful.


THE ACTION at *Mademoiselle* was up front, where the editorial offices were. The promotion department, where I worked, was down the hall. A lot of the staff up front was around my age; here I was with my elders, except for a girl named Audrey, who strangled her every word. I thought it was a speech defect. It was, I found out later, something called Locust Valley Lockjaw, which I had never heard before because the girls afflicted with it went to schools like Bennett Junior College and Finch rather than Connecticut, where the accents were mostly West Hartford and Shaker Heights. I have heard it countless times since, and have always found behind it someone who called her mother "Mummy" and grew up with good furniture.

There was a pretty woman named Joan, too, who lit her cigarettes with Stork Club matches and spoke in hard, fast sentences. And a much older woman named Jean, the promotion director's secretary and the only person in the department who could take shorthand. Only the promotion director and the editor-in-chief had real secretaries. The rest of the editors had to make do with people like me: forty words a minute, a habit of obedience, and a willingness to start at $195 a month.

Audrey never spoke to me or to anyone else in the office—she was forever on the phone, conversing through clenched teeth—and Joan spoke only to be rude. Jean's mind was on her shorthand, her filing, and her home in Queens. So when I talked, which was seldom, it was only to my two bosses: Joel, the press editor, and Hugh, the special projects editor, middle-aged men whom I would not have dreamed of calling Joel and Hugh.

All I ever did for Hugh, who was tall and thin, with the spine of a Grenadier guard and several impeccable pinstriped suits, was order theater tickets, make restaurant reservations, and type the occasional letter. The letters were personal, not professional—I think he wanted their recipients to realize he had a secretary—and in one of them he introduced himself by a completely different name, something that smacked of the Baptist Church and parents named Hazel and Dwight. Until that moment I thought only movie stars changed their names, and I had spent long hours in childhood wondering how to abbreviate mine for a possible marquee. But changing one's name, or having had it changed by one's father or grandfather, turned out to be kind of a New York thing. So, if you were a woman who had a career as opposed to a job, was having three names: Christian name, maiden name, and married name. *Mademoiselle* was a monument to three-named women, although sometimes the married name was that not of the present husband but of one or two back. A lot depended on euphony.

Joel kept me busier. For him I clipped and read and typed the letters he had painstakingly written out in longhand because I feared dictation. Once, when there was an extra seat at something called a Fashion Group luncheon, to which he assured me I must go because it was the most professional fashion show I would ever see, he scurried around the office and found me a hat. None of the "ladies," as I was learning to call them, would have gone to Fashion Group without a hat, and B.T.B., true to the legend, often wore one at her desk.

The luncheon, as they all were and still are, I guess, was in a hotel ballroom. The younger fashion editors wore Seventh Avenue, the most powerful of the older editors wore whatever had debuted on the Paris runways a few weeks before, and the store buyers wore too much. Carmel Snow, who was editor-in-chief of *Harper's Bazaar,* spoke. Or maybe it was Andrew Goodman, who was, the ladies said, "a great merchant." The one had a small head, a slight sway, and a thick Irish accent; the other ended a speech on the American woman's fashion needs with a ringing "If she wants satin, give it to huh. If she wants cotton, give it to huh." They are the only speakers I remember from what turned into years of going to Fashion Group luncheons.

Joel sent me on little errands, too, but most of the time I sat at my desk, listening to the occasional ring of a phone, to Audrey's tortured vowels and Joan's café society snarls.

Life in the promotion department was strange, silent, and lonely. But at least it was safe. Up front was a foreign country. C.A. was a slicked-up version of the ladies on the Connecticut College faculty, but the rest of the country's citizens were like nothing I had ever known before.

The fiction editor, Rita Smith, was the younger sister of Carson McCullers. A plump woman with sad brown eyes and an alcoholic past, she was forever rushing to Nyack, where "Sistuh" moaned and reigned. Afraid of elevators, Rita climbed the stairs to *Mademoiselle*'s sixth-floor offices, would not travel on a subway un-accompanied, and believed that her constantly burning, and forgotten, cigarettes would one day set fire to the whole build-ing. Every evening after five, her assistant searched their office looking for a telltale cinder. Finding none, she would send Rita home relieved. "Sistuh," I was reliably informed, had ruined Rita's life.

Leo Lerman, the entertainment editor, sat in a sort of railed-off den behind an enormous mahogany desk, taking phone calls from Marlene Dietrich and Truman Capote. A plump, bearded man, he lived in a house so assertively Victorian it defied the century, which was the point, and had a collection of friends so dazzling I am still dazzled by it. I knew about them only by hearsay, however, from the acolytes who clustered about his desk and giggled over his every word. Stiff-necked and shy, I studied him more or less from afar, wondering at a social life that was so busy he kept his invita-tions in a faille shoe rack—each little bag represented one day—on the back of a closet door.

C.A.'s editorial assistants, all of them tall, brainy, and badly dressed, had long, hilarious lunches at a restaurant called Barney's and spoke out of the sides of their mouths. The chief assistant's husband was planning to run for mayor of New York on the Labor Party ticket, provided he could get enough signatures on a nomi-nating petition. When she, older than the others and deliberately plain as porridge—her looks were in themselves a political state-ment—showed up at my desk with the petition, I wouldn't sign. No way was I going to get the chair.

The head of the fashion department, a scant-haired fluttery woman in her forties, was said to ask her maid to iron her stock-ings. I'd also heard that she had had Greta Garbo and—here the speaker's voice deepened to signal a significance lost on me—her "friend" for Sunday dinner, and that Garbo had carved. That any of these fascinating people might have anything to say to me, or I to them, was past imagining.

A week or two after my arrival, Joel sent me across the border for the first time. I was to take a press release to the fashion copy editor, a tall, rather handsome woman with eyes that rolled like a maddened stallion's. Kathy was temperamental—she had thrown a telephone book at a hairdresser named Enrico Caruso because she didn't like the way he had cut her hair, and had led a kind of peasants' revolt against management—so Joel said, "Approach her carefully."

Past the college and career department I walked, past the pretty, peppy girls who wrote about working in Washington and living in Georgetown and the pros and cons of joining a sorority. Past the fashion department, with its clothes racks and ringing phones and editors who wore necklace piled upon necklace and Italian shoes. Past the deep green room—she called it her boudoir—in which B.T.B., who was also rumored to wear ironed stockings, proofed copy with a bright red pencil (C.A. used blue) and broke out ice cubes and a bottle of vodka every day at noon. Past the bullpen where C.A.'s assistants were talking smart talk. To Kathy's office, where I paused at the open door.

She was typing, and she kept on typing until the sun went down and the lights came on all over Manhattan. Or so it seemed. Cold sweat trickled down my back and my stomach fell to my knees, but still I stood, incapable of advance or retreat. Finally she looked up. "Don't you know any better," she asked in a voice that rejected reply, "than to disturb a writer while she's working?"

I muttered something about her door being open, put the press release on her desk, and scuttled back to kindly Joel. But I had learned a lesson, which, unfortunately, I forgot by the time I traveled on to *Vogue*. To survive eight hours of producing "tangerine linen crossed with a lime-green slice of belt" or "Mrs. Randall Oakes, an enchantment of a woman with a gallant list of good works to her credit," it is necessary to call it "writing."

Still, I wanted to do what Kathy did. Or what Nancy and Rachel in the college and career department did. Or what Jane in C.A.'s bullpen did. I wanted to write something. I didn't care what, nor did I care about bylines. I just wanted to see something that had been in my mind transformed into print. I wanted to see a miracle.

◆ 2 ◆

$\mathcal{T}$HE CORNER OF Fifty-seventh and Madison is still quite glamorous, what with Tiffany's down the street and Hermès and Chanel
around the corner. But it seemed even more so when 575 Madison
housed *Mademoiselle* and *Charm,* the building across the street
housed *Harper's Bazaar,* and the Checker cabs were forever unloading magazine editors, who were sometimes ugly but always
chic.

At lunchtime the editors-in-chief were dining at places like
L'Aiglon, on bifteck haché and Bloody Marys. C.A. was in the
Bayberry Room of the Drake Hotel with the writer of the moment,
Dry Sack for an apéritif and something wholesome, like calves'
liver, for the entrée. The copywriters and other literary types were
eating saucisson at the French Shack, unless they were at Barney's
knocking back martinis. I, with as yet no office pal, was dining
alone at Henry Halper's Drugstore.

Which is not to say that I was sitting at some rundown soda
fountain picking at tuna salad on white. Henry Halper's was where
all the young fashion editors went for a quick bite (they were always either going to or coming from "the market") and employed
a middle-aged black man just to push one's long-legged chair in to
the counter. The egg salad sandwich, which was heaped with wa-
tercress, was "the best in New York."

So was the devil's food cake at Hamburg Heaven and the coconut cake at the Women's Exchange and the sundaes at the
Schrafft's on Fifty-seventh Street, where one could see the famous
designer Charles James sitting with his right leg crooked up under
him and his hands flying about like frightened birds. The people at
*Mademoiselle* and *Charm* and *Bazaar,* people around whom my
ears were like morning glories or the big horn of an old Victrola,
had made finding "the best in New York" their life's work. Some
choices were obvious; others were not. I had thought, for instance,
that if you wanted a pair of gold earrings, you should go to
Tiffany's. Not at all. You went to a little place called Olga Tritt.

Out of the office I would saunter at noon—Joel was never too fussy about when I came back—and cross the street to Halper's or go around the corner to Hamburg Heaven, where one slid into a wooden chair whose right arm curved around to form a little table. The men who worked at Hamburg Heaven were black, with the classy mien of sleeping-car porters, and the customers wore gold circle pins and spoke of Junior League dances and wedding receptions at the Georgian Suite.

Then it was up to Bonnier's, to look at the Swedish glassware, or over to Bonwit's for the ladies' room, or down to Steuben for a chat with a classmate who worked there. Never once did I spend a cent except for lunch, because I had no money whatsoever, and never did I go to the art galleries, because I didn't know about them. I simply drifted, studying the pretty girls in their Anne Fogarty dresses—they had "wallpaper waists," *Mademoiselle* said, and "great flous of skirts"—and wondering if I could ever look that bright, that bouncy, that New York. The humidity stuck my hair to my head and my face turned red and sweaty and my lips moved in silent conversation with somebody who wasn't there— my father, usually, and sometimes my grandmother. Never mind. I had done what I had planned to do since I was—oh, God—twelve, I guess. I had given my small town the back of my hand.

I wish I could say that as a child I had lain in bed listening to the siren song of train whistles. But no trains had come to our town since the Hurricane of 1938 had torn up the tracks, and the old station had been a small bottling plant for as far back as I could remember. Or that I could claim to have read my parents' *New Yorker* for hours on end and dreamed of strutting down West Forty-third Street. But the only magazines that came to our house were my mother's copies of *American Home* and *Better Homes and Gardens,* and although I longed for my father to subscribe to *Life* and *The Saturday Evening Post* and thus realize my dream of a proper American dad, he persisted in reading novels (mostly Graham Greene) and poetry (mostly Yeats). My father was very Catholic and, despite a Scottish father, very Irish.

No, what pulled me to New York, apart from the young man I was to marry, was my father's promise. "Don't you change, don't you dare change," he would say when I came home from school in tears because I hadn't been elected to this or that or because somebody had called me a showoff for writing so many book reports. "Someday you'll live in a place where there are lots of people like you." My guess is he meant academe, a world that he revered and that he believed welcomed the chatty, the gaffe-prone, the people with more brains than sense. But I, bored with tests, bored with papers, and cursed with a mayfly's attention span, thought of something speedier. I thought of a world in which you "raced" to the subway, "hopped" the shuttle, "grabbed" a cab. Infatuated with its pace, I thought of New York.

Now here it was, sprawled, half-dressed, in the heat. And here I was, opening my eyes every morning in a "studio" that had once been the kitchen of an 1840s row house and, only a few weeks after I'd gotten off the train at Grand Central, racing for the subway.

As I was racing uptown, the young man I was to marry, B., was racing downtown from the railroad flat on Ninety-sixth Street he shared with a friend named Jerry and an art historian named Sidney, with whom he was splitting the $28-a-month rent. He was going to his job in the mailroom of an advertising agency. The Puerto Rican revolutionary suit had been put aside with his first paycheck, and now he was wearing gray flannel and a black knitted tie. The tie, he said, was "sincere."

The money, everybody said, was on Mad Ave; B. had once written a short story whose hero had "come to harvest in the golden field of advertising." He had wanted to be a writer then, and most of all he had wanted to be F. Scott Fitzgerald. But now he wanted to be Maxwell Perkins. Or Edmund Wilson. Or Malcolm Cowley. He knew about every little magazine that ever was. He knew about *Broom* and *transition* and the Black Sun Press; he knew about Djuna Barnes and Kay Boyle and Robert McAlmon; and like everyone who spent his junior year abroad, he came out of Paris with a copy of *Tropic of Cancer* hidden under his train seat. He gave me *Tropic of Cancer* to read and I tried, I really tried, but he might as well have asked me to dash a communion wafer to the floor. Mrs. Grundy I was, he said, as he chipped, chipped, chipped away at my stubborn puritanism. One might have thought he'd have gone for somebody more his type. But the truth is, I was his type.

"I knew what you'd look like the minute B. told me about you," Jerry said. "He always goes for girls who could model for Pepsi-Cola ads."

Jerry was the smartest man I'd ever met, one of those people who knew everything and could do anything. We expected great things of Jerry, without being able to define exactly what form his greatness would take. He had so many choices. For now he was making a living designing textiles freelance (B. acted sometimes as his salesman), but he wrote like George Bernard Shaw and painted like Wilfredo Lam, at the same time being a monument to each and every practical skill. He could build bookcases and fix leaks and rewire lamps, and he even knew what to do when I had food poisoning: "Feed her cottage cheese to keep her digestion going and ginger ale every time she vomits."

Jerry sent us to *Les Enfants du Paradis* and *Le Diable au Corps,* and there was nothing playing at the Thalia and the Beverly, both of them revival houses, that he hadn't seen. Because of Jerry we subscribed to Cinema 16, a group that showed old and experimental films, and we spent every Sunday morning—those were the cheapest subscription days—in the Needle Trades Auditorium watching Buster Keaton in *The Navigator* and garbage can explosions and once a kind of homemade movie in which a bit part was played by a girl in my office. I was never comfortable in the Needle Trades Auditorium, because the audience was almost wholly Jewish, including B. and Jerry, and I half expected a raid. In college, B. had seemed like everybody else. Now, association with him struck me as dangerous.

I couldn't tell him, though; I couldn't tell him where my mind went when it wandered. He would say I was crazy, and because I valued his opinion more than I did my own, I would believe him. Besides, I couldn't bear to have him think me an anti-Semite. Once he had stood in the old playroom of my home in Rhode Island with tears in his eyes and asked, "What's wrong with me? Why doesn't she like me?" He was asking about my mother, to whom a Jew— apart from the textile brokers who had been my father's Providence friends—was Roy Cohn.

My mother was Catholic, so she feared the pope, and mostly Irish, so she feared the WASP. She saw my future—barred from the Greenbrier and the Homestead, unwelcome at country clubs, and eventually cast into hell—and she wept. Of course my mother didn't like B. He was endangering my immortal soul. I, though, didn't worry much about my soul. My eye was on the chair.

If I wasn't comfortable in the Needle Trades Auditorium, neither was I comfortable in the apartment on the Lower East Side that Jerry took us to one night. There were a lot of painters there, some of whom are probably famous now, but the only person I remember by name is a woman named Sorietta who sat with her knees apart and had dirt between her toes. We drank tea from glasses while she sang "Come 'Way from My Window" in a basso so profundo I was afraid the neighbors would complain and the police would come and lead us off to jail, because everyone there was Jewish and probably selling nuclear secrets on the side. I was merely a muddled Catholic, but who would believe me?

I wasn't comfortable the night we went to a loft on Sixth Avenue for something called Folksay, either. I have never figured out what Folksay was, only that we had been taken there after an Equity Library Theatre production of a Depression-era play called *White Wings,* which it had partly sponsored. The room was set up with folding chairs, and soon after we sat down, a large black man strode along the aisle to shouts of "Here comes de Lawd." He'd played the lead in *Green Pastures,* had just been released from imprisonment on a rape charge, and was now returning to the hosannas of the faithful. I didn't care whether the charge had been trumped up, as Jerry said, or not. All I knew was that things were looking pretty pink in there.

Then another man, an actor—it may have been Will Geer— stood up with his guitar and his reedy tenor to sing some old Wobbly songs, all of them dedicated to Big Bill Heywood. For someone who'd been told by a classmate from Shaker Heights who had money, a horse, and a forehead a quarter of an inch high that her playing of the Weavers' "Kisses Sweeter than Wine" was tantamount to treason, this was terrifying.

The evening's climax was the apperance of Woody Guthrie, small, narrow, stiff, already encased in the disease that killed him.

Now I brag about having seen Woody Guthrie, as one would brag about having seen Shelley plain, but then I just wanted out of that loft and into my apartment at 148 Waverly Place, with Allie in her striped pajamas and pincurls and Vivaldi on the phonograph.

In the midst of the "Here comes de Lawd"s and the Wobbly repertoire and the adulation of the rigid, silent Woody, a plump young man in pinstripes leaned toward me and whispered, "I wish to God we were at the Bon Soir."

"So do I," I whispered, and wondered if there were not still time to turn back to young men who called their dates "really great gals," and evenings in smoky rooms in which someone was singing "Down in the Depths" and "Love Walked In," where all I had to be was polite and nice and a bit of a *bon vivant*. One night when I was leaving our apartment for tea (in a glass) at a friend of Jerry's, Allie said, "I'll bet there's nobody in that crowd who even knows how to mix a martini."

Jerry had sat in on some Communist trials in Seattle, on the side of the accused, and the young man I was to marry had had a cousin who had died with the Lincoln Brigade. Together they hammered at my allegiance to the religion that had produced Francisco Franco and Joseph McCarthy, not to mention its having prevented the residents of the state of Connecticut from getting birth control information. I myself had a diaphragm, and when the doctor was fitting me with it, the ring sprang from his hands like a mouse and bounced across the room. I hated putting it in and hooking it out, and all my defenses of Catholicism were hampered by the knowledge that my legs were crossed over a gasket-sealed womb.

Not that it made any difference, really. I was not as quick and glib and bright as Jerry and B., and never sounded more ridiculous than when I was attempting to describe the doctrine of transsubstantiation or rub their noses in Duns Scotus. What I really believed I could never have said aloud, not even to myself. What I really believed was that if I said my prayers nightly, my father would be freed from purgatory and ascend into heaven.

ST. JOSEPH'S CHURCH was just around the corner, on Sixth Avenue, and the building next door to 148 Waverly Place was a convent. Never had I lived so close to nuns and clergy and incense. But trusting in magic is not the same as having a faith, and I would not have gone to mass if not for Allie. She was contemplating conversion.

Allie's mother, whom I had met at graduation, was tall and thin, so attenuated that she seemed to sway when she walked. That she had converted to Catholicism struck me as logical: she looked like she needed a mooring mast. Allie was also tall and thin and smoked Pall Malls—"Pell Mells" we called them, not knowing we were aping the English—right down to the stub, so I assumed she also needed a mooring mast.

St. Joseph's was the kind of church that would appeal to a potential convert, especially one who, like Allie, had belonged to one of the fancier Protestant sects. The windows were the usual stained glass, but the architecture was Greek Revival, so the flamboyance of the first was cooled by the rationality of the second. The statues were few, the stations of the cross inoffensive, the sermons short, and saccharine hymns like "Mother at thy feet is knee-eee-ling" never sounded from the choir loft.

Most of the choir members belonged to a group of musicians called Pro Musica Antiqua, and the choirmaster was Pro Musica's harpsichordist, so the music was on a level I, and Allie, had never heard in a church before. Here the hymns were born in the fifteenth or sixteenth century or earlier, and listening to them was like licking an icicle: the same chill, the same purity. Their chastity made me understand why Allie wanted to convert, why Clare Boothe Luce had converted, why my father had kept a breviary by his bed. But hidden in my suitcase at home was a sin made tangible: that diaphragm. To give it up would mean giving up B., and to do that would be like losing my father again. So I never saw the inside of a confessional at St. Joseph's, never knelt at its communion rail, never again knew what it was to have one of those flat, dry wafers stick to the roof of my mouth. Instead I marveled that Allie, or anyone, would actually choose Catholicism. There'd been no choice for me—I had only been in the world a few days when I was baptized—but I think I would have picked something simpler if I had had the chance.

Nevertheless, I loved those Sunday mornings in St. Joseph's, with the hot summer slipping in over the tilted stained glass windows and the doors open on the traffic noises from Sixth Avenue. I loved walking over to Washington Square with the Sunday papers afterward and sitting on a bench to watch the old Italian men playing chess and checkers on the scored cement tables. Allie did the crossword; I closed my eyes against the elm-dappled light; pigeons scurried after bits torn from somebody's breakfast bagel. Still marooned in English muffins, we had yet to taste one.

Along about one o'clock, we would rise, push the papers into a trash can, inhale deeply of the only grass we would smell all week, and walk back to Waverly Place to struggle with Sunday dinner. While Allie made martinis out of the Dixie Belle and a drop or two of Noilly Prat, I fought with a stove whose flames were always close to dying, and together we gloried in the grownupness of it all. Once we even entertained.

On a steaming Sunday in August, B. and Jerry came for dinner. Unfamiliar with the vast terrain between egg salad sandwiches and Thanksgiving feasts, we served roast turkey with stuffing and mashed potatoes. Our motives were different, of course, but we had as frail a sense of the appropriate as Alice Adams's mother. No matter. Turkey meant gala to us, and to B. and Jerry, too. Jerry carved. Needless to say, he knew how.

The following weekend Allie's father came up from Bethesda and promised us dinner at the Plaza. Leaving 575 Madison that Friday night to walk the four blocks to the hotel, I felt for the first time like one of the pretty girls at Henry Halper's counter: on the town and on my way. But when I got to the Plaza I couldn't find the desk, and fearful of revealing my gaucherie even to a bellboy I would never see again, I slunk out past the Palm Court and subwayed home. Already I was possessed of the New York disease: a feverish desire to appear knowing, no matter how deep one's ignorance.

The next day, another scorcher, Allie's father took us to a famous fish house, Sea Fare I think it was, on Eighth Street, and I ate some clams that must have spent a few hours in the sun. At least I think it was bad clams that had me rushing out of the Thalia—Jerry had sent us to *Major Barbara*—a few hours later, my cheeks puffed over my returning lunch and B. in tow. We got into a cab, and I remember regretting that I was in no condition to enjoy the

very first cab we had ever taken together before I vomited. I vomited, in fact, the length of Ninety-sixth Street, vomited again when
we got to B.'s apartment, vomited long past the time there was anything left to spew. Meanwhile, as I lay heaving on the rollaway cot
Jerry kept for guests, B. stood at the kitchen sink, rinsing out my
gingham skirt. That he would handle that stinking skirt, that he
could bear looking at a woman with sticky hair, a flushed face, and
underwear as grimly practical as a mop and pail, was as great a
proof of love as I could ever ask.

That night, too weak to return to Waverly Place, I lay on the
rollaway cot, between the kitchen sink and the kitchen table. To
my left was B., asleep on the studio couch in his tiny bedroom. To
his left was Jerry, asleep in his tiny bedroom. To Jerry's left was
Sidney, asleep in his tiny bedroom. My skirt was draped over the
sash of the kitchen's one window, moving slightly in the hot, sooty
breeze. My pink shirt, also damp, was on the back of a chair.
Nobody had thought to find me a pair of pajamas, nor had I
thought to ask for any. I was still wearing my underwear.

Lying there, listening to the rumble out on Ninety-sixth Street
and the snores and snuffles of my three companions, I realized
there was no turning back. In losing my virginity to B. during my
junior year in college, in the front seat of his Plymouth, wedged
against the steering wheel, I had lost my freedom. And in lying here
in this railroad flat in my underwear, cheek by jowl with three
young men who'd been witness to my vomiting, my dry heaves,
and my diarrhea, I had passed the point of no return. There was no
bathing me in the blood of the Lamb. I had crossed over.

❖ **3** ❖

SOMETIME TOWARD the end of September the heat began to lift.
Now the air was laced with a thin, cool thread and by five o'clock
the light was blue. The weddings were winding down—Allie and I
had gone to three in July alone—and the classmates who had spent

the summer after graduation in Europe were getting apartments on the Upper East Side. Only Allie and I were in the Village, along with everybody else who didn't want to get dressed up on the weekend. Even today there is something about the Village—a certain seediness, a certain raffishness—that makes its residents feel unbuttoned, ungirdled. The Village is more than a home. It is a hangout.

When we had moved into 148 Waverly Place, Allie and I had had a few plans for the garden—a couple of chairs, maybe, and a little table. But the weeds and the cracked cement and the broken glass defeated us. Seldom did we sit outside, and the night the weather took a chilly turn and had us shivering on our studio couches was the night one of us got up and locked the back door for good.

The closing of that door marked the end of college more surely than that hot June afternoon when we sat in Palmer Auditorium drowsing through a commencement address by a former United States commissioner of education. The past three months had been a postscript to school—we were still wearing the same clothes, after all, and we still thought going to the movies on a weeknight was somehow illicit—but that part of our lives was finally, officially over. One Saturday afternoon we strolled through the College Shop at Lord & Taylor, checking out the Shetland sweaters and the Bermuda shorts and the camel's hair polo coats, sorrowful that they would never be ours again and even a little frightened. We had outgrown them, without yet having anything else to wear. Neither of us knew what we should look like now.

Some women, of course, never give up the wardrobe. I see it wherever WASPs gather, in the headbands and gold bobby pins that hold back still pageboyed hair, and in little Belgian shoes on little bony feet. But that uniform would never have done for *Mademoiselle*. Now at lunchtime I studied the clothes at Bonwit's, puzzled because I couldn't seem to find anything resembling what the fashion editors wore and ignorant of the fact that not one of them ever went retail for anything. Eventually, when the fabric department had a remnants sale, I bought a length of green tweed, took it to a tailor on West Seventy-second Street (I had found his name in the Yellow Pages), and had it made up into a stern suit which I believed announced intelligence as well as chic.

The parents of the young man I was to marry arrived from Seattle. The father looked a bit like Fiorello La Guardia and the mother looked a lot like B., and neither of them looked Jewish, which I knew would be a great relief to my mother. We sat together on a bench in Central Park while Mr. L., nearly seventy, teased me and was avuncular and Mrs. L. told me about how her son's favorite song when he was a boy had been "The Girl That I Marry," and now here I was.

One of B.'s twin sisters moved to Paris with her young sons and wrote to us about our wedding present: "I have in mind, for linens, a really good tablecloth . . . perhaps an organdy job from Madeira, or cutwork from Florence. Or would you like a pair of English blankets? Also, if you'd like a complete set of crystal, the one thing that seems to be cheaper in France, let me know and I could bring it back with me."

His other twin sister, who wanted to be in the theater but was in advertising instead, said, "Well, you've got your man, but I've got to go on looking" and gave a cocktail party. One guest recited Vachel Lindsay—"Boomlay, boomlay!" he shouted across the canapés—and my soon-to-be sister-in-law spoke of how Martha Graham had raved about her plié when she was a student at Bennington. I had a nervous moment when I heard some people talking about how you could get off the blacklist if you had the money, but mostly I marveled at how far I had traveled.

Meanwhile, B. was making the rounds of priests, seeing if there was one who would marry us without his agreeing to sit through religious instructions and sign his children's lives away, and wherever he went he was received rudely. Or so he said, and I believe it. A rich friend of my father's tried to bribe the Catholic chaplain up at Columbia into marrying us without any prenuptial fuss. Or so I heard, and I believe that, too. And I just wanted everybody to go away and leave me alone, because while I did not care about offending God, I did not want to disappoint my father. "Oh, Lulubelle," he would have said, "it's a terrible thing to lose your faith."

"But not," I would have told him, "as terrible a thing as losing you."

Allie and I didn't discuss my impending wedding. We never discussed religion, we never discussed love, and goodness knows we never discussed sex. Doing so would have implied that the speakers knew something about it, and if we did, we 199 graduates of Connecticut College Class of '53, we kept it a secret. We all knew that the Playtex panty girdle was the finest of all chastity belts, and Allie and I had known a girl who always inserted two tampons before going out on a date. By the time they were dealt with, she figured, the impulse would be gone. We had also known a girl—she lived down the hall from us—who thought she was pregnant by a boy from Yale, took pills, and then set fire to her room. The smoke, which somebody saw, saved her. But if we gossiped about the girl with the Tampaxes and the girl who tried to incinerate us all, we never gossiped about ourselves. Instead we were silent about where we slept when we went to Yale or Wesleyan or Brown for the weekend, and if we panicked when we studied our calendars, we kept it to ourselves. The night B. became a part of me—indissolubly, I believed—in the parking lot behind my dormitory, I walked on tiptoe afterward to my room. Were one of my dormmates to open her door and see the blood on my legs, she would know the truth about me. But nobody knew the truth about me or, I suspect, about anybody else.

So Allie kept silence and I kept silence, and one evening, while she buried her nose in a book and pretended deafness, I quarreled with B., who loved debate but hated emotion. Lose one's temper or burst into tears and he would say, "I never realized how sick you really are" and leave. This time I let him go, and as I did I felt a great weight rising off my back. After two years, I was finally free of hands that went where I did not want them to go and assaults on the faith of my father and people who seemed to believe in nothing at all but brains, their own in particular.

The room was quiet, and Allie, still faking deafness, was brewing tea. In another hour she would be asleep, and the only sounds would be her soft, slow breathing and the occasional yowl from whatever tomcat was strolling in the garden. This was how I wanted to live, in peace, in the light of a reading lamp, with "Glory be to God for dappled things" on my lap.

My share of the phonograph records was piled next to my couch, and I started to separate those B. had lent me from those I had bought for myself. I would give his back, the Marlene Dietrichs and the Edith Piafs, the Yves Montands and the Jean Sablons, all of them souvenirs of the Paris in which he had lived and for which I longed as ardently as I had once longed for the kind of college at which girls rolled hoops on May Day. I separated out the books, too, the Hopkins he'd given me at Christmas of my senior year and the Woolfs with which he was trying to educate me and the Tristan Corbière with which he was trying to improve my French.

If it hadn't been for him, I thought, I would not have heard Montand sing "Les Feuilles Mortes" or read *Mrs. Dalloway* or tasted Brie or drunk any wine beyond sherry. I would not have known about Shakespeare and Company or Harry and Caresse Crosby or what it was like to live up near the Pantheon and breakfast on croissants. I would never have smelled a Gauloise. Maybe I would not even have had my job at *Mademoiselle*; he had told me how to behave during the interview. I would not have anything, really, except my virginity. I would be back in the town in which I was born, bouncing from pillar to post because Papa was not there anymore to say, "When you do this . . . when you do that." Weeping, I went out into the dark hallway, up the shabby stairs to the parlor floor, to the pay phone hanging on the wall. "I'm sorry," I said when he answered. "I don't know what I'd do without you."

THERE IS ONLY ONE NIGHT that sticks out between that evening and my wedding day, the night Allie and I went to the theater on press passes and she lost me. Misplaced me, really. One could say that I misplaced her, of course, but since I am five-five to her five-nine, I continue to think of myself as the overlooked item.

She lost me in the lobby of City Center, up on West Fifty-fifth Street, after the curtain fell on Jose Ferrer in *Cyrano de Bergerac,* and since she was carrying our bus money, she left me with no way to get home. I panicked for a few seconds, hating this place where I knew nobody and nobody knew me and where there was no help on heaven or earth. Then I did what I had always done when I was a child and two or so miles lay between me and the skating pond or the hill for coasting or the meadow for hunting arrowheads. I walked.

*Down Fifth Avenue,* I said to myself, *that's the best way. There'll be people out, looking in the store windows.*

Only there weren't. Midtown Manhattan, I found out during a hike in a city so quiet I could hear my heels clicking on the sidewalk, shuts down at about eleven, maybe even ten o'clock, and the cars are so few that one can hear the swishing sound their wheels make on the pavement. Elsewhere in the city people were drinking after-dinner coffee in the restaurants I had not yet seen, hanging out in the jazz joints I had only read about. But there was no one on Fifth Avenue besides the mannequins gesturing in the windows of Saks and Lord & Taylor and Franklin Simon and B. Altman, and after I crossed Thirty-fourth Street, the only lights were from the streetlamps. The Flatiron Building, looming like a tall ship in the distance, seemed as desolate as the *Marie Celeste.*

Now it is past believing, that I walked those forty or fifty blocks without a hiss from a doorway or a whisper of footsteps behind me. The cars swished, my heels clicked, the rest was silence. No figure slouched against a building; no heap of rags was sleeping over a steam grate. Over on the Bowery drunks were lined up on the sidewalks like sardines in a tin, but Fifth Avenue was the Fifth Avenue of the Steichen photograph: as unsmudged as the moon.

When I was an adolescent, coming home from supper at a friend's, I often walked through a landscape as still as this one. In Rhode Island I had feared strange men leaping out from behind the elms and maples and oaks and privet hedges. In New York I feared strange men leaping out from behind mailboxes and the old doors that fenced construction sites. But now it seemed that there was no more to fear in this vast city than there had been to fear in my small town. I was relieved when I saw Washington Square Arch, just as I had been relieved when I had seen my grandparents' big, awkward Victorian beaming like a lighthouse, but sad, too. The only time I ever think about death is on long walks like that one, when I realize that what I am seeing does not depend on me for its existence.

I never did it again—walk like that in New York, I mean, alone for miles in the middle of the night. But I did it then, taking in the dinosaurs that were those old empty buildings as avidly as I had once taken in rustling trees and sleeping clapboard houses. I took in the smell, that curious confluence of asphalt and automobile exhaust and swill and, surprisingly, tidal flats, and most of all I took in the swollen, purplish sky, in which, in all the years I have stared at it, I have never seen more than two stars.

B. WAS READY to settle down; it was as simple as that. So were the boys he had gone to school with. They were all still boys, some of them even younger than he, and they were all as eager to embark on domesticity as he was. First you got your life in order, that was the idea, and then you lived it. Twenty-four, which B. was, was more than old enough to have a wife, have a home, have a real job, and there was no reason to believe you wouldn't keep all three until the day you died. I, however, had never traveled, never truly been on my own. I wasn't old enough for anything. But marrying young, a classmate used to say, was like getting to a sale on the first day. God knows what, if anything, would be left if you waited till you were twenty-five or -six.

Besides, I had slept with him, and the flesh, I believed, was an unbreakable link. Furthermore, he had delivered an ultimatum. If I did not marry him right now, he was not going to hang around any longer.

We went to Saks Fifth Avenue together for the dress, and he, so pleased and excited to be a groom, lingered for a while over something in green wool, with fake leopard cuffs. Young, and as innocent in his way as I was in mine, he had no idea of what, besides ten yards of tulle, women got married in. Finally we picked a cocktailish kind of thing in beige silk taffeta, with a high neck, a low back, and a big bow. I was wearing my new Capezios, dark red suede with black heels, when I tried it on, and the saleslady, not knowing it was to be my wedding gown, said, "Be sure you wear these shoes with this. They look wonderful."

"Oh God, this'll be a nine-day wonder in Bristol," my mother said when we called her, but she came to New York anyway. My sister, who was in her senior year at college, came with her, along with my oldest friend and some friends of my father's with their wives. They, all Protestants, were distressed for Papa's sake that a judge was to perform the ceremony but determined to do their best for my mother. So they took an enormous suite at the Essex House and made believe they were at the Rhode Island Country Club.

Allie, my future sister-in-law, and I made the canapés and iced the petits fours, and B. ordered the wedding cake from a Yorkville bakery. My sister-in-law also went down to the flower district on Sixth Avenue for dozens of carnations with which to frame her fake fireplace. The judge was a Supreme Court judge, the gift of a friend of B.'s father's.

Before I left the office on Friday night, Joel and Hugh each gave me a ten-dollar bill. "Buy yourself a spatula," Joel wrote on the accompanying card. "You won't be able to live without one." But I spent most of the money a few minutes later, at Best & Co., on two sheer nightgowns, the first I had ever owned. They constituted my trousseau; the green suit was my going-away suit for our one-night honeymoon at a hotel on the corner of Fifth Avenue and Eighth Street. Number 1 Fifth Avenue was the closest we could get to the old Brevoort, which was torn down before it was our turn to be Greenwich Village bohemians and only a block from Washington Square.

B. had bought a new blue suit, nicer than the Puerto Rican revolutionary suit and the gray flannel, and on the morning of the wedding got a haircut and his first manicure. Jerry, seeing him reclining in the barber's chair with his hand stretched out to the manicurist, said he looked like a gangster.

And I? I awakened in a room that I would never see again. My oldest friend was asleep on the other side—Allie had given up her studio couch for the night—and a damp chill was, as usual, seeping in under the back door. My records and books were gone, and so were most of my clothes. The mirror, which the landlord had promised to hang and never did, still leaned against the fireplace, and the light was dim and dirty. It was time to go. I had exhausted this place. Even so, it took my oldest friend to urge me out the door and into her car. "I always thought I'd be with you on your wedding day," she said as we went up Fifth Avenue, "but I never thought I'd be driving you to the ceremony."

When we got to the Essex House, my dress needed hemming,

my hair needed doing, and my nails were unpolished. The wife of one of Papa's friends summoned the hotel housekeeper and handed her the dress. She called the beauty parlor on the first floor and booked me a shampoo, set, and manicure. Another wife took my mother to Bergdorf's, where Mother bought a lacy garter for my something blue. The same wife gave me a dime to put in my shoes, the red Capezios. They were my something old; the dime was my something borrowed; the dress was my something new. There was nothing for it now but to marry. My reluctant mother and her friends had, without knowing it, put me on a conveyor belt.

At the wedding reception, the maid who was opening the champagne bottles that my sister-in-law had deposited in ice in her bathtub said she had never seen so many pretty girls. They were my friends from college—triumphs, all of them, of orthodontia and orange juice and poached eggs on toast. They were pretty, I was pretty, everyone was pretty in the Class of '53. Some years later one of our crowd, or maybe she was a year ahead of us, jumped into the airshaft of the Biltmore Hotel and landed in the Palm Court. I have always thought it was the perfect Conn. College death: she just missed ending up under the Biltmore's famous clock.

How could he resist me, a brown-haired shiksa who read Gerard Manley Hopkins and knew all the college songs? How could I resist him, a dark-haired Jew who looked like Montgomery Clift and had studied in Paris and carried a copy of *Orlando* in his raincoat pocket? Resistance was out of the question. Not walking into the living room, which is what I wanted to do, was out of the question, too. Everyone—my mother in borrowed navy blue crepe, my sister in her best taffeta party dress, the groom in his new suit with polished nails and a hope he would never have again—was waiting for me. On the dot of three, with the back of my head looped by a wreath of white roses and my gloved hands clutching a matching bouquet, I walked out of my sister-in-law's bedroom.

The judge, his back to the fake fireplace, looked around at the boys from Wesleyan and the girls from Conn. College, at the three-piece suits that were my father's friends and the silk crepes that were their wives. "I can see you are all educated people," he said, and began the ceremony.

# *301 East Twenty-first Street*

### ❖ 1 ❖

*B.* FOUND THE APARTMENT. It was at 301 East Twenty-first Street, on the thirteenth floor of a building named the Petersfield. "Guess what?" he said when he called the office a few days before the wedding. "It's got walk-in closets!" There had been no closets in his place on Ninety-sixth Street, only a cheap wardrobe, and Allie and I had kept our clothes in our old college suitcases. Walk-in closets told us more surely than my wedding ring, for which we'd spent $18 at Cartier's, that we were now embarked on adult life.

Finding a place was not hard, even though B. started only a week or so before the wedding. Nothing seemed to be very hard then. East Twenty-first Street was a nowhere part of town, and although the el was no longer running, the elevated tracks still traveled, dark and spidery, along Third Avenue. But the rent was only $89.90 a month, including utilities. I loved the term "including utilities." I would roll it over on my tongue. It was New York talk, like "I grabbed the shuttle" and "He works at 30 Rock," and speaking it meant I was settling in.

All the apartment's windows—one in the living room, another in the bedroom—faced an airshaft, and when it snowed the flakes drifted into the warm air toward the bottom of the shaft and then rose, so that looking out a window during a blizzard was like looking into a popcorn machine.

Sound drifted upward, too, from the apartment directly below us, where a woman whose romantic life kept us sleepless fought with a long series of boyfriends. "*That's* what I think of Latex International," we heard her say one night, and we got to the window just in time to see a female hand fling an open briefcase into the airshaft and the papers spiral as they hit the updraft. Which of the women we saw leaving for work in the morning was she? we wondered. And which of the men was the homosexual who had gone to a costume party naked but for a coat of gold paint on his penis? Living in a big apartment house, with our ears forever to the wall or out the window, we knew more about our neighbors than our parents knew about the people with whom they had exchanged "Good morning"s and "Looks like we've got another nice day"s for years. But we preserved silence in the building's elevators, as did the rest of the residents of 301 East Twenty-first Street, and we could not have matched a voice to a person to save our lives.

We could not have said what we liked in the way of furniture, either, although we had spent hours in Bloomingdale's looking at the rosewood room dividers and the Paul McCobb couches and B. had bought a home improvement magazine whose pages he marked with "What we do want" and "What we don't want." So, but for a table from the Door Store flanked by four unpainted captain's chairs from Macy's, Jerry made most of it: a couch, which was merely a wooden frame on black iron legs on which was set a mattress and three pillows covered with fake nubby linen; a rosewood coffee table; and a so-called easy chair, which was not easy at all because it was only a wooden frame pillowed with two squares of Naugahyde-covered foam rubber.

Jerry's masterwork was a black boxlike structure he had designed and built to house a Ro-tiss-o-mat, our major wedding present. Once you pulled down a lid, the Ro-tiss-o-mat was revealed, and when a roaster was revolving on the spit, you could no more take your eyes off it than you could a fireplace. We treated the box like a fireplace, too. On cold nights of that first married winter—the wedding was just before Christmas—Jerry and B. and I would sit around it, staring into the dripping fat and marveling as the chicken went from white to gold.

We also had a Swedish crystal bud vase, silver-plated candle-

sticks, and, at the far end of the living room, a wall (again Jerry's
work) that combined bookshelves, a niche for the Columbia 360,
slots for the records, a plywood writing surface, and, cleverest of
all, a small coffin into which one could slide the typewriter table.
My only contribution to the room's décor was a pair of brown,
black, and white curtains made, badly, on a rented sewing machine
with fabric from B. Altman's Young Homemaker's Shop. B. con-
tributed three lithographs he had bought in Paris, two Rouaults
and a Matisse: proof positive of the junior year abroad, about
which I could never hear enough. "Tell me again about the night
your uncle took you to the Café de Paris," I would say. "Tell me
again what snails taste like." He would smile and begin. "Well,
the Café de Paris—I think it's closed now—had men dressed like
Cossacks standing at the entrance, and. . . ." I would smile, too, the
best audience then that he could ever hope to have.

Jerry gave us our plates, red Russel Wright rejects a friend of
his was throwing out, and B. found our serving platter, the lid of a
broken oval pottery casserole a friend of his was throwing out. Oh
yes, there was a shag rug, deep green, over which I occasionally
pushed the old Hoover B.'s sister was throwing out. The silver, a
stainless steel imitation of Danish work, came from the Pottery
Barn and was paid for by my mother's $50 wedding check.

If the apartment had a flaw, aside from its perpetual gloom, it
was the kitchen, which was the size of a closet and painted mud
brown. The refrigerator was under the stovetop and the oven on
the wall. I knew nothing about cleaning ovens, and the day ours
caught fire and the doorman came up with a fire extinguisher, I reddened with shame, because when he opened the oven door he saw
two frozen dinners sitting inside. By that time I fancied myself quite
a cook, having gone through every recipe in a book called *Quick
'n' Easy Meals for Two* that B. had given me, and I kept telling the
doorman that we hardly ever had frozen dinners. He nodded and
walked out, leaving me desperate for the casual chatter that had attended my childhood's every transaction. Was there no one in this
city who, as my mother would have put it, "took an interest"?

My specialties were beets with caraway seeds and veal scaloppini rolled around Jones Dairy Farm sausages. We were very fond
of Kraft's Seven-Minute Dinnér, but I always made a salad to go

with it, and never with iceberg lettuce, and I always used red onions, which I had never seen before New York. Once or twice a week we would have wine with dinner—usually a Tavel, because rosé seemed to go with everything—and it began to look as if I might really be a wife. Certainly I was a wife on the nights I stopped at the small Gristede's near the Petersfield on my way home. Emerging from the store after a bit of byplay with the butcher, I would hug the groceries to my chest and feel myself a virtual Ceres. I was going home to feed my husband, and no more was there anyone to tell me that it was time to come in or to tap on a car window and tell us to stop that stuff. A policeman did that once to us in New London, when I was still in college. "It's all right, officer," I said, sobbing. "We're going to get married."

The bedroom. Can I go into the bedroom? It held a three-quarter bed, the iron frame and the springs throwaways of my sister-in-law's and the mattress a Simmons from Macy's. There was another bed, too, very narrow, with a foam rubber mattress, the duplicate of the couch in the living room. Two unpainted bureaus, also from Macy's, one long and low, one short and high: both were stained mahogany by Jerry. Glass curtains shielded us from the men working in the cigar-band factory across the airshaft, and because we did not have a bedside table, the telephone was on the floor. The sheets and pillows, two for $25, half goosedown, came from Bloomingdale's January white sale. And the yellow blanket was a wedding present from my aunt, who inscribed the card "To keep my baby warm."

What else? Oh yes. Imagine a woman staring at the ceiling until her husband, young and aroused and in love, finally rolls off and away. She gets up, to run scalding water over her hands in the white-tiled bathroom, and returns not to the three-quarter bed but to the little one, where she can tell herself that she is in the maple twin at 232 Hope Street, Bristol, Rhode Island, and that her parents, both of them, are asleep in the next room.


WE STARTED ENTERTAINING. Jerry, of course, and a few people from our respective offices. I learned to make boeuf bourguignon, and we discovered that you could hardly go wrong with a Beaujolais. I bought linen napkins in lots of colors, but all of them colors that would go with our jute placemats, and put a Spanish earthenware pot into which I had stuck a bunch of strawflowers on the Door Store table.

Burlap was big then, so I contemplated making bedroom curtains from the brightly colored burlaps at a place in the Village called Bon Bazar. But making the living room curtains had more or less done me in, although I never ceased to be proud of them, so I contented myself with a burlap coat, and wore it to weddings. The rest of our classmates were marrying, and those that had not yet, like Allie, lived uptown with roommates and gave cocktail parties that reminded me of Wesleyan's after-the-game fraternity parties. Unskilled at keeping conversation going for two hours without a lot of help, the guests, myself included, always got drunk.

But there were other friends. No, they were not friends, not really. Rather, they were people we were trying out. There was, for instance, the young man who knew everyone, the kind who looks good leaning on a fireplace with a drink in his hand. We thought he was a possibility.

He claimed to be a protégé of Frank O'Connor's, one of the names C.A. was fondest of dropping, and took us one night to O'Connor's vacant apartment in Brooklyn Heights. Now I wonder at his, and our, gall and the way we poked around O'Connor's small bare living room. *So this,* I thought, studying the four-square furniture and the pile of paper beside the office typewriter, *is where genius resides!* B. was as thrilled as I. Neither of us had ever met a famous author, and my only sightings were of Louis MacNeice and Robert Penn Warren when they spoke at Connecticut. We would not have crossed the street for a movie star, and I had already seen quite a few on Fifth Avenue, all of whom seemed to think that keeping their eyes on the sidewalk made them invisible. But we thought good writers were gods.

One evening I came home giddy and silly from an office cocktail party and found the young man having a drink and listening to the Columbia 360 with B.

"I'll choose the next record," the young man said. "Any requests?"

"Anything but Palestrina," I said, giggling. "Palestrina makes me cry."

I don't remember anything after that, because I was drunk, though since I carry liquor well, it is hard for others to tell when I'm smashed. But my husband said the young man put on Palestrina, sat down, and waited for the tears.

I didn't cry. I couldn't even hear the record above the buzzing in my head, and remember nothing but B. finally ushering the young man out the door. He never asked him over again.

When B. told me of the way the young man watched me, like a hawk eyeing a sparrow, I was frightened. Cruelty I had associated with major events, like the Nazis gassing the Jews, or childish hurts, like the gang going to the movies without me. But adulthood, I had assumed, with World War II over and Girl Scouts behind me, was a plateau on which one walked safely until one fell off into death.

There were other tryouts. There was the couple from my husband's office who lived in Queens and had us over for dinner. The hostess said "the girls" would do the dishes while "the men" sat and talked. Not our class.

There were the two sisters in their thirties who lived on the Upper West Side and kept a radio on the kitchen table. Not our class.

There was the young Viennese writer, the protégé of Thomas Mann, who lived weekends on Washington Place in the Village with his girlfriend and during the week with his parents in Washington Heights while he finished a novel. Our class.

My Parisian sister-in-law came to town with a Yale professor, and they took us to Luchow's. The Yale professor, already half seas over, disliked me on sight—I have always aroused hostility in heavy drinkers, maybe because, as one of them said, "You look like the goddamn Virgin Mary"—and was abusive. Angry, I rose from the table and walked home, to throw myself on the bed and cry until I was ill.

An hour later, when B. arrived, he said, "Why are you crying? You were right to get mad. You did so well up till now. I'm ashamed of you."

I was ashamed of me, too, but not for crying. I was ashamed of showing anger, of walking out. "Never let them see they've gotten to you," my father used to say. "Don't give them the satisfaction."

We went to a cocktail party where, at last, we saw celebrity up close. Everyone there was famous, except for the pretty young men, most of whom seemed to sell books at Doubleday and who turned out to be de rigueur at every party that had a legendary writer or two as its centerpiece. The verbal equivalents of boutonnieres, they dressed up the room, scented the conversation.

My husband moved easily among the tweedy men and the women in the rump-sprung skirts, among the people whose faces I had seen on dust jackets and whose names I had read in book reviews. He was charming. He belonged there. But cold sweat was chilling my back, and self-consciousness had pinioned my tongue, and I ended up doing what the shy always do at cocktail parties: I toured the host's bookcases, staring intently at row after row of titles, no one of which I actually saw.

It was better at Joel and Mil's. I still called Joel "Mr. Graham" and always would—after a while it turned into a kind of nickname—but I could manage "Mil" for Mildred. They lived in a one-room apartment on Minetta Lane, to which we would go once or twice a month for dinner and stories about the New York they had known when they were our age. Joel would talk about Sandy somebody or other at the Group Theater and John (he called him "Julie") Garfield, and he told us we could never claim to have seen a great actress because we hadn't seen Laurette Taylor in *The Glass Menagerie*. We heard about the Lower East Side, where he grew up after his parents emigrated from Russia, which he could not remember as a country, only as a place in which he had slept, swaddled, on an enormous stove. He and Mil had seen Gene Kelly in *Pal Joey* and Marilyn Miller in *As Thousands Cheer,* and listening to them was like watching a thirties movie: young men in felt fedoras, young women in cute little print dresses, brownstones outside of which milkmen left bottles at dawn, and cobblestone streets that shone like black satin when it rained.

One night while we were eating Joel's version of beef Stroganoff, a dish I was dying to add to my own repertory, B. announced that he was leaving his slot in the advertising agency's mailroom. "My God, kid," Joel said, "you don't know what it's like to be out of work."

Joel and Mil had known the Depression, which we knew only through movies and songs like "Remember My Forgotten Man," and it had left them fearful in the way my mother was fearful. A job, any job, was the only sure bulwark against chaos. But our world was one in which a young man with a college degree would never have to go without a salary. As for his wife, her mind would have been so enriched by her college education that no household task, however mundane, could possibly bore her, because she could always escape into her well-stocked head.

"Don't worry so much, Joel," B. said, already dressed in a professional confidence that would never show a crack. "I'll manage." And of course he did. He got a job in the textbook department of a publishing house, not where he wanted to be but a handhold nonetheless. He had tried—my God, how he had tried, with his letters and his suggestions and his outlines—and he had made it. B. was on the circuit.

My father had gone on many business trips, and now here was my husband packing for his first: his shirts strapped to their cardboard backs, his knitted ties laid out on the bed, and his wife folding back the shoulders of his extra jacket so that only the lining showed. He was Odysseus, a joyous Odysseus, at the start of a lifetime's journey through hotels and expense accounts ("swindle sheets," my father had called them) and breakfast meetings. And I, who had never spent a single night alone, was terrified.

I GOT THROUGH THE FIRST NIGHT, waking every hour or so to watch the alarm clock's minute hand jerk its way around the dial, but on the second there was a knock at the door. A middle-aged stranger stood in the corridor, silently extending a card. Screaming, I slammed the door in his face. The next day the doorman told me he was a deaf-mute who lived in the building and did watch and jewelry repairs at home. Knowing we were new tenants, he had been trying to give me his business card.

*If I see him again,* I told myself, *I'll smile. I'll find a bracelet or something he can fix.* But of course I never saw him again. In the evening the residents of the Petersfield disappeared behind their deadbolts, and by the time I emerged to take the garbage to the service stairs, the corridor was as silent as a crypt.

You could live in New York, I had begun to realize, without ever having to open your mouth except for life's necessities. You could even be invisible, not because you were hidden by the crowd but because the crowd was blind to your being a part of it. And unless you were in a park—there were none near us except for Gramercy Park, which was private—you could not sit down. You had to keep on walking until you got home, and if your home was like mine—two rooms in which I could not seem to find a place for myself—you had to go out and start walking all over again. You had to walk and walk and walk until exhaustion set in, and once it did, home—the apartment that faced the airshaft or the basement flat that seemed as dark as a coalhole or the studio that was the size of a closet and maybe even had been—looked good. It looked even better if you could turn it into a fortress. My fortress was built with pots and pans.

I phoned my grandmother for her baked beans recipe and invited people for Saturday night suppers. Friday night I put the beans, California pea beans and yellow-eyes, into a bowl to soak, just like Ganny did, and Saturday morning I stuck them in the oven, and by evening the apartment smelled like her kitchen at 232 Hope Street. The scent loosened my tongue, set me talking.

"In Bristol," I would say, "there are four funeral homes. There's the one for the Italians—that tends to be showy. Then there's the one for the Portuguese, and Connery's, which is for the local Irish and puts on a very muted, sober production. Strictly speaking, my family should be buried by Connery's, since we're Irish, but we're also old settlers, so we're buried by Wilbur's, the Protestant, not to mention society, mortuary, which makes us, on dying, instant Yankees.

"Then there are the churches," I'd continue, warmed by the guests' silence and the discreet little Beaujolais I was waving in my hand. "The lowest rung meets in a former dry-goods store. They're mostly fallen-off Baptists and swamp Yankees, and they've all got cotton-batting hair and blinky blue eyes.

"On the next rung is the Portuguese church, St. Elizabeth's, which is across the street from the rubber factory and is attended only by the Portuguese, who are, according to Bristol, very clean, good hard workers, and possibly mulattos.

"The Italian church, Our Lady of Mount Carmel, is on the north side of the common and is very cozy, since it's small and has a baby-blue ceiling painted with gold stars. The Italian church also has a ten o'clock mass, which is handy for the Catholics who go to St. Mary's, the Irish church, because the service is shorter than St. Mary's eleven-fifteen high and later than St. Mary's nine o'clock low.

"On the fourth rung is St. Mary's, my church, which is a fancy Gothic on the east side of the common and a block from the rubber factory. Some Protestants have been known to attend weddings and funerals at St. Mary's. We always feel honored.

"Next up is the Baptist church. It's on the west side of the common and looks like the Parthenon, but half Bristol thinks Baptists are possible snake handlers and speak in tongues, so even though it's Protestant, it's not a classy church.

"Now, the Congregational church is another thing entirely. It's super-respectable. Congregational men tend to show up only once a year, to pass the plate, and Congregational women run the best church suppers and crochet the best Christmas bazaar potholders. The Congregational church is also the one that the Italians join when they have a fight with the priest. As for St. Michael's, the Episcopal church . . . it's the same as Bailey's Beach and the Agawam Hunt. It's more than a church. It's a club."

On and on I would go, revisiting a town I would never truly leave, glad I could finally, or so it seemed, laugh at it. And as I did, I felt my bones taking on flesh and my skin taking on color. But when the guests left, I would drop into a crying jag and tell my husband about my father, about how much I wished they had known each other, about how he had had a crush on Margaret Sullavan, about how he used to say that just walking around the ground floor of Brooks Brothers could cheer him up, about how we read poetry together and cried together; about how much he had wanted to name me Maeve and about how he was overruled by my mother, which is why I was Mary. And B. would clear the table and pile the dishes in the sink and fold his lips into a long thin line and go silently to bed. Until, that is, the night he opened them and said he couldn't stand hearing about my father anymore.

I could not stop, I could not give it up. I gave him the packet of letters my father had sent me my sophomore year in college, the letters I had tied with a black grosgrain ribbon and kept with my handkerchiefs.

Papa wrote about money. There wasn't much. I was desperate to stay in school. He was desperate, too, wanting to equip me and my sister for the world and knowing he would die before he could finish the job. "I may have to will my massive brain to Harvard Medical or something, but don't worry, I'll keep you in college. . . . I'm enclosing a check to pay for your *Herald-Tribune* subscription, and please don't go broke. I won't be able to send much but I'll always be able to scrape up a buck or two. . . . Sorry to hear you didn't order a class ring. It's part of school life to have it in later years, and I'll see that the balance is paid when necessary. . . . Sorry you had to call yesterday and use that money. You could have had a hamburg sandwich or something with it. . . . Enclosed is your vacation check. I wish I could send more but I can't. You won't need to pay it back. When your tax refund comes I'll deposit it in your account which now has $82.93, $1.16 interest as of Feb. 1. Your train fare should be $10.00 or so,

| hotel | $ 7.50 |
|-------|--------|
| shows | 15.– |
| meals | 15.00 |
| total | 47.50 |

Then you'll have tips. Your plans make me homesick for New York. How I love that town."

His own life almost over, he held on to the future by planning mine. "I was very pleased to hear of your good marks, have always wanted to wear a Phi Beta Kappa key. . . . Any As lately? . . . Have you asked yet about graduate schools, maybe Yale? . . . I am proud of you. . . . Your success means a great deal to me."

He asked about my boyfriends. "That new one sounds nice. . . . Don't pass too many up. . . . There's no reason you can't do graduate work and marry, too. . . . I don't care who or what you and Diana marry, so long as he's a nice guy."

He busied himself with minutiae. "Have ordered your new stationery. . . . Judy's mother is knitting knee socks for you. Do you want cable stitch? . . . Is your desk lamp all right? . . . Have already bought your Christmas presents: a green sweater to go with your new skirt, and a long wool scarf."

He talked about his health, but because he had not told me yet that he was dying, I did not understand what he was telling me. "Am going into the hospital for a transfusion. Don't worry, it's just that my blood is a little thin. . . . Couldn't go to work today because I felt so tired, but don't worry. I guess I won't be as cute in my old age as I had hoped. . . . My hip ached today. Can you imagine? I think I have neuritis of the backside."

Descriptions of movies to be seen were replaced by radio programs to be heard. "Rudolf Serkin is playing the *Emperor* today. . . . T. S. Eliot is reading his poetry this afternoon." He no longer climbed stairs. "My bed has been moved downstairs to the bay window and it's nice—I can see everything going on. . . . Today the weather is bad, just a good day to listen to good music, some smart talk, and perhaps have someone read to me. . . . I love you very much. . . . I am so proud of my daughters. . . . Good night, sweet princess."

B. read all the letters, from the first, with its big, exuberant handwriting, to the last, almost illegible hen track, and came into the bedroom. He was crying, and he said, "I'm sorry. I didn't know what it was like."

❖ 2 ❖

SOME MARRIAGES, at least in the beginning, take three people. The third provides the glue. Our glue was Jerry, who came down every Sunday to use the shower and join us in perusing the real es-

tate section of the *New York Times*. I had assumed, because I had
seen movies like *Mr. Blandings Builds His Dream House*, that after
a certain age—thirty-five, say—every New Yorker who could afford to moved to the suburbs. The kind of people we had begun to
know would have died first. Instead they mostly stayed put in
one or another inadequate apartment and read the real estate ads
over their Sunday breakfast. On the whole, I was told, it was an
academic exercise. Anything good was gone by noon, snatched up
by somebody who had managed to get a copy of the section before
it hit the newsstands. Acquaintance with a *Times* employee, then,
was highly valued.

"My God!" Jerry would say, his eyes running down the two-
and-a-half-rooms column. "If only you could afford $125 a
month, you could get anything." We would sit silent for a moment,
each of us visualizing the same thing: an apartment in the Village
with a white marble fireplace, dentil moldings, and windowboxes
in which I would plant geraniums and trailing ivy. In winter the
firelight would dance over the American country furniture that we
did not yet own, and in summer a breeze would set the ball-fringed
curtains that I would make someday to stirring, and then, finally, I
would sit down. Living here, in this faceless apartment in this faceless part of town, was not living at all.

On this dreary stretch of First Avenue, across the street from a
cement playground and two blocks south of a rundown A & P, our
only entertainment was each other. In summer, the sun beat down
on the musty secondhand bookstores on Fourth Avenue which
were our sole diversion and turned them into ovens. In winter,
while we waited for the Madison Avenue bus, the wind drove us to
huddling together in a quadrant of a bank's revolving door. At
night, with no place to stroll, B. would try to make himself comfortable in the easy chair and I, defeated by the foam rubber couch,
would retreat to the bedroom. Oh, we knew we were lucky, especially in those walk-in closets, but we wanted to be cozy.

Jerry made us cozy. When he was in the apartment, with the
Sunday papers scattered at his feet and some cheese he had just
discovered at some shop nobody else knew about stinking on
the Door Store table and his chatter rising to our low ceiling, we
melded. We were young Mr. and Mrs. L. at home. Mr. L. was light-

ing a cigarette and Mrs. L. was lighting the gas stove and their guest, opinionated, talkative, not-yet-settled-down, older-than-they-were Jerry, was evoking their mutual amusement, their mutual adulthood.

He was also that invaluable addition to any marriage, the man who would do what the husband was too busy to do. What I wanted to do, more than anything, was find the Ilium that presented itself whenever one drove down the West Side Highway at dusk and saw the lights going on in the skyscrapers and the sun dropping into the Hudson. What I found, however, was infinitely more interesting: all Europe, a bit of Asia, some of Africa, and three centuries dropped indiscriminately on one small island.

I do not know if Jerry liked me, and I do not even know if I liked him, and he left New York for good while I was still making up my mind. But if I remember him kindly, and I do, it is because we both believed—though neither of us would ever have said anything quite so fancy—that the best way to possess a place was to eat it. We never went uptown. It was years before I saw Morningside Heights, and I knew Harlem only as the place in which, on our one trip to New York, my father told me to push down the lock button on the car door. Downtown was our destination: that was where the food was. Piroghi, cannoli, and dim sum were a kind of sympathetic magic. In consuming them we were consuming the Little Ukraine that was lower First Avenue, Little Italy, and Chinatown.

We wandered over to the other side of town, too, to Dey Street, which was lined with plant nurseries, and to narrow, musty shops that sold spices and fresh-ground peanut butter, and to a store called Cheese of All Nations, where everyone who had immigrant grandparents or who had spent their junior year abroad went for Muenster and Camembert. Once we went to the old Washington Market. It was soon to close, and half the booths were empty, but I talk about having been there as I would talk about having been on the dock when the survivors of the *Titanic* came down the gangplank. I cannot remember much, though, only a ceiling like a cathedral's and light that was like a cathedral's, too, and hanging chickens, row on row, and eggs still stuck with straw.

Sometimes we would stumble upon an early nineteenth-century, maybe even late eighteenth-century house that the march of progress had missed. More often we would see its shadow outlined on the wall of the building it had once stood beside. It had never occurred to me till then that New York had so many strata, that the city that I was trying to know was only the top layer of an enormous archaeological dig, and that no matter how fast and far I traveled, I would never get to know it all.

Walking across the Brooklyn Bridge was like walking into an enormous spider web, and the financial district on a weekend was as bleak and barren as a desert. One dark afternoon, when a cold wind was sweeping its empty streets, we entered a saloon with white-tiled walls, a shirtsleeved man pounding on an upright piano, and a line of red-faced topers drinking boiler-makers and cracking hard-boiled eggs at a long mahogany bar. Now the saloon seems a hallucination, but I will stake my life on its reality. Somewhere in downtown New York, in 1954, was a room in which it was always 1905.

Sometimes, in Little Italy, we would glimpse old men playing boccie on a scrubby patch of grass behind a coffee shop or restaurant, and one day, in Chinatown, we ran into a funeral procession led by a small band. The music was brassy, like jazz, but sinuous and scary, too. My God, but I was far from home!

A Michelin is tempting. Two stars for Mother Seton's convent! Three for the Battery! But I could not concoct one. Half the time I did not know where we were, although I am sure Jerry did, and I was vague about the names of streets because I was always looking at the tops of buildings or peering into windows. In childhood I had tried to swallow the town in which I grew up—"Your eyes are too big for your belly," my grandmother said, and she meant more than food—and now I was trying to swallow New York. Of course I would never be able to: that was the blessing of it. There would always be another street to turn down, another roofline, another Chinese funeral.

On Sunday nights the chicken twirled on its spit and the cook, happy because she had worn herself out with walking, rubbed a clove of garlic on the wooden salad bowl. The wine-glasses tottered on the lumpy placemats, and Jean Sablon or Charles Trenet sounded sonorously from the Columbia 360. The Rosenbergs were dead, and the young man was on his way up, up, up, and it did not matter that there was nothing but an airshaft to see from the windows, because night had come down and smoothed a blanket over the whole city.


ONE AFTERNOON in late winter I was sitting at my typewriter when my head began to ache, on the left side, just behind and around my eye. Confused and a little dizzy, I asked Joel if I could go home. He nodded and murmured the requisite "Hope you feel better," and I left, to wait for the Second Avenue bus. By now I could scarcely see out of my left eye, and lunch was pushing its way up my throat, but it never occurred to me to take a cab. The only times B. and I had ever taken cabs were when I had food poisoning, on our wedding day, and on the day his office sent him to Brooklyn with a manuscript and he called, excited, to see if Joel would let me out long enough to share the ride.

Memory, I am told, is selective—but not mine. "Selective" implies choice, and I have none. I recall completely or I am afflicted with amnesia. There is no in-between. So believe me when I say that I can remember how gray the sky was that afternoon, and how bits of paper were scudding across Second Avenue, and how the smell of my egg salad sandwich kept exploding in my mouth. Above all, I can remember the pain. It was as if someone were hammering a spike through my eye socket.

The light in our bedroom was gray, too, and the cigar-band factory across the airshaft was clanking out its product, and, desperate to lie down, I could not stop to take the dusty-rose cotton spread off the bed. Instead I lay on top, careless for once of wrinkles, and felt my back arching, almost into a bow. Locked into that curious arch and unable to turn my head, I reached my right arm straight behind me, pulled the phone to my side, and managed to dial B.'s office.

The woman who answered said my husband was away from his desk. "Then get him, get him!" I screamed. I had just enough time to say, "Get home. My head!" before I dropped the phone and rolled off the bed to crawl into the bathroom. I vomited into the toilet, pulled myself up by a towel rack, and stumbled back to the bed, where I lay down again, back still arching, head digging into the pillow, my left eye bulging, and tears streaming down my face.

The key sounded in the lock and in came B., pale, with his raincoat flapping behind him. He had called Jerry, who knew of a doctor at Beth Israel and would meet us there. His arm around my waist, he dragged me the few blocks to the hospital and a doctor who took me into a dingy cubicle and injected something in my arm. My back released, the throbbing dulled, the film—or so it seemed to me—over my left eye slowly cleared.

"Has anything happened to upset you?" the doctor asked.

"No. Why?"

"You're having a migraine attack."

"What's the cure?" I asked drowsily.

"A psychiatrist."

Home, sinking slowly into that serene sleep that follows migraine, I could hear B. and Jerry moving about the living room and the push of the captain's chairs. But I could not hear what they were saying, because they were whispering.

I did go to a psychiatrist—as always, Jerry knew of somebody—one who had positioned his desk against a light-filled window. He could see every pore of his patients' faces. They could see little of him beyond a bulky outline, out of which came the voice of God. I would say that I hated him on sight, except that I cannot claim to have seen him.

"Last week," I said, "I had a very bad headache, and the doctor my husband took me to said it was a migraine attack and that I'd have one again. Can psychiatry cure migraine?"

He didn't answer. Instead, having been prepped by Jerry, he asked me how and when my father died.

"Four years ago," I answered. "But migraine. If I go to a psychiatrist, will that get rid of migraine?"

He asked me again about my father; I asked him again about psychiatry. In childhood I had always done what the doctor had told me to do, and now I was willing to do what this doctor told me to do. If only he would tell me.

But he would not. Over and over again he asked me about my father, until finally I did what I always did when forced to remember Papa on his bed, thin where he'd been fat and jaundiced where he'd been ruddy and with a pillow rolled and placed beneath his double chin because now he was dead. I cried.

The next day the psychiatrist called my husband, which I know only because, emptying his suit pockets for the cleaner's, I found the notes he had scribbled on scraps of paper during their talk. "Cannot accept father's death," they read, and "anxiety neurosis," and "close to complete collapse."

The first I realized, the second I had never heard of, and as for the third, I knew with a certainty that surprises me now that, inviting though the abyss might be, I would not lose my balance. I knew something else, too: that I had been betrayed.

"DOES ANYONE have anything to say about the photograph on page eighty-seven?" B.T.B., her pearls and her diamond brooch at the neck of her Adele Simpson and her feet squeezed into and slightly overflowing her Delman pumps, is sitting at the head of the conference room table. The beauty editor, who has a nose you could slit envelopes with and a tart tongue—"The rich, they ride in chaises," she murmurs whenever she contemplates B.T.B.—is fluttering a fan. She is bored.

So are the fashion editors, but they are always bored when they're not out in the market or on the phone or at a sitting. They are, they claim, "visual," which is why they have nothing to say about any of the magazine's fiction or articles. Most of them don't even know they're there.

C.A.'s assistants and the girls from College and Careers have plenty to say, since they are verbal. If the rest of the world divides people into those who like sugar and those who like salt, magazine editors divide it into those who are visual and those who are verbal. Since *Mademoiselle* is a fashion magazine, the visuals think the verbals are dowdy. The verbals think the visuals are shallow. When the staff meets once a month, as it is doing now, to review the current issue, the visuals speak solely of the photographs and the verbals speak solely of the prose. The only people who have to look at both, besides B.T.B. and C.A., work in the art department and do not like anything they see or read. For them, perfection is a page on which there is nothing whatsoever.

B.T.B. turns to this month's fiction. *Mademoiselle* and *Harper's Bazaar* are unlikely repositories for some of the best American short stories. Everybody thinks those are in *The New Yorker.* They aren't. They're in *Mademoiselle* and *Bazaar,* somewhere between the Claire McCardells (*Mlle.*) and the Balenciagas (*Bazaar*).

This month's story is "The Geranium," by William Goyen, and the assistant art director hates it. "Honest to God," she barks. "Save me from the sensitive."

She looks around the room for the expected laugh, and gets it. But not from me. The assistant art director sounds just like the bullies I knew in third grade, the ones who used to back the brightest boy in the class into the coatroom corner with their derisive "Think you're so smart!" I had defended him; I would defend William Goyen.

Someday I mean to track down that story, because all I can recall of it now is its title and its author. But whatever I said about it (and truly, I have no idea) caught C.A.'s ear. The next day a messenger from up front, one of the tall, brainy girls who talked out of the sides of their mouths, arrived at my desk with several manuscripts and a blue-penciled note. Would I please read these for the fiction editor, it said, and let her know what I thought of them.

The names on the cover sheets startled me. I hadn't realized that the famous had to submit stuff like everybody else, that being published once was not a ticket to being published forever. Nor had I realized how much I missed the nights when I sat up late in my dorm room with some obscure sixteenth-century poet or seventeenth-century polemicist whispering in my ear. Mostly, though, I hadn't realized how much I needed to use my head, and that if I did not, my head would use me. "Look what I've got," I said when I went home that night. "Work!"

A few years ago, weeding out a desk, I came upon copies of those careful little reports—I had been so proud of being asked to do them that I had made carbons—and was pleased by my seeming judiciousness, my seeming good sense. Still, it is sobering to think that the bench before which so many writers, some of them distinguished, had to appear was occupied by somebody who was barely out of college. "Rejected John van Druten today," I would tell B., "and passed Tennessee Williams on for a second reading." The nerve of me! The gall! Yet had I ever met John van Druten or Tennessee Williams in the flesh, I would have been speechless. If I could look at the product with a cool critical eye, I could not look at the producer without awe.

To me, *Mademoiselle*'s fashion copy also constituted literature, though on a far lower plane. Kathy and her assistant, whom one of the fashion editors described as dressing like an assistant buyer, that is, strictly à la mode, favored literary conceits along the lines of "Put these flowers in water immediately!" under a photograph of a floral-print swimsuit. So I was joyous the day Kathy left her office to stroll languorously down the long corridor to the promotion department. "My assistant's leaving to get married," she said. "Do you want to try out?"

At home I spread the photostats, rejects, and merch sheets— clothes were "merch," and merch sheets listed sizes, fabrics, and brief descriptions—on the desk and, skipping supper, struggled for hours over five or so captions. Then I passed them on to B., who studied them as intently as he would *The Partisan Review*. "I don't think you need 'glossy,'" he said, and "Haven't you got a better word than 'snappy'?"

"They're a start," Kathy said.

I took home a second set of stats, rejects, and merch sheets, and once more I wrote and B. edited. "Better" was Kathy's response. "But there's a lot of competition for this job. You'll have to do another."

I could not do another. I was tired, I told B., and it was hopeless anyway.

"Jesus!" he yelled. "You're a goof-off! You'll never amount to anything, because you just won't *try*."

I cried, and sat naked at the plywood writing surface all one hot July night, writing a third tryout. A few days later, Kathy, who always walked as if preceded by altar boys, arrived at my desk to say I had the job.

Without B.'s prodding and pushing, I was nothing. With them,

I could be anything. I had lost God, lost my father, and now, thank you Lord, I had recovered both.

JOEL AND B. WERE THRILLED FOR ME: I was, in the old re-port card phrase, living up to my potential. But B. was also angry. While talking to an employment agency from which he was hiring a secretary, he had found out that *Mademoiselle* had listed the job with the agency and offered to pay $10,000 a year. I, young and "promoted from within," would make less than half that. B.'s out-rage rolled right off my back. Like most of my friends from college, I thought being offered a job for which no one was going to check my typing speed a great compliment. We knew we were bright, but we did not think we were worth much.

The window of my new office faced Fifty-seventh Street, be-tween Madison and Park, and since the magazine was only six flights up, I had a good view of the browsers and the strollers and, occasionally, the famous. One afternoon, for instance, Queen Elizabeth and Prince Philip crossed Fifty-seventh from east to west in an open car. The secretaries and assistants from C.A.'s bullpen rushed in, and when one of them, peering over my shoulder, mourned that she had nothing to throw—confetti, say—another said, "I can give you a phone book." At last I was in the land of smart talk.

Another time I saw the Duke and Duchess of Windsor, he the size of a jockey, she the width of a hatchet, marooned on a street corner. Whoever was supposed to pick them up was late, so they, helpless as beached fish, stood motionless while pedestrians pe-rused their every inch. Looking out that window was like being at the movies, and I could not get enough of the spectacle. Being ju-nior to Kathy, however, I had the desk by the door.

Actually, the view out the door wasn't bad either. After Dylan Thomas died, a girlfriend of his—tall, dark, and lachrymose—sat one long afternoon beside C.A.'s desk (C.A. had known him, and devoted almost an entire issue to *Under Milk Wood*) and sobbed. Carson McCullers, the fiction editor's sister, lurched in, tall, pin-headed, and on crutches. Françoise Sagan, too, after *Bonjour Tristesse,* small and wan and stared at by everyone who suddenly found a reason to be in the bullpen. Living legends called Leo Lerman. When Cary Grant gave the girl who answered the phone his name, she said, "Oh, my God!" and hung up. And everyone was kind to me because I was such a relief after Kathy, who, although keeping dibs on the desk by the window, was now working from home. Kathy had struck terror in the heart.

I even made it onto the pages of *Mademoiselle*, in a spread on short haircuts. The beauty editor had me photographed, and there I am for all time, uncharacteristically elfin and slightly bucktoothed. I am also wearing the green suit, but it was on its way out. After going to a few showings—Kathy believed that copywriters should actually see clothes once in a while—I was slowly acquiring samples out of the back room at Claire McCardell. In them I looked like the kind of woman who could dance *Appalachian Spring,* and that struck me as just about perfect: a little to the right of Village boho and way to the left of Peck & Peck and the Bermuda Shop.

The fiction editor's assistant was living in sin, and Rita blamed herself, because she had introduced the girl to her seducer. Sometimes there was sobbing in the ladies' room, and there were rumors of abortions, all of which seemed to have been performed in Hoboken. Fetuses were swimming in the sewers of New Jersey, and what was spinsterhood after all but cold and rain and a wind that blew up your skirts and chilled your legs? Thank God I was spending my lunch hours in Bloomingdale's, not knocking back martinis at Barney's, and thank God for B., who had known better than I what was best for me. I was safe, I was warm, I was married.

Still, there were those days and nights when I lay in bed in darkness, tears seeping out from under my closed eyes, and B. sat in the living room, hurt and lonely because migraine took me to a place where neither he nor anyone else could follow. Finally, shy and embarrassed but trusting because she was older than I was, I asked Kathy if she knew of a psychiatrist. Of course she did. She had visited one from every school, for disabilities ranging from broken heart to writer's block to chronic itch. "Rita's been looking pretty good lately," she said. "Let's see who she's going to these days."

Rita's psychiatrist was named Dr. Franklin. He was plump and pleasant and spoke with a middle European accent that in all the many years I knew him he could not conquer. He did not inquire about my husband, my father, or my sex life. I simply asked him, "Can you help my head?" and he said, "Yes."

And then we moved from Twenty-first Street.

# *224 West Eleventh Street*

## ❖ 1 ❖

*A* DAY OR SO after the Blizzard of 1888, a photographer named Cranmer C. Langill focused his camera on Eleventh Street, west of Seventh Avenue. A man in a white apron and visored cap—he probably works at the grocery in the foreground—is shoveling snow. Two men in overcoats and tall hats stand beside him, and a little girl in a coat with shiny buttons is in front of them. The snow in the gutter is piled higher than their heads, and there on the left, next to the portico of the Church of St. John the Evangelist, is 224 West Eleventh Street. Our new home.

In 1888, 224 West Eleventh Street probably housed one family. In the mid-1950s, it housed five. The minister who was our landlord—or, rather, St. John's Church was our landlord—lived with his family in the bottom duplex. A childless middle-aged couple who seldom made a sound lived in the third-floor back. A Scotswoman had the fourth-floor front; somebody we never laid eyes on had the fourth-floor back. We ourselves had the third-floor front, $120 a month and acquired, as most such apartments were acquired, by word of mouth. It had belonged to *Mademoiselle*'s office manager and her husband, who were moving to Connecticut, and she passed it on to me.

There was no proper entrance hall. Open the door and one was in the kitchen, small and painted my favorite mud brown. The refrigerator was full-size, thank God, though the freezer was tiny, and we put a hook on the wall for our first important cooking utensil, a copper-bottomed Revere Ware skillet. The sink leaked, and the only way I could ever get it fixed was to tell Father Graf, the minister, that I was afraid something terrible would happen to his ceiling. The stove was a Royal Rose.

The living room was the room we had imagined when we sat around the Door Store table, resting our elbows on the *Times* real estate section: a large square with two tall windows facing north and a white Italian marble fireplace on the east wall. All the walls but the south wall, which was forest green, were white. The white ball-fringed curtains were made by the seamstress at the Little Homemaker Shoppe in Bristol, Rhode Island, and the long quasi-mahogany bureau was now the quasi-mahogany sideboard. In it were towels and sheets, and on top were the sterling silver coffeepot, sugar bowl, and cream pitcher that my Parisian sister-in-law had finally decided on for our wedding present and that we finally had a chance to display.

The black Ro-tiss-o-mat holder was gone, along with the shag rug, the Door Store table, and the captain's chairs, but we had brought the couch and the easy chair from Twenty-first Street. There was a real couch, too, a pumpkin-colored Paul McCobb loveseat from Sloane's, and a real desk, an eighteenth-century pine slant-top from an antique shop near Bristol. A real mahogany table and four real Hitchcock chairs from the same place were between the windows. We had a few prints, by French artists, a floor-to-ceiling bookcase in the southeast corner, and a pair of tiny silver-plated candleholders from the Museum Silver Shop. We were beginning to acquire style.

The bedroom was just big enough for the three-quarter bed, a bureau (the short Macy's unpainted) at its foot, and across a narrow aisle, a bookcase jammed with my detective stories. Two walls were painted white and two the pale blue of the Lautrec lithograph we'd hung above the bureau. There were long white ball-fringed curtains here, too, a windowseat, and a millefleur quilt. "Look," I would say, feeling racy as I said it, to friends peering in the bedroom door. "Did you ever see anything quite so virginal?"

I HAD WANTED to come back to Greenwich Village ever since I had left Waverly Place, and since moving to West Eleventh Street, I have never lived anyplace else. I do not want to. That is not because of what the Village is but because of what I have made it, and what I have made it depends on who I am at the time. The Village is amorphous; I can shape it into any place. The rest of Manhattan is rectilinear, its grid an order, a single definition, that I dislike. But the Village is a collection of cow-paths and landfill and subterranean rivers, visible, if you know about them, because they are traced by streets paved to mask them.

If some areas have a certain architectural unity, it is not because an architect had a grand scheme but because row-houses with common walls were put up hastily for people fleeing a yellow fever epidemic downtown. One of the streets is called Little West Twelfth, which distinguishes it from West Twelfth and is a distinction that makes no sense whatsoever, because the two streets are unconnected. Everything in the Village—the way Waverly Place takes a right turn, for instance, and West Thirteenth Street's sudden transformation into Horatio—seems haphazard, accidental. When we first moved there, the old-timers told us the Village had changed. People still tell me the Village has changed. The Village does not change, not really. The Village—the *real* Village, the one bounded by Fifth Avenue on the east and the Hudson River on the west—remains an accident.

In the years on West Eleventh, it became the Europe I had yet to see. On Saturday nights we would walk along West Fourth Street to a store that sold Scandinavian modern everything and served free glogg. I didn't like Scandinavian modern anything, and I hated glogg, but I loved the store owner's accent. It and the glogg and the Swedish candleholder that was his best seller—six metal angels that revolved around a candle when it was lighted—raised possibilities, unveiled horizons.

When we went to the Peacock to drink espresso, it was because I believed there were a million Peacock Cafés in Italy, and if I sat in this one, on West Third Street, staring at a waitress who looked like a Veronese, I was sitting in all of them. If we had a drink at the San Remo, it was because of its name and not because everybody hung out there. A lot of famous and about-to-be-famous people hung out at the San Remo. I must have seen them all, and cannot remember any of them. They were not the point. Even if they had been, I would have been too timid to strike up a conversation. Working for a fashion magazine, however distinguished its fiction, separated me, in my eyes and doubtless in theirs, from the literati.

I started walking again, alone. In Bristol I had walked all the time, long walks that would take me to solitary picnics on the low stone wall surrounding an estate a few miles from our house, or to the meadow a mile further on where the grass seemed a thin skin between myself and the Indians I imagined lying in layers beneath my feet. Walking in the Village, I would quickly exhaust the import shops and the bars, into which I peered, believing that all of America's young literary life was being lived in them, mostly by fast, fluent talkers like Jerry, and head for the docks.

There was nothing over there then—no gay bars, no young men in leather jackets and button-front Levis—but nineteenth-century warehouses, a few houses, some vacant lots, and beyond them the river. One block I liked especially. It had two trees and ten or so tired old houses, was paved with cobblestones and littered with whatever the sanitation trucks had missed, and led to the garbage pier. The street was wholly desolate and, for someone who was slowly developing a taste for the seedy and the out-of-season, a magnet.

The garbage pier was precisely that, the pier where the tugs that lugged garbage out to sea made their pickups. No one ever went that far west then, not on weekends anyway, but myself and the young Italians from the South Village who would park their cars on the dock and curry them as if they were horses. They never bothered me; I never bothered them. They would curry their cars, I would lean against a piling and watch the boats, and all of us would allow ourselves to be wrapped in silence. Silence was the cure, if only temporarily, silence and geography. But of what was I being cured? I do not know, have never known. I only know the cure. Silence, and no connections except to landscape.

HAPPIER THOUGHTS! I learned to cook! And what a cook I was! Rolling out pastry on the quasi-mahogany sideboard because the kitchen had no counter. *The Joy of Cooking* replaced by *Gourmets I* and *II. Quick 'n' Easy Meals for Two*, with its inscription "To my *wife*, in gastronomic appreciation," gathering dust.

We entertained, sometimes as many as six at one time, and B. bought a wooden spice rack, which I hung over the sink and filled with a lot of herbs I never got to use. Fenugreek was one of them. What did one do with fenugreek? I didn't know, nor did anyone else, but we all had a bottle of it, we apprentice gourmets, in our spice racks. God forbid that we should cook the food of our forebears. Instead we bought chorizo and tortillas at Casa Moneo on West Fourteenth Street, and Polish hams over on Second Avenue, and fillets of beef at a place that sold them cheap on Sixth, and by the time we got dinner on the table we felt as if we had run a marathon. Already we were giving up hard liquor, except for martinis. We were attempting wines, and dry vermouth on the rocks.

The people we had known in college had begun to harden into types. A friend of B.'s, for instance, had gone to work on Wall Street, and when he walked upstairs to our apartment, his steps were slow and measured, his suits were sober, and he was always carrying a dozen roses for his hostess. So predictable!

After a dinner party, an editor at a publishing house insisted we play "What novel speaks to you?" "Not a novel," my husband said, "F. Scott Fitzgerald's *The Crack-up*." I said, "Anything by Graham Greene"; and the book editor said, "*Fiesta*. The original title for *The Sun Also Rises*," he added when our faces blanked. So pretentious!

The wife of B.'s friend the medical student kept her diaphragm on the toilet tank, and whenever a man lifted the seat, the box was knocked to the floor, where it opened. Such a showoff!

We went out—to the theater, because that was what you did in those days, and to cocktail parties, which always ended with someone saying, "Let's all go to Monte's" or "Let's go to the Gran Ticino." So off we'd go to MacDougal Street, to eat veal scaloppini and drink Soave and order zabaglione—because we loved watching the waiter make it, right at the table!—for dessert.

We did not watch television, because nobody we knew did, and we did not own one, besides. But we fell in love with *What's My Line* and on summer Sunday nights would walk over to Gay Street to watch the show with a man, a classmate of B.'s but older, who was "in theater" and had been given a Mexican silver cigarette lighter by Tennessee Williams. The flame heated the silver to scorching, but never mind. It put us in touch with genius.

My husband's aunt and uncle from Montreal came to call and thought our apartment awfully small. The son of a viscount came to call, and he, too, found it awfully small. But what could they know of New York? My secretary (twenty-four and I had a secretary!), who was crazy, recently tossed out of Radcliffe and into Reichian therapy, came to call and brought Isaiah Berlin's stepson. He said I had delightful feet. I do.


IN COLLEGE, almost everyone I knew spent the summer before their senior, or maybe their junior, year abroad, and Allie had even spent a winter vacation with her parents there, embarking on KLM, I remember, all done up in her sheared beaver coat. Some were part of the Experiment in International Living and spoke soberly of sharing chores with their host families, but most just traveled around Europe, getting lost a lot, marveling at the toilets ("You should have seen the ones in Marseilles! I thought I'd die!"), and soaking their feet in bidets. When one of our English professors, lecturing us on Henry James, said, "When you're in the Uffizi, you must . . . ," he was assuming correctly. Of course we would be in the Uffizi someday. Next summer, in fact.

B. had been in the Uffizi. B. had been everywhere. B. had even cruised to Scandinavia, in a ship so notorious for its bad food that gulls knew better than to track its garbage.

He had spent his junior year at the Sorbonne, where he'd run into Jerry, whom he had known slightly in Seattle and who had been living in England. They took rooms in a place called l'Hôtel des Grands Hommes, near the Pantheon, and then they looked for Hemingway's Paris.

B. had sat in *caves* where one drank cherry brandy and applauded the entertainment—young, leftish Americans, many of them, singing "We are climbing Jacob's ladder, ladder, LADDER"—with repeated snaps of the fingers. He had eaten crêpes and used *jetons* and been accosted by young men whispering that if he was interested, he could see an *exhibition* just around the corner, two flights up. I ransacked his memory for details. "What *exactly* does crème fraîche taste like?" I would ask.

For my classmates, for B., for our friends, Europe was a rite of passage. Once you had been to Europe, you could settle down—but not before. Because if you did not go, you would be haunted all your life by not having run the bulls at Pamplona while you still had the legs to do it. You would not have the demitasse cups you could trot out after dinner, saying, "We bought these in Venice before Muffie was born." You would not be able to say to your old roommate, "Remember Pierre? That boy we met at Versailles? Remember that terrible friend of his? Philippe?"

B. and I saved money and vacation days, and at last, during our first September on West Eleventh Street, we went to Europe, with our clothes in two cheap green plaid suitcases I had bought in a luggage shop that gave discounts to magazine people and a maroon leather diary, gilt-inscribed "Trip Abroad," that my mother had given me. I was frightened of flying, but Jerry, who came to see us off at the East Side Airlines Terminal, told me to imagine that I was rolling across an empty highway, and by the time we had been two hours in the air I was a familiar of the aisle, a sightseer who crab-walked from one side of the plane to the other to peer at the Atlantic, which looked marceled, and at minute boats, which I believed to be strung across our route, ready and able to pick us up if the plane dumped.

In Paris our hotel was on a quay and our room faced the Seine, and below the tiny balcony on which I stepped on our first morning an old man was pushing the water that ran along the gutter with bunched twigs tied to a wooden handle. "It's like François Villon," I said with a gasp. "François Villon!" I loved Paris, I loved everything about Paris, and above all else I loved my husband most in Paris.

Both of us spoke French with awkward American accents, but B.'s was fluent and idiomatic, so he did all the talking for us. He knew how to order breakfast from room service—"*Deux cafés complets, s'il vous plait*"—and how to go where on the métro and how you ordered *une fine* rather than a cognac. I was dizzy with worship.

We walked to l'Hôtel des Grands Hommes in the rain, in our trenchcoats, my Kodak dangling from my hand, and he said, looking at the tattered building, "The day Jerry and I went to our first class, the landlady took one look at us and muttered, '*Il n'y a plus des grands hommes.*' " I smiled—I knew better—and positioned him against a wall and took a picture of him lighting a cigarette in the rain. His eyes are toward the camera, his hands cup the flame, his trenchcoat sags with water.

Sometimes, when I am with women of my age and, I suppose, my kind, we reminisce about the images that stamped us, we claim, for life. They are all French.

"Jean-Louis Barrault in *Les Enfants du Paradis*. Remember? My God, that face! They talk about Garbo's face. But not in a league with Barrault's."

"Gérard Philippe in *Le Diable au Corps*. When he leaned his head against Micheline Presle's stomach. Do you know I have never loved *anyone* like I loved Gérard Philippe?"

"That picture of Camus lighting a cigarette. *Not* bad."

I nod, smiling, at that last. I know that photograph. Only I replace Camus's head with my husband's.


WE WENT TO IRELAND, too. Once, long before he knew he was ill, my father had said, "Ah, Mary Lee. I want to walk on Stephen's Green before I die." So now, I told my husband, I have to do it for him. Loving me, always treating me like a student, just beginning to treat me like a patient, B. agreed.

We walked on Stephen's Green and saw the Book of Kells and shopped for linen placemats, and one night we called on a friend of B.'s, an English professor from Berkeley who was living in a rundown Dublin hotel while he worked on a Yeats variorum. B. had known Tom at Wesleyan, where he taught for a year or so after refusing to sign California's loyalty oath. So had another of B.'s English professors, as had one of mine, and since all three were livelier than most of our respective college's English faculty, we found them yet another reason to feel superior to the West Coast. Such a stupid place, to force its best to flee eastward!

Because Tom was older than we, and B.'s former teacher besides, we treated him with a certain deference. He lectured; we listened and sipped Irish whiskey out of tooth glasses.

Tom knew Yeats's daughter and his widow, the spirit-writer, and one day they had invited him to dinner. He asked, "May I follow an old California custom and bring the wine?" and Mrs. Yeats said, "Do you think the unicorn will mind?"

"And I thought to myself," he said, laughing and rocking on his long crane's legs, " 'My God, this is *it*. I'm at the source. It was the unicorn that guided her hand, and that in turn guided Yeats!' And then I found out the Unicorn was the name of the restaurant she was taking me to!"

I looked around the room, at the faded ceiling decorations, which I liked to think were by Angelica Kauffmann but probably weren't, and at the pile of manuscripts on his desk. They were Yeats's, in small crabbed writing, and mine for the touching. I looked around at the other guests, young men mostly, in raincoats, half of whom seemed to be named Padraic. The dim room, the Irish cast: they could have shot *The Informer* in that room.

There was a lot of backtalk and backbiting and a lot of high-flying hopes tempered with cynicism, and an unspoken but audible conviction that nobody and nothing in that room would ever get off the ground. (One man, a poet and anthologist, did, and I see his name sometimes, but flying low.) That evening was one of a thousand like it, I suppose, for most of the people in that room. But not for me. For me, it was like being at the heart of Ireland—the bitter heart, my father would have said.

We had read about a spa named Lisdoonvarna and went there, to find a small town, gray and ugly and smelling of peat like most Irish towns. When we saw its shabby old hotel we laughed, and when we asked a little girl standing in the doorway if that candy store on the corner sold newspapers, she said, "By God they do!" and again we laughed. We laughed some more when we saw the swaybacked mattress and the net curtains and the chipped bureau, but I stopped laughing when my husband led me to the bed.

I did what I was supposed to do. I always did, watching while the softness in B.'s face slid into rock and then out again into near-tears.

"Why, Mary Lee?" he asked. "What's wrong with me?"

"It's not you," I said. "It's me. I can't get *out.*"

There was another hotel, in the countryside, a nineteenth-century version of a medieval castle that looked like a cardboard cutout pasted against Ireland's forever clouding and unclouding sky. Whether it was actually run by nuns or just had an order living on the grounds we never knew, but we would pass a clump of them every morning—red-faced, hearty, plopping through the mud in big rubber boots. "Chaucerian!" we would say, delighted.

Meals were taken in a dismal, drafty, high-ceilinged hall that stank of disinfectant and were served by shy young girls with soft voices and thick, wind-reddened legs. We slept in a cottage down the road that had one room, so small that the double bed nearly filled it, as crowded with holy pictures and mass cards as a chapel at Lourdes. Fornicate in a room like that? Better Castel Gandolfo.

During the day we drove over treeless hills, past pewter-colored ponds and midge-tented bogs and tumbles of limestone while I read aloud from the guidebook about what battle was here, which queen buried there. It seemed that we were driving through an enormous boneyard, that Ireland had a subterranean scaffolding made of skeletons. And because there were no houses between us and the soil, no human barriers, I felt myself sliding into that soil, slithering past the bones.

We drove to Sligo, to a graveyard on the outskirts of town. Chickens were pecking their way through the rough grass and the dried wreaths, and the stones all bore inscriptions like "Here lies" and "Sacred to the memory of." Except for one. That one stood tall at the head of a long, sunken slab and read, "Cast a cold eye / On life, on death. / Horseman, pass by." My husband photographed me standing beside Yeats's grave, wearing an odd belted coat we called my Gertrude Stein coat and a silent face. Not surprising. I am talking to my father. I am saying, "Look at me, Papa. Look where I am."

◈ 2 ◈

$\mathcal{O}$NCE B. SAID that if I had not married him, I would have spent my life alone in a room cluttered with old I. Miller boxes (shoes were my only extravagance) stuffed with dollar bills. I believed him. I think I was dependent from the beginning, but maybe I was being drained of will. Certainly I was being drained of blood. My menstrual periods had turned into hemorrhages, and coming home at night, I would have to sit and catch my breath on the second flight of stairs before going into our apartment. But if I was Mina Murray, it was because I wanted to be.

No, this discussion is too fanciful, the comparison too arty. Besides, the subject is academic now, serving only as an amusement on evenings when I cannot sleep and conduct dialogues with this woman I used to be but have never understood. All I am sure of is that by the time I went to work for *Vogue,* my husband was to me what a piling is to a barnacle and I, dangerously anemic, weighed 103. "You're so *thin,*" the stubby little woman who was my boss would snap, slapping my waist with a flat palm. She was jealous, I think.

I was at *Vogue* because one April evening while I was bent over the begonias in the windowboxes Jerry had made us, which I cultivated as assiduously as if they were gardens, B. came home with some news. By now he was in the trade department of a big publishing house and in on all the gossip. The literary editor of *Harper's Bazaar* had told him that *Vogue* was looking for a feature writer. Maybe I should apply for the job.

My rich great-aunt, who (like others of her ilk) dressed mostly in bouclé suits slung with dead foxes, scoured *Vogue* every month to see what "they"—an indefinable entity to whom she and my mother paid constant obeisance—were wearing. "Why don't you enter that contest, that Prix de Paris?" she had said. Uninterested but obliging, I entered the competition, which was for college seniors and involved questions like "What is style?" Having done the bare minimum on the assignments, I was startled when I was named a runner-up. *My God,* I thought when I received the congratulatory letter, *I might have won this thing.*

Working for *Vogue,* like working for *Mademoiselle,* would be like eating marshmallows all the time. Even so, writing "Jerry Lewis, thin, dark, and crazy-nuts funny" struck me as a big step up from writing "Plum-perfect silk taffeta, pleated to within an inch of its life."

B. unearthed tear sheets of my only example of nonfashion copy—eight hundred or so words about four female novelists—and dictated the letter with which I sent them to Condé Nast's personnel director, a former gym teacher with the manner, and command, of a mother superior. A few weeks later I found myself sitting in *Vogue*'s enormous waiting room, which was furnished with the kind of spindly chairs and tables I knew from Miss Dutton's Tearoom in Providence, Rhode Island, and painted eau de Nile and silver. "Found myself" because, strictly speaking, I had not really arrived there under my own steam.

Would that I had had a sense of the ridiculous! Would that I had not been as sober as an owl, as judgmental as Cotton Mather! I might have dined out on life in *Vogue*'s feature department. Instead I stayed in to cry.

What a cast! Were the women who worked on fashion magazines like *Vogue* in the late fifties crazier than the ones who work on them today? (*Mademoiselle,* but for its fashion editors, attracted more bookish types, the kind who later staffed publishing houses.) Or is it that I, small-town and shy, saw anyone whose sophistication exceeded mine as exotic? I have given the matter much thought, another of my dialogues for sleepless nights, and have decided on the former. The late fifties at *Vogue,* and presumably *Bazaar,* represented the madwoman's last hurrah.

My researcher—the title given to secretaries at the magazine so they would not realize they were secretaries—was small, pretty, eager, and married to a homosexual. She had met him in Paris during her (and his) junior year abroad, and with its being Paris and her having read a lot and him wanting to write a lot, she confused him with André Gide and was wed.

They lived on the Upper West Side, next door to the fiction editor of *Esquire,* into whose apartment they could peer from their bedroom window. The fiction editor, who didn't know of their presence and indeed never met them, worked nights at his kitchen table under their constant surveillance. Aided by binoculars, they would try to spot the moment when his eyes fell on one of the husband's manuscripts and thereby study his facial reactions.

Their night watches struck me as peculiar, as did her happy smile when she told me she was leaving him of whom she spoke so lovingly, so I wasn't surprised when her parents swept into New York and had her committed to a sanatorium. She was a not atypical employee.

I should add that on the second day I worked at *Vogue,* I was told never to use her as a researcher, since she was unreliable. Since good typing was beyond her as well, I soon decided that her real role, apart from bringing in the tea and cookies that arrived on our desks every day at four, was to be one of the cloud of butterflies hired by the personnel department to decorate the place and disguise the fact that the rest of the employees were worker bees or praying mantises.

The second researcher was a butterfly, too, a tall dim girl from Bernardsville, New Jersey, who spent every weekend in Maine with her fiancé's family, flown there by the family plane. Once, grumbling slightly about having lost a brooch at a wedding reception, she brought me the insurance form so I could check her spelling and I saw that the pin was valued at $3,000, or more than half her salary. Again, a not atypical employee.

She had literary ambitions and wrote occasional captions, which, like all our captions, were thick with adjectives and strong verbs and adhered to the rule of three: each subject got three modifiers. A movie actress might be "beautiful, brainy, and unexpectedly bizarre"; a movie actor, "russet-haired, impish, and crinkle-grinned." Eighteenth-century artists were often called upon. All fair-haired women looked like Greuzes to us; and Brigitte Bardot was compared to Boucher's Mademoiselle O'Murphy. A small woman was invariably a Tanagra figurine, and when in doubt we relied on "extraordinary."

The woman with whom I shared an office—a perfect cube with two old desks, a cracked ceiling, peeling paint, and a travel poster depending from one strip of Scotch tape—was a rarity, a combination butterfly and worker bee. Her hair bubbled blond and her eyes flashed blue and she spoke with an international accent, crisp and faintly British.

Her former husband, the author of "the definitive book on the Argentine pampas," she said, had run through all her money, and she was living in a small apartment on Park Avenue. She slept there, dressed there, received her dinner dates there, but never saw the inside of the kitchen unless she was pouring herself a morning glass of orange juice. No embassy gave a dinner party without her, since she spoke four or five languages and could be depended upon to beguile all visiting foreigners. She had been the girlfriend of a famous movie star and a close friend of a famous conductor and, desperate to remarry, would one day land a French diplomat—"It was a *coup de foudre*, Mary, an absolute *coup de foudre*"—whose previous marriage she dismissed by saying, "The first was when he was very young, so we'll overlook *that*, and the second was to a Pole, which doesn't count because nobody can stay married to a Pole."

Under the bubbles, however, was a hard head and, I found, surprised because she prattled of her Virginia birth in such a way as to make one think she was every Byrd, Lee, and Carter rolled into one, a lapsed Catholicism of the Irish variety. Whenever one or the other of us was called to the mat by our editor, we exchanged signs of the cross and laugh-punctuated Hail Marys.

Down the hall worked Margaret Case, the society editor, though she was never known by so definitive and essentially déclassé a title. A friend to the rich, a brute to her researchers, she was not unkind to me. When I had to write about Newport, she hovered over the phone while I called the wife of the man who had revived the old Newport Casino to ask about the exact color of the new shingles, and, satisfied that I had not shamed *Vogue* with my gaucherie, proceeded to put a little trust (not much) in my intelligence. When she finished the draft of a letter to the princesse de Rethy, the king of Belgium's consort, for instance, she brought it to me for editing, although I was, still am, the last person to ask about protocol and royalty. When she had to make phone calls about a sad, poor sister, I think it was, she made them from my office, trusting that I would not talk.

When I wrote of somebody's "magnificent Venetian palazzo," she told me to strike "magnificent." "I've seen better," she growled. And when (or so I was told) she talked the archbishop of Canterbury into being photographed by Penn or somebody like Penn, she ended the telephone conversation with a peremptory "And wear your robes!" One month she went to Greece, and I, excited at the prospect of anyone's going to Greece, asked her if she had been there before. "Only on the Onassis yacht," she said.

Miss Case had no jewelry, no jewelry that counted anyway, and whenever I went into her office she was phoning someone called "Darling Vava" and telling him that Mrs. Luce said she could borrow her sapphires for that evening and would he please get them out and she'd send her researcher for them. There was something noble about her, I thought, struggling into a girdle and an evening gown night after night and smearing orange lipstick across her thin, impatient mouth.

A long time later, after she had forgotten my name and where she had known me, we shared an elevator. She remembered my face and said, "Tell me. I just got a letter from a friend's daughter who wants to work for a magazine. Tell me. Was typing a great help to you in your career?" "Yes, it was," I said, and we never spoke again, although I often saw her hailing cabs. When she killed herself, jumping fourteen stories naked under the plaid raincoat that was her all-weather uniform, I was truly sorry, because she had been nice to me, knowing that I knew she was an outsider, never mind the rich friends, and liked her anyway.

Now we come to my editor, Allene Talmey, Allene who was as short and firmly packed as a Boston bull and had a Boston bull's bright brown eyes. She never showed up before eleven in the morning and never left before seven at night, and she worked out of a small, plain office with a Tamayo of a watermelon on one wall. Her desk and desk chair were mounted on a thick pad, presumably to save the rug. But the pad also served to raise her above whomever she was talking to, which always struck me as the point.

On my first day at *Vogue,* she dumped on my desk a pile of research, all of it in French, which was to help me in my first assignment: deep captions, as we called them, for some Penn photographs of elderly French notables. No one, certainly not she, had ever asked me if I read French. It was an assumption, as taken for granted there as one's washing one's hands before leaving the ladies' room. It was also, less innocently, a way of separating the sheep from the goats.

I do read French, so I passed the test. The test I could not pass was lining up the requisite modifiers, at least one of which had to be unexpected, tap-dancing through the middle and coming up with a smash finish. When I would go to Allene for help, she would tell me that what I had done was wrong, all wrong, but she would never say or show me why. I would study the caption and, not having been given an exit from my sentences and unable to find one on my own, would grow as dizzy and frantic as a rat in a maze.

Where to go for research was another problem. One of the notables was a sculptor of whom I had never heard. When I asked Allene where I could get more information, she told me to go to the owner of the gallery that showed his work. But when the same problem arose with another artist (the notables were certainly that, but they were also obscure) and I suggested going to his dealer, her reply was "Don't you know that's the worst gallery in New York?" She said nothing further, so I returned to my desk, stared at the material, didn't know who else to call, and felt the start of the paralysis that eventually swallowed me.

I would go out to interview the famous, become so involved with talking to them that I forgot their fame and my fear, and return with good, often funny notes. But once I was back in the Graybar Building, where *Vogue* had its offices, and aware that Allene's sharp tongue was about to rip my back, I was terrified. One day she outdid herself—outdid everyone, really, who has ever disliked me. "You have more talent for the quick phrase than anyone I've ever hired," she barked, "but you're not capable of a sustained piece of work."

Using my notes—"After Loren, bones are boring" was perhaps my finest moment—Allene would write the captions, bring them out to be typed, and then, always running scared, wait for our reactions to them. Since they were good within their context and entirely predictable, I had nothing to say, having been raised never to gush or, in my family's parlance, be "Judas-friendly." My silence meant acceptance, but it was construed as criticism, and I was stunned the day she asked, "Do you know how many people you've hurt?"

When I joked of the horror of having to write my fifth caption in one day about women about whom there was little to say except that they had "skin as translucent as a Limoges cup" and "a brave list of charities," she heard of it within seconds and raged at what she called my betrayal. Her secretary and her assistant, linked in the camaraderie of survivorship, let me flounder. Only my friend the bubbly blonde implied that Allene was difficult to work for. "The first few weeks I worked with her . . . well, my dear, I used to go home, sit in the tub, and *weep*. My dear, the bathwater was pure salt." I wish I had known about the walking wounded who were my predecessors, or that one of them had spoken of wanting to kill Allene and claimed she lay in bed at night trying to figure out how to leave the Graybar undetected. It might have given me a new perspective.

By then, however, I had no perspective on anything, and certainly not *Vogue*. I had even begun to believe in "People Are Talking About." This was a page, written primarily by Allene from material collected by her minions, that ran in almost every issue. Finding "People" items was a nightmare. If we were lucky, we could come up with sentences like "People Are Talking About . . . the bluesy, cigarette-rasp with which the astonishing Elaine Stritch saws through 'You Took Advantage of Me' . . . the way the brilliant young senator from Massachusetts, John F. Kennedy, is capturing the nation's imagination." Unlucky, we were reduced, as one contributor once was, to ". . . the music piped into the treatment rooms at Sloan-Kettering during chemotherapy."

I wrote a "People" page all by myself once, when Allene was on holiday—"on holiday," so snugly British, was *Vogue*'s preferred term for two weeks with pay—and Jessica Daves, the magazine's faintly frumpy editor-in-chief, suddenly wanted one. With the bull terrier no longer a room away, my pencil flew. Once she was back, it traced boxes and initials and trees with fluffy tops, but no sentences. Allene threatened to fire me, but I said no, you must not, because I have never failed at anything and cannot bear to.

One autumn afternoon I walked to Saks Fifth Avenue to buy a dress I had seen in an advertisement. I had never cared much about clothes, except for the samples I bought from McCardell's back room, and was vain only of my very narrow feet. The one mirror in our apartment was on the door of the medicine cabinet. Mornings, I would sling on something, twist my head over my shoulder to see if my slip showed, and that was it. So I did not know what I looked like until I saw myself in the dressing room's full-length mirror: ghastly in orange, my cheeks as hollow as if I had lost my back teeth, my eyes as staring as my father's just before he died, my arms like sticks.

Only Jell-O would go down at lunch, Jell-O and the occasional nutted cream cheese sandwich at the Chock Full O'Nuts across Lexington from the Graybar, and the Dexamyl that Dr. Franklin had prescribed was robbing me of what little appetite was left. B. joked about my logorrhea, about how I would elbow him awake at midnight with "Did I ever tell you what my grandfather said to me when I was ten?" and "Do you remember the time we went to the basketball game and . . . ?" but he could not joke any more after he took me, for a treat, to a restaurant named Teddy's.

Teddy's was a treat because it was expensive and because we had convinced ourselves the other customers were Mafia. It was a treat, too, because it was somewhere around the west end of Canal Street, and the kind of New Yorkers we were turning into love nothing more than eating in a nowhere part of town. The walls above the banquettes were lined with photographs of Teddy's movie-star diners, and we sat directly under one of Elizabeth Taylor, who was at that moment supposed to be dying. It should have been a wonderful evening, what with the rain falling sadly on Canal Street and the beautiful young actress so tragically breathing her last and B., who looked so much like Montgomery Clift in *A Place in the Sun,* sitting beside me. But when the steamed lobster I'd ordered arrived, out of its shell and lying naked on a bed of lettuce, I thought it looked like a boiled baby. Perhaps it was the Dexamyl; perhaps it was Allene. All I know is that when I saw that lobster nestled in its iceberg lettuce cradle, I saw a murdered child.

I lasted for about nine months, or maybe it was seven, until the winter morning when I wrote a deep caption about an actress. It was a monument to adjectives, strong verbs, and the rule of three, and Allene liked it. She even smiled. Still, there was something wrong—she didn't say what—with the last sentence. I slid the paper off her desk, stood up, and did what I should have done a long time before. I said, "I quit."

"You can't do that," Allene barked, then, terrier to the last, added, "I don't care if you spend the rest of the week in the infirmary, but no one just walks out of here."

"I do," I replied, and left her office.

Pausing only to pick up the stone from Prince Edward Island that I was using as a paperweight and the cellophane bag of dried apricots with which I was trying to beef up my blood, I ran for the elevator and home. There I did what I always did when I had lost my temper. I cried.

B. took me to the Berkshires the following weekend, to an inn that served up roast ham and raisin sauce and four-poster beds and cranberry-glass tumblers. We had longed to go to an inn like that, and to auctions, where we could at last buy the hutch and dry sink that would make us feel calm and cozy and truly married. But by now I was seeing the world through the wrong end of a telescope. Everything and everyone was very far away, too far away to touch or be touched by. One afternoon, so late that shadows were already bluing the snow, I took a long solitary walk beside the river. Walking, the mere act of moving my legs, had always brought me back into connection with the physical. But this time I returned shaking, because I believed that someone, shielded by the tall snowbanks that margined the water, was tracking my every step.

A few months later, a woman, a stranger, called me at home. My replacement at *Vogue,* she had found my name in the files and was wondering if I could tell her something about her boss, because no one else would talk. I didn't talk either. I thought the phone was bugged.

Years later, I ran into Allene at a cocktail party. She congratulated me on what I was doing and I congratulated her on what she was doing, half expecting the playful slap and the sputtered "You're so *thin!*" Then we both disappeared into the smoke and the chatter and the palazzo pajamas and the dry vermouth on the rocks, and I never saw her again. I never forgave her, either, not for being demanding but for being unable to resist piercing an all-too-visible jugular vein.

A MAN AND A WOMAN are sitting at night in a living room in Greenwich Village. It is nicely furnished and so are they. Both are reading. The woman is lonely, she is always lonely, and she would like to ask her husband if she could sit in his lap. He would like that. But if she does, she will feel his penis rise and push against her buttocks, and that will shock and sicken her. When he stands up she would like to go to him. But if she does, he will press his groin against hers and his penis will swell and she will loosen her arms and push him away. She would like to look at him. But if she does, he will mistake the glance and cross the room to her. Therefore she does not dare to ask to sit in his lap or hug him or even look at him. So she is silent and motionless and he is silent and motionless, and the one keeps her head bent over Ngaio Marsh and the other keeps his head bent over Philip Rahv.

It is a few days before Christmas. The woman has put up a tree and the man has helped decorate it and both are especially pleased with a jeweled butterfly she bought on Madison Avenue. Christmas cards march across the quasi-mahogany sideboard and wrapping paper spills from the couch. She has made cookies and he has made elaborate efforts to hide his presents to her in their apartment's one closet. She was excited about Christmas coming and December's briskness and her forays along Fifth Avenue, because he is beginning to make enough money for them to spend a bit. But now she has stopped talking and cannot hear when he speaks, because today she saw a man holding a little girl's hand while together they looked in a window of FAO Schwarz and suddenly she wanted to be dead.

An evening a day or two later. The man and woman are walking home from dinner at a friend's house. There was a girl there, younger than she and even shyer, and because the woman felt sorry for her she "brought her out," as her mother would have put it, and made her comfortable. The man is proud of his wife. "You couldn't have done that a few years ago," he says, and the woman grins. She has just received an A+.

Any Tuesday or Thursday at 4:30 in a psychiatrist's office in Schwab House, on the Upper West Side, which is where all psychiatrists seemed to have their offices. Given the Jewish and Austrian accents that overlay the area like icing on a cake, the woman assumes the placement brings Freud's acolytes closer to him.

The woman is sitting, arms and legs crossed, on a Barcelona chair. The couch to her left, also from Mies, has a clean paper towel, changed for each patient, at its head. But not for her. She has never lain on the couch and she never will.

The doctor is smiling, because the woman can be rather amusing, but although she talks a lot, she says nothing. After their fifty-minute session, she walks to the Seventy-second Street stop of the IRT and descends the narrow stairs to the track. When she hears the train coming, she steps behind a pillar and closes her eyes. She is afraid that if she sees it, she will jump.

The woman loves her husband. No, incorrect. She worships her husband. But she wants to go to her father. Suicide, however, is out of the question. She is a coward, and besides, her church, whose grasp she has never quite managed to elude, will not let her. So what is she to do? Writing is out of the question: she believes what she was told, that she is "not capable of a sustained piece of work." Another job is out of the question: she has already worked for two magazines and where else can she go? A baby is out of the question: her gynecologist says she is too underweight to risk pregnancy. There is nothing for it but to move.

# 21 Perry Street

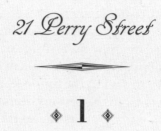

SOMEWHERE I have read that an image John Fowles could not get out of his head, of a hooded figure alone on a dock, was what prompted him to write *The French Lieutenant's Woman*. There is an image I cannot get out of my head, either, that of a man standing in the areaway of our third apartment, and although it has never prompted me to write a novel, it has always struck me as a compelling first page.

The page, in précis, would read something like this. A young man and a young woman are walking home from the late show at the Waverly Theater in Greenwich Village, where they live. It is a hot summer night, and their steps are as slow as their conversation is lazy. As they round the corner of Perry Street, they see, silhouetted against the white petunias the young woman has planted in an old concrete urn, a man standing in the areaway of their apartment. He is motionless. Perhaps he is listening to something. Or waiting.

In reality, the young man and woman keep on walking, passing their apartment as if it were not theirs at all. When they return, ten or so minutes later, from their circuit of the block, the man is gone. The hands that gripped their hearts relax. They can enter the areaway, unlock the second gate, go home.

On my first page, however, the young couple decide to dare the intruder in the areaway. Maybe it is just that he is at the wrong address. The night is dark, and all these houses, brick with tall stoops, look alike. So they open the first gate, the latched one that abuts the sidewalk, and ask the man if they can help him. He mutters something, then moves toward the gate they have just opened. Relieved, they turn to the second gate, and the young man brings out his keys. Then it happens. The stranger swivels and plunges a knife in the young man's back. The woman, her shoulders hunched and her own back pressed against the areaway's brownstone facing, watches her husband die. Meanwhile the stranger, the sound of his footsteps diminishing as he hurries west, runs toward the Hudson River and the docks.

I see that man standing there, against those blazing white petunias, every time I pass 21 Perry Street. Suppose we had taken the dare, suppose we had not circled the block? Maybe what happened on that first page would have happened in fact. Maybe I would have been a widow; maybe there would have been no Kate, no Mag, no memories. That I might have been the one with the knife between the shoulder blades never occurs. Like most people, most Westerners anyway, I have a sneaking suspicion I am immortal.

But why—aside from the fact that there was indeed once a man lurking in the areaway—bring so heavy an imaginative burden to so innocuous a place as the basement apartment of 21 Perry Street? Easy. That is where my life as an adult began.

St. John's Church owned a lot of property: five or six houses on West Eleventh Street and seven or eight more on Perry Street, which ran parallel. Between the two, and hidden from passersby, was perhaps the most secret of all the Village's secret gardens. It was very large, with two fountains, a small stone altar, private sitting areas at the rear of each basement apartment, a towering catalpa tree which in spring had a haunting, peppery scent, rose of Sharon bushes and spirea and a community of box turtles, invisible in winter and shy in summer. Once there had been peacocks, too, spreading their tails along the paved pathways.

All St. John's tenants had keys to the garden, and on summer Saturday afternoons B. and I would unlock an inconspicuous wooden door on Eleventh Street, carry our cheese sandwiches through the cool dark tunnel that led to the minister's small enclosure, cross it, and enter the garden, to sit for hours on the stone bench that circled the catalpa and dream about getting a basement apartment. It was hot and still in the garden—street sounds rarely penetrated—and though our butts were pocked by the bench's granular surface and our backs ached, we seldom left before sunset.

Finally a family on Perry Street moved out and we leaped, signing the lease before we even took a good look at what we were getting. The previous tenant was a set designer, with a presto-chango approach to décor. The furniture, for instance, had been spray-painted *in situ,* which meant the walls it hid were blotched with various colors. He had made a dollhouse for his daughter by building shelves in an unused fireplace. Filled, it was charming. Empty, it was a fireplace clogged with splintery boards. The kitchen stank of cats.

No matter. We scrubbed and deodorized and hung wallpaper along the kitchen's long east wall, and Jerry built bookcases in the small back room we called the study. He built bookcases in the living room, too, on either side of the fireplace, while B. hefted the shelves and handed out nails, as eager as he had been on Twenty-first Street to make himself a home.

An interior decorator could not date that apartment—B. and I were equally unwilling to enter department stores and indifferent to trends, but for our Paul McCobb couches and line-shaded standing lamps—but I think a cultural historian could. The little foreign matchbooks came from West Fourth Street and were very Village. The Chinese export porcelain cups, each of which had at least one hairline crack and held cigarettes, were very New England, as was the white ironstone pitcher crammed, depending on the season, with chrysanthemums or laurel leaves. The Spode dinner service spoke of a trip or two to London, the copper pots in the kitchen of a trip or two to Paris, and the reproduction eighteenth-century silverplate of an inability to afford sterling combined with a rejection of stainless steel modernism. The two wine racks in the coat closet told of someone venturing beyond Soave and Chianti, and the copies of *Tropic of Cancer, Tropic of Capricorn,* and *Les Amours Jaunes* argued junior year abroad. Almost everything from West Eleventh Street had come with us, and now we had a real Windsor chair.

In the house next door lived May Swenson, a stocky woman whose hair was cropped short over her bullet head and whom we used to see peering from her second-floor window into the garden. Justin O'Brien—"the Gide man," B. explained—had a duplex a few doors down but was seldom in residence. His Chinese cook, though, was forever getting drunk and forever setting fire to the kitchen.

A family with a lot of money moved in across the way, and when the husband made what the head of the garden committee, a skinny little woman who wore high-top sneakers, perceived as encroachments on the community space, she chased him down West Fourth Street with the hatchet she'd been using to kill privet. The tall, Slavic-looking woman who had the floor-through above O'Brien and claimed to be a Russian princess had French perfumes delivered from Bigelow's Drugstore and, seemingly unacquainted with cloth diapers, kept her young son in so many layers of disposables that one could have driven a truck between his legs.

The middle-aged woman who lived in the garden apartment to our right was a buyer of notions for a large department store and had never married, she told me, because everyone in her family was crazy and she did not want to pass on the taint. Al, an ex–tap dancer, and Bud, who hooked rugs, strung their terrace with fairy lights ("Ho, ho," we chortled) at Christmastime and gave tasteful little dinners, more tasteful even than ours. The garden apartment next to theirs was lived in by a former nightclub singer and girl-about-town in her late thirties who got herself knocked up by a young stranger. She married him and promptly turned from continental layabout to Italian mama, a switch so startling to her amiable, fat-necked groom that he, starved for glamour, had an affair with Al.

I loved living at 21 Perry Street. Finally I could do again what I had done for all the years of my childhood. I could spy.

My family spied. If my aunt was looking out the window and a neighbor's car drove by, she would say, "I wonder where the Armstrongs are going this time of day." The lights going on next door would evoke my mother's "Guess the Tingleys are home," and my grandmother, who spent every afternoon sitting in her bay window, was timekeeper for the twice-weekly meetings of the woman who lived across the street and the man with whom she was having an affair. "There goes Ralph," Ganny would say as he turned his car into her driveway, and "There he goes again" an hour later. But they never gossiped, not even among themselves, nor did they want to know more than what they had seen with their own eyes. Watching the play was sufficient, and the house, with its two porches and big windows, gave them front seats. Small wonder that I, too, grew up a spectator. I had spent too many hours with my grandmother to be otherwise.

Now, instead of sitting with Ganny, with my head, like hers, turned toward Hope Street, I walked the paths of St. John's Garden, watching for shadows beyond the windows, pausing to chat with whoever was sitting under the catalpa tree. If I was not really at home with everyone, neither was I a stranger to anyone, and if all my acquaintances were slightly skewed, well then, so was I.

It was strange, being idle. A skinny little black man—"dustman to the literati" we used to call him, because he worked for a lot of Village editors—did the cleaning while I lay on the chaise longue we had bought for the bedroom and read. I read Dorothy Sayers and thought myself Harriet Vane, I wrote a fan letter to John Dickson Carr, I became the self-styled "greatest living expert" on the British working-class novel, and I argued with B. about Salinger, whom he loved and whom I, with the plodding Gentile's instinctive distrust of the quicksilver Jew, found too clever by half. Once outside the house, though, I seldom delivered an opinion. It would not have done, not with my not having an official position in our world. The wives I remember from dinner parties, the ones around my age, at least, were usually silent, and those who were not talked too much, anxious to get a word in, anxious to show that they, too, had read Wellek and Warren. The worst of the latter were those married to writers. Tell him you liked chapter seven in particular and she would say, "We worked awfully hard on that one." Eventually, "writer's wife" became the term B. and I used for all suckerfish.

None of us had mastered charm, and the only time we saw it was when the dinner guest was English. A visiting English editor never had to buy a meal or a drink or pay for his own theater ticket, nor did he ever try to. He simply opened his mouth and let the clipped vowels roll out.

My dinner parties grew ever grander, culminating in the evening I served beef Wellington. "*Gourmet*'s," I said, when asked. That was how one answered culinary questions then. Another guest, usually a woman, would raise an inquisitive eyebrow, and the hostess would say "*Gourmet*'s" or "Dione's," and, later, "Michael's" or "Julia's." We all attempted mousse au chocolat, we all aspired to Pavilion, and we all reveled in Joseph Wechsberg. If we had read M. F. K. Fisher (but none of us had yet), we would have reveled in her, too.

Who were "we"? Mostly we were bright young men and their first wives, and now I can scarcely remember anyone's name or face, because we were all interchangeable. What I remember better is the recipes clipped from the *Times,* because this was the age of Craig Claiborne, and copper pots from Bazar Français on Sixth Avenue, and the timid progression from an after-dinner cognac to an after-dinner marc because the latter was earthier, more real somehow. "I am measuring out my life with coffee spoons," I would say to B. when we came home from that night's dinner party, and together we would preen our feathers, serene in the belief that we spoke the same language. Certainly we shared allusions.

But what was I to do with myself? Maybe this was my chance to *write*. If I italicize the word, it is because the act was something I approached on my knees. Turning out copy and captions took only cleverness, but *writing* took—oh God, it made me nervous just to think about it. B.'s parents sent me a check for a course in short-story writing at the New School. Terrified at being put to the test, I spent the money on clothes.

I—we, really, because it was B. who invariably propelled me to action—wrote to Columbia for the graduate school catalogue. It was not too late to become the academic my father had always wanted me to be. But reading it, sprawled as always on the chaise longue, I suddenly remembered how it was to have to scrawl teeny-tiny notes—"outgrowth of Copernican cosmogony," "antithetical contradiction in metaphysical tradition"—in the margins of my anthologies, and how the late-afternoon sun caught chalk dust and suspended it in midair. I remembered how hard it was to keep one's lids from dropping over one's eyes and that I never wanted to read Thomas Hobbes again. The next day I stuck the catalogue in the wastepaper basket under the kitchen sink.

"Mees Cantwell," said Dr. Franklin, plump in his Barcelona chair. "Tell me one thing that you want." As if I knew! If I had known, I would not have been sitting in this small office, clearly the "junior" bedroom of 4 1/2 rms., util. incl., while traffic whined on West End Avenue and other people went about their business.

Maybe it's different if you were born here. Maybe then you are deaf to the buzzing and the beating of wings. But I had come from out of town, and to me New York was a hive. You could not just live here. You had to be somebody, do something, it didn't matter what. You were not a part of the city unless you were on a bus or a subway and on your way to an office or a factory or a school-room. How could you know New York if you had not bolted your lunch in a coffee shop or had not had your subway stall under the East River or had not had to stand on the bus for thirty blocks be-cause it was rush hour? You could not. The best way to know New York, to learn to love New York, was to let it wear you out. When B. came home at night, I envied him his exhaustion.

I had always assumed that someday I would have a baby. Once, when we had lived on East Twenty-first Street, we had even had a scare. At least, it was a scare for me. A doctor thought I was pregnant and insisted on a test, and over the weekend while we were waiting for the results, I stared at the ruin of my undefined ambitions and B. smiled foolishly and called me his "little seed-bearer."

By now, though, a lot of our college classmates had had chil-dren and I had taken to staring at Best & Co.'s ads for its Lilliputian Bazaar. They were of fat-cheeked babies, dream babies, like the babies in *The Blue Bird,* who toddled about heaven wait-ing until their names were called for the journey down to earth. When I visualized a child of my own, I visualized one of those ba-bies. I never gave it a gender; I never even gave it a face. I simply saw myself with something to love lying swaddled in my arms.

"You may have waited too long," my gynecologist said, the same gynecologist who had told me that I must not get pregnant because I was too thin and anemic to carry a child. Now he was telling me that I probably had endometriosis, which he described as a "premature aging of the womb." I was still in my twenties. Stunned and dizzy, I wept, and he, eager to get me out of his office, called B. and told him to take me home.

We went to Europe for five weeks, but all that remains of the trip is an image of myself taking a shortcut through the food section of Fortnum & Mason on the way to our hotel, a shabby old place on Jermyn Street. It was about five o'clock, and customers were flocking the counters to buy vol-au-vents and those ghastly English gateaux before going home to happy families. I was going to a high-ceilinged hotel room that lacked only a hanging man to perfect its décor, and nobody needed me anywhere. That my husband might have needed me was beyond imagining.

I thought I could be necessary to a child; it was impossible to believe that someone like myself had anything to offer an adult. I was sterile, mentally as well as physically, and I was sick. B. had said so. By now his "I didn't know how sick you really are" had the force of my mother's long-ago "Why can't you be like everybody else?"

When I looked into a mirror, I was surprised to find a face looking back at me. I know I was skinny, but I do not know if I had nice breasts or a flat stomach or firm thighs. But my hands I remember: the nails short and neatly filed, the only ring my wedding band, the fingers long as a spider's legs. How my husband and I complemented each other! His certainties fed my nothingness; my nothingness fed his certainties; and to this day I can find no fault in either of us. We could not help it.

At the end of the five weeks, B. was to return to New York and I was to take a month's tour of Italy. He had worked out the itinerary with a man who had lived in Rome for many years and knew each and every odd corner, right down to which doorway I should peer through for which view, and was excited for me. What an introduction to the Italian Renaissance! What a way to improve my mind! But a few days before I was to leave, while we were still in London, I canceled the trip.

It was the cold. I was so cold if B. was not there to give me blood. Sometimes I wonder if he knew that for me, being away from him was like being severed from a transfusion tube. It is odd. I never used my married name and bristled when other people did. Alone, however, I whispered it over and over again—"Mrs. L., Mrs. L."—putting myself under its protection.

Back in New York, I applied myself to the asexual, unloving acrobatics of a woman bent on pregnancy, and once a month awoke to the same slow trickle. I would jump from the bed before the blood spotted the sheet, rummage for the Kotex on the closet shelf and the stringy elastic belt in the bureau drawer, and slide into five days of depression, watching my life drain into a boxful of sanitary napkins.

Coincidentally I saw a second gynecologist—I never again wanted to lay eyes on the first—about the recurrent cysts in my breasts. They were painful, but I could not keep my hands away from them, certain that in touching them I was touching my death. The doctor said they were unimportant, but why did I keep covering my chin?

"I guess I'm self-conscious about these pimples."

"Have you ever had acne before?"

"No."

"Are you taking any kind of medication?"

"Yes."

I described the pills the first gynecologist had given me to regulate my menstrual flow.

"Did you know they prevent conception?"

"No. He never mentioned that."

"Do you want children?"

"Oh, yes."

"Well, stop those pills and let me check you out and we'll see what happens."

The next month my period didn't arrive.

On the Saturday night of the weekend over which we waited to hear if the frog had died—"the frog died" was code then for "pregnant"—Jerry, B., and I saw *The Nun's Story* at Radio City Music Hall. "You are, you are," my husband said. "I *know* it." I knew it, too, and made B. and Jerry shield me from the crowds as we left the theater. One bump and that fertilized egg might be dislodged.

On Monday morning I called the doctor's office, and yes, the frog had died. I do not remember whether I called B. I do not re-member whether we celebrated; I do not remember anything ex-cept feeling as cleansed, as scrubbed and laundered and turned inside out, as I did when, in childhood, I left the confessional. I thought God had punished me for having sealed my womb as if it were a Mason jar. But he had not. God loved me.

❖ 2 ❖

My FACE WAS green and nausea was constant, and before the obstetrician prescribed some little pills that were pink on one side and blue on the other, I lived on crackers and mashed potatoes and Schweppes tonic water. At night I would lie in bed fingering the small bumps that surrounded my nipples and pressing my inter-laced hands just above the pubic hair to feel that minute swell. And Jerry disappeared.

No, he did not really disappear. He went back to Seattle, I think, but I am not sure, because I was blind and deaf to anything that did not have to do with my baby. There must have been a leavetaking, and probably a farewell dinner, too, but memory stops at *The Nun's Story* and his guiding hand on my elbow. So Jerry left without my noticing, on what I suppose was a summer day, while the Vermont shopkeeper we met a few months later, a gimpy little bird who said, "That's the stuff!" when B. told him I was pregnant, is stamped forever on my mind. My husband photographed me that afternoon, standing beside our tiny car, exultant, hair flying, Shetland pullover caching the tiny bulge. Our first photograph: my daughter's and mine.

Now when I lay on the chaise longue it was to unpack and pack again the little sweaters knitted by my mother-in-law and the lucky booties sent me by the old woman who lived next door to Ganny and the lacy white blanket, sweater, and cap I made for the day we brought the baby home. Each was held up, smoothed out, refolded, then laid reverently in white tissue paper and returned to the quasi-mahogany sideboard, which was once again a quasi-mahogany bureau. I read Alan Guttmacher on babies until the book was tattered, showing B. line drawings of the fetus at four months, five months. "Now she's got fingernails," I'd say. "Now she can suck her thumb . . . has hair . . . would live if she were premature." At a cocktail party, a man told me I was the most attractive woman in the room, not remembering (though I did) that we had met a year before, when I was thin and empty and invisible.

My happiness was a blanket around our house, around B., too. The night the diaper service man came, B. marveled at the choices and was tempted by polka dots. I, matronly and self-assured, smiled fondly at my little boy, my husband, and said the plain bird's-eye would do.

She was "Michel," this dolphin that swam inside my belly, rolling and diving and kicking, because we thought the name non-definitive, but she was really Katherine because we were sure she was a girl. Even so, it was "Michel due"—no sense in tempting fate—that I wrote in my pocket diary under March 17, amused by our baby's birthday. Papa would have laughed and sent her green carnations.

I, too, was swimming, covering the city with the slow, easy crawl with which my aunt traveled Bristol Harbor, accompanied by my baby. We would go for walks, my child and I, and converse for miles. I had always talked to myself, moving my lips and tightening my eyebrows and catching odd glances from passersby, and now I talked to her. "Look, Michel," I would say when we passed the old Northern Dispensary down on Christopher Street. "This is where Edgar Allan Poe went when he had a bad cold." And, as I settled heavily into my seat at Carnegie Hall, "Now, Michel, we're going to listen to Beethoven." My baby was safe, so safe, because she was enclosed in me, and nothing and no one could hurt her while I lived. And if I died? Well, then, we would die together and neither of us would be lonely in paradise.

Old ladies were to the left and right of me in the balcony at Carnegie Hall, old ladies who said, "Oh, that Lenny," even when Lenny wasn't conducting. To them, any dark-haired young man on the podium was Bernstein, and to me, too, who never really heard the music, only floated in the sound.

Before the concert—I had subscribed to a Friday afternoon se-ries—I invariably lunched with Sally, a copy editor I had known at *Mademoiselle,* and caught up on the gossip in a country from which I was now very far away. *Charm,* "The Magazine for the Working Woman," had folded, and its editors had been shipped over to *Mlle.,* which meant two people for every job. C.A. had lost her chair early, to a former Hungarian baroness who, blond, blue-eyed, and zaftig, was said to look like something painted on a ceil-ing in Dresden. But B.T.B. was prepared to outsit everyone, and did. So was the beauty editor, the one with the nose that could slit envelopes.

"Really, Mary, you've got to have nerves of steel to survive the tension," Sally would say, and I, knowing that I did not have nerves of steel, would count myself blessed for being able to sit on Ararat and watch the flotsam and jetsam pass by. There was no place I had to be, no appointment but for the doctor's I had to keep, no demand I had to make on myself. All I had to do was be. Be, and prepare a place and a wardrobe for my baby.

Lord & Taylor would not do for a layette, being inextricably linked with the sweaters and Bermuda shorts of a girl I was begin-ning to forget and would not remember again for a long, long time. Saks Fifth Avenue appealed, because both my high school gradua-tion dress and my wedding dress had come from there and I was in-fatuated with what seemed a sort of symmetry. But on the day I went to the children's floor, customers, too many for me to have a saleslady's undivided attention, crowded the long counters. I wanted a serious talk about undershirts and sacques and those lit-tle nightgowns that tie with a string at the bottom. I wanted to know about snowsuits.

The Lilliputian Bazaar did not live up to its newspaper adver-tisements—nothing could have—and in the end I wandered into Bergdorf's, where my wedding garter had come from. Here was a cushioned chair, and a perfumed hush, and a middle-aged woman who spoke of receiving blankets and terry-cloth bibs and baby's lit-tle bonnets.

"You'll want at least three or four of these little sheets," she said, "and I like these little shirts that tie at the side—so much eas-ier than pulling them over baby's head. Oh, and diaper pins. I'll bet you never even thought of diaper pins. See these, how the point is covered so that baby can't possibly be pricked, even if the pin opens by mistake? And then, of course, you'll need rubber pants. Aren't these cute?"

I was joining a club; I was learning the rules, the secret code even. I had never heard of a receiving blanket or a special pin for diapers or a little shirt that tied at the side. "See, B.?" I said when the packages, along with a bassinet, arrived from Bergdorf's. "These shirts are much easier to use than the ones you have to pull over their heads, and the thing about these diaper pins is that they. . . ." He was as thrilled as I.

What a husband he was in those days, what a wonderful father-to-be, poring over Guttmacher, reading and rereading *Thank You, Doctor Lamaze.* If we could have, we, too, like Marjorie Karmel, would have called our doctor from the Café du Dôme in Montparnasse on a night that "was fresh and full of the smell of earth that blows over Paris on a summer night." Instead we would be calling him from a basement apartment in Greenwich Village. Never mind. Hadn't we always told ourselves, and everyone else, that living in the Village was a lot like living on the Left Bank?

I would not be able to Lamaze till the end, we figured, but surely I could do it for a few hours before caving in to twilight sleep or whatever it was they gave you. And wouldn't it be wonderful if I could spare our baby from being born drowsy! So off we went to someplace on the Upper West Side, some small, shabby room with folding chairs, to watch a film on the birth of a baby according to Lamaze.

Being there was like being in the old Needle Trades Auditorium—the same audience, mostly Jewish, with the same fierce thirst for information—and for one sick second or so I was once again waddling down the long corridor to the chair. But when the baby's head began to show, a scarcely visible darkness between the thighs of a grimacing, panting woman, I cheered like the others and exchanged shy smiles with my companions in fecundity.

My Lamaze instructor, Mrs. Bing, was, predictably, on the Upper West Side as well, in an apartment near the Museum of Natural History that was milky with light and had geraniums blooming along the windowsills. Later on, Mrs. Bing got rather famous for being a Lamaze pioneer, and when people told me they had been in one of her classes, I would let drop that I had known her when and had been tutored alone. I was boasting, of course, but I was also giving myself an excuse to recall those winter mornings and the sun scouring Mrs. Bing's uncurtained windows. "Sink contraction, not pain," she would order—her accent, like Dr. Franklin's, was faintly Germanic—and I would obey. "Huff! Now puff! Now do your *effleurage*."

I huffed, I puffed, I did my *effleurage,* brushing my hands in a circular movement over my belly, and when I got home I did it all over again. After dinner, B., my *monitrice,* would sit in the chaise longue, watch in hand, timing me while I, supine on the bed, practiced the three stages of breathing.

"Not long enough! Do it again!" I'd do it again.

"Did you do that *effleurage* right?" Yessir!

It is curious. I can see the white light and the bare floorboards in Mrs. Bing's living room, and the pots of geraniums on the windowsills, but I can no longer see the building. Which one of the big apartment houses up by the museum is it? I cannot tell. No doorway catches my eye, no trees or clumps of bushes clutch at my memory. But it is there somewhere, I know, the place where I huffed and puffed and rubbed my stomach and held my breath for . . . how many counts was it? One of those old behemoths still holds that big, high-ceilinged room, and that room still holds my joy, and if I am sad whenever I am in the neighborhood, it is because it is a cruelty to have known perfect happiness. Up there, up near the dinosaur eggs and the trumpeting elephants, I am once again that young woman with the big belly and my Kate is once again sleeping peacefully in the amniotic sac, and my heart breaks for both of us.

I AWOKE ON MARCH 17, waiting. "They never come when they're supposed to," I told B., and sent him off to work. All day long I waited, dusting the furniture, scrubbing the bathtub, longing for the moment when, like somebody in the movies, I would bend over, clutch my stomach with both hands, and say—to whom? I was alone—"I think it's time." Meanwhile the baby was quiet, scarcely moving, hardly even stretching her legs. I know she could hear, but could she see? Do babies keep their eyes closed until they're born? Or do they open them, look around, study the terrain?

After supper, we went to the movies. With no baby yet in view, of course we would go to the movies. We saw *Our Man in Havana*, in Times Square, where Irish and Irish-for-a-day drunks were roistering down Broadway.

The next morning, on the dot of 8:30, I felt a dull ache in my back, which was repeated about fifteen minutes later.

"The baby's coming," I said, as cool and know-it-all as I had been the day before. "But it's going to take hours, so you just go off to work." My husband, obedient to the superb creature I had become, did as he was told.

So much to do! I had to go to the A & P so that B. would have something to eat for the next few days. Then I had to pick up the slipcovers I had left at the cleaner's so the living room would look nice. Waiting for the cleaner to find them, trying to distract myself from the contractions ("Don't sink pain!" Mrs. Bing was hissing into my ear. "Sink contraction!"), I studied the little plastic bird on the counter. It kept dipping its head, up, down, up, down, toward a glass of water. *I will never forget this bird*, I said to myself. *I will never forget this moment.*

"I'm in labor, I'm in labor," I wanted to shout to the people I passed on Seventh Avenue on the walk home. "Look at me, look at me, look at how it's done!"

On my hands and knees, I crawled around the couch and loveseat, closing the snaps that held the slipcovers to the tapes sewn to their undersides. Finished! I washed every dish, did a last run with the vacuum cleaner. Finished! I ate my favorite lunch, egg salad on white. Finished! And at last I crawled onto the chaise longue with Rose Macaulay's *The Towers of Trebizond*. I loved that book. Who wouldn't love a book that began " 'Take my camel, dear,' said my aunt Dot, as she climbed down from this animal on her return from High Mass"? But after a while I could no longer rise to Macaulay's High Anglican empyrean and dialed B. "Come home," I said, still calm, still grand.

Because we thought overnight cases tacky, bourgeois, my

nightgowns and toothbrush were in a paper shopping bag, along with a handful of lollipops that were supposed to provide glucose when my energy flagged during labor. Together, with B. carrying the shopping bag, we walked out the door and up Perry Street to Seventh Avenue, and together we directed a cabdriver: "Doctors Hospital."

"Doctors Hospital?" the driver said. "I hear that's some place. Jackie Gleason was just there, and they tell me the parties were *something*."

Judy Garland dried out in Doctors Hospital, I believe, and it was a nice place to go after a suicide attempt and an even nicer place to go if you were having a baby, because it had room service. Queenly in my wheelchair, I watched while B. fumbled in his wallet for his Blue Cross card. Gracious even with an enema tube dangling from my backside, I chatted with the nurse while she shaved my pubic hair, faithful to my parents' creed that small talk could raise you above anything. Because I felt the pains—oh, no, the contractions—in my back, B. and my doctor did the *effleurage* for me, circling their hands over my spine while I lay on my left side, facing a bureau and focusing on a drawer pull. Only once was there a break in my Lamaze breathing. B. had ordered a sandwich, and the crunch of the pickle he was chewing distracted me. "Stop that pickle," I said. He stopped.

"Look," the doctor said, rolling me on my back and shining a bridge lamp between my parted knees. What pleasure to lie with my legs spread, pubis shaved, blood trickling, stomach swollen, an inch or so of dark head visible in my vagina, and nothing on a man's face but love and joy.

In the labor room, or so I understood, there were rails on the beds so the maniac maternals wouldn't fall to the floor. But here I was in a wooden four-poster, while a light snow drifted past the window. The window was slightly open, and through it I could hear the faraway whine of traffic fourteen floors down on East End Avenue. Sometimes the curtain rustled; sometimes there was a footfall in the corridor. There was no other sound beyond my "Huh, huh, huh, huuuuuuh." "The baby's crowning," the doctor said to B. "Help me wheel her to the delivery room."

Something happened next, a coincidence, which would be unacceptable in fiction and is barely acceptable in fact. But for one who believed then that the mills of the gods do indeed grind, it seemed reasonable, predictable even. On the way into the delivery room, we were stopped by a doctor who said to my obstetrician, "Do you want any help, Elliott?" He did not recognize me, but I did him. He was the doctor who had said I was too frail to carry a child and medicated me with a contraceptive. "No," I replied before my doctor could open his mouth, and we sailed on.

I had imagined bright lights and white-robed, white-masked nurses flanking the table, not a small, quiet room empty except for a nurse who was putting kidney-shaped bowls in a cabinet. No matter. I needed no encouragement, no towels dabbed on the forehead, only the doctor's "Push . . . stop . . . pant . . . push . . . stop." And at last, "Here's the head . . . I've got the shoulder . . . Mary, it's a girl."

"It's Katherine," I said, and let go of the handgrips.

Dying, even if the crossover is accomplished with a fanfare of bugles and the raising of a golden curtain, cannot be so profound a shock as the birth of a child. Nothing, not all the reading, not all the line drawings, not Mrs. Bing's big cardboard-mounted pictures of a baby traveling down the birth canal, had prepared me for the sight of a human being emerging from between my legs. Katherine had dark hair, two deep dimples, and was yelling.

The nurse, through finally with the kidney-shaped bowls, dried the baby with a towel, slid her into a diaper and a slightly tattered, too-big shirt, and said, "Ooh, look! She's got dimples."

"Will she keep them?"

The doctor, sitting between my knees with his head bent over a needle and thread—he was sewing up the episiotomy and looked like a tailor—laughed. So did the nurse, as she tried to hand me the baby.

"No," I said.

"Don't you want to hold her?" she asked, and again I said no. "I might drop her."

They started laughing again but stopped abruptly, because I had started to shake. There was no controlling it; even my legs were trembling. The nurse gave up and took the baby away. I gave up, too, and closed my eyes while the doctor wheeled me back to my room and to B., who had just become a father.

"Shut the window," I said, trying to talk over what was happening to me. "Shut it. Don't let me get near it. Please, I want bed rails."

A carpenter came and nailed the window to the sill. *Ridiculous,* I thought as he hammered. *I can jump through the pane.* I heard the sound of breaking glass, felt myself hurtling with the baby in my arms, heard the splat when we hit the ground.

"Don't leave me alone. Get a nurse. Put me out."

A fat Irishwoman came and settled herself into the chair in the corner. Another doctor came in and injected something into my arm. The last thing I saw was the light and the hope fading from my husband's eyes, and the last thing I thought was that my baby, ejected now from the fortress that was myself, would never be safe again.


FOR YEARS, I could not think about, much less talk about, those weeks that followed my first child's birth. Now I can report, but I cannot interpret. Compulsion, depression, anxiety: I can work up a song and dance about them. Psychosis—there! I took the easy way out, I gave horror a name—is beyond analysis.

Dr. Franklin arrived the next morning. He came every morning after that and held my hand, and although I cannot remember what I said to him, I do remember that I said nothing to B., afraid that if I diverted one word from my psychiatrist I would weaken the lifeline that was slowly, and finally, beginning to connect me to him.

Besides, Dr. Franklin would not be horrified by what he was hearing, any more than he would have fainted while watching an operation. My husband, however, was not equipped to deal with sickness, or so I felt and so I still believe. If he could look into my head, I figured, he would run away. Still, my having excluded him from my madness must have seemed yet another way of excluding him from my life.

I begged my obstetrician to tie me to the bed. He would not. I begged him to move me to the psychiatric floor. He would not. How could I nurse the baby, he asked, if I were that far from the nursery? Strange. I, mad, knew what should be done. He, sane, would not do it.

One night the fat Irish nurse fell asleep in the chair and I, staring across the bed rails at her plump, pink, piggy face, panicked and woke her. "I saw on your admission form that you're a Catholic," she said. "Pray."

The hospital was full of wanderers, most of them diaper service salesmen popping up unexpectedly in one's doorway. But once a woman dispensing religious tracts slipped into my room and spilled badly printed exhortations all over my bed. She was trying to enlist me in Jehovah's Witnesses. Another time a nurse, young and pretty and so thin she scarcely left a shadow, slipped into my room and told me that nerves were the price one had to pay for being as delicately attuned, as sensitive, as we. Meanwhile the fat Irish nurse mumbled her Hail Marys and then, nodding off, as always, at midnight, left me to the devil.

When the nurse who worked the evening shift in the nursery, and who brushed Katherine's hair into different dos—sometimes parted down the side, sometimes down the center—brought her to me for a feeding, I would not let her leave, because the old Irishwoman ran off down the hall then to her cronies, leaving me free to crash the window with my beautiful, innocent baby in my arms. Early one morning, when the Irishwoman left to get my orange juice, I got out of bed and baptized my daughter with water from the lavatory faucet. At least she would go without original sin.

Friends came to visit. I smiled, I chatted, and if any of them wondered why there were rails on my bed, they never did so aloud. B. came every night, stopping first at the nursery to peer through the glass at his daughter, and told me who had called, who had written, what his parents had said, who had invited him for dinner. When my breasts swelled to blue-veined white globes—"You've got enough milk to feed every kid in the nursery," the night nurse crowed—he arrived, unasked, with nursing bras. "Size 40C," he said proudly, taking my abundance for his own.

"If you'll just let me out of here, away from this window," I said to my doctor, "I'll be all right." So he released me from the hospital a day early, and back I went to our basement apartment, frantic to feel nothing but Manhattan underfoot. But first we watched while the nurse dressed our child in the clothes B. had brought from home, gasping when she broke off the withered stub of the umbilical cord. Then she swaddled Katherine in the lacy knitted blanket and stuck the lucky booties on her feet and handed her to B., who smiled to see his baby, his lamb, in his arms.

JUST AS I HAD THOUGHT overnight cases bourgeois, so I thought a baby nurse a sinful self-indulgence. So I had asked our cleaning woman, Mamie, who claimed some acquaintance with infant care, to come in for a few hours every day for the week after I came home from the hospital. She came once, then never again, and when chided by a neighbor said cheerfully, "You know me, Miz Gibney. Can't handle responsibility."

For two days I sat alone, holding the baby until B. came home from work, afraid that if I put her down for more than a minute, she would stop breathing. I nursed her, too, although my nipples were cracked and bleeding, because I was afraid I would make mistakes with a formula. On the third day Hoppy, a practical nurse, arrived.

Hoppy was Jamaican, short and round and brown, and when she walked, her starched white uniform crackled and her spotless white shoes squeaked. She slung Katherine over her shoulder, rather like a dishrag, and commandeered the apartment, whistling or singing ("You've got to get them used to noise") as she moved from room to room. When Hoppy swaddled Katherine in a receiving blanket, it was because she "needs the comfort"; when she made me nurse the baby every time she cried, hungry or no, it was because she "needs the comfort"; when she asked Katherine, "Do they speak Latin where you come from?" I knew that like me, she believed in a room up in heaven where babies waited to be called to earth. When Hoppy was there, my daughter was safe, and until the night B. told me about Lewis, so was I.

Lewis, the first child of another editor and his wife, was four weeks old. "Kate's got a date for the junior prom," his father said when Katherine was born, and he sent her a split of champagne in his son's name. A few days before her birth, we had had dinner at their house and I had given Lewis his bottle, "for practice," his mother had said. Now he was dead, B. said, with tears in his eyes, and he had not wanted to tell me but had to for fear I might call Lewis's mother one bright morning and say, "How is Lewis? How are his burps?"

There were tears in my eyes, too, but Hoppy said, "No, no, Mrs. L., you'll spoil the baby's milk if you cry." So I didn't cry, and wondered if there had been something wrong in the way I had held the bottle.

That night, lying beside my daughter, whose bassinet I had put next to the bed so I could listen to her breathing, my right hand holding down my left so that I could not close them around the tiny neck and squeeze, I resolved that whenever I felt the urge to kill someone, I would redirect it and kill myself instead. The relief was tremendous.

Many nights I slept on the living room couch, leaving my husband alone in the bedroom with Kate. She was safe with him. Often I would stare at the tiny, pulsing fontanel, thinking of how easily my long strong thumb could crush it. Her neck was so little one hand could break it. I would not bathe her. My husband did. He thought I was afraid she would slip. I was afraid I would push. But every time I felt my hands moving or realized that my eyes had been too long on her neck, her head, I determined again to harm myself before I could harm her. The decision to die is a great restorative.

After six weeks the sickness trailed away, dispersing in shreds, like clouds lifting. The fear of heights did not. Day after day Dr. Franklin stood me next to his twelfth-story window, put both his arms around me so I would feel secure, and said, "Tell me what you see."

"There's a man with a raincoat and a shopping bag, and I can see a woman pushing a baby carriage. There's a little girl crossing the street, and three cabs at the corner." Naming. I kept naming things, people, eventually emotions, and the naming gave order to chaos.

But the fear of heights—ah, the fear of heights. Even today I stay away from windows on high floors, and when circumstances push me onto terraces, I sidle along the walls, my fingers looking for crevices among the bricks. It never leaves me, that reminder that once upon a time I was crazy.

◈ 3 ◈

THE FIRST TIME I took Katherine on an outing, on a Sunday afternoon in May when she was six weeks old, the wheel came off her green plaid baby carriage. A garage mechanic repaired it—"On the house, lady," he said—and set me, grinning, back on West Tenth Street. There could have been no stronger line of demarcation between me and those people up on the Upper East Side, I thought, infatuated with my fecklessness, than the distance between a fabric carriage with dodgy wheels and a Silver Cross pram. Actually, B. might have preferred a Silver Cross pram, but it would not have gone with the new identity I was coining for myself: Village mother.

That day and many days thereafter I took my daughter to Washington Square, to the southeast corner, where a big sycamore that I came to call the baby tree spread its branches over a large, grubby sandpit. A certain kind of Village mother spent hours there, offering chunks of raw potato to her teething child. The purest example (all struck me as variations on a type) was a sallow, stringy-haired young woman who, talking constantly, made much of her Jewishness and her husband's blackness. She brandished his color, in fact, as if it were a flag. Meanwhile the baby, scrawny and dun-skinned, was treated with the rough affection due a puppy. But then, rough affection—dumping one's offspring in its carriage, carrying it more or less upside down on one's hip—was, like the raw-potato teething tool, a function of Village style.

I would have loved to talk to someone, especially about Beechnut's as compared to Gerber's and whether pacifiers made for buckteeth, but I was too shy to start a conversation, and nobody was inclined to start one with me, probably because my face is stony in repose, and forbidding. Still, it was pleasant under the baby tree—the drunks mostly clustered by the fountain, and the folksingers who preceded the drug dealers hadn't yet arrived—and membership in the club to which I had so desperately wanted to belong was glorious.

About four o'clock, about the time the air began to turn blue, I would rise from the bench and kick up the carriage brake and off we would go, past the stern, beautiful houses that were all that was left of Catherine Sloper's Washington Square to Bleecker Street, where strolled another kind of Village mother. This one pushed an enormous perambulator in which lay, banked in pillows and laces and fleecy wools, a fat little boy who was almost always named Anthony. I know this because a silver tag on a chain, reminiscent of the kind that drapes decanters, invariably swagged his coverlet. There it was, inscribed for all to see: ANTHONY.

Lucky Anthony, to be going home to a crowd. Like a lot of people with small families and without a strong ethnic identity, I thought the spirits were higher and the sentiments warmer in big Italian and Jewish households. Not in B.'s Jewish household—he had never even had a bar mitzvah, and if his parents knew a word of Yiddish, I never heard it—but in the kind I had glimpsed in old photographs of tenement life. Snug as bugs in a rug those families were. I couldn't see the poverty for the coziness.

So when I saw Anthony after Anthony moving like Cleopatra on her barge through the dusk of late afternoon on Bleecker Street, I saw their grandparents and their aunts and uncles and cousins lined up to greet them. I saw first communions and weddings and funerals at Our Lady of Pompeii, and statues of saints dressed in dollar bills, and a network of Philomenas and Angelas and Roses stretched over the whole South Village. I envied Anthony all of them, for Katherine's sake. For my sake, too.

My mother, who was forever reminding me that she personally had scrubbed my every diaper and strained my every beet, was nonetheless rich in household help—her mother and her sister and her widowed great-aunt—and when she had walked uptown with me, it had been "Good afternoon" and "Is she teething yet?" all the way. But these were strangers on the streets of Greenwich Village, and I, who had never lost my provincial chattiness, had only an infant to talk to. "Okay," I would say as I turned the carriage into Ottomanelli's meat market, "this is where we get the veal scaloppini for Daddy and me. And you, you're having cereal and banana."

Once I had wrestled the carriage into the areaway of 21 Perry Street, however, the miracle overtook me, the miracle that always overtook me when I unlocked the door to my own home. The stove, its pilot light like a votive candle, was waiting; the refrigerator was purring; the turn of a faucet would set a pot to filling. "Poor Butterfly, though your heart is breaking," I sang while I settled Katherine into her baby butler; "The most beautiful girl in the world," while I maneuvered her small silver spoon into her small stubborn mouth; "Bye Bye, Blackbird" as, one hand firm under her rubber-pantied rump, I waltzed her to her crib.

While I wished that my father had lived to see his grandchild, I no longer felt the curious pain—a strange, slow tearing-apart— that had crossed my chest whenever I thought of him. I gave up the hope, too, never quite lost, that someday he would walk into the room. And, blessedly, a recurring dream gave up on me: a dream in which I met him, in one of his Brooks Brothers suits and a felt fedora, walking down Fifth Avenue.

"Papa!" I said. "You're alive!"

"Yes, I am, Mary Lee, but you must never tell anyone or try to find me, because if you do, I will die." So I left him in the middle of a crowd on Fifth Avenue and woke up crying.

"But Mary," a friend said once, "your father *can't* have been flawless."

"He was till I was twenty," I replied.

Perhaps if he had lived just a little longer, it might have been long enough for me to have grown away from him. But he did not, so I am forever the daughter looking for the lap that disappeared. It is the same with Katherine. If I had not gone back to work, if I had been locked up with her until the morning she left for kindergarten, I might one day have seen her as distinct from me. But I did go back, before she could even talk, and so I retain an image of my baby and myself nestled into each other like a pair of *matryoshka* dolls. She is perfect; so am I.

"SIDNEY," B. SAID, naming the owner of a small publishing house, "needs someone to read for him." "Sterling," naming a literary agent who was striking out on his own, "needs a reader." "Jack at Coward-McCann," naming an editor at a large publishing house, "needs someone to look at this and see if it can be salvaged." The manuscripts stacked beside the chaise longue, between it and the playpen, constituted the slush pile, the over-the-transom stuff, the stuff that people like me were hired, for next to nothing, to skim through. Only two—a novel and a curious little biography of a bat, both of which had been published earlier in England— were worth consideration. But I read everything, all the way through, remembering Yeats's "Tread softly because you tread on my dreams."

One woman had written a biography of Ruth Chatterton, based on clippings from old movie magazines and a brief dressing-room how-do-you-do when Chatterton was touring and played in her town. I saw it three times—she had submitted it to each of the people for whom I was working—and there cannot have been a publisher's reader in the city who had not seen it once. In truth, every publisher's reader in the city had probably seen all the manuscripts beside the chaise longue. If, working on a magazine again in years to come, I was to defend the reading of the slush pile, it was not because I believed it hid a gem. It was because I thought its originators were owed the courtesy. Most of them, after all, were not trying to get rich. They were simply trying to join a church. It was a church I had thought of joining once, but no more. Better to do what I was doing now: read in the morning light and watch my Katie roll over, stand up, spit up. We kept her crib in our bedroom until she was a year old, unable to give up the sight that greeted us when we woke. At dawn her starfish hands grasped the bars, she struggled upward, and her face appeared, like the sun rising.

Several days a month I lugged the manuscripts uptown in shopping bags, taking the bus because I was not about to spend money on cabs, and curiously nervous about crossing Fourteenth Street.

Uptown, I told B.—taking my allusion, as usual, from my reading—was the world of telegrams and anger. It was also a world in which we went to a lot of cocktail parties on hot summer nights. Cold winter nights, too, I suppose, but I do not remember those. I remember the summer parties, though, because usually I was the only wife (the rest were in Amagansett with their children) among a flock of pretty young women, many of whom were sleeping with the young editors whose wives were in Amagansett. The pretty young women were in publishing, too, often fresh out of Radcliffe's summer course, and I have sometimes wondered what happened to them. They came along a bit too early for publishing houses to place them anywhere but in their textbook departments, and a bit too early for the young editors, too, who did not acquire their second wives until ten or so years later. But whatever became of them, I am sure they remained good sports, just as I am sure that none of them, to this day, would leave the milk bottle on the kitchen table.

I remember a summer Saturday afternoon, too, when we rented a car and drove to Westport for lunch with Sheilah Graham. Sheilah was a Hollywood gossip columnist whose affair with F. Scott Fitzgerald had lent her a certain literary shine, and B. was her editor. She was plump and blonde and blue-eyed, the kind of woman who looks as edible as a bonbon, and when Katherine was born she had given her a pleated nylon bedjacket. *So Hollywood,* I thought, and tied it round the baby's tiny shoulders whenever we had dinner guests.

Sheilah made me laugh—she was sharp as a needle—and never more so than that afternoon. Katherine was in her infant seat, on the kitchen table, when Sheilah called her teenage son in to see her. "Fair warning, Rob," she said, pointing at Kate. "The wages of sin."

But there was no sin in Katherine's conception: a judge had sanctioned it. Rather than being the restriction I had feared, marriage had turned out to be roomy. It allowed for all sorts of stuff. Except, of course, for flirtations. When a young man who had not noticed my wedding ring spoke of seeing me again—we were at a cocktail party—I backed away as if presented with a snake. "Lock Mary Lee into an igloo with Mastroianni for two years," B.

boasted once, "and *nothing* would happen." At least, I thought he was boasting.

I remember something else as well, the nights when Katherine squalled and condemned me to blurred and stumbling walks around the living room. I remember a paperbound copy of Dr. Spock hurled against a wall, the spine splintering on impact and the pages cascading to the floor. I remember thinking I would do anything for sleep. And because of all that, I remember Bloomingdale's as I would paradise.

There was a morning when I was tired, so tired I was having dizzy spells. *I'll faint, I told myself, and something terrible will happen to the baby. She'll catch her head between the crib bars or pull herself over them and fall. Or she'll stop breathing, like little Lewis did, because I am not watching. If I take my eyes off her, she will die. But I am going to take my eyes off her, because I cannot keep them open.*

We seldom had a babysitter unless we were going to the movies or to someone's house for dinner. But the woman who usually cared for Katherine then was home, thank God, and free. I was dizzy until the moment she walked into the kitchen, all white uniform and rubber-soled Oxfords and competence. I was about to say, "If you could just watch Katherine while I nap" when my head cleared and exhaustion dropped from my shoulders. I would go to Bloomingdale's instead. I would look at the model rooms.

I have never known the name of a plant that has long stems and round leaves and that, dried, smells of spices and pepper. Antique dealers love it. So do the owners of "country" shops. But Bloomingdale's was the first place I ever smelled those leaves. Smell them now and I have just traversed the Directional couches and the rosewood room dividers to join the shoppers who, barred from entrance by a velvet rope, are viewing the model rooms.

Even when they were supposed to evoke the South of France or a corner of Tuscany or somebody's Maine hideaway, the model rooms evoked New York. It was their scale and their extravagance and sometimes the sheer nonsense of them. All I ever bought at Bloomingdale's, besides white-sale linens, were lamps with black paper shades and cheeses from the delicacy department, but I returned again and again to those rooms. None of them, really, were

to my sober, strait-laced taste. Still, I was proud of them, even proprietary. "You don't see raisin bread like this at home," a visiting
friend of my mother's said one day when I gave her tea and toast.
You didn't see rooms like these, either.

Once in a while a salesman would unhook the rope and escort
a customer inside. The customer was always a woman, always
thin, always ash blond, and almost always, I assumed, from out of
town. She and the salesman would pause over a fruitwood ar-
moire, a terra-cotta urn deep enough to hide a thief, an enormous
Rya rug. He would whip out his order book; the viewers' eyes
would shift to the right, where a discreet sheet of plastic-covered
paper listing items and prices hung on the wall. God! That woman
had just spent $500 on—oh, let's say a beaten copper tray from
Morocco.

Together they emerged, the woman flushed with the pride of
someone who can spend $500 on foolishness, the salesman saying
something about delivery in ten days. The line of viewers parted to
let them through, then moved slowly on to the next room. No one
spoke; we were too busy inhaling opulence.

Dreamily I would descend the escalators and eventually the
stairs to the basement. Lackadaisically I would make my way to
the subway and the Fourteenth Street stop of the West Side IRT.
Emerging at Twelfth Street and Seventh Avenue, I was still se-
dated—by the scent of the dried round leaves and the rip-rip-rip of
sales slips being torn from order books. A few blocks south, a few
yards west, and I was unhooking the gate into the areaway, as re-
freshed as if I had been hours in deep sleep. I had not spent a cent.
I had not wanted to. The bustle was sufficient, and the traffic and
the noise, and above all the Lethe that was Bloomingdale's fifth
floor.

THE ROOMS I THOUGHT OF, still think of, as my kind of
rooms I never saw. But I know where they were. They were in one,
or maybe all, of five houses that stood on the corner of Greenwich
Street and Dey Street in 1810. The first, at the left, is white clapboard with two dormer windows, green shutters, and a Dutch
door, on the bottom half of which a man and a woman are leaning

their elbows. Next to it is a brick house, much bigger and grander, with a rail-backed bench on either side of the front door. A boy is sitting on one of them.

The remaining houses are on Dey Street. The one at the corner, which is also brick, is big and grand indeed and has two entrances. Maybe the second—two men are standing on its steps—is for servants. But the one next to it, and the one beyond that, both of them white clapboard and comparatively modest, also have two entrances. So I am confused. It is a winter day, though, I am sure of that, because the trees are naked, and the sky is the same dull gray I wake up to on January mornings in New York.

But the rooms? What do I know of these rooms, some of which are shuttered? Nothing, really, only that they are spare and clean and that they have wide floorboards and small fire-places. These are the rooms in which I have always wanted to live, the material equivalent of Jane Austen's prose, and that they once existed in Greenwich Village is reason enough for me to believe that some of them still do. Up and down the narrow streets and all the way down toward what was later called SoHo we would go, Kate in her carriage or, later, her stroller and me in my pants and sneakers. Sometimes I could see the outline of a pitched-roof house on the bigger, newer building that had stood next door and survived it. I saw boarded-up dormer windows, too, and incised stone lintels crumbling before my very eyes.

Nothing of those five houses, however, remained at the corner of Greenwich Street and Dey Street. I had been there with Jerry long before I had bought a print of that 1810 watercolor at the New York Public Library's gift counter, for plants for the window-boxes at 224 West Eleventh. The nurseries that were there then, though, are now as vanished as those five houses, and I suppose that whatever is there now will have vanished in another few decades, too. Fix it before it disappears! Fix it before it disappears! I knew I was never going to live in those rooms. I knew I was never going to find more than their traces. But what I could find I would fix, so that one day I could walk those streets again whether they had lasted or not.

I have fixed Kate and me, too, on our long late-afternoon strolls along the western shores of Greenwich Village. The boat

horns—one does not hear those anymore—are lowing, and the police are riding their horses to the stables (they are vanished, too) on
West Twelfth Street, and the three old musicians—Italians from the
South Village, I think—who used to play songs like "Deep Purple"
for change thrown from Village windows are just starting out for
their evening tour.

It is time to go indoors, time to get under a roof, time for the
cereal and the banana, the bath and the waltz round the living
room, and if I speak as if we, too, have vanished, it is because we
have. Never again would I be Kate's alone, nor would Kate be mine
alone, because when she was eighteen months old I went back to
work. For me to do that, she had to be born again, into another
woman's care, and I had to be born again, too, to become someone
who was not wholly, solely a mother. The Kate who is here now is
not the Kate who was there at the beginning. That one is still in a
stroller, being pushed along Hudson Street. And the woman who
pushed her is still gripping the stroller's handles, still looking for
rooms that are as clean and spare as a bone.

◆ 4 ◆

*I* AM NOT really sure what it was that drove me back to work,
although I think loneliness was part of it. Except for when I was
talking to Katherine—"That's a good girl" and "Let Mommy button up Katie's sweater"—I kept a Trappist's silence. Mostly,
though, it was probably pragmatism, pragmatism and a need to
own New York as surely as I had owned the town in which I was
raised.

I had not spent all those days in classrooms and all those nights
with John Donne so that I could spend my time washing Kate's
little shirts and nightgowns and hanging them on the bathroom
shower rail, separating B.'s shirts (they went to the cleaner at the
corner) from the sheets and towels (they went to a big pick-up-and-
deliver commercial laundry), and waiting for the diaper service

man. Of course not. Somebody else could do that stuff. Why should I?

Besides, I knew a man who would do the heavy cleaning. And Nanny Schaefer, who babysat for us, was tired of working out of an agency and was happy to have a regular morning job. Maybe if it had not been so easy to walk out the door, I might have stayed at home. But if I had, I would have been unhappy, and not simply because a college education was going down a drain. To live in New York, to be part of New York, I had to work.

In Bristol, I had joined the Girl Scouts and sold their cookies door to door. I had stood in our high school gymnasium wearing a blue bloomer suit and waving Indian clubs at the crowd in the bleachers. But not because I believed in the truth of scouting or the virtue of exercise. It was because I wanted to weave my life with the town's life. Traveling, I have spent more time in street markets and butcher shops than I have in museums and churches, and have imagined myself behind every closed door I have ever seen. Home with, say, a cold, I watch the five o'clock news and regret that I have not been out on the street that day to see the traffic jam at Times Square, the arrest at Grand Central. I had to work, because to someone who comes from out of town, that is what New York is for, and what it is. No matter how late at night I open my window, I can hear the streets and the sky and the buildings emitting a dull, constant drone. The hive, whatever the hour, is always buzzing.

But what should I do? I envy those for whom the world holds infinite potential, who are as flexible as whips. Except for a few weeks or so when I was ten and wanted to be an archaeologist (a few thrusts with a spade, I believed, were all it took to bring up glory), I have never wanted to be anyplace but around words. My father's cousin was a critic for the *Providence Journal;* her house burst with books piled on tables, sitting two rows deep on shelves, lining the staircase to the second floor. Papa and I thought she lived at the heart of light.

The reading I did in the chaise longue, though, was as near as I wanted to come to book publishing, and a part-time job at the Washington Square Bookstore—sweet little lending library, nice customers, lots of time for browsing—would not pay Nanny

Schaefer's salary. So, fearful lest she remember that three years before I had left *Vogue* in disgrace, I made an appointment with the former gym teacher who was personnel director at Condé Nast.

"Welcome home," she caroled when I went in the door. No matter that I had walked out without giving notice, no matter at all. Half the people who had worked for Allene, she implied, had done the same. But that was what you had to deal with when you dealt with the creative. They had . . . quirks. The gym teacher smiled, serene in the knowledge that she had no quirks whatsoever.

"Now, Mary," she asked. "What have you been up to?"

"Well, I have a baby. Katherine. She's eighteen months old now, and I've been thinking that maybe there was something here I could do part-time."

"As a matter of fact, there is," she said. "Do you think you could do your old job at *Mademoiselle* in half the time?"

Of course I could, and at half the pay, too.

Among the women I worked with on fashion magazines when I was young, there must have been one who was shrewd about her salary. But I never knew her. We took it for granted that the people who worked in the art department had higher starting salaries than the rest of us, because they, having gone to art school, were presumed to have skills. We also took it for granted that the women who worked in merchandising and the men who were space salesmen made more money than we did. A successful store promotion or a few new advertising pages were evidence of their worth. But there was no way we traffickers in taste could prove our value; so most of us didn't even try. "We *never* match salaries to keep people who get another offer," the former gym teacher would say to someone who proposed to jump ship for, say, *The Ladies' Home Journal,* and—although she didn't say this bit aloud—"we never take them back."

*Mademoiselle,* which had been bought by Condé Nast, had not yet moved its offices to the Graybar Building, so I met C.A.'s successor, the ex-Hungarian baroness, at 575 Madison. Nothing had changed. B.T.B. was still holding court in her boudoir, the fashion editors were still wearing Italian shoes, the writers in the college and career department were still peppy. There were a few new faces—the editors from *Charm* who had succeeded in edging the editors from *Mlle.* off their chairs—and some of the old faces looked up from their desks and waved as I passed by. Before I was ten paces down the corridor, somebody told me the baroness didn't wear underwear. Somebody on a phone in the fashion department was telling one of the photographers—they were all out on college campuses photographing the August issue—that it wasn't possible that *everybody* at Wheaton had acne. Somebody else was telling Leo Lerman, in his lair and surrounded by the usual acolytes, that Mr. Capote was on the line. I was indeed home.

"There's just one thing," I told the baroness after she said she would be only too happy to have me join the copy department. "I have to go to Paris first."

Now *that* was the kind of excuse a former baroness and former editor of *Harper's Bazaar* found acceptable for almost anything. "My dear," she said in her whiskey baritone, "of course you do." Happy day! Happy Mary! Back in the lobby, the same lobby in which eight years before I had stood clutching my mother's old handbag, I said to myself, "I will never leave this again." I did not mean *Mademoiselle*. I meant work.

BUT IF I HAD LIVED IN PARIS? Oh, if I had lived in Paris, I would have sat all day in cafés drinking citrons pressés and staring at passersby. I would have walked up and down those pearl-gray streets, stopping only to lean my elbows on the parapet of the occasional bridge and watch the *bâteaux mouches* slide by. On a night when B. and I were standing on the Pont Neuf, one slid by empty of passengers and sounding of "Jesu, Joy of Man's Desiring" from, I suppose, a record player. How I remember that night, that encapsulation of everything I loved most about this world: that there was a city like Paris and a composer like Bach and that I had been lucky enough to have married someone who had introduced me to both.

We all went to Paris, all the time, B. and I and our friends, clutching the clips of Craig Claiborne's most recent tour of France and lists of boutiques and the addresses of Baccarat's factory salesroom and the best perfume discounter. I could not write about

New York if I were not to write about Paris as well, because Paris was what we, our crowd, wanted New York to be. If we longed for sidewalk cafés, it was because we'd sat in them in Paris, and if we were forever lugging boughs of mountain laurel from the florist down on Greenwich Avenue to our walk-ups, it was because they were the closest thing to the bouquets we had found on every Paris corner and lugged to our hotels. We dared the nasty salesladies at Guerlain, and we bought copper pots at Les Halles, and whenever we returned home, it was with the name of a new shop or a new restaurant to pass on.

"There's this place," we'd say, "Chez l'Ami Louis. It's in an area with a lot of laundries, stuff like that, and you have to call a cab before you leave, because you'll never find one otherwise. They do this little leg of lamb. . . ." Or "Go to the Monoprix, or maybe it's the Prisunic. Anyway, it's on the Boul Mich. They have these knives and forks with plastic handles in *wonderful* colors. . . ."

In Paris I bought a present for Allie's first child (she had married an Irish Catholic from Boston, and the wedding reception, at the Plaza, was a meld of flamboyant Irish toasts and her relatives' high-nosed "Hear, hear"s), a little boy for whom I got a striped bikini. Where but in Paris could you find a bikini for an infant, or a woven straw crib lined with ruffles and flourishes? And what better place to conceive my next daughter? That B. and I might have a son was past imagining. He, like my father, was meant to sire girls.

"Don't you think we ought to quit while we're ahead?" he said, as cautious as those acquaintances—invariably Jews streaked with pessimism—who had warned me that in knitting little sweaters and assembling a layette before Katherine was born, I was thumbing my nose at the Fates. Then he warmed to the romance of it all. We would be able to tell our next child that she had come into being in the city of Notre-Dame and the Sorbonne and La Tour d'Argent.

When our first child, our Katherine, was born, we took her to Bristol to introduce her to my grandmother. Ganny was sitting on her porch, I remember, and held out her arms for her great-grandchild. She examined her closely, running her fat little hands over Katie's honey-colored hair, poking a finger into one of her deep dimples. Then she turned the baby so that her profile was on a line with the railing.

"What on earth are you doing?" I asked.

"I just wanted to see her nose."

"What made you think she'd have a big nose?" I said, pretending I couldn't guess.

"Because," Ganny said soberly, "that's the mark the Lord set on them."

My grandmother wasn't anti-Semitic, I knew that. But I also knew that she saw all children as compendiums of those who had gone before them. I had my father's hands; my sister had my mother's; my aunt was the dead spit, she told me, of an aunt on Ganny's side, just as my mother was the dead spit of Aunt Mame, on Gampa's side. Those were the marks—an ancestor's cheek-bones, the narrow Cantwell foot—the Lord set on us. But the Lord had stamped my daughter not with a beak but with a button, and now I would have another button-nose, to relieve me of the strain of loving the first one so much. Having to stretch love to cover two children would, I thought, thin it out, make it bearable.

So we went to Paris, to a room on the top floor of the Hotel Bisson, which we had read about in Liebling or Wechsberg or whoever it was that we and our fellow Francophiles were passing around those days. B. was excited by my new sexual sophistication, or, rather, carelessness: the swagger with which I had tossed out my diaphragm, my no-nonsense, knees-up, pelvis-tipped style in bed. Sex was okay now, because now I knew what it was for.

I did not get pregnant in Paris. "Next month," I said to B., having proof in Katherine that we were capable of launching legions on the world. "Both of us had rotten colds, and we had to climb four flights of stairs to our room! What can you expect?"

A few weeks later, in New York, the colds cured themselves, the egg dropped, the sperm swam, and off I went to my new job. No matter that in nine months I would have to take a few weeks off for childbirth. A pregnant editor was a commonplace at *Mademoiselle,* trundling her belly in and out of meetings, saving up her vacation days so she would get paid for the few weeks she was home with a newborn. The "office babies," we called our progeny, and today, when some of them are parents themselves, some are disappointments, and several are tragedies, we still do.


THE SPORTSWEAR EDITOR, a thin young woman with a narrow fox face, is going through a rack. "It'll be shipped shorter than it is here, and it comes in a myriad of colors." That is the invariable ending of her presentation of the pick of her market: "It comes in a myriad of colors."

"Would you *look* at those buttons!" screeches the fabric editor, whose hair is a kind of Seven Sisters pageboy (though she herself dropped out of someplace on Long Island) moored with a silver barrette. "Those buttons are *impossible!*"

"Listen, it's the best thing on the line, and I think it'll photograph okay." The dress editor is using a code which all of us understand. We have to show something from this manufacturer because he advertises, and this is his most inoffensive garment.

"Well," one or two or three of us say, because this is the prescribed response to the ghastly, "it's a look."

The room is windowless, the table is littered with packs of Cheez Doodles, the smoke from a dozen or so cigarettes rises to the ceiling. The fashion department is holding its monthly meeting, and I, being a copywriter, am sitting in. B.T.B. is sitting in, too, but only for an hour or so. Other duties call, among them her punctilious red-penciled reading of copy and manuscripts (she is quite possibly the world's greatest copy editor) and the correspondence entailed by her membership in the Women's Republican Club.

The sportswear editor holds up a silver evening sweater. Everybody likes it. "Group order," somebody says. "Group order, group order!" Ten or so of us are going to get it wholesale, that's what that means. But not me. I couldn't pull that sweater over my bulge. No matter. I will participate in plenty of group orders before my time is up at *Mlle.*, or "Millie!" as B.T.B. is forever sighing. "Such a silly name."

The first editor-in-chief of this magazine lasted only a few months; by the time B.T.B. is retired, she will have lasted nearly forty years. "Dearly Beloved Family" is how she addresses the staff in the long letters she writes to us during her annual holiday in the Grand Caymans. The morning after her beet-faced, Old New York husband's sudden death, she came to the office and sat at her desk, a red pencil in her hand. Nobody interrupted her: we knew she was holding a wake in what was more surely her home than the big apartment on upper Fifth Avenue in which, we still believed, her housekeeper ironed her stockings every morning.

I have been in this meeting long enough for my eyes to water and my feet to fall asleep. Soon after B.T.B. leaves, I leave, too, for the shoebox I share with a woman who is even more pregnant than I. Short and fat, her eyes gray behind big glasses, she is a poet and playwright. Like half the people at *Mademoiselle,* she aspires to other things.

"Do you *believe* those ruffles? And would you check out those buttons?" The fabric editor is at it again; the laughter and "a myriad of colors" are crossing the hall and seeping into my office. The baroness's assistant sticks her head in my door. "I may go mad," she says, and withdraws it.

Now there is no C.A. to order the troops, and B.T.B., whose faith in her staff is beyond sublime, asks only that we stay out of jail. Leo Lerman is in the doorway. Do I have time for Schrafft's before going home? It is drizzling slightly, so as we leave the Graybar he knots the four corners of his handkerchief and places it on his bald head. Down the street we go, Leo either oblivious to or shrewdly aware of—I have never quite decided which—the sight he is making. I am laughing; I am always laughing. This is the season of my content.

A NIGHT IN APRIL. We are dressing for a dinner party, I in a black skirt with a porthole over which I have dropped an empire-waisted blue *schmatte. Schmatte,* along with "merch" for merchandise and "matchy-matchy," as in "That sweater and skirt are too matchy-matchy," is among the words I have picked up at *Mlle.* I have resisted pronouncing beige "behj" and kimono "kimina," but on the whole I am beginning to sound like a fashion maven. My transformation, however, is not yet complete. It is years before I discover that "maven" is Yiddish.

The dinner party is on the Upper West Side, and it is safe to say we will be eating boeuf bourguignon. It is also safe to say that after coffee, somebody will put Chubby Checker on the record player and everyone will start twisting. Everyone, that is, but me, who has learned how—"Make believe," I was instructed, "that you're drying your backside with a towel"—but who is considered (though not by me) to be *hors de combat* on account of pregnancy.

This is all anybody does after dinner parties anymore: twist. Conversation among the literati (I, of course, am not one, but B. is) has been suspended for the next two years.

TO THE RIGHT of the kitchen sink in the house in which I live now is a menu, slightly stained, in a narrow brown frame. "A la Halte de l'Eperon," it says at the top, beside a drawing of a duck on a platter staring fearfully at a carving knife. It's the menu for "10 mai 1962" at a restaurant called Chez Allard, and by now it has hung on the walls of four apartments. May 10 was my birthday, my second child was two months from being born, and once more we were in Paris, where, too pregnant to wander alone through Venice, as I had first planned, I was making believe I lived by taking cooking lessons from Julia Child's coauthors, Mesdames Bertholle and Beck. Every morning I took a bus up to just beyond L'Etoile, climbed a flight of stairs, tied on an apron, and, standing in a small, simple kitchen, realized the dreams of everyone who had ever read *Mastering the Art of French Cooking*.

As usual, our stay in Paris would in memory have mythic proportions, because we would have spent time with Alice B. Toklas. Alice was very real to us, especially to B., but she was also someone who had another reality, in the pages of a book. At this point the two Alices seemed one, but I have always wondered whether the Alice we knew was not the Alice Gertrude had known but the Alice Gertrude had invented.

B. wanted Alice to write her own autobiography, and a few years earlier, before I had had Kate, she had granted him an audience. She lived on the rue Christine then, in a house behind a tall wooden door that was approached through a shabby courtyard. "G. Stein, *ecrivain*" was the name above the doorbell, although

Gertrude Stein had been dead for at least ten years (I seem to remember that she was still listed in the Paris phonebook, too), but there was no answer when we pushed that bell or the one beside the door to her flat.

Remembering that someone had told him Alice was slightly deaf, B. ran off to find a kiosk—he knew she could hear a telephone's ring—leaving me to stand on the stair landing, staring down at the courtyard. Suddenly the door to the right of the window opened, and there she stood, "a tiny, hunched woman with dark hair, round glasses, and a Boston voice," I wrote in my travel diary. "Deaf, closes her eyes when she laughs."

Alice asked me if I was Mrs. L. I explained that my husband was in a phone box, and she ushered me down a long dark passageway paved with Picassos. I gasped. I had not known, or perhaps I had forgotten, that these were Alice Toklas's property now.

They were hung in no particular order; some were framed, some were not, and when I paused in front of a portrait of a naked young girl holding a bunch of red roses and said, "How beautiful," Alice said, "That was the first Picasso Gertrude ever bought."

I felt like the publisher-lodger in *The Aspern Papers* when he met Miss Bordereau and first heard the voice heard, and loved, by Jeffrey Aspern, a feeling made even stronger an hour later when B. had returned and we were sipping sherry. Not knowing either of us, Alice was hostessing with anecdotes, most of them about Gertrude. "When T. S. Eliot said to Gertrude, 'And from whom, Miss Stein, did you learn your habit of splitting infinitives?' Gertrude said, 'I learned it from Henry James.'"

Because her hands were crippled by arthritis, Alice no longer cooked. But she loved to eat—one good meal a day, the rest coffee and an endless consumption of Pall Malls—and the three of us went to a restaurant near the rue Christine. It had banquettes along the walls, flowers on every table, and waiters who genuflected at the sight of Miss Toklas.

She was fussy about the food—"This sauce," she said, rolling it around her tongue, "has *flour* in it"—and anxious to see that B. got enough to eat. I would not hazard offering any theory about Alice B. Toklas's division of the sexes, except for one. A man, being a man, had a completely different digestive apparatus from a woman and must be stoked like a furnace.

How proud I was of B. that day, how proud I am still. His appetite was equivalent to mine, but Alice would not let him stop after the *langoustines au gratin* and the *loup sur fenouil* that sufficed for her and me. She insisted that he follow them with an entrecôte and the appropriate red wine (we had been drinking a lot of white with the fish) and said that he could not say he had dined there without sampling the *glace au vanille,* which was sprinkled with the restaurant's special praline powder. On and on he ate, dying I knew, and I loved him for his courage.

Alice liked B., as well she might. He was charming, intelligent, and devoted to her book. In the years when she could no longer see to write, he found secretaries to whom she could dictate, and the last few pages were dictated to him. What surprised me was that she appeared to like me, too. But I am not sure: Alice hid extraordinary perversity under a seemingly helpless directness. When the book was published, she wrote in B.'s copy, "To——L——," giving a wrong first name, "who made only one mistake and never knew what it was."

A devout Catholic, devout as only a convert can be—although Alice claimed that hers was no conversion but a return, given that the nurse of her infancy had had her baptized without her Jewish parents' knowledge—she found a certain link to holy order in my own born Catholicism. Liking clothes—her only coat was made by Balmain—she approved of mine. Very much a lady, she responded to my shyness and good manners, although she may have found me dull.

There was one day, though, during those two weeks in May when I carried my second child *in utero* around the city in which I had hoped she would be conceived, when I think Alice truly liked me. The three of us were walking down the rue Christine, which was very narrow, to Lapérouse for lunch. A car came along, and since Alice was too frail to step out of the gutter quickly, I picked her up and put her on the sidewalk. She was mortified: to be lifted like a baby, and by a woman so hugely pregnant.

"But I do this all the time," I said. "My grandmother is very fat, and the only way she can get out of her rocker is by rocking back and forth very quickly until she gains momentum. Then she launches herself forward, like a rocket. I always catch her just before she lands in my lap."

Alice closed her eyes and laughed, knowing that I was telling the truth, that I thought little of picking up eighty-year-olds. Since her fragility meant little to me, it could, for a little while anyway, mean little to her.

She was sentimental about my pregnancies. Maybe she thought I was doing what a woman *should* do, unless she was a Gertrude or a Janet Flanner, in which case other rules applied. I remember her praising Picasso's wife, Jacqueline, because, or so it sounded to me, she was a slave. When she heard that mutual friends were finally divorcing—Alice seemed to be the only person in Paris who did not know they had not spoken in years; or did she?—she told me of her concern for their children, then wondered aloud if anyone who dressed as badly as the wife did could have made any man happy.

When she died, she was buried in a dark Balmain suit ("Pierre has given Gertrude a black bride," Janet Flanner, or somebody like Janet Flanner, said) in Père Lachaise, to which I plan to go sometime, to put flowers on her grave. We always took Alice yellow roses, in memory of Gertrude. I will take yellow roses that day as well, in memory of her, and in memory of me. In memory of Paris, too.


ALICE WAS NOT TO DIE for nearly ten years yet, though, and now we are sitting in Chez l'Ami Louis, watching as she tips a snail shell to her mouth and drinks the garlic butter. Tomorrow B. and I will lunch at La Tour d'Argent for the very first (and my very last) time, sitting by a tall window and watching raindrops dimple the Seine. In the afternoon we will take the boat-train to Le Havre, to the United States. We have bought a case of Taittinger Blanc de Blancs, more copper pots, and a pile of *tabliers,* those little smocks French children wear, for Kate. B. reclines in the top bunk reading manuscripts and I recline in the bottom bunk rereading Evelyn

Waugh, and together we are as rich as Croesus and as soigné as Gerald and Sara Murphy.

Six weeks later, on a hot July night, our second child arrives, on a sea of Richebourg because we have been at a dinner party and all that talk about alcohol in pregnancy is far in the future. She is the girl we knew she would be, and right away we name her Margaret, after my grandmother.

Margaret is very plump, has a thicket of black hair and no space between her eyebrows. "She looks," B. says, "like an Armenian innkeeper."

"She has my father's eyes," I say. Brown (eventually), turned down at the outer corners, they are the mark the Lord set on her.

# 44 Jane Street

## ◆ 1 ◆

KATHERINE, who had just learned to drink from a cup, returned to the bottle, pulling desperately on the nipple, her eyes anxious and her fat hands gripping fiercely. But she was kind, so kind, brushing her sister's hair at bedtime and retreating quietly to her little back bedroom after we had put on her sleep cap, a felt cone that had come with her copy of *Goodnight Moon*. But first we had taken her out to the areaway to wave to the one star (I think it is Venus) that faithfully shines upon New York City. Margaret, sleepy as a dormouse, was ensconced in the bassinet beside our bed. And we had begun the hunt for the most elusive of all Manhattan spaces, a Village apartment big enough for four.

On the Upper West Side you could find big apartments—"If worse comes to worst, we can always move to the Upper West Side" was said at least once during any Village dinner party featuring new parents. But giving up Greenwich Village would have meant giving up not only its sweet, seedy streets but a certain self-image. B. and I were Villagers; we bore (I told myself) a noble heritage. Never mind that the cobwebs at Julius's bar were fake, or that the historically literary Chumley's seemed as fusty as a provincial museum. Marianne Moore had worked at the Hudson Street branch of the New York Public Library! Mary McCarthy had lived on Bank Street! And e. e. cummings still lived on Patchin Place! Once, as I was leaving a Sixth Avenue grocery, I noticed that the brown paper bags that were to be delivered to me were nestled against the brown paper bags that were to be delivered to Djuna Barnes. "You'll never guess whose order was next to ours," I said to B. when I got home. "Djuna Barnes! *Nightwood!*"

Early one morning, about to share a cab to our respective offices ("My talent is my bank account," B. would boom when I complained of the extravagance. "I can't afford to arrive frazzled"), we walked instead into a real estate agency. The agent was on the phone. "It doesn't have anything right now but space," she was saying to somebody, "but the landlord's willing to do some work on it. So let me know if you're interested."

Ten minutes later we ourselves were looking at the place that didn't have anything but space: a basement and parlor floor on Jane Street, way over west near the garbage pier.

Jane Street is in an area of docks and warehouses, a few tenements, a few big apartment buildings, and a lot of nineteenth-century houses. Some Irish still lived there then—it was the old Eighth Ward—and even though it had started to "come up," as the real estate agent put it, it was so far from the subways and so close to the meat market (where turn a corner and you were apt to run smack into a carcass dangling from a chain) that many people regarded moving there as the same as moving to hell and gone. Still do, for that matter.

Not I. When the wind blows from the west one can smell the Hudson, and the houses are low, and there are field mice in the gardens. Even now, when the old refrigeration plant and some of the old livery stables have been turned into apartments, the only night-walkers tend to be drunks shaking their fists at fire hydrants and yelling "Motherfucker!" at the dust-obscured sky.

Dogs bark as in the country here, deep-throated roars from collies and big mongrels, and the soprano yips of Yorkies and Lhasa Apsos are only just beginning to be heard. In those days there were not even any supermarkets near Jane Street, only one newsstand, one delicatessen, and a tattered triangular park with metal swings and a sandpit. Jane Street was on the edge—of the city, of the river, of respectability—and it was a hideout. Walking home from the subway, the houses and people dwindling as I traveled west, the trees growing fewer, the river smell coming up stronger, the traffic quieting, almost disappearing, I felt as if I were entering a stockade.

The house faced north, an ordinary red brick with a fire escape that spoiled its facade. I have no idea what the interior looks like now, but once the first two floors were beautiful. Or so we thought, and so I still think, even though the ground floor was torrid in summer and the parlor floor, with an air conditioner blasting from either end, like a meat locker.

Our landlord was a small, skinny Irishman with five children (a year or two later they were six) and a small, trim wife on whom he doted. His grandparents and their parents had worked the docks and run the livery stables, and it was from them that he had inherited the house. "The minute anybody around here got any money," he told us, "they put down parquet floors. On Saturday nights you'd get a trio—a sax, maybe, and a drummer, and if you had a piano, a guy to play it—and there'd be dancing in the living room. Now the Italians . . . they liked to put down linoleum." The Village was to him what Bristol was to me: a place where the streets were as thronged with the dead as with the living.

Matty—his name was Matty—had had to gut the top two floors of the house to make bedrooms for his kids, most of whom were at parochial school. But our two floors he could return to what they had once been, balking only at ripping up the parquet to expose what I was convinced would be pumpkin pine floorboards beneath.

He installed a new kitchen sink, out of which rats ran until the plumber discovered an unplugged hole that led to a tortuous tunnel that led to the sewer system. He had some of the stones in the little drying yard raised so we could plant a garden and replaced the sagging board fence with wooden palings. He cut off a corner of the parlor floor linen closet and put in a small second bathroom, and he had the old shutters prised from their niches in the dining room and our bedroom.

And we? We were giddy with wallpaper, which we put in the hall and the children's room and the tiny guest room. We installed stair carpeting, a washing machine that emptied into the downstairs tub, and a dryer that was vented out the bathroom window.

B. and a friend of his worked night after night building bookcases, then gave up and let a carpenter take over. "Please, Matty," we begged, "can we have a new refrigerator?" He smiled and gave us $150 toward a fourteen-cubic-footer from Sears. Oh my! Let me walk through that house again. It makes me happy to walk through that house.

The dining room was on the ground-floor front, but it was not really a dining room yet, because we did not have a table. We visualized something oval, something mahogany, something, we said, "like an Irish hunt table." Not that we had ever seen an Irish hunt table, you understand, or had the foggiest notion of how to go about finding one. But we loved the term "Irish hunt table." We loved it like we loved "Georgian silver" and "Chinese export porcelain." Own them, we thought, and you are armored for life.

The walls were cream, and on three of them were floor-to-ceiling bookcases, packed with books left over from college, books we had bought at the secondhand stores on Fourth Avenue, books sent to B. by friends in publishing, and what B. called "*The New Yorker* collection," which is to say the collected works of Liebling, White, McNulty, and Mitchell, all of whom we idolized. The slate fireplace on the west wall didn't work, so we put an old metal milk-bottle basket sprayed yellow on the hearth and stuffed it with dried flowers. The slant-top desk and Windsor chair were in a corner by the window, and an outsize blue wing chair lighted by one of the standing lamps from West Eleventh Street was by the door.

The big square kitchen had a brick fireplace that didn't work, either, an old Chambers stove (no more Royal Rose for me!), enameled cabinets brought from Perry Street, a round deal table and rush-seated chairs, a high chair and a playpen. In that roomy kitchen, I told myself when I first saw it, I would put up jellies. I would attempt croissants. I would finally make the veau Prince Orloff, from *Mastering the Art of French Cooking, Volume One,* that I and all my fellow cooks aspired to.

The living room, on the parlor floor, was a measure of how far we had come. The wing chair, couch, and loveseat traveled with us from Perry Street, but now we had a Portuguese needlepoint rug and a mahogany sideboard (eighteenth century, English) and a

round, cloth-covered table centered by a lamp from Bloomingdale's that had cost $75. There were many more pictures and, even-
tually, tucked in a drawer in the sideboard, a pen-and-ink by
Andrew Wyeth (gift of the artist), a Cruikshank sketchbook (gift
to me from my husband), and a caricature by Max Beerbohm
(gift to my husband from a friend). The living room also had,
as did the bedroom, dentil moldings and a slate fireplace that
worked.

The living room opened onto the bedroom, which was actually
the front parlor, and although they could be closed off from each
other by huge sliding doors, they seldom were, because we liked
the long view into that serene white room. Also, we liked to show
it off.

Like all my bedrooms, this one was impossibly virginal, suitable for a nun with a passion for pillows. The walls, curtains, bed-
spread, the flokati rug, even the flowers in the ironstone pitcher on
the fireplace mantel were white. A wing chair and the chaise longue
were blue and white toile. The three-quarter bed had been replaced at last, by a brand-new Bloomingdale's queen-size with an
artfully rustic Spanish headboard, also Bloomingdale's. The quasi-
mahogany sideboard had gone to the dump, and now we had an
early eighteenth-century American pine blanket chest. All that remained of Twenty-first Street, but for a few glasses, prints, and
odds and ends of china, was the quasi-mahogany bureau.

With a fire in the fireplace, B. on the chaise longue with one
book, and me in bed with another, we could imagine we were in the
ultimate country inn, the inn that, in the autumn I was pregnant
with Katherine, we had looked for all over Vermont. Here it was,
just like the bluebird of happiness, right in our own back yard.

Meanwhile, as we read, two little girls slept as if couched on
zephyrs on the south side of the parlor floor, in a room that had
bunny wallpaper, a nightlight that looked like a Staffordshire cottage, and a bookcase crammed with the collected Beatrix Potter.
Snow White was in a youth bed and Rose Red was in a crib, and
next to them was the little blue and white guest room that one of
them would have one day.

Because I recognize emotions only in retrospect, I didn't know
that I was happy. As always, there was something nagging at my

mind's corners. But I did know that I had all that it is proper in this world to wish for.

SOON AFTER SHE WAS BORN, and just before we moved to 44 Jane Street, our little one, our Margaret, got funny patches on her face. Her hair started falling out in huge clumps, with bits of her scalp attached, and we became afraid to comb or brush it. Her eyes shrank to slits, and stuff oozed from under the lids and out her ears. There were cracks at the creases in her elbows and behind her knees, out of which the same stuff oozed. Eventually the cracks widened and began to bleed. The pediatrician said she had eczema and sent us to a dermatologist. When he saw her, tears sprouted in his eyes and scared us into speechlessness. "This is bad," he answered to our unasked question. "She can't retain skin."

The dermatologist sent us to an allergist, who said infant eczema was inherited, and did either of us come from families with a history of eczema or asthma? My husband said he did. I called his mother. Oh yes, she said, B. had had asthma as a child, and his nephews had had eczema. I had married a killer.

My mother had said that I had a nasty tongue, that someday I would call my husband a dirty Jew. The words were not in my head until she put them there, and I had spent so much of my life keeping my mouth shut that I didn't know what kind of tongue I had, if any. But now I feared that this dreadful mouth of mine would open and devils would leap out. So I clamped my lips, and "If I had known about those allergies I never would have married you" was written all over my face. My husband was silent, too, because he was ashamed and guilty, and because there was no way to expiate original sin. Between us lay our baby, who we thought was dying, and words that, unspoken, were as loud as cymbals clashing.

I kept the hood up on Margaret's carriage, even in the supermarket, so strangers could not see her clearly. If they did, they asked what was the matter, should she be wearing a bonnet, was she getting enough sun?

A second doctor, the head of a hospital's allergy department, kept losing Margaret's records and confusing her with her other patients. She said she wanted to take blood from Margaret, reduce it to a serum, inject it into a paid, allergy-free donor, and test the donor for the baby's allergies. "You mustn't let her do it," said a mat-mate (I never knew her name) at Kounovsky's Gym, where, in leotard and tights, I tumbled, trapezed, and swung on the rings twice a week. "The blood loss is terrible."

"Rosehip tea and beef broth cure everything," an ex-ballet dancer said, making me hate her for her mindlessness.

"My son used to look like that," the old Italian contractor who was painting 44 Jane Street said.

"How was he treated?" I asked.

"He died."

In the office—I had gone back to work when Margaret was four weeks old—I could lose myself in work. I have always been able to lose myself in work. But if someone asked me how the baby was coming along, I grew nervous, desperate to leave my desk and go home. *She won't die,* I told myself, *if I keep my eyes on her. If I close them for a second, though, she'll slip away.* (Years later, the old maternal griefs having returned, I stayed up all night with a sick kitten, believing that keeping my eyes on it as I had on Margaret was a way of pinning it to life.)

In the evening B. and I sat in the living room, Margaret sleeping on my lap, in a silence thick as heavy dust. How could we have spoken? All we had to talk about was his guilt and my rage. When we met he used to tell me how he felt, but he had stopped, because although I listened, I could not absorb. I, however, had rarely spoken of how I felt about anything. I did not want him to know, let alone anyone else to know, afraid that if I plunged into my head, I would come up with a forkful of worms. So we sat silent, Dr. Franklin once again dispensed with, Jerry moved away, and neither of us able to leap over the wall to the other.

At last we found the right doctor, the one who knew how to care for our baby. "She's allergic to *everything,*" he said, "so right now I'd rather treat the symptoms than the source." Margaret, slathered with cortisone cream, sluiced with tar baths, switched from my breast to soybean milk, grew curly black hair and cheeks like pink peonies. Once, when her doctor was lecturing to the class he taught at University Hospital, he used Margaret as his subject, pointing to her as she sat, fat, naked, and happy, on a table in the classroom. I stood in the corner beaming, as proud as if she had just won a contest for Most Beautiful Baby.

But as the eczema disappeared, asthma surfaced, and sometimes at night we heard her breathing turn to rales. Then B. would sit for hours in the bathroom, Margaret on his lap, the shower pounding and the room steaming and his eyes a misery. Meanwhile I pretended sleep and turned my back when, the baby no longer wheezing and back in her crib, I felt him sliding into bed.

It was too much. When the baroness, soon to leave *Mademoiselle* and devote herself to biography and opinionated gardening, asked me if I would consider working full-time, I said yes on the spot. I was flattered, of course, and proud to be earning my own money. But the real reason I leaped was that those months of standing over Margaret, watching and crying, had convinced me that I was not fit to deal with crises. Hoppy had returned, Hoppy who had slung Kate over her shoulder like a dishtowel and sung and whistled her into sleep, and my children would be safer with her than with me. But I am telling only half the truth. Maybe only a quarter of it. The rest of the truth is that I was unable to bear loving my children so much. Loving left me weak, skinless. Ideally I would have liked Katherine and Margaret sewn to my armpits, secured to me. Or, better yet, kicking and turning in my stomach, where I could keep them safe forever. I had to be away from my daughters because loving them was making me crazy.

B.'s being around—if together we had sat between the youth bed and the crib, as I did every night alone, singing "Rock-a-Bye, Baby"—might have eased my obsessiveness. But he had been offered a job in Boston a few months before Margaret was born. "See if they'll let you be there part-time," I said, and consigned him to a room in some club or other. I was not about to move anywhere, but especially not to Boston, which was too close to the permanent three-o'clock-in-the-afternoon that I imagined a life in Bristol would have been. Besides, I loved my job, not because it was engrossing—although it was usually amusing—but because it was all mine.

So he was gone from Tuesday at dawn through Thursday at sunset, and when he came home on Thursday nights I was rattled, resentful of an intruder into my beautiful circle of work and children. By the weekend I was glad he was in the house; I'd gotten used to him again. But when Tuesday arrived he was gone once more, and then I would reenter the magic place, all females, two of them babies, and all of them smelling sweet.

"Mary," a friend asked, "aren't you nervous? Didn't you see *Captain's Paradise?*"

I laughed, not yet having acquired imagination. My husband and my father were the only men I had ever known well, and Papa was faithless only in dying. Since B. had taken over where Papa left off, he would be no different. He was not the same man, I knew that. And yet, in a way, he was.

I DO NOT KNOW NOW how I discovered that I should have been nervous. All I remember is a civilized conversation in the living room, my hand shaking whenever I lifted a cigarette to my mouth and B.'s eyes opaque behind a pipe which kept going out. "How could a woman with children," I am asking him, "do that to another woman with children?" What had I ever done to deserve such treatment from a perfect stranger?

I absolved him, poor man alone in Boston because his wife refused to move. But not her, not that traitor to her own gender. Nor me, the wife who hadn't packed up her children and chattels and left town with her husband. And if I had? Best not to think of the boredom and, I suspect, the drinking that would have ensued. But something my father had often said when my sister and I left for parties and proms started sounding in my ears again. "Always come home with the man what brung ya," he had charged, and I had disobeyed.

MARGARET GOT WELL, Katie got beautiful, the girlfriend was discarded—how and when I never knew, being too courteous to ask—and Boston dissolved into the past. It was no place for someone as fast-paced as B. or, for that matter, for a Jew. When his boss heard that I had come from coastal Rhode Island, he said, "Oh! She's maritime." That was his way of saying, "She's okay." B., I knew, because a childhood spent next to New England's old money had thinned my skin almost to transparency, would never be okay.

No, B. was better off in New York, which is infinitely capacious, and better off as a literary agent wheeling and dealing and caviling and cajoling and doing it all with seamless charm. One of his colleagues called him "the Master."

Deep into the evening, flopped on the chaise longue, he took call after call from writers who depended on their agents like patients do on their psychiatrists. Their wives, too. Writers' husbands I knew little about—there seemed so few of them—but they struck me as docile. Writers' wives were not. They were martyrs to literature, all of them, and God forbid you shouldn't know it.

One night the ultimate martyr phoned. During an argument her husband had chased her through the room with a hammer or a chain or an axe or some other piece of heavy equipment. Somehow she had diverted him out the front door and locked it, and he was now circling the house, weapon in hand, feet occasionally entangled in pachysandra. Calling the police never entered her mind. Instead she called his agent, who lived one thousand miles away. "This," I barked, "is the limit!"

The husband was coaxed inside, weaponless, with the promise that his agent, the Great Healer, was on the phone, and B. lured him to tranquillity with his Thorazine voice. I, distracted from my book, my beautiful bedroom, my beautiful life, said I was sorry the writer and his wife hadn't shot it out, thus leaving us in peace.

In truth, this particular writer's wife was one of the few I really liked. I liked her because she was frightened, because she always expected the marriage to slip out from under her, because she knew about the abyss. Other wives, most wives, I disliked. They had, it seemed to me, certain tools I would never possess, the marital equivalent of street smarts. They could wheedle, they could pounce, they could own. I, who would have made some lucky woman a fine husband, didn't know how to do any of those things. My father's daughter, I had been a gentleman all my life.

I was afraid of wives—I saw them as smug, smooth-feathered hens—and the wives I feared most were astronauts' wives. There they were in *Life* magazine, with names like Joan and Annie: stalwart and true, and the first ones to be phoned after their hubbies had spoken to the president. Why do I think they all had sons named Chip? What was their secret? What did they know? What was the sorority grip, and why was I never taught it?

B., gregarious as well as deeply involved in his work, stayed out late at dinners and at parties. I, being neither, stayed home with the babies and the books. My husband, overworked and high-strung, would vomit late at night. I, who tend to conduct my illnesses as do dying dogs—sitting alone, staring into corners—did not realize that grownups as well as children need to have their heads held as they bend over the toilet bowl, and left him to his retching.

Work exhausted me, too, but not intellectually. How could it? I was, after all, sitting at a desk writing "Pink brocade, its skirt plumped with layers of petticoats." But it was difficult for me to talk to too many people for too long, or to listen to the endless nattering on the Graybar Building's elevators. What I wanted from marriage, apart from the children and the pleasure of knowing that I was not out there on the street alone, with the wind lifting my skirt and the mud speckling the backs of my legs, was a clean, well-lighted tomb in which I could spend the evening restoring myself for the next day. I was tired, too. When at last I finally drifted into sleep, I could feel the bed falling into the center of the earth.

◈ 2 ◈

E̶very january, B.T.B. went to Paris for the collections, installing herself in a suite in the Plaza Athénée and hiding her liquor on a ledge inside the living room fireplace. "Why tempt the help?" she used to say. Then, companioned by *Mademoiselle*'s Paris editor, a taut, thin Frenchwoman who was aunt to Leslie Caron, she did Dior and Chanel and everybody else worth covering that season. Mrs. B. had been going to Paris for years—her first trip was on the *Berengaria*—and although she never learned to speak French, she loved the tag lines. *"Merci millefois,"* she would say in thanks, *"A bientot"* in leaving.

In July the head of the fashion department made the same trip. Both sent sketches, by a man named MoMo, and notes for copy and captions back by overnight flight to New York. We—the art director and two copywriters—then worked all the next night to squeeze them into the next issue. The result, four pages of undistinguished drawings and telegraphese, was invariably ugly. But not to B.T.B. and the rest of the fashion department. *Mademoiselle,* like *Vogue* and *Bazaar,* had reported Paris!

Our second winter at 44 Jane Street, I suggested an article that would track a young designer for the two weeks leading up to his first show. The baroness's replacement, a middle-aged woman with famous friends, who always put on lipstick before answering the phone if told the caller was a man, liked the idea. "Now let me see," she mused. "Who do I know who's in Paris right now?"

"But *I* want to do it," I said, surprising myself as much as I surprised her. Never before had I said "I want" about anything that had to do with work. "Yours," a friend had pontificated, "is a passive personality."

I had been afraid to fly—"Which one of us is going to be on the ill-fated plane?" B. would ask about the tortuous travel plans that would assure that our children did not lose both parents in a crash—and afraid to write, and now both fears had evaporated in the face of that furious "I want."

The night before the flight, I lay in bed beside my husband as frightened as if it had been execution eve. I do not understand why I thought I was taking an irreversible step. I had no goal beyond writing that one article, no ideas for others, and little interest in advancing what I would have been embarrassed to call a career. The term was pretentious, even low-class—the kind of word used by the kind of people who called a college economics class "econ" rather than the Ivy League—preferred "eck." So when I cried and apologized to B. for leaving him, and said over and over again that I was sorry I had to go, I can only assume it was because my gut was telling me something about myself that my head was not ready to hear.

B. was proud of his wife: at last she was living up to her potential. I must not forget to call on Alice, must not forget some tinned truffles at Fauchon, must not forget his sandalwood soap.

He had written to so-and-so, so there was at least one good dinner on tap; and surely so-and-so would be free for lunch one day; and no, I must not worry that people would not like me, because of course they would. I left the next morning, blessed with my husband's good will and competent child care and possessed by a sadness that has grayed a portion of every day I have lived since. Why did I have to make that trip, when all I had ever wanted (or so I still tell myself) was to be a good wife and a perfect mother and to sleep in peace?

My room was on the Left Bank, on the top floor of the Hôtel Pont-Royal, and its ceiling slanted like a garret's. It was small, too, just big enough for me and a typewriter and a tiny portable radio, which I stuck in a wooden bureau drawer so the sound would be better. Because it was January I had packed warm flannel nightgowns, and laughed every night on seeing that the chambermaid who turned down the bed and laid a nightgown athwart its pillows invariably pinched in its waist. Sexy granny gowns! Too funny! "You brought flannel nightgowns to *Paris*, Mary?" B.T.B., who arrived a week later, said. "Suppose something unexpected should arise?"

I was flattered that B.T.B. thought me capable of racy conduct, thereby admitting me to the company of the dashing, but the idea of sharing my bed was incredible. There was no one in the world, no movie star even, for whom I would have sacrificed the pleasure of sleeping alone in that room with its view over the rooftops and its scent of disinfectant and Gauloises and Jolie Madame.

I had never been alone before, unless not having a roommate in college counts, and I kept discovering new things about myself. The pleasure of my own company, for one, and the curiosity that sent me bravely out into the streets with bad French and no sense of direction. But I never got lost, not once, and I began to acquire a trust, still with me, in my feet's wisdom. My body was becoming my house. I ambulated as securely as a turtle.

And I was happy, so happy I was afraid to acknowledge the feeling lest, once named, it would fly away. Sitting one noon in a restaurant near the Madeleine with my omelet and my packet of Disque Bleus, wearing my fun fur and my Pucci dress and my I.

Miller shoes, I said to myself, "Now you've got everything Papa and B. ever wanted for you."

So what if I had run my entire life on my husband's and father's engines? Who is to say that my own engine, assuming it ever existed or was distinguishable from theirs, would have been preferable? Not I.

SOME EVENINGS I spent in my room, bent over a bowl of soup, my notes, and the phone. The article had to be finished before I left Paris, and since the only criticism I trusted or would abide by was B.'s, I spent a fortune calling New York and reading him the day's work. If he said it was okay, it was. Anyone else's opinion was unimportant. The reading over, we would chat about the children and what he was doing and what the weather was in New York (it was gray and rainy in Paris), and then I would do something I had not done since we were in college and he had called me every night on the dorm phone. "You hang up first," I would say. "No, you hang up first," he would say, and then, unwilling to be the first to cut the connection, we would arrange to put our receivers back in their cradles at precisely the same time.

In college, once I had hung up the phone, I would feel as though I had lost an arm. But not now. Now I felt whole again, because of the bliss of returning to a silence broken only by the type-writer's hesitant staccato and an occasional *whoop-whoop-whoop* from a passing police car. I was concentrating at last, and all my bits and pieces were coalescing into one self-sufficient self.

Other evenings I dined with B.'s friends, or with new friends I had met while following the couturier around. They liked me, they asked me out again and again, they thought I was amusing. Maybe I was, but mostly I was a new face, a new audience for the old act. No matter. I was working without a net—my husband—and I was not falling down.

There was one man, Philippe (I cannot even remember his last name, and in any case it was never important), a few years younger than I, who took me dancing. He wore Cardin suits and came from Provence, was small-boned, elegant, and faintly reminiscent of

Colette's Chéri. More than that I cannot say, because I knew no more of him than that, only what my imagination made of him. It turned him into France, and Paris, my Paris, in particular.

In Paris it was the month of the Beatles. They were performing at the Olympia and were reliably reported to have just left every discothèque one had just entered. "The Beatles were here only a minute ago," I heard in every dim, smoky room. "You just missed them."

I can't remember ever smoking or drinking in any of those discos, only dancing and looking back at my little round table to see if my quilted Chanel bag was still there. Actually, every little round table bore a quilted Chanel bag. They were membership cards.

The big word was *"yé-yé,"* used to describe everything from the cut of a skirt to the curve of a curl, and the big song was "Et Maintenant." When that was played, conversation halted, hips ground together, partner eyeballed partner, and the sound of heavy breathing swamped the room. When Philippe and I danced, my groin hurt, and although we kept a proper inch or two apart, I confused the thought with the deed and deemed myself an adulteress.

Toward dawn he would drive wildly through the empty Paris streets. Or maybe he was not really driving wildly. Maybe it was only the smallness of his car and the screech it made when he took corners that made me think we were speeding, heading for a crash, careless of our lives. One evening he stopped in front of Notre-Dame, which, the illumination gone, had returned to medieval darkness.

"This makes me think of François Villon," I said, "and the wolves that stalked the walls of Paris."

*"Vous êtes formidable,"* he breathed, and took my hand.

I cried. I was not *formidable.* I was simply the virgin mother of two experiencing the late adolescence she had never had, too naive to recognize the melt in the stomach, the sense of shiver, as the sensations of the twenty-year-old she had never been.

On the afternoon I left Paris, Philippe took me to the airport and stayed on the observation desk waving until takeoff. I cried again, cried all the way home. I was on Air France, stretched out on three seats, and an old babushkaed Polish woman across the aisle kept looking over at me, sighing and clucking and nodding and wanting to help. But she had no English, and the babushka and her anxious monkey eyes and baggy coat and fat, spread feet only made me cry the harder.

B., the children, and Hoppy were at the airport. Margaret, sitting on my lap, wet my skirt on the cab ride into the city. She was eighteen months old, and too hearty even for double diapers and rubber pants. Katie's hair ribbon was flying and Hoppy was chatting and my husband was silent. He knew me, much better than I knew myself, and he saw my pink eyes and the way they dodged his.

I am not much given to playing "If I had" or "If I hadn't," much preferring to stay with "It would have happened anyway." But that last is usually a lie, and I am not one to kid myself. I am sorry I went to Paris, because when I returned I was full of myself and starved for more of me. Or am I sorry? I do not know. I am mixed up. But I do know that there have been many years when I wished I could have walked into that little group at the airport, never to emerge again. I see them—the husband who looked like Montgomery Clift in his Harrods' raincoat, the nurse in her white uniform, the little girl dancing in her hair ribbons, and the baby bulwarked in her diapers—and they haunt me, still there, still waiting at Kennedy.

MY MOTHER HAD SAID I was born an old maid. My husband had told me I would make a wonderful widow. Always eager to accept others' definitions of myself—they saved me the boredom, and the pain, of having to make my own—I argued with both, that being my way, and silently agreed with both, that also being my way. But now I had to think, and I could only do that if I was alone. So I made what seemed to me a perfectly logical request: I asked B. to move out for a few weeks.

So B. moved to a friend's apartment down the street, more dwindled by my request than I had been by his adultery. Which does not imply that I was the larger character, only that he was, for a while anyway, the more human. And I lived for a month the life that a few years later became the only one I knew.

In bed at night, the children asleep, I had long talks with me.

So satsifying! I said, *Papa would not have wanted me to have mourned him for so many years.* So I buried him. I thought about Philippe. Who was he, anyway? A figment of my imagination, really. So I buried him. I thought about B. Who was he? The only man I had ever wanted to marry. My father's surrogate. My floor. My door to the world. So I asked him to come home.

He came home, and he cried. But I did not know it then. He cried because the relief of being away from me had eclipsed the hurt of being asked to go. He had met someone, or, more likely, someone had been served up to him—when a formerly unavailable man is suddenly made free, all the world turns Pandarus—and he had had fun. He had had a good time. But I am guessing. I do not know what his life was without me, but I think it was like being on parole.

A few months later, in December, we gave a party to celebrate our eleventh wedding anniversary. "For this I'm coming wrapped in the Israeli flag," Leo Lerman said. "I never thought you'd make it."

Neither did I, and I was tremendously pleased with myself, with my husband, and with the exceptional sanity and staying power that had put us beyond anything so weak-minded as divorce. One could defeat anything, death only excluded, if one just put one's *mind* to it. Not enough people put their *minds* to things.

I had spent the previous evening making pâtés and dips, deviling eggs, stuffing mushrooms, and baking a ham. We had hired a bartender, but everything else was done by me. My grandmother's contemptuous "store-bought" had left me with the style of a house-proud nineteenth-century New England housewife.

My office assistant said our friends were absolutely glamorous. Our apartment was jammed with writers and editors and agents and their pretty, thirtyish wives. No one was divorced or dying yet—that started a few years later—and our children, in their best dresses and hair ribbons, were made much of. Almost everyone there had children, too, all of them about to be launched toward New York's private schools.

No one had bad breath; no one was overweight but for one literary agent, who was discovered in the kitchen picking at the hambone. But since her weight served as a metaphor for her arrogant charm, her two hundred plus pounds were considered okay. No one got drunk, since half the guests were drinking dry vermouth on the rocks with a twist of lemon. Several of the writers were stars of the month, just about the right number, because too many of them and everyone would be wondering if he was standing in the right orbit, only one of them and you got awed and silent guests.

The hostess has had her hair done in a kind of Jackie Kennedy bouffant at the Tempo Beauty Salon on West Twelfth Street (stingy, practical, she will never drop a cent at Kenneth's), and is elegant in a long gray Donald Brooks cut low over breasts so small (though sweet) that she looks dressed even when she is naked. She is balancing a glass of dry vermouth and a cigarette, keeping an eye on the children, counting the stuffed mushrooms, and greeting all and sundry. She is a wonder. She has crested.

CASTING YOURSELF in character parts is a pleasant way to trundle through life. It promises continuity. Those were the years, I say now, when I was a young matron, thus implying that there were other years when I was a this, other years when I was a that, years to come when I will be something else entirely. Young matron. Yes, I was certainly that.

Early in the morning I walked Kate and Mag down Hudson Street to their little Episcopal school. Like all our crowd, we had abjured the public schools. They were all, except for the legendary P.S. 6 on the Upper East Side, for which parents fought and killed, "impossible."

Rose Red hung on to my right hand, Snow White hung on to my left, until they broke free and ran through the gate and into the little playground. The school was banked by a very old church and early nineteenth-century brick houses—Bret Harte had lived in one of them—and in my memory yellow leaves are forever scudding along the sidewalk and the air is forever crisp and blue.

Next I would step off the curb, hail a cab, and pick up B., who was waiting, attaché case in hand, on the corner of Jane Street. He would drop me off on Park, next to the alleyway that led to the back of the Graybar Building, with the incantatory "Good luck, I love you" I insisted on before I could start work. Then I would enter the office I shared with two assistants, to laugh a lot and write copy between spurts of gossip.

Two nights a week I stopped at the Tempo Beauty Salon for a shampoo and set. The Tempo was cheap. Even better, it was reminiscent of the place my mother went to in Bristol for her permanents and manicures, but where hers had a radio on the windowsill, this one had a television set on the counter. I saw that Vietnamese colonel, I think he was, blow a hole through a captive's head on that television set. Then I walked home, to Snow White and Rose Red, who were gobbling down fried whiting and collard greens. Hoppy had retired. Our new housekeeper was from North Carolina, and I was running, although I didn't know it and had not even heard the term, the greatest soul food kitchen in New York.

We entertained quite often, and if I did not shine in conversation, I did not care. B. was the shine; I was glad to be the chamois. Feeding people was what pleased me. I thought myself a goddess when my hands were in dough or skinning a chicken or hulling strawberries.

We were invited to many parties, too, but I skipped most of them, and the only evening that sticks in my mind was a New Year's Eve in the dark, crowded apartment of a literary agent who chain-smoked cigarettes clamped in a roach holder on her index finger. "There we were," I told my assistants the next workday, "like the audience at a bullfight. The wives were sitting around the ring, and the matadors, the husbands, were strutting in the center. The only woman who got out there with them was Elaine Dundy, but of course she'd had a bestseller."

No, there's another evening that also sticks in my mind. We were dining, on the Upper West Side, with a man who had been famous because of his talent and was famous now mostly because of his eight wives. The eighth was there, a former movie actress whose eyes swam in their sockets like guppies in a bowl and who kept repeating, her fist pounding her palm, that her husband was *a real man.*

He, balding, was on the other side of the room talking about

Spinoza, about whom he could quote reams of other people's opinions. You could not beat him in debate. Disagree with one of his assessments, which were never his to begin with, and he would hit you with Kierkegaard, say, quoted *in toto*.

Later, in the cab, I told B. that if I had ever been mad enough to marry that man, I would still be his first and only wife. "I can't see that divorce solves anything."

"I know you can't," he said, and kept silence all the way home.

THE SILENCES are what I remember, not conversations, not even arguments. But then, we never did argue, not really. We had too much in common.

We read a lot, for instance, and we were as one when it came to our children's educations. We were accomplished eaters, drank only grape derivatives, and enjoyed driving through Europe. We even looked a bit alike. "If we were meeting for the first time," I said the day before he left, "you'd like me."

Perhaps it was, in the end, a matter of style, not content. Myself, holding Kate's hand, emerging on Easter Sunday from a church he hated as only a man whose cousin, the Lochinvar of his childhood, had died in the Lincoln Brigade could hate it. Myself, bustling in from a Sunday afternoon movie in which quantities of cognac had been consumed, pouring myself a stiff two fingers in emulation of the heroine and describing the film in the breathlessly chatty manner I had osmosed in assorted country clubs (no Jews allowed, Catholics, provided they looked and talked like me, only bearable) and Connecticut College. Myself, enthusing about a gymnastics class and demonstrating a headstand to a man whose last participatory athletic event had been a softball game when he was twenty-three. Myself, anxious to get sex over with so I could get to sleep. Myself, desperate with migraine and nursing an ulcer and smilin' through. Myself, talking, talking, talking to reach someone who was receding, irretrievably, into the distance. Suddenly there was so much of myself, so much to choose from, and none of it wanted.

◆ **3** ◆

*T*HE MANAGING EDITOR, the one with all the famous friends, resigned. She was going to *Seventeen,* where the increase in salary would more than make up for no longer being able to publish such unlikely contributers to *Mademoiselle* as Cabot Lodge and Alistair Cooke, and the personnel department—mysterious women stuffed with more secrets than the Sphinx—was shipping candidate after candidate to B.T.B.'s boudoir. All we ever saw of them was a coat, usually expensive, folded over a chair beside B.T.B.'s secretary's desk, but that was enough to set the office, Leo Lerman in particular, to trembling. We liked *Mademoiselle* just the way it was.

Leo's kingdom was a shoebox of a room crammed with a filing cabinet that might have come out of *Front Page,* an old glass-fronted bookcase, an ancient typewriter, and a big desk spilling over with papers, photographs, pens, pencils, and once, in a drawer, a family of mice. I had never known him to like any of *Mlle.*'s managing editors—they either threatened his pages or cramped his style, or both—so he was pleased when I suggested myself for the job. It was about then, I think, that he, who lived and breathed every English novel that ever was, started calling me "our Mary."

There was a certain amateurishness, a beguiling raffishness to *Mademoiselle.* One of the fashion editors was hanging out at Tim Leary's place in Millbrook, forever racing out the back door as the police were racing in the front; another, fresh from California, had framed her bulletin board with lollipops and wore skirts so short the world gasped when she bent over. B. claimed that if he was standing around the Graybar Building's lobby, he could always identify the *Mademoiselle* girls by the way they dressed ("oddly," he said) and by "something funny about their knees."

So if I felt a bit timid about going to the gym teacher who still ruled the personnel department and telling her I would like to be the next managing editor, I was not the least timid about thinking I could handle the job. *Mademoiselle* was the kind of place where you could make things up as you went along, not because anybody was ever thinking seriously about innovation or would even dream of using the word but because most of the staff was imbued with the spirit of a Mickey Rooney/Judy Garland musical. We were forever planning a show in the back yard.

Magisterial behind her bosom and her desk, the gym teacher pondered. Could I, she wondered aloud, "handle" B.T.B.? I was younger than my predecessors, had two small children, and could not be counted on to stay an hour or so after the staff went home, chatting in her office and sharing a nip or two of vodka.

"Oh, yes," I said, and got the job.

In truth, I never had to "handle" B.T.B. We got along because she was always loyal to her editors in public, even if she disagreed with them in private, and because I was not remotely duplicitous. Sometimes, though, I think I puzzled her, being perhaps the only Irish Catholic she had ever known who was neither the cook's daughter nor the child of a family like the Kennedys or the McDonnells. "But of course, the Irish *ruined* Southampton," I had once overheard her say to the managing editor with the famous friends. The latter, born in Boston and raised among the pink-cheeked and high-nosed, shared the sentiment.

Not being able to place me forced B.T.B. to put me on something like par; and besides, her snobberies were essentially innocent. "Did you know her mother was a *trained nurse?*" she once asked about an editor who, eager to ingratiate herself with a woman whose son had belonged to the Knickerbocker Grays, was overfond of mentioning her own membership in the Junior League. Trained nurses, I knew from childhood eavesdropping, had seen men who were not their husbands (assuming they had any) *naked*, and knew more than they should about birth control.

"Take me to the Plaza!" I said to B. when I phoned to tell him that I was the new managing editor. The Plaza was in honor of Fitzgerald, just as the Ritz was in honor of Hemingway. "Take me to the Ritz Bar!" I had said on the day six years before when I arrived on the boat-train from Le Havre, seven months pregnant and glowing like a lamp. I had two martinis and stole an ashtray, and B. caught my every word and tossed it into the air. Now, though, he smiled and said the right things, whatever they were, but my words never reached their target, not really. Instead they simply dropped into space.

If it wasn't like the day at the Ritz, neither was it like the last time I had been in the Plaza. That had been a few years before, when Leo Lerman and Roger Schoening, who was the art director, and I sneaked out of the office late one afternoon to see *The Leather Boys*. Suddenly the screen went blank and the little lights at the end of the aisles died and we went out onto Fifty-seventh Street, where people were scurrying like ants just dislodged from an anthill. The sky was a chill November gray, still light enough for us to see clearly, and all that told us that something was very wrong were the darkened windows of Tiffany's and Bergdorf's and Van Cleef. "Let us go to the Plaza," Leo said grandly. "They will know what is happening."

Roger and I followed him—it was like following stately, plump Buck Mulligan—into the Palm Court, where the waiters were bringing candles and the little orchestra was sawing away at Viennese waltzes. "The last night on the *Titanic*," Leo said, delighted, and waved us to a table, where we sat for hours, Roger and I drinking whatever the waiters came up with and Leo abstemious as usual, in what we learned later was the great blackout of 1965.

The phones were not out yet, so after a long wait in a line downstairs I managed to call home and tell B. that I was not only not stuck in an elevator but ensconced in the Palm Court. Then there was nothing to do but enjoy the shadows and the candles and the Blue Danube waltz.

Once we realized that the electric power was not going to come back anytime soon, Leo started the long walk home, fifty or so blocks to his house, a raddled old beauty way up on Lexington Avenue. Along the way, he informed us later, he helped direct traffic. We were stunned.

Roger and I walked him as far as Fifth Avenue, then waited at what we assumed was a bus stop because of all the people clustered there. When a bus came, perhaps an hour later, it was as crowded as a Mexican jitney. The mood was Mexican, too. Or rather, what I imagined a Mexican mood to be. We were cheerful, we were happy, we all but danced in place.

Once in the Village, we walked west through a city that was

close to invisible. I do not remember stars (although I have been told there was a full moon), or people, or sound, only Roger falling over a fire hydrant in front of the Greenwich Theater. He left me on Jane Street, then limped to his place on Greenwich Street, and I walked into a house that smelled of the chicken Hoppy had roasted in the gas oven. Her daughter was there—B. had fished her out of a nearby subway station—and was to sleep on the living room couch. Hoppy was taking the little bedroom next to the children's. A smile split B.'s face when I came in the door, and the children, bathed and in their bathrobes, capered around my knees. There we all were, safe under one roof, and there was nothing the darkness could do to any of us.

"WELL, WHAT DO YOU THINK I ought to do first?" My new secretary, who has just arrived from *Vogue,* where mostly she answered the sportswear editor's phone, is standing in the doorway. "Maybe I should go through the files."

"That sounds like a good idea."

She laughs. I laugh. At lunch I tell a chum from the copy department that I just love my new secretary's face. "No wonder," the chum says. "She looks just like you." Back from lunch, I stare at this girl who has buried herself in the file drawers and is turning them upside down. She could be my niece, or a much younger sister. This resemblance, I figure, is a good omen.

Everyone in the office is forever looking for omens, good or bad. We read the horoscope column in *Elle;* several of us, including myself, toss the I Ching every morning; and one of us is studying numerology. Nobody takes any of this seriously, but we love having a couple of tools with which to grasp life's vagaries. That B.T.B. and I are so unexpectedly harmonious, for instance, is laid by the office seers to our both being Tauruses.

When I tell B. that evening of what my secretary had found in the file drawers—manuscripts going back through two of my predecessors, often accompanied by angry letters from their authors demanding to know when they would run—he says, "Get rid of them."

"But they must have paid thousands for this stuff."

"Don't worry about it. The worst thing you can do is publish something that doesn't represent your idea of what this magazine should be."

Something else was bothersome. There was a certain fuzziness around the edges of the letters with which articles were commissioned. The terms were never quite spelled out.

"What you should do," B. said, "is state the kill fee very clearly. Since you people pay miserably, make it half."

His were the only two lessons I ever got in managing editorship, and all I really needed, because the world was shoving subjects in my face.

*Mademoiselle*'s readers bought it because it was a fashion magazine. Anything else, the fiction as well, was lagniappe. Since we didn't have to use the features to sell an issue—if we had, we couldn't have run much beyond articles on sex and diets, because only they made surefire cover lines—we could commission whatever interested *us*. What interested us was eventually codified as "popular culture," "the counterculture," and "feminism." But we never used those terms; we never even knew them. Instead we said, "I heard about this commune in the Berkshires that's led by a kid who's the reincarnation of Saint Peter, so I thought I might go up there for a weekend. . . ." or "How about we use rock stars on the fashion pages? Grace Slick is pretty, so we could use her for a beauty shot, and if Aretha Franklin wants to model something, we could always stick her behind a tree." Which we did.

We ran articles on what we called the Women's Movement, and when *Ms.* was born, we yawned and compared it to *Popular Science* at the same time that we were angry because of all the press it got. Why wasn't anybody looking at us? Why hadn't anyone noticed that we ran articles with titles like "No More Ms. Nice Girl" and writers like Rebecca West, not to mention a passel of very young writers on rock, most of whom could not write well but who for a brief time had cornered the market because nobody else knew anything about the subject? We grouched, we complained, and eventually we relaxed. We were true amateurs, and what we did, we did for love.

Here is Roger, come to my office with his morning coffee, brewed by a black woman named Cora, whose job it is to stand in the hallway behind the coffee urn from nine to ten and greet us white warriors. Roger has transferred his coffee into his big pewter cup and is settling down for our daily chat.

Between us, Roger and I have seen almost every bad movie made between 1935 and maybe 1960, and they form the substructure of our every conversation, especially when we are in the art department. "Don't you find her just a teeny bit reminiscent of the unforgettable Vera Hruba Ralston?" I say, peering through the magnifying glass at the Ektachromes spread on the light table. He looks through his glass at the blonde model. "I don't know," he answers. "I would have said Marie Windsor." Were we not to see each other again for thirty years, his first words on meeting me would be something like "Seen any good Faith Domergue movies lately?"

Later today he and I and B.T.B. will be looking at the cover tries. B.T.B.'s response is predictable. "She's got a mutt face," she'll say of the pug-nosed and strong-chinned. Our response is predictable, too. If the sitter is a crop-haired girl much beloved by the fashion department but not by us, we will once more point out her resemblance to Flora Robson. "God, you people are cruel," one of the editors in the college and career department always says when she hears us talking. But we are not cruel. It's just that people whose business is fashion look at models with the same eyes with which they look at a bust dart ("Godawful") or a Rudi Gernreich ("divine!"). One way or another, everything is merch.

There is a clatter in the corridor. Leo, wearing the shaggy coat (it looks like a bearskin) he bought on sale at Saks, has arrived, scattering bon mots as he goes. "Tell all," he commands as Roger and I walk in his door.

I spend a lot of time with Leo. His career, and indeed his identity, depend on keeping up with what's going on. Nobody's going to catch Leo napping! No sir! Mention a new group, a new book, or a new art gallery and Leo's heard it/read it/seen it first.

It is to keep up that Leo climbed endless steps to the balcony of a Lower East Side Loews where Tim Leary, barefoot in white pajamas, told us to turn on and tune out or something like that while a girl in a leotard attempted Martha Graham movements behind a backlighted scrim. Later we went to Ratner's for farina pudding.

"I've seen better high masses," I said airily.

"But that, our Mary, is what this was all about."

He had nothing to say, however, when I dragged him to the Ike and Tina Turner Revue. Ike talked dirty, Tina humped the mike, and Leo sat impassive. "I am," he told me once, "a Jewish puritan. Whereas you, our Mary, are a Catholic prig."

Returned from movies, he gave us capsule reviews. The cast of *Ship of Fools,* for instance, he described as "everyone who was not otherwise employed." Staying in London, he sent us letters to be read aloud. "I can't go into details now but you must remind me to tell you about Cecil Beaton's party for Audrey Hepburn where I had a long talk with Princess Margaret. . . ." Yes, we would remind him. We would hang on his every word.

Tonight Leo is taking me to a screening. What is nice about a screening, apart from the facts that it is free and that the seats are as comfortable as club chairs, is the sense it gives the audience of belonging to a fraternity. I am not at screenings often enough to recognize anyone, but I can recognize the tie that binds. The viewers loll in their chairs, they exchange few words in the elevator going down, but no matter how long they have done this, no matter how boring the film is, they have experienced the exquisite pleasure of seeing it first. First! God, how tired I will get of that word—and that obsession—one day!

Around noontime I am taking a writer out for lunch at a restaurant in the East Forties called Cheval Blanc. Cheval Blanc has the kind of French food that reminds me of the days when our crowd, B.'s and mine, had innocent mouths, when we found any pâté, however cold and dry, exciting and always ordered crème caramel for the joy of giving the proper Yiddish-sounding, soon-to-spit "khr" to "crème." The woman who runs Cheval Blanc is strict about men wearing jackets and keeps a spare for those who do not. Once she forced it on our rock columnist, a very short young man whose fingertips barely emerged from its gorilla-length sleeves. But at least she does not forbid women in pantsuits a table, like some of the restaurateurs farther uptown, although she did frown the day our sex columnist showed up in rayon lounging pajamas. The exterminator had arrived unexpectedly, the columnist announced in her piercing Australian chirp, and she couldn't get to her closet for the bug bombs.

Now, though, there is just enough time to make a few phone calls and dictate a few letters. No, wait. B.T.B. is calling a short meeting in her office. She is not at all happy about our photographing swimsuits in Miami instead of Bermuda. Isn't Miami just a little bit . . . common? The fashion editor explains. It's been raining in Bermuda. Chilly, too. And the magazine's got a due bill at a hotel in Miami, which is a good thing, because we've just about exhausted the travel budget.

There! That's settled. The photographer, a fashion editor, and two models will leave for Miami at the end of the week, along with a stack of swimsuits packed in a long box called the coffin. B.T.B. reaches for her lipstick. So do I. So do the fashion editors: they're on their way to the market. Our perfumes—Diorissimo and Madame Rochas and Femme and my Vent Vert—meet and mingle; the sun hits B.T.B.'s Georgian chandelier; B.T.B. slides a tortured foot out of her Delman pump, then slides it back in again. "Women!" she says fondly. "We *are* a silly sex."

B.T.B. WAS PUNCTILIOUS about my hours. On the rare evenings I worked late, I could put a cab on petty cash, first having fought with the feral boys who lined up outside the Lexington Avenue entrance of Grand Central, grabbing taxis and demanding ransom in the shape of a tip before they would take their hands off the door handles. But most of the time I could leave the office at rush hour, swept up with half the city toward the subways and the buses.

The lobby of the Graybar Building debouched directly into Grand Central Terminal, so there was no need to go outdoors to get home. Instead I descended a dark, broad staircase near the Lexington Avenue entrance, walked the equivalent of a city block or two, then went down a narrow staircase to the shuttle. My father used to talk about "hopping the shuttle," and now I was hopping it, to careen across town to Times Square.

At Times Square, I press my shoulder bag to my side with my

right arm, grasp it with my left hand, and, holding my breath against the stink of urine, walk quickly to the IRT-Seventh Avenue line.

Across the way, on the uptown platform, people are packed as densely as sardines, and when a subway arrives they will move in one mindless surge toward its doors. Getting on an uptown train at rush hour is both a game and a shoving match: you can either get into the spirit of the mob or be enraged by the crush and, all too often, the feel of a stiffening penis against your back. To live downtown, however, is to be always going against the traffic, until Thirty-fourth Street, where the Macy's shoppers arrive, lugging their shopping bags and—many of them—composing their souls for the long haul to Brooklyn. They settle their shopping bags along the floor, stare dully at the ads for hemorrhoid cures and cigarettes. The youngest of them bring out paperbacks; the scattering of men lean forward, their elbows on their knees, and study the morning's tabloids.

Fourteenth Street! I rise, skirt the shopping bags and the occasional extended leg, and leave the car. Straight ahead is the Twelfth Street exit, my exit, and the entrance to another world.

At my left is a big community garden, built on the site of the old Loew's Sheridan, from whose balcony I saw *Rock Around the Clock* and *The Rains of Ranchipur* and *Them!* At my right is the Maritime Trades Building, its porthole windows dark and empty. Ahead is the Greenwich Theater and a thin line of ticket buyers, and beyond it West Twelfth Street, which, in just one short block, has a huge garage, several decaying tenements, and a string of nineteenth-century houses. The only sound is that of my heels on the cement sidewalk.

The traffic is light on Eighth Avenue, and there is none whatsoever on Jane Street. No strollers either. It is a little early for the gang at the No-Name Bar to gather, and the fat man who runs the delicatessen at the corner is looking at an empty store. I lift the latch on the iron gate that leads to the areaway of 44 Jane, unlock the metal grille that is the outer door, relock it, and unlock the wooden inner door. Nobody shouts, "Mommy's home!" Snow White and Rose Red, bathed, fed, and bathrobed, are sitting in the kitchen with Ann, the housekeeper who arrived when Hoppy retired, watching an *I Love Lucy* rerun.

It is not that they are not glad to see me, because they are, and they will be especially glad when, later on tonight, I read them *Eloise* or tell them once again the gripping story of Mary Lee Cantwell, Lost in the Hurricane. But since nine o'clock this morning, they have lived a life to which I have no access. Parents have limited access to their children's lives anyway, but my exclusion is absolute. I am not around.

Rose Red, however, tries very hard to keep me informed. Snow White is old enough to be a charming companion to her father, and on the Saturdays when he is around he takes her out to lunch or to a matinee. *She Loves Me* is her favorite show; she will sing "A Trip to the Library" at the drop of a hint.

Mag, though, is too young for theater. When she and I and her sister went to a revival of *On the Town* (they squealed when they heard "Christopher Street, Christopher Street/Right in the heart of Greenwich Village"), she sat politely on her upfolded seat, the only way she could see over the heads in front of her, kicking her bored legs up and down, up and down. So we spend our Saturday afternoons on long walks, retracing her week.

"This," she says, pausing at a house on West Fourth Street, "is where Ann stopped to tie my shoe." We move along to West Eleventh. "This is where I lost my ball." We enter a variety store for a new one. "They know me here!" she crows.

At Abingdon Square, a dusty triangle with a sandpit, several struggling trees, and some faded benches, I lift her into one of the metal swings and pull down the safety bar. "Have you ever seen the squirrels that live here?" she asks. No, I have not.

When their school reports from St. Luke's arrive, I read about the red skirt that Katie likes to put on during dress-up hour and that she tells her teacher is beautiful. She likes to cook at the play stove in the kitchen corner, too, and pretend to put on makeup from the bag of make-believe cosmetics I gave her for her birthday. Mag, I read, sleeps very soundly at naptime. But I have never been there when Katie rushed home from school to talk about what she cooked on the cardboard stove, nor have I ever seen Margaret flushed and sleepy after an hour on her little cot. I do not even know which blanket she took from home to cram in her cubby. I am stuffed with memories, so many memories that today they spill over into my dreams and strike me—right across the face—when I am not expecting them. But I do not have these.

I doubt that those two little girls who are watching Lucy and Ethel fill their faces with chocolates, who are soon to be tucked into what I—and my mother, and indeed all mothers—call "your own little bed," have spent a day that was darkened by my absence. Although we will never know this for certain, the day may even have been the brighter for it. But tonight, when they drift off to sleep and into a place where no one can follow them, they will take with them bits and pieces of lives in which, almost from the beginning, I, their mother, have played no part.

◈ 4 ◈

THERE WAS QUIET, and there was no sex. And a marriage without sex, I realized at last, is a desert.

I had always liked sleeping alone in monkish little beds. Their narrowness helped exclude everyone who had brushed up against me during the day. Once B. had objected to my dark and silent steals, pillow under arm, clock in hand, to the small bed in the small room next to the children. He did not object any longer. When I did sleep in our bed, no hand came out and touched my belly. I asked if there was another woman. Yes, yes, those very words; there are no new ones. He said no.

In February, B. went to Guadalupe for "a rest," and to "lie in the sun." There was, as he knew, no question of my going. I have my father's pale Irish skin, and a beach is a skillet to me.

The day he was due back, a storm came and shut down the airports, and I, not knowing whether he had left the island, called his hotel. The desk clerk spoke an incomprehensible patois, so I called B.'s office and asked for his secretary, a plump young girl who often babysat for us and about whose weight he fretted. Certain that the problem was glandular, he had even sent her to our doctor. When I, who had written reams of copy about diets, said idly that almost all excess weight was due to overeating, he barked, "You don't know what you're talking about," then closed his mouth in a thin, mean line.

His secretary, I was told, was in Florida.

I did not know who was where, did not know for sure for years, and in any case it does not matter now. But I can still feel the cold that iced me, the cold that Emily Dickinson called "zero at the bone."

I can still feel the cold on Hudson Street, too, and the way the wind was whipping up off the river, and the tunnels of snow through which I walked all the way down to St. Luke's Place, trying to exercise away something my body knew long before the message reached my brain.

When, a few hours later, the key turned in the lock of the front door, I jumped up from the kitchen table, where Kate and Mag and I were having supper, ran into the hall, and hugged him. His eyes were opaque. Years before he had gone to Jamaica with friends, and sung "Take me to Jamaica where de rum come from" for the children and me, and done a little dance, and spoken hilariously, happily, of lizards and beaches and mysterious insects. I asked about Guadalupe. "You wouldn't have liked it," he said.


"MAYBE IF YOU BEHAVED like Irene Dunne in *The Awful Truth*," Leo suggested. "You know. Lively laughter and all that."

I tried lively laughter. I sat in the living room chattering. B. sucked on his pipe. But sometimes he, too, tried lively laughter. "There are all kinds of people you could marry if you got rid of me," he said.

"Name one."

He named a few bachelors. We laughed immoderately. Such fun!


IN JUNE the guest editors arrived at *Mademoiselle*, eager to work on the August issue, which in truth was already close to complete, and after a few weeks of hanging around the office, even more eager to speak of being "exploited." Part of their month in New York now involved a week in a foreign country. For years I had hankered for a free trip with what we called the g.e.'s. Israel was not what I had in mind.

I hated Tel Aviv, of which I recall little but stucco apartment houses built on stilts, with balconies closed by corrugated aluminum doors. The women's army camp we toured was similar to the Girl Scout camp I had gone to when I was twelve, and struck me as about as serious. Israeli men, I decided, would kill rather than queue, and the food left me seven pounds lighter. But everything—the heat, the dryness, the militarism, the chauvinism that had a guide claiming that even the stars were brighter over Israel—receded in the face of my realization that I was in the Holy Land.

I became a pilgrim, returned to Sunday school, returned to stations of the cross and purple-wrapped crucifixes on Good Friday and quick childish prayers to Jesus to "please help me be a good person." We stayed in a kibbutz on the Sea of Galilee, and one evening before dinner I went out to the dock, took off my sneakers, and stuck my feet in the water for a kind of inverted baptism.

For three days I walked through the old quarter of Jerusalem, which is sixteenth century, Turkish, built on ruins, and probably unmappable, through sudden spills of light and fly-covered fruit and taunting, stone-throwing Arab children and rug sellers and Arab men with blue eyes (Crusader remnants, I told myself) who wore gilt-edged burnooses over their striped robes and kept their hands cupped over their crotches.

Walking along the Via Dolorosa, I touched my fingers to its walls, and when a man excavating a trench near the Temple of Solomon tossed up a pot handle he had just uncovered, I wrapped it in my underpants and hid it in my suitcase for the journey home.

A guest editor and I went to the Wailing Wall and, shy and scared, stood well back from the chanting women. Finally I said, "Let's go to the wall. It's ours, too," and we moved forward to face the stones. Tearing a page from my pocket diary, I scribbled a prayer that our family be kept together, and watching to see how the murmurous, davening women did it, I shoved it in a crack.

That night I wandered into a park near the hotel and could find no exit. It was very dark and the trees had no foliage, only white bones of branches. Panicking, I ran along what seemed miles of wire fence until a gate loomed and freed me.

I bought small wooden camels for the children and a Bedouin's embroidered caftan for myself and a blue-and-white-striped robe like those I had seen on the Arab men for B. He smiled awkwardly and, even before he tried it on, said it did not fit. But it did fit, I knew. It would fit anyone short of a dwarf. So I gave it to Leo, who said he would wear it for his at-homes. And I pinned my future on the paper stuck in the Wailing Wall.

A MONTH LATER. A Saturday afternoon in a little house, no more than one room, really, in Provincetown. The children are in Rhode Island with my mother for a month and I am spending the weekend with a friend from the office. I have just put down the telephone. My sister is expecting a baby at any minute, so I keep checking on her. Using my impending aunthood as an excuse, I keep checking on my husband, too. I need to hear his voice, to know that he is still at 44 Jane Street and that life is proceeding as usual.

My hostess is weeping. She has been twice married, but she has no children. Doesn't like them. Doesn't want them. She has, though, been a mother to men, over and over again.

The first of her men that I remember was very young, with red hair and a shiftiness so apparent one could sniff it. Properly nurtured, she claimed, he would turn into the most adventurous of entrepreneurs, which he did. In a sense. He lifted her credit cards.

The second, who was very handsome, had had a rotten childhood, for which she, in return for companionship (and sex), was prepared to compensate. That rotten childhood, however, had left him with a child's instinct for the jugular, and the more she built him up, the more he tore her down.

My friend is weeping because her boyfriend, a homosexual she was determined to straighten out, has left her for a man. "Why?" she is asking me. "Wasn't I enough?"

The next evening, near midnight. A bedroom in a house in Greenwich Village. The phone rings, waking me, who has returned from Provincetown a few hours earlier. It is my brother-in-law, announcing the birth of my first and only niece. I go to the kitchen, pour a cognac, and toast her alone. My children are, of course, in Bristol. And my husband? I do not know. The front door of 44 Jane Street opened on an empty house. Even so, I, like my friend with the little house on Cape Cod, still believe that there is nothing in a man that a hug and a kiss cannot heal.


WITH THE CHILDREN AWAY I hoped we could talk, but what about? The few times I mentioned his secretary, he made me feel ashamed of my tortuous, tentative sentences.

"But why did she stay at the house while I was in Israel?" I asked. (A friend of his had told me.)

"I needed help with the children," he said, and shut me up.

I tried sex, hoping that my body, which he had loved so much, could serve as a bridge. He always responded, or rather, his penis did, but his disgust with his ever-ready self made ours a sickbed.

It was hot that August, so hot the kitchen was unbearable, so I would suggest little dinners in Little Italy. Out into the steamy streets we would go and hail a cab to downtown and the perilous flight of steps that led to the Grotta Azzurra. The stuffed artichokes and spaghetti were no better at the Grotta Azzurra than at anyplace else in Little Italy, but during the years when, like babies, we were testing the world with our tongues, the restaurant seemed to us the most "authentic," the most evocative of a southern Italy about which, in truth, we knew nothing whatsoever.

The Grotta Azzurra was invariably noisy, but the only sound I recall is that of my voice, reasonable, charming, skating over hysteria, ashamed to plead when he spoke of moving out. In bed after one of those dinners, I said, "But I could never forget the way your skin smells."

"I have ambivalent feelings about you, too."

That was not what I meant at all.

At Dr. Franklin's I cried until I retched, stuttering about how I had brought my whole life tumbling about me, just like my mother had said I would.

"You should get out of the house," Dr. Franklin said. "You should go to a hospital for a few days and rest."

"No, I can't," I said, nose streaming. "He'll say you put me in a hospital because I'm insane, and he'll take the children away from me."

Dr. Franklin thought I was being paranoid, but time proved me right. A long time later, when words like "separation agreement" and "alimony" and "Mexican judge" flew, batlike, through our home, "custody" was accompanied by a threat to question my sanity in court—"unless you sign." Unless you sign, unless you sign, unless you sign. So many heads, accused of so many crimes, have bowed to "unless you sign."

In the end there was a September night when I sat, legs crossed under me, in the big blue wing chair in the dining room and cried until it seemed my intestines would spill from my mouth, afraid to put my bare feet to the floor, afraid the chill would be irreversible. My husband stayed upstairs. He would not leave until I gave him permission.

*How can you hear this? I could never stand to let you cry like this,* I thought, and huddled in the wing chair until morning.

When I went upstairs, B. said, "You're killing me," and I, finally guilty of the murder I was always afraid I would commit, said, "Then I guess you'd better leave."


IT IS ALWAYS A SOAP OPERA. The backgrounds, because I was peripatetic, were more exotic than most, but the dialogue and the situations were the usual. No matter who you are or what has gone into your life, the end of a marriage becomes, when meted out in words, the same old story.

Once in a while one surfaces to courage, one makes a stand. But most of the time one is talking and living the banal. You listen for footsteps coming down the street, but you don't hear the ones you recognize. You wait for the key to turn in the lock, and it does not. The bed seems a prairie and the sheets still smell of him, and in the supermarket you stick your hand in the meat bin for a roast and withdraw it when you realize that a chop is enough. Your married friends avert their eyes if they run into you and do not invite you for dinner, because they figure losing is contagious. Besides, you might cry. You will not, but never mind. It is always the same.

I DID NOT BELIEVE IN DIVORCE, at least not for people with two young children. I believed in marriage counselors and psychiatrists and will and, above all, responsibility. When B. telephoned and said, "I want a new life and a new wife," I was incredulous.

Blind to his transgressions, I proceeded, with the logic I used to block hysteria, to define my own. The definition was rigidly, exasperatingly Catholic. "There is a difference," I said to Dr. Franklin, "between sins of omission and sins of commission. The first are negative acts, the second positive. You see, it's not what I *did* do, it's what I *didn't* do, so I am guilty of the first."

"Get *mad*, Mary, get *mad*," friends said when I reported on midnight phone calls from my husband—exhortations to see a lawyer, pleas—no, orders—to release him to the bliss promised by a life with his secretary. "I can't," I would whimper. "I drove him to this. It's my fault. I . . . ," and then I'd stop, unwilling to speak of the nights I got into bed and turned my back, of the day in Bristol many years before when, faced with my mother's unspoken but unyielding opposition to my marrying a Jew, he stood in my old playroom and cried, "What's wrong with me, Mary Lee? What's *wrong*?"

I remembered too much: his tears when he saw me in the pale blue nightgown a friend had given me for our wedding night; the day when I was in a cab stopped at a traffic light and he, coincidentally crossing on the same light, walked up to the cab and slid a book he had just bought me through the half-open window; the boy in the Puerto Rican revolutionary suit carrying peanut-butter sandwiches to Central Park.

"He's behaving like a monster," the same friends said.

"If he is, it's because I made him one," I said, knowing myself for a sinner. The only kind of absolution I understood or could accept now came with the *clap!* of the confessional window.

THERE IS A CHURCH on West Fourteenth Street, Irish-immigrant Gothic, with a parochial school, Saturday night bingo, and electric vigil lights that snap on when you put a dime in the slot. I went there one October night when the children were away.

It was raining very hard and I was wearing a trenchcoat and a scarf, conscious of the fact that being tear-stained and black Irish, I probably looked like an IRA widow. It is that self-consciousness, not courage or religious convictions, that keeps people like me alive. How can we watch our own high dramas if we are not around to see them? We are always two people, the star and the spectator, and it is the latter that keeps the former working.

It was the usual rectory office—cheap lace curtains, a desk, old plush chairs, the smell of disinfectant and floor wax—and he seemed the usual priest—in his forties, plump, one leg struggling to cross the other at the thigh. But he was not the usual priest. He was a psychology professor on leave from a midwestern university to do fieldwork among the urban poor.

He did not scold me for my apostasy or for the civil ceremony that was my wedding or for my not sending Katherine and Margaret to Sunday school. He said instead that he regreted what the Catholic Church, his Church, had done to me. When I said that I wanted to die, he did not tell me that I had to live for the children's sake. He said, "Jesus would be kinder to you than you are to yourself." When I told him I thought myself an adulterer because I had lusted for Philippe, he said, "You are confusing the wish for the deed. Did we teach you to do that? If so, I am sorry." He was a nice man, but he did not give me four Our Fathers, three Hail Marys, and some rules to live by, so I left with my sins intact.

Somewhere in this world there was an Irish priest with a face like Samuel Beckett's and a mind like St. Paul's. He was laying down the law, confirming the verities, and scaring his parishioners. That was the kind of priest I had known as a child and the kind I looked for and did not find on Fourteenth Street. Raised in a church that manufactured crutches for its communicants, I had thrown mine away. Now I needed them again. But during the years that I was out courting damnation, the church, it appeared, had gone out of the business.

A FEW MONTHS LATER I went to Europe to work with a photographer for three weeks. For years I had kept travel diaries—notes on where we had been and what we had eaten and what things had cost—and now they were filling up with prayers and pleas and fragmented memories of dreams. "Dreamed I was walking through the Sahara. . . . Dreamed I saw B. kissing a tall, thin, pretty girl. . . . Dreamed about Papa. He was wearing a brown suit and a felt hat." During the day I interviewed fashionable young women about their lives in London and Paris, and at night I would scribble in the diaries, crying, then turn to the detective stories that since childhood had lulled me to sleep. "To bed with Michael Innes," I would write. "To bed with Nicholas Blake."

After twelve days, the photographer and I went to Amsterdam. I hate Amsterdam. I hate cold ham and cheese at breakfast and the car-clogged streets and the damp that rises from the canals, and I have memories of the ladies' room in the Rijksmuseum that put the lie to the legend of old Dutch cleansers. I had been in Amsterdam once before. This time and then, the rain was constant.

One evening when it was dark but too early for dinner and my room was getting colder and grayer and quieter and I had nothing more to add to those half-hysterical travel notes, I felt I had to move or die.

I called New York and spoke to Ann, who said my husband had taken the children out for supper and told her that he would never live at home again. The kind of woman who would be in the front row at a hanging, she bustled about, a self-appointed emissary between my husband and myself, dispensing poison. She bore me no malice, but her allegiance was to the male heads of households, and she loved theater. "I knew something was up, Mrs. L. . . . You're too innocent, Mrs. L. . . . You'd better hurry up and marry again, Mrs. L., 'cause once those children grow, ain't no man comes to this house gonna look at you."

Then I spoke to the children. Kate said she missed me, and

Margaret, who was reading *Winnie-the-Pooh*, said nothing but "Tiddly pom pom pom, tiddly pom pom pom." I sat on the edge of the bed, crying as always, wanting to die, wishing the decision would be taken from me, and, also as always, mocking myself. *How like you, Mary Lee,* I thought, *to have made sure you were cracking up in Amsterdam rather than in Westport, Connecticut.*

Oh yes, move or die. When in doubt, walk. I went to the hotel lobby, asked for the nearest Catholic church, and went outside to cross an enormous cobblestone square. The church was several hundred yards up a neon-lit street.

Once I would have been able to fantasize myself into a romantic figure moving, lonely and mysterious, through a foreign city. This time the magic didn't work. I was just a woman in her thirties whose husband didn't want her, looking for a priest who would take her out of the pain and put her back in a world where a good act of contrition equaled morphine.

A man and a woman were praying at the back of the church (married! kneeling together!), and when they rose to leave, I asked how I could find the priest. I was crying again, obviously not a person one would want to be around, so they pointed to a bellpull and fled.

The sexton was old and lame, and when he saw the tears asked if I wanted to make a confession. No, I mumbled, I just want to see a priest. When he limped back a few minutes later and said, "The father will see you now," I felt a weight sliding off my body, a kind of thumb-sucking, milk-glutted peace. The father. To me, as I followed the sexton to a door near the altar, the word meant God, the priest, and, above all, Papa.

The father was a small blond man in a pale gray flannel suit and a necktie. He lit a gas fire, then sat silent while I spoke incoherently of the husband to whom I had been a bad wife and the children to whom I did not believe I could be a good mother. I told him that I had been married by a judge and that I had not taken Communion since I was twenty-one, and that I would like to come back to the Church but that if I thought there was the slightest chance my husband would come home, I knew I would reject Catholicism all over again.

His English was thickly accented and hesitant, and he stared at me all the time he spoke—his eyebrows and lashes were, I remember, white—trying to make his eyes help his clumsy tongue. He said he would pray that I would have the strength I needed for my children. He said strength was what I should pray for as well. He said I must be more merciful to myself. And he said that I was honest, and that he would rather have me honest and outside the Church than dishonest and within it. I left, both frightened that I could not find my way back to the nest and giddy because a priest, a *priest*, had given me permission to fly. It was an absolution, of sorts.

◈ 5 ◈

*T*wo AND THREE and even four times a week (it took two years to pay the bill), I emerged from the IRT at Seventy-second Street to walk to West End Avenue and Dr. Franklin. The elderly people who had sat on the benches on the scruffy grass median that ran along Broadway were companioned now by junkies; the pastry shops that had sold strudel and hamentaschen and those little butter cookies that, judging by the bakeries, Jewish families eat by the thousands were starting to disappear; the lights were off behind the big window in the shop of the tailor who had made my green tweed suit. Seventy-second Street was going down, down, down, and living on the Upper West Side had begun to take a certain bravado.

My dreams, I told Dr. Franklin, were awful. In them my husband and father were so confused that I did not know which was which, or who had died, or what was dead. Describing them, I became even more confused. I said "When I died" when I meant "When my father died." I would start to say "B." and it came out "Papa." I babbled, but I never really talked—except, maybe, about others. By now everyone I knew had a psychiatrist—always called a headshrinker—and where once what was said between the two of you was as sacred as confession, it had now become the stuff of lunch-hour conversations. But not my conversations. Even if I had wanted to, I would not have known what to say. Because I never really said anything, besides those curious slips of the tongue, to Dr. Franklin.

Introspection, I figured, was a luxury reserved for those who could afford a peek into the subconscious. I could not. Better I should allow myself the pleasure of opacity and, with Dr. Franklin's help, scuttle along as best I could. Otherwise, like a child taking a watch apart to see how it works, I might stop the tick.

Dr. Franklin had become impatient—I think—and he had changed, presumably with the times. Where once he had sat silent, his notebook in his lap, he was now vocal, even physical. When I cried so hard I bent my head to my knees and wet my skirt with tears and the run from my nose, he put his arm around my shoulders and raised me back into the world. When I tried to run from his office, enraged because he said that now I seemed a woman, and a sexy one at that, compared to the sexless child he had once treated, he wrestled me back to the chair, locked the door, and said, "You're going to sit there and tell me why being called a sexy woman terrifies you."

I did not tell him, because I pretended I did not know. But I did have half the answer. Being told I was sexy made me sick to my stomach, partly because it was my psychiatrist who said so and mostly because it was anathema to someone who was, however lapsed, a true child of a church that was far more Irish than it was Roman. But a woman? What was that? My secondary sex characteristics were not such as to drive the point home, and the brain, I had assumed, was androgynous. The discrimination practiced by New England Protestants in the name of God and by New York Jews in the name of Spain had kept me aware that I was a Catholic. But an education at a women's college and jobs on a women's magazine had kept me innocent of sexism. My father's daughter, oblivious of my mother, I inhabited an indeterminate sexual territory, not wholly female, certainly not male, unconsciously neuter. If anyone had ever asked me what I was, I might have replied, "A Mary."

Some women at the office were joining consciousness-raising groups. When they suggested my coming along, I drew back, afraid to have anyone but Dr. Franklin picking at my head. I was interested in feminism as a subject to be explored and exploited for magazine articles, but faced with a crusade, I was, as ever, detached. The only authorities I had accepted were God the father and God the husband, and I felt a chill—still do—whenever I heard someone preaching. So if I embraced feminism, I did so in the name of economics and editorial intelligence and not for the sake of illumining the inner life.

One day a minor movement star came to the office. Pretty, articulate, impassioned, she was a thorough fraud. On being introduced, she snubbed me until she found out who my husband was, then cozied up like a cat looking for a scratching. Thanks to a man whom she knew to be successful, I had acquired an identity—his—and was thus a desirable acquaintance. She was forming a new consciousness-raising group that night, and asked if I would like to sit in at the birth.

There were about twenty women in her apartment, but I recall only three. A belly dancer who said that she used men sexually as casually as men used women, and that it was a sensible arrangement, on the whole. A recent medical school dropout, dropped out because she could not stand the jibes and pressures from her male teachers and fellow students. A young, well-dressed mother who was eager to join a group in New York because the summer she had been part of one on Long Island had been the happiest of her life. "We petitioned the mayor to let us parade on Equality Day and we won. It was the first time I'd ever really defied a man, and I was so proud."

I could not identify with any of the women. In fact they puzzled me. I did not believe that the belly dancer was as casual about sex as she claimed. It was unlikely that any male could have driven me out of school, and the only men I was conscious of having had power over me were my father and my husband, neither of whom I lumped with men. A few months later, however, when I wanted to tape a group for an article, I called one of the women. Would the group allow it? And would they discuss their sexuality?

I do not know why they permitted the intrusion. Perhaps it was my unexpected eloquence when, at a prior confrontation (we used that word a lot then), I said, "I've never known the left or the right not to grab a soapbox when it was offered to them. So here you are—you call yourselves the mainstream of feminism—turning one down. No wonder the people in the middle aren't heard. You don't know how to use the media." "Media" was another word we used a lot. So, for that matter, was "used."

We met in an apartment on East Ninety-sixth Street, which is the great divide. Cross it and you're in Harlem. The group, shrunk to eight women, was so uniformly white, middle-class, clean, and well syllabled that we looked like a Junior League steering committee. I could not imagine any dialogue coming out of this evening that could not be reported in an alumnae magazine.

The first speaker, the woman I had met at the office, had separated from her husband a few months previously. In the interim she had gone to bed with her husband's closest friend ("He kept making noises—*unh, unh, unh*—and it was wonderful") and nine other men. Only one experience had been unsatisfactory: "He came like within a minute or two, like immediately." Temporarily between men, she had mastered masturbation. "Now I feel autonomous, my own woman. Besides, any way you get it, it's nice."

Another woman, blond, pink-cheeked, a monument to Peck & Peck, was a teacher at the city's fanciest girls' school. She had been taught to masturbate when very young by her boyfriend and could not attain orgasm any other way, although she had tried every other way with all kinds of men, one of whom said she reminded him of his daughter. "I think he was using me," she said.

A third, the ex-wife of an editor I knew slightly, had spent her childhood in closets and under bushes with a flashlight, checking out male and female genitalia; her adolescence in bed with other girls; and her maturity in bed with men other than her husband. The last, she told us, was "purely satisfying."

The fourth . . . no matter. For years I kept the transcript in a file, and now it is hidden, assuming it still exists at all, in a place always referred to as "Forty-fifth Street." Forty-fifth Street is where Condé Nast sent old manuscripts and letters to die. This manuscript, however, should be in a time capsule. Words jump out of it, I remember—"orgasm," "autonomous," "beautiful, that's really beautiful"—that mark its year, 1970, as surely as a date stamp.

Now I would not be surprised by what was said that night, but I was then, because I discovered that I did not know much about women. That nobody knew much about women. I began to think

about myself as a woman. What is one, besides the obvious? Or is
the obvious what one is? Where did I fit in? *Did* I fit in? If feminism
did nothing else, it gave me a sex, my own. Whether that is one step
forward or one step back depends, of course, on how you look
at it.

BECAUSE I FOUND WORKING easier than living (I was still
making a distinction between the two), I assigned myself and a
close friend. Amy Gross, to an article about Stephen, a former se-
manticist who, guru to hundreds, had piled his disciples into
schoolbuses and led a caravan across the United States, preaching
the gospel according to himself. His lesson was that "we are all
monkeys living on the same rock" and that we have to keep the
rock clean or die in the garbage. I could not fault the message, but
Stephen's disciples were dismaying. They sat numbly, dumbly during his discourses, they followed him as donkeys would a carrot,
they had given themselves up to his Word. They were kind, sweet
people, and talking to them was like eating air.

All the long train ride to Providence, where Stephen was speaking, Amy and I played the sixties games. We compared our horo-
scopes to our photographer's: the conjunction promised perfection.
We tossed the I Ching: the goat was, as usual, in the brambles.
And, graduates of the same college, we tried to dig up what little
we remembered about Jung and the collective unconscious. When
Stephen made his entrance into Brown University's Sayles Hall—so
skinny that he looked pumiced, and soaring on peyote—and took
off his boots, lotused himself onto the floor, and sounded his ram's
horn, my "Om" was as sonorous as any in that perfect Episcopal
room.

The next day I was sitting cross-legged on one of the mattresses
that carpeted Stephen's bus, tape recorder between my thighs,
dodging the ritual joint, nervously eyeing the dope box, praying the
state police wouldn't come over the hill and cart me to jail ("Editor
held on drug rap," the headline would read. "Estranged husband
sues for child custody"), and listening to Stephen talk about tantric
yoga, satanism, Freud, Hindu chakras, acid, energy, and craziness.
"What's insanity?" I asked.

Insanity, it seemed, was optional. "I've been crazy every way imaginable, and I found insanity's just like ticktacktoe. After you've been through it enough times, you know who starts, who finishes, and where it all goes—and it's no longer insanity. It's more of your head. There's a choice about going crazy. You decide it. It's not something that just happens."

Remembering the bed rails, the nurse telling me to pray, that splat when my baby's body and mine hit the pavement, the horror ten years back, I told him that he was wrong, that once I had had the choice taken from me, that—and then I stopped, because Amy and the photographer were overhearing something I had not wanted anyone to know. Stephen did not count. More priest than person, he had heard everything. Once again I was trying to confess.

"You're afraid sanity is a little teacup that you carry around like this"—his hands cupped—"but sanity is really tough. The secret about the mind is, you can't blow it. I can't cop to insanity, and I can't cop to anything that human beings can't handle. There's no refuge outside yourself."

But there was. There was Stephen, at least for the disciples who sat in a circle with us, sipping peppermint-alfalfa tea, sticking wood in the little stove, silent as Trappists. I looked around the bus and imagined giving up the books, the furniture, the job, and moving the children and myself into narrow wooden bunks, leaning on Stephen's perceptions so I would not have to grapple with shaping my own. Stephen was better than opium. I wish I could say it was self-reliance that finally made me turn my head. It was not. It was a sudden desperate wish to be out of that pond and back in the maelstrom, back in the place where there were lots of people like me.

WE ARE IN THAT PLACE, Amy and I, sitting at my dining room table, the pages of the transcript scattered about us, cursing the vagaries of the typing service and chortling as we listen to the tapes with their undersounds of kindling being halved and teacups rattling. Throughout them my voice is a brisk, clear soprano, rather snotty; Amy's is slow, sonorous, sexy. "You *see* what marijuana does to you," I am shouting. "You *see!*" Amy laughs. We bend our heads to our lined yellow pads, congratulating each other when we hit a phrase we think especially apposite.

Without work, who or what will tangle your head, your hands? Everybody needs a tangle. Especially when she can no longer depend on a sideways glance and a cute little laugh to act as a grappling hook.

Women without tangles. Once, on the Costa del Sol, I met three of them. The first had a son in Hong Kong, a daughter in Manhattan, a small condominium on the beach, and a little alimony. She went on quickie package tours ("Badly arranged, my dear, I can't tell you how badly arranged") of Tangiers and Gibraltar and points south, never missed a maid's wedding or a baby's baptism (in a flowered hat and a garden-party dress), and started with gin before noon. She called it "Mr. Juniper."

There was a plump blonde in her fifties who hung out in the midnight bars, the young Spanish fishermen clustered about her like flies about fruit. There had been an evening when she had changed her mind, I was told, and the man who had taken her home bit her naked breast. From then on I never looked at the woman's face. My eyes were fixed on her caftan's deep V, hunting for the scar.

A third, another blonde, had the older woman's little pot-belly, that false pregnancy that blossoms after menopause. Her long thighs shook when she walked, and no amount of swimming, jogging, compulsive housework, and compulsive dieting could bring her back to what she had been. She was not one for Spanish fishermen. She inquired after widowers.

Women without men, women without work. There but for the grace of good typing go I. "But you'll never be like that, Mary," the people whom I was with protested when I confided my fear of ending up on a Spanish barstool with teethmarks on one breast. "I am, I am," I insisted, laughing. They thought I was kidding. I was not.

But I am jumping. Spain and ten days on the Costa del Sol came later. Now I am at 44 Jane Street, bent over a table and a transcript, afraid to look up, because if I do I will see a house with no husband in it and two confused children, one of whom clings to me, the other of whom is slowly, too slowly for me to catch the motion, drifting out to sea.

THE SADDEST THING about sorrow is that it is as evanescent as everything else. One day it dies, leaving a hole as empty as the socket left by an extracted tooth. You keep searching the socket with your tongue, hoping to lick a nerve, hoping for the old shock. But you feel nothing.

A night in a church in Amsterdam, an afternoon in a guru's bus, rise up and take line and color like the visions conjured by acid, but for the rest it is one long night. I snatch at rags. Myself sobbing, pleading with two women who had stolen the cab I had been hailing for blocks because I was late for Dr. Franklin and to miss him was to die. They stared and slammed the door, and the driver rolled up his window before they drove away. Dreaming the old dream about Papa met in a Manhattan crowd. Hearing the telephone ring after midnight, when the children were asleep and I was dozing into the darkness: he demanding a divorce, I alternately begging for another chance and scourging his secretary. But they are rags, and they touch as lightly as rags now. Once snatched, they can be brushed away. They leave behind only a few fibers, little filaments of pain that twinge when I have forgotten to anesthetize myself with talk or work.

A long night, a few rags, a few scenes, and, finally, a day when my head, my body, and—can I say my soul?—were once more in the same place.

It was January, and my mother had been calling all week with reports of Peggy, relayed by Peggy's sister Julia. Peggy was sixty-four, an art teacher in the public schools whom I had known since my childhood. She loved painting and reading and talking and Ireland and Portugal, and ran through life highlighting everyone she knew, like an artist touching up a sitter's hair and skin. Because of Peggy, all of us became a little more beautiful, a little more romantic, a little more interesting, to ourselves as well as to others. To know her was to be presented with infinite possibilities. That was her gift to her friends.

"Julia says Peggy is very tired. She sleeps a lot" . . . "Julia was at the hospital today. She said Peggy's getting very quiet" . . . "Peggy asked Julia to brush her hair, but it hurt her scalp too much and Julia had to stop" . . . "Peggy died last night."

The evening before I went home for the funeral, B. called. Had I seen the lawyer, had I agreed . . . ? My eyes on the clothes I was packing and wet, for once, with grief for someone else, I snapped, "I'm not interested in our divorce or your marriage. Peggy is dead and I'm going home and that's all I care about." As I talked, I realized that Peggy was indeed all I cared about just then, that the death of my friend was more important than the death of my marriage. Of course, if I were married to a friend . . . but I was not, not anymore.

As we walked up the aisle after the service the next morning, my oldest friend whispered, "Whenever I come to a funeral here, I think of your father's and how beautiful it was. Do you remember?" "Yes," I said, and we went to the cemetery and stood by Peggy's grave, a few hundred yards from Papa's.

It was a day like every January day in Bristol: no snow, bare black branches spearing the gray sky, matted brown grass underfoot. In this cemetery my married name was irrelevant, probably unknown or forgotten. I was the Cantwell girl, to some old-timers Mary Lonergan's girl, Margaret Guinan's grandchild. It is possible that someone there was old enough to know that I was Bridget McCarty's great-grandchild. But for a chipped front tooth, I had no feature that had not belonged to them or to my father. My accent was theirs. I was as shocked by divorce as they would have been, and as little equipped to deal with it. I was all of them, and home again, I had slipped imperceptibly into the spin of their lives.

Several days after the funeral, B. agreed to join me at Dr. Franklin's. They had never seen each other, this man I had known for nineteen years and this man I had known for fifteen. My life was divided between the two, and they had never met.

Again I talked and cried, and then I heard my husband's silence, though he spoke, and watched his eyes, which, though they looked, could not see me. "You don't know what it was like for me," he had said a few months back, during one of his midnight phone calls. "All those years of Dr. Franklin and the migraines and that time after Kate was born." And I, stung and sick with memories, said, "But you don't know what it was like for me." That's all it was, really: neither of us ever knew what it was like for the other.

B. left the doctor's office a few minutes before me. I was not cool enough to share an elevator with him, or for us to part casually in simultaneously hailed cabs. Dr. Franklin put his hand on my arm and said, "It's no use, Mary. Let him go."

So I did.

## ❖ AFTERWORD ❖

$\mathcal{F}$OR A LONG TIME, I have lived on the street down which I used to walk to the garbage pier to watch the Italians from the South Village grooming their cars. The garbage pier is inaccessible to all but sanitation trucks now, and the old pilings are slumped against the supporting rocks and covered with barnacles and that green slippery stuff of which I have never known the name but which is like aqueous moss. Looking down at them, I might imagine that I am in Bristol. The rocks and the lapping water and the smell of brine are precisely the same. But I do not want to imagine an elsewhere. These, the Hudson River and the towers on the New Jersey shore and the Circle Line boats, are what I want to see.

At my back is the meat market. During the day large men in bloodstained coats and hardhats load beef carcasses into trucks and take lunch breaks on the loading docks. At night the prostitutes—young men mostly, usually black and sometimes in drag—come out. They stand in the shadows cast by the warehouses' old metal awnings or, if it's cold, around the fire somebody has started in a rusted metal drum.

They are visible, but the other habitués of the meat market are not. They have disappeared behind unmarked doors and down flights of stairs into the leather bars that have made this place ground zero. At least, I think most of the bars have reopened—one sees the occasional notice posted on a streetlight—but they are as transient as the sea gulls that sweep the streets for garbage when the river is frozen. One night you see a cluster of men at a doorway; the next night, maybe not. A certain decorum prevails in the meat market. The men in clusters do not look at me, I do not look at them, and the prostitutes keep custody of their eyes.

The street itself is nicer than it used to be. The refrigeration plant at its foot has been turned into an apartment house, as have some of the derelict warehouses, and the block association has planted pear and cherry trees and put evergreens in great big terracotta pots. Even so, the street is almost always empty when I come home at night, and my eyes are searchlights, sweeping it from side to side until I reach the front door. My key is out, I look behind me, I turn the knob. Whew! I have trumped the predators again.

My building is one of those that underwent transformation—transfiguration, really. A livery stable built in 1907, it eventually became a warehouse for a meatpacking company. My piece of it, two thirds of the first floor, was its garage. When first I saw it, oil stains had sunk into the cement floor and iron shutters were closed over its tall windows. But two columns stretched sixteen feet to a ribbed tin ceiling, and the space seemed limitless. Two years after I moved in, real estate prices escalated, and I realized that selling it would mean money enough to buy the little house that I had sought all over Greenwich Village. But while I could have crammed my possessions into small rooms, I could no longer have crammed myself. Besides, I had labored for this place as doggedly as Jacob had labored for Rachel.

The thing is, in New York you are always at someone's mercy. The children and I had to move from 44 Jane because Matty needed our duplex for his mother-in-law, and after seven years' residence we had to move from our next place because the landlord wanted it for himself. But we were glad to leave. He beat his wife and she drank herself into slurred speech and ankles that swelled and spilled over her shoes, and sickness soaked their walls and trickled all the way down into ours. But then there was a kind of sickness in our rooms, too. One midnight I had to search the basement, terrified lest my flashlight land on a pair of small, sneakered feet limp and useless on the floor. But that is another story, and one that is not mine to tell.

We had no place to go, not for the fifteen months it would take to turn the garage into an apartment. Curiously, this was no hardship, for me, at least. Night after night I wrapped cups and saucers and shell frames and a Staffordshire goat and toys long outgrown in sheets of newspaper. I tagged the furniture and put all the sheets and pillows into bureau drawers, and when the truck came to take everything into storage, I was lighter by a million years. Then we started traveling, Rose Red and I (Snow White had gone away), all over Manhattan.

First came two weeks on the top floor of a narrow house on Jane Street, two doors west of the house to which Mary Rogers—Edgar Allan Poe's Marie Roget—said she was going on the August day in 1841 when she disappeared. That house, which belonged to her aunt, is gone, but the one that remains is almost certainly its twin, as are the five other twelve-footers on the south side of Jane Street.

From there we moved to a house as old as the one on Jane Street and a torrid summer on Eighth Avenue. Here we had all four floors, but the living room was so formal we were afraid to sit down, and the kitchen was visited by winged bugs we called Puerto Rican flying cockroaches. We had never seen them before, we have never seen them again, and one day they vanished as suddenly as they had appeared.

After Eighth Avenue, there was Thirteenth Street between Sixth and Seventh Avenues and a few weeks in a basement apartment. All basement apartments are dark, but the landlord had built a staircase from the parlor floor into the garden, which made this one even darker. I cried here all the time, and Rose Red asked timidly, "Is this menopause, Mom? Is this menopause?" "No," I said, "it's only the dark," and cried some more.

Then we moved into the light: a bedroom, living room, bathroom, and kitchen on a high floor in a high-rise on Hudson Street. I had not lived in a place with a doorman since East Twenty-first Street and had forgotten the silence of apartment-house corridors and the secrecy that attends a long line of closed doors. There was safety in living behind a guarded lobby, but we could hear the toilet flushing in the next-door apartment, and the kitchen was no more than a closet. In New York, unless one is very rich and maybe even then, one is always a Goldilocks, trying rooms on for size and seldom finding a "just right."

By now we had run out of sublets, and there was nothing for it but the Chelsea Hotel.

I had passed the Chelsea, which is on West Twenty-third Street, often over the years and been in it three times. The first time I was at a party given by Virgil Thomson for, he said, "the friends of Alice B. Toklas." His suite was a monument to horse-hair upholstery and stained glass windows, and the guests a monument to intellectually posited frumpiness. I remember a lot of women in late middle age with flyaway hair, crocheted sweaters stretched over breasts that had never known bras, and strings of amber beads.

The second time was for a dinner given by a couple who were between apartments and making the best of it. They had draped crepe paper around the tiny dining area and across the peeling ceiling, and the hostess had managed to produce a roasted chicken and a lopsided cake out of an oven that never went above 350 degrees. Still, there was no jollity, no celebration. There couldn't be, not in a room that promised no exit.

The third time I was interviewing an actress in town for a play. Her suite was presentable—"because the producer coughed up a piano and some pictures"—but on leaving it one walked through scarred corridors to a street where old black men, and a few old white men, held sad travesties of cocktail parties with cheap wine in paper bags and a brave bonhomie.

I had a horror of the Chelsea, yet here we were, with three cats, a dog, a few clothes (I kept the rest in trash bags in a corner of my office), our portable television set, and my hot rollers, lodged directly above the room in which Sid Vicious had murdered his girlfriend, Nancy, a few days before. "Did you hear anything?" the plainclothes man who knocked on our door asked. "We're new here," I answered, and tried to make it clear that we were only passing through.

We were not. The next day I shared the Chelsea's one elevator with Thomson, who didn't seem at all surprised on hearing I had moved in. *Maybe he sees me as the kind of woman who sooner or later ends up in the Chelsea Hotel,* I thought. Then I laughed. Obviously, I *was* the kind of woman who sooner or later ends up in the Chelsea Hotel. For eight months.

It was a cold winter, but the radiators shuddered with heat, and in the fireplace the Dura-Flame logs from the delicatessen shook with flame. The water was always hot, and dinner simmered on the stove and scented the room. Rose Red had her schoolbooks, and I books borrowed from friends, and together we watched *Masterpiece Theatre* on the television set. The dog and the three cats nudged us in our sleep, jubilant because they were never more than five feet from their owners, and I felt as if I were pregnant again, not only with Rose Red but with our pets and our few possessions. On the nights that Snow White, slowly returning from sea, stayed over and shared a studio couch with her sister, I would lie awake and listen to their slow, deep breathing. My babies were folded into their mother again, where nothing—short of her death—could harm them.

Then spring came, and with it opened windows that let in the sound of radios and quarrels across the courtyard and the screech of cats. We moved to the Upper East Side, to a friend's apartment so meticulously planned that a cigarette ash blindly dropped would hit an ashtray and light bulbs multiplied like mice. Here there was no sound of flushing from the next-door apartment, the maintenance men moved as swiftly and silently as if they were on wheels, and the doorman's hand was quick to the cab's rear door. But it was not the Village. We could not find any cheap Asian-Cuban restaurants. Everybody dressed to go to the supermarket.

We moved again, a few blocks north, to a bigger apartment, big enough for the man who lived there—with his wife, another of my friends—to spare one room for an office. At eight-thirty, just when I was sitting down to the paper and a second cup of coffee, his staff arrived. There could be no lounging about *en déshabillé*. I was combed, lipsticked, and immaculate by eight.

Finally, the last move, to an apartment in the South Village, in the district of the old printing plants. Rose Red had fled, for two weeks in Connecticut with a classmate who had proper parents and proper beds, and once again I was hanging around, hanging out. One night I walked past an Italian luncheonette that normally closed at seven. A light was burning in the back, so, curious, I peered through the plate glass to see a scene that might have been taking place in Naples: the luncheonette owner's family stripping piles of basil of its leaves for next winter's pesto. The first time I had ever tasted pesto was in Little Italy, only a few blocks away, when B. and I went to the San Gennaro Festival and a band played "I'll Take Manhattan." We danced to it, on a raised platform roped off like a boxing ring. "My God," we kept telling each other, "this is like a movie."

At last the new apartment was ready. The furniture was sprung from storage and we settled back into our own beds. "You must be thrilled," people said. "All that moving around!"

Rose Red was. I was not. There were still so many streets we had not walked, so many stores we had not entered, so many lives we had not tried.

ALMOST NOTHING has been discarded, not even the photographs and drawings and mottoes kept on my bulletin board at *Mademoiselle*. I took them with me when I left, all that I retain of that job besides the way my lips, without my willing it, curve into a smile whenever I remember the chatter and the I Ching and "Group order! Group order!" I missed them when I moved on to the *New York Times*. But not much. They had been outgrown.

Where I am now is a very grownup place, and writing editorials is a very grownup occupation. But to me it seems that I have come full circle, that I am copywriting all over again. Describing a dress and describing a social policy take the same set of knacks: the ability to analyze, clarify, and compress. One has to have a point of view, of course, and I am no more skilled in debate now than I was when I tried to tell B. and Jerry about transsubstantiation and Duns Scotus. But once I am seated in front of my computer, everything comes clear. If I have spent a lifetime writing one thing or another, it is because it is the only way I can figure out what I am thinking.

Sometimes I am invited to a publisher's lunch, and then I sit at a long mahogany table staring at the distinguished guest and his (or, occasionally, her) inevitable aides, worrying about forking the

baked chicken breast off the platter presented at my left shoulder
and wondering if I should put the spoon for my iced tea (the recipe
for which is said to have come from the famous Iphigene) on the
damask tablecloth or the little plate the glass stands on. The silver
is Tiffany's Hampton, the conversation is equally polished, and the
guest, seated at the right hand of the publisher and an old pro at
forking chicken off platters, exhales success.

When I leave, after the cigars have been passed, the demitasse
sipped, and the guest's hand shaken, it is with the momentary illusion that all's well with the world, or could be. Haven't I just been
at civilization's epicenter? Haven't I just sipped a perhaps historic
iced tea?

Little now can be experienced on its own, not even in Times
Square. There is always a point of reference. Walking along
Broadway at lunchtime, I am reminded of Allie and me, also at
lunchtime, searching for an I. Miller outlet we had heard was in the
area. Our college shoes—Bass Weejuns, sneakers, and suede pumps
for fraternity parties—were not suitable for the office.

After dark, heading for the subway at Forty-second Street, I try
to figure out where Toffenetti's Restaurant was. This corner? That
corner? Back there? B. and I never ate at Toffenetti's, but we
thrilled to the menu posted in its window, not for its offerings but
for the purpleness of its prose. When B. sent a sample to *The New
Yorker* (everyone we knew was forever looking for funny bits of
prose to send to *The New Yorker*) and it was published, we were as
excited as if he had produced a short story.

Strolling down Fifth Avenue after a movie at MoMA, I remember, we would pass the Olivetti typewriter on a stanchion outside the nearby Olivetti showroom. But how nearby? There was a
paper in it for passersby, and on it B. would type "the quick brown
fox . . ." and I, "My name is Mary and I live on. . . ."

I called Olivetti a few years ago. I wanted to know exactly
where that showroom was. Nobody there knew, or had even heard
of it. But that typewriter existed, I'm sure of it, as surely as we did
once.

There is no bulletin board in my *Times* office, only Piranesi
prints left by my predecessor. My sole addition to the décor is a big
color photograph Kate took of Bristol Harbor. But buried under a

pile of leaflets on a shelf in back of my desk is a photograph torn from a magazine. It is that famous one of the little Jewish boy who, with his hands up, is being led away to what one supposes was his death. I love that boy in the photograph, because had he lived to adulthood, he would have looked like B. In fact, he *is* B., more surely than the stranger I danced with a few years ago at Margaret's wedding.

At the bottom of the in box on my desk is another photograph—a Xerox, actually, of a photograph—from the May 7, 1961, issue of the Sunday *Times Magazine*. It accompanied an article about Greenwich Village, and is of me and Kate.

I did not know a camera had been aimed at us until I read the article on a Saturday night at 21 Perry Street. I turned to the runover and there it was, a picture of a thin, square-shouldered woman in a Lacoste shirt, white pants, and sneakers pushing a stroller, the kind with a fringed canopy. The child in the stroller is obviously a girl; you can tell by her bonnet.

We have been at Washington Square, I am sure, and now we are going home for supper. Along the way I have been looking, as always, for the little house to which we will move one day, the house that is the material equivalent of Jane Austen's prose. And here it is, in the newspaper of record, a record of one New York woman's stroll with her daughter on a hot spring day in 1961.

I still stroll, all the time, but I doubt I shall ever move again. I will never find a better place. Besides, maybe I do not want to open any more doors. But that is silly. They will open anyway. Still, sometimes I imagine living where Margaret lives: a pretty little backwater in Brooklyn where every stray cat gets a bowl of Friskies put out for his breakfast and householders sweep their sidewalks every morning. I go there often, for dinner, and breathe deeply of the peace.

The dream lasts only for as long as it takes my cab to cross the Manhattan Bridge, travel west on Chambers Street, and round the corner onto what remains of the West Side Highway. What I see then, at the right, is a line of massive buildings, and what I feel is their power. It is as if I have been given a shot with a kick like a donkey's, a shot of something to which I am terminally addicted.

"Could you wait till I get inside?" I ask the driver. He nods, and stays in place until I unlock the front door of my building. A short flight of steps, and I unlock the door to my apartment. The cats are waiting as I enter; the barely audible pad of their paws is the only sound.

An hour or two with a book, and it is time for sleep. I open the bedroom window, not on a street but on a garden. The noise from traffic, pedestrians, quarrels, late-night drunks cannot penetrate the trees and bushes and these thick brick walls. Even so, I can hear it. The hive. Buzzing.

# SPEAKING
# WITH STRANGERS

FOR AMY GROSS
WHO IS ALL AND MORE
THAN IS MEANT BY THE WORD "FRIEND"

---

"If one cannot close a book of memories on the
deathbed, any conclusion must be arbitrary."
— GRAHAM GREENE

## ❖ PROLOGUE ❖

*J*HE TIDE WAS WRONG, I think, and maybe that was why the tenders couldn't come in to the pier and take us out to what I believe was the old *Queen Elizabeth*. Or it may have been the *United States*. Maybe the ocean liner, which at that distance and at twilight recalled a resurrected *Titanic*, wasn't ready to take on the people who were boarding at Le Havre. Or it may have been Calais.

I am sorry to be so vague, especially because I am proud of my good memory, and many have remarked upon it, but all I can remember is sitting on my one suitcase (I travel light) and waiting for hours to get going. Anywhere.

Neither can I remember how I got to the pier, although obviously it was on the boat train from Paris. I can't remember what I ate, or what I was wearing, or if I spoke to anyone, or any landscape except vast fields of yellow mustard. What I do remember is the pier and the man sitting on the suitcase beside me. He, too, had only one, old and wrapped with rope, because otherwise it wouldn't have closed. He was old as well, and dressed with the kind of decency that proclaims that traveling is an event to be treated with solemnity, respect.

"Have you ever read the great Polish writer Joseph Conrad?" he asked me. I turned, startled. We had never even exchanged glances, and, besides, the pier, for all the hundreds waiting on it, was very quiet. We might as well have been waiting for Charon.

"Yes, I have," I answered, but in truth I had forgotten almost everything but the "fascination of the abomination." It was a tag line of mine, trotted out for any and all revolting occasions and lending me (I thought) a certain literary aura.

"I am from Poland," he said. "I have just come from there."

Then the story came out, in slow, thick English.

When the old man was twelve or so, his mother and father and a brother or two had emigrated to the United States—to Chicago, as I recall. What his life was there—his work, his family, his dailiness—I have no idea. But I did hear about how he had saved for years for this trip. He had planned to see the town in which he was born, of whose houses he still had faint images and along whose streets he was sure he could still find his way. But when he arrived at the place to which memory and an old map had taken him, there was no town, only a crossroad where it once had been. The war had erased it, and with it erased his origins. Joseph Conrad was his Poland now.

I am not sure how much Conrad he himself had read. He talked about the person, not his work, and not in detail. I doubt he knew any details. But he knew that Poland had produced a great writer, that it was his Poland that had produced the great writer, and as long as the great writer was talked about and read, his Poland still existed. The more he spoke of Conrad, the more I saw the crossroad turning into a town again, the houses taking shape, the streets emerging from the raw landscape.

Finally, the tenders arrived at the pier and we boarded, but not together. In fact, I never saw him again. I was traveling cabin; he was probably traveling third class. His journey had not been a success. Even now, so many years later, I can imagine him tracing maps, exercising his rusty Polish, counting and recounting his money, riding springless buses and cranky trains, only to arrive at nowhere.

Still, for those few hours on the dark pier, when we were without landmarks, without anything but that distant, almost mythical ship to give us a sense of place, he managed, because of "the great Polish writer Joseph Conrad," to put us in his country. His country was built with words, and for a little time, while we talked, he lived there. I wish I could say I am happy about his momentary repossession of his roots, but I know far too much about traveling back in time not to discount the pain that is so often the aftermath of the journey. It must have been hard for him to have lost that town. It must have been harder to have been wrenched from it again.

THAT WAS A LONG TIME AGO, when my children were small and my husband, about to be my former husband, was desperate to replace me and I seized every chance I got to leave home. I was lucky. I had a lot of chances, because I was working on a fashion magazine and was handy when it came to writing travel articles. There were other chances, too, not necessarily involving travel articles but always involving work. I would not have traveled without the work. I could not have borne the loneliness. But work drove me out into foreign streets to talk to people with whom I would have been much too shy even to share a nod. Work took me to places—the Anatolian plateau, for instance, and Siberia—to which I would not have dreamed of going. Work drove me to restaurants and airports and to hotels in which I was sometimes the only guest. And all the time that I was making notes and asking questions and taking pictures with my little Brownie Starmite, I was promising God that if only He would get me out of this hell-hole I was in—Tashkent was the worst—I would stay home and be a good mother and never again leave my children, my wonderful, beautiful, innocent, and abandoned children. But then the chance would come once more, and, a bag slung over my shoulder, off I would go to the airport, so swollen with excitement it seemed I would push out the sides of the cab. At takeoff I would press my feet against the plane's floor, urging it into flight. Once I got to wherever I was going, though, I was so stripped of the familiar that I was skinless and would promise God once again that if only He would get me out of this hellhole I was in, I would stay home and be a good mother and never again leave my children, my wonderful, beautiful, innocent, and abandoned children.

Eventually the day came when I didn't have to do it anymore; travel like that, I mean. I could stay home. I didn't have to sit with strangers anymore, talking about Joseph Conrad and creating a country whose only boundaries were words. Piety would have me

say that it was my daughters who brought me back into the land of
pots and pans and beds and pillows and homework that had to be
checked and suppers that had to be cooked. The joy on their faces
when they saw me making Sunday pancakes or unpacking groceries while singing a song my younger had invented, a song that
involved endless repetitions of "Oh, juicy spaghetti, oh, juicy
spaghetti," put something bubbly, something like ginger ale, in my
veins. But that day was long in coming, and during the five or so
years in which I rolled about the world like a billiard ball looking
for a pocket, watching my girls was often like looking at them
through the wrong end of a telescope.

Even when the three of us were together in front of the television set, the two of them huddled against me like cuddling cats,
they seemed far away. Everything and everyone was far away. In
the office and on the street I had to wear dark glasses even when
there was no sun, because crying had my eyes chronically swollen,
and what I saw through those shaded lenses was almost always in
miniature, too distant to seem real. It was only when I trailed my
children to school in the morning (they wanted their classmates to
think they were allowed to walk alone) that I saw them full size:
one fair, one dark, their little rumps twitching under their pleated
skirts and their knee socks starting the slow descent toward their
shoes.

Now, when I look at old photographs of my daughters, I see
the desolation on the face of the younger, sitting on her rocking
horse and clutching our impossible dog, Fred, and am touched by
the little ribbon the older used to tie around her throat in imitation
of a choker. But then, except for those minutes during our carefully
distanced walks to school, I might as well have been gazing from a
star.

Often I was deaf as well. "Mom, Mom," my children would
cry when I settled into silence, trying to pull me back into their
world. But I didn't want to see, not really, or to hear or talk. I
wanted to be with Papa, buried beside him in St. Mary's Cemetery
in Bristol, Rhode Island, reunited with someone who was faithless
only in dying. But I couldn't go, couldn't slide beneath the grass
that covered him. Being a mother denied me death and made me

resentful. Sometimes I would look at my girls, my beauties, and think, "If it weren't for you two, I could leave."

No. To return to my children and to sight and sound and speech, I had to go far away and become acquainted with the only companion I have ever been able to rely upon. As long as I had a pencil and paper and notes to make for my insignificant little articles, I was not alone. With work to do, I could exit a world in which I was restless and confused and, above all, haunted by people who are shards and ashes, if they are anything at all now, and enter one in which it seemed morphine was dripping on my soul. Here I was calm; here, although I was actually more awake than in any elsewhere, I could sleep.

# *One*

---

$\mathscr{T}$HE MORNING OF THE DAY my children and I left the house we had lived in with their father—the house with the bunny wallpaper in their bedroom and the wooden valet from Brooks Brothers in ours—to move farther west on Greenwich Village's Jane Street, I was sitting with a friend in its tiny backyard.

"Would you ladies please move your chairs forward?" one of the moving men called out. "I've got to do some work with this window."

Obedient, we moved our chairs out of the shade and into the sun. Behind us, only two or so feet from where we had been sitting, the air conditioner fell to the ground. Had we not been told to move, we would have been killed. Still, neither of us paled, neither of us scared up so much as a tremble. "It's an omen" was all my friend said. "You were *meant* to leave this place."

Some hours later, with the children at my family's home in Rhode Island and the house bare of all but my bed and a few cartons, I went to a cocktail party way uptown, grateful that someone from my office had thought to invite me on a night when I would otherwise have been walking through the empty rooms, crying, maybe, and feeling the strange pain that seemed to twist my ribs whenever I thought of my husband—my husband who was happy now and free of the marriage that I had ruined. "How did you ruin it?" friends would ask, but I could never answer. I just knew it, that was all, knew it just as surely as I once had known that to step on a crack was to break my mother's back. I did not believe in fate or happenstance, only in my power to destroy. "That tongue of yours . . . those hands of yours . . . that temper of yours will get you into trouble someday," I was told in childhood. My mother was right. I was a killer.

Some of the guests were friends, the rest were strangers, and one of the latter was drunk. In those days I was a pretty woman, but there was something about my face, something that seemed to condemn, I guess, that aroused hostility—and, at the same time, attraction—in those who had had one too many. This man was no different. While his wife stood by, smiling limply, he made a few rude remarks about my having arrived late, tried to goad me into responding to a couple of dirty jokes, and finally said, "Who stuck the stick up your ass?" Then he dared me to drink a full glass of Scotch. I took the dare. "You're dealing with an Irishman here," I said, trying for a tough sophistication that I had never possessed, had never had to possess.

When I was halfway through the Scotch, another man took the glass from my hand and told the drunk to cut it out. The wife kept smiling, the drunk moved off, and I left for what remained of my home, feeling as helpless as my mother did the first time she had to balance a checkbook. My father had died. He had always paid the bills, and when, not realizing that she had to figure in the ten cents for each check, she couldn't match the bank's tally with hers, she put her head down on the desk and cried the only tears I had seen her cry since his death. Now it was I who was unprotected. Without my husband, with whom I had spent my entire adult life, I had no defenses against drunks and their brutalities. I didn't even know how to come to a cocktail party unescorted. How could I know? In the past, when I had entered a party by myself, it was always with the knowledge that my husband was soon to appear, rushing in from the office and about to feel my proprietary hand on his arm.

I shall call him by his initial, B., because it is boring to repeat *husband* again and again. Also, I have a bad habit, one that leads strangers to believe I am still married. In speaking of him, I always say "my husband," simply because he is the only one I have ever had. Besides, it is hard for me to believe that a piece of paper can end a marriage, any more than it can end a motherhood or a sisterhood. My mother is my mother, and that is that. My sister is my sister, and that is that. My husband was my husband, and he still is. True, I am unacquainted with that man who lives across town, that man who has gained a little weight, a little hearing aid, and—as they seem to me, in the few times I have seen him—capped teeth. But the boy who bought me books to improve my mind and a linen blouse and a cashmere sweater to improve my wardrobe when I was a junior in college: I am bound to him until my last breath.

"You're always lighting little candles to that guy," a man who once fancied himself a possible suitor said not long ago. Yes. They are to someone who occupies the same niche in my mind as the plaster saints before whom—the dime pushed in the slot, the flame fluttering—I knelt in childhood. Pray as I might, I never really believed in them. As time passes, I grow less and less able to believe in him. But I want to. If I go on lighting candles, it is because I cannot bear thinking that he was, in the end, only a figment of my imagination. To think that would be to do myself a kindness. But I have never been very kind to myself. I am my own Simon Legree.

During that childhood, in a town where the only official entertainments were the bowling alley and the movies, I spent every Friday night at a little stucco theater called the Pastime. When the movie—and the news and the serial and the short—was over, I was still not only at it but in it. Walking home, gripping my grandfather's hand, the elm trees soughing overhead and the salt air surrounding us, I was not Mary Lee Cantwell but Alice Faye or Betty Grable or Lana Turner. Thin, dark-haired, my teeth armored by braces, two elastic bands, and a plastic retainer, I even thought I looked like them. Years later, the elms and the salt air long behind me, I subwayed home alone to B. from an evening at the Royal Ballet (it was Sadler's Wells then) and *Sleeping Beauty*, and tried to show him how a man named Brian Shaw danced the Bluebird Variation. My arms flapping, my leaps a mere six inches off our shag rug, I truly thought I was dancing. Once, leaving a Broadway show with B. and an acquaintance who proclaimed himself "a truth-teller," I so persisted in unconscious mimicry of the heroine that the truth-teller told me to cut it out.

Retaining my edges was even more difficult when I was reading. Then, if the story was powerful enough, it erased my reality. The people I have been! Emma Bovary and Daisy Miller, of course. Lily Bart. Judith Hearne. I have been real people, too. Edith Thompson, who was hanged for killing her husband, and for whom I wept because her only crime was silliness. Madeleine Smith, who probably should have been hanged for killing her lover, but with whom I sympathized because he was a leech. And a woman, or several women, described in an article in *New York* magazine.

The article was one of the magazine's usual 1970s exposés of the tragedies of urban life—life as a Puerto Rican pimp, for instance, or life as a black hooker. This time the tragedy of urban life had to do with the divorcées who, hair fresh from all-day rollers, buttocks molded by Lycra slacks, congregated at a roadhouse near the Long Island Expressway for five o'clock drinks with the men— married, most of them—who stopped there on the way home from work. I cried for those women. I was one of those women, not a magazine editor but a jobless housewife with teased hair and a pneumatic butt who cadged drinks, smokes, and feels from men in leisure suits. Leaving the party where that drunk had dared me to down a Scotch—how I had loved our cab rides home from parties, the New York streets glistening in the night and B. solid beside me—I remembered that article. There it is, I said to myself, my fate.

My true fate, for a while anyway, was invisibility. A few weeks before my last day in the old house, a friend of B.'s had stopped me on the street and said solicitously, "Moving to a smaller place?"

"No," I snapped, "bigger," hating him for his curiosity and distrusting his concern. He and his wife, after all, had dispensed with me months before. So why the worried eyes, the voice dripping sincerity? I knew. Showing an interest in my future was akin to going to church once a year—Easter, say, or Christmas. The knees had been bent, the money dropped in the collection basket, the duty done.

But, then, everyone except my friends at the magazine had dispensed with me, and the world in which I had lived seemed imagined but not experienced. The seat I had occupied at dinner parties was still warm when my successor slid into it. If I wasn't surprised, it was because I had seen it happen so many times before, that curious disappearance into purdah that seemed so often the fate of first wives. It was as if we were all trial runs. Even our children were sometimes trial runs. "With my first two children, there was never time . . ." says the semifamous man to the newspaper interviewer, glorying in the issue from his aging loins. "But now I am discovering what it really means to be a father."

I might have missed that world more had we stayed in our old house. But our new house brought new vistas, new corners to turn. The first time we saw it (I was responding to an ad), my older daughter peeked around a closed shower curtain to see the tub. "So nosy!" I said, attempting to blush, but my embarrassment was faked. Had the present tenant not been there to show us around, I too would have peeked around the shower curtain. For I, like my eleven-year-old, was excited about unfamiliar faucets, foreign tiles. As time has proved, it is, above all else, what we have in common.

To remember life in our new house is to think of small blocks of color in a long gray ribbon. The blocks were the days and weeks when I woke up in countries in which, without a language to share with those along whose streets I walked, I was condemned to silence. I was condemned to envy, too, because those were their front doors they were opening and their groceries under their arms and their tables at which they would have their evening meal. Even so, I wallowed in the silence because it sharpened my senses. My ears were a fox's, my eyes an eagle's, and often I forgot I had any identity but that of traveler.

But I could not have survived without the long gray ribbon, the ordinary, to be deprived of which is my definition of hell. Still, on nights when I have run out of books, and all television palls, I sometimes bring out the colored blocks and play with them, freezing time, watching the woman I used to be in performance.

Soon after we moved in, I heard the leader of a Sunday-morning walking tour tell his charges that the house (Number 83, as it was known to the neighbors, who identified themselves by their addresses) was "Anglo-Italianate." But the neighbors, most of whom were standing about in what looked suspiciously like a receiving line the evening I emerged with the landlord after signing the lease, said it was a made-over stable. Whatever it was, it was built in 1856 and had an enormous mahogany bar in the cellar. "If worse comes to worst," said a friend who knew I was worried

about the rent, "you can always open an afterhours club." Over
the bar was inscribed: "On this site overlooking the majestic
Hudson stood the William Bayard Mansion, where Alexander
Hamilton, the first treasurer of the United States, died July 12,
1804, after his famous duel with Aaron Burr."

The rooms were tall and airy and painted my usual white, but
it is the cellar I remember best: the bar and the tattered posters
from rock concerts thumbtacked to dirty plaster walls and the cartons of 45s and rotting paperbacks left by the previous tenants.
The landlord and his wife hoarded food. They came back from
New Jersey supermarkets (no taxes) in what seemed a clown car, so
crammed was it with staples and what they called "paper goods,"
then stored them in closets in the front. Once, curious, I opened
one and saw what must have been fifty boxes of Social Tea Biscuits.

My old dishwasher was in that cellar, and an old wing-chair,
along with, in the back, the washer and dryer, around which
crawled an army of shiny waterbugs. I was in that cellar constantly,
hauling laundry and, bookish as always, quoting something appropriate from Yeats. Surely this, this unspeakable slum above which
were rooms arranged as starkly and as beautifully (I thought) as a
museum, was the foul rag-and-bone shop of my heart.

Because of a curious conjunction of streets, the block seemed
cut off, isolated. Entering it, I always felt as if I were entering a
stockade, a stockade that smelled strongly of the vanilla wafted
through the open windows of the wholesale bakery at the corner. I
liked that scent. I liked even better that, no matter how late I came
home from work, some of the bakers would be sitting on the fire
escape, taking a break from the ovens. Sometimes I'd wave at
them, and sometimes they'd wave back. We were too distant and
the sky too dark for us to recognize one another if we ever met by
daylight. Still, on a street where little houses, their windows
shrouded in curtains and blinds, turned blank faces to the world
and the sidewalks emptied after eight, I thought them my compa-
triots, my *landsmen*.


IN A TOWN AS OLD and settled as the place in which I was
raised, one is known simultaneously by one's maiden name, one's

husband's name, and, to some old-timers, by one's mother's maiden name. So it is not fatal to lose that second one. In fact, it is not fatal if you never acquire it, because identity also resides in your house, your street, your church, your great-grandfather's occupation. My grandmother had a cousin famous for her angel cakes, door prizes at many a church fair and the centerpieces of my every childhood birthday party. When she died, at a great age, there were enough people left to remember them, and therefore her, for the next twenty-five years. But in a city as provincial as New York, how are you identified except by your husband, your job, or your money? I loved my job, not so much for what I did at my desk but for what being at my desk did for me. It gave me a face, a voice, a manner. It gave me a personhood.

Even office friends, though, friends who'd been barely conscious of my having a husband, sometimes treated me as an amputee. "The one thing you musn't do," said the worldliest of them, a woman who herself had never married and had a long string of sexually uncertain escorts, "is give brave little dinner parties."

I didn't understand what she meant.

"*You* know," she continued. "You've always got to have a man at the foot of the table."

However, I didn't give dinner parties, brave or otherwise, although I liked to feed people, had memorized a book on carving, and could mix most drinks if they weren't too fancy. Raised with ritual, I held a wake instead. I did not think of myself as divorced but widowed, and when B. called about the children or a check, the man I heard was a stranger. The voice was familiar—he had a beautiful voice, dark brown and as accentless as a radio announcer's—but I didn't know the speaker. I mourned the boy, I dreamed of him constantly, but I could not connect him with the man who had threatened custody suits and sanity hearings. Or I chose not to.

"Did I tell you about Shirley?" asked a woman whom I will call Rachel, herself recently separated from a husband who'd jumped everyone from assorted secretaries to their *au pair,* and eager to salve her miseries with those of the *salon des refusées* who seemed to constitute her friends. "Her ex-husband used to make notes in book margins with a red ballpoint pen. Well, last week I borrowed a book from her, and guess what? She'd written in the margins with a red ballpoint pen! And did I tell you what she did the week before he divorced her in Mexico? He's a photographer and used that week to finish an assignment. And she, right behind him, drove all over the Southwest, staying in the motels he'd just left."

A few weeks later, Shirley telephoned me. "Rachel says we've had a similar experience, and I was wondering if you'd like to join me and some other women who've been through the same thing for lunch so we could talk about it."

I hung up as quickly as was decent. "No, it is not the *same thing*," I wanted to yell. "Nothing is the *same thing*. And, no, I don't want to talk about 'it.' "

It would have been like eating my vomit or leaving a corpse too long unburied. I had to inter my husband. Then, years later, I could resurrect him and make him a part of my past, to be discussed with the same nostalgia with which I discussed my former boyfriends and my former schoolteachers. I hadn't realized yet that a former husband, unless he'd been a cipher, will never slide into the same category.

So I held a wake, for myself as well as for him. Oh, my God, this reads grim; it wasn't grim. It just meant being an animal again; not even an animal, nothing quite so complex. Our new house had a garden in the back, and one summer morning when the sun was too bright on my book, I looked down toward the bluestone with which the garden was paved and saw an inchworm insinuating itself across a square. One of the children's cats tracked it with her nose, and the worm stopped and flattened itself into a still U. The cat lifted her nose and walked away, and the inchworm started moving again, right through the tiny space under the paw of another, sleeping cat. My style.

Cats. A dog. My younger daughter, the one I shall call Rose Red because her hair was black and her cheeks pink, loved pets, so at our previous house we'd had goldfish, a series of turtles, and an enormous snail who ceaselessly suckered his way along a big glass bowl. We had accidental pets, too, small brown mice who could slide through hairline cracks. I grew adept at trapping them—the first time I disposed of a mouse, I felt I had achieved man's estate and was proud—but the children were appalled by my blood lust and could be appeased only by funerals. All the corpses got names. I remember only Mousie Brown Eyes.

Frustrated by the intractability of the furless (she had tried time after time to train her turtles to sit on the steps of their terraced plastic bowl), Rose Red languished for a dog and, tearless, stiff-backed, endured countless patch tests until declared only mildly allergic to animal fur. So we acquired Fred, a mongrel who looked like a Schnauzer on stilts and who, if left alone, avenged himself by toppling wastebaskets and chewing bed petticoats. Then Rose Red found "the most beautiful kitten in the world" at a block party and named her Eliza, and her sister, whom I shall call Snow White, because her hair was fair, appeared one day with Melanie, a half-grown tabby who'd been living in a vacant lot. When I objected, Snow White cried and said she wanted something of her own. So of course I said yes to this cat, who couldn't believe her luck and whose every meal was accompanied by furtive glances over her food bowl.

The calico up the street had kittens, one of which, its mother's clone, Rose Red acquired when it was weaned and which, after an evening with the dictionary looking up words that began with *cal*, she called Calypso.

So many pets were nuisances, especially the temperamental Fred, and Purina Cat Chow graveled the kitchen floor, but they gave life to a house in which the mother had none. I was keeping silence, playing dead, and if my daughters survived, it was because they were determined on all the little rituals—the bedtime stories, the Sunday breakfasts, the momentous trips to the supermarket—that made up the substance of their lives. But sometimes my children came home from school crying, because these were the days before every other mother was a single mother, and listening to what Mom and Dad had done over the weekend or hearing how the whole family was to gather for, say, Thanksgiving dinner was torture to them. My children did not want to be different from other children. My children were still young enough to want, desperately, to be like everybody else.

Some nights, though, I found myself unexpectedly happy because there was no body between me and the river-scented air that drifted through the open window. "I wonder if anyone will ever love me again," I would ask myself, but only because I thought I should. "You want to be like your mother, rocking on the porch all these years?" a cousin asked. I started to explain, then stopped, realizing suddenly that there was no longer an adult in the world to whom I owed an explanation for anything.

Except for my daughters, who invariably say, "You did the best you could," then laugh, there are still no adults to whom I owe an explanation. But I do indulge in description, because I like to tell stories. This, I am telling you, is what it was like to hold a wake for the living. It lasted, by my rough count, about six years, and much of it consisted—as do many wakes—of speaking with strangers.

THERE IS A THING I have noticed about New Yorkers, many of them, anyway. Asked a direction, they will stretch a conversation that should have lasted one minute into three. If they are on a bus, they will stretch it even further. Perhaps it is because so many of them live alone. Words pile up behind their closed mouths like clothes that have been crammed into a too-small suitcase. Words were piling up behind my closed mouth, too, but because I was reluctant to utter them, I began to listen instead. I eavesdropped, although never on anyone I knew, resuming a habit of my childhood when, unnoticed in a corner of my grandmother's living room, I had listened to her and her friends speak of illness and death and wills, all of them growing more cheerful by the moment, so healthy was their interest in mortality and money.

Sitting on the bus, listening to people talk about their boyfriends or their jobs or the building super, who they were sure was in their apartments when they were out, was like reading novels whose endings one would never know. Did the girl who was going to Lincoln Center ever make up with Joe? Did the man who was worried about his company's sales ever get his raise? Was I accurate in believing that people who lived on the Upper West Side, by far the most vociferous of my fellow passengers, had the most tumultuous relationships with their landlords, supers, and block associations? I envied the people on the Upper West Side. Loneliness could not possibly be part of a life that involved so many phone calls, meetings, and rent strikes.

I began to listen to friends and acquaintances in a way I could not do when I was married. B and I had given dinner parties, many dinner parties, which were like tennis matches, but for the balls being *aperçus* and the net, leg of lamb or *vitello tonnato*. The rallies were always long unless somebody, usually B., served an ace. Often there was no way to distinguish one voice from another—hardly surprising, since the guests, writers and editors for the most part, hewed on such occasions to the same intensely literary mode. Once I had made my own contributions to these tennis matches, lobs usually, and once B. had been amused by them. But eventually I could see the corners of his lips tightening when I talked, and grew afraid to open mine except to say, "More salad, anyone?" and, "Oh, yes, I saw a good review of that in the *Times*."

Now, because I never gave and seldom went to dinner parties (potential hosts, I figure, may have feared I might talk about "it"), I was usually alone, except for the children, with whoever was speaking to me. My daughters squeezed themselves between me and the guest. They lingered in doorways or, courting invisibility, secreted themselves on the stairs. They wanted to hear chatter, bathe in the sea of normality, and I was, in a sense, asleep. But my hearing was coming back, sharp enough for me to drown in dialogue, savor style. It was never sharper than on a June afternoon a few weeks after we had moved into our Anglo-Italianate stable.

I had been divorced (and B. newly married) for four months, and was about to leave for Australia for the magazine. I was longing to go, longing to leave the Saturday night trio of Archie Bunker, Bob Newhart, and Mary Tyler Moore, and the hours behind my closed bedroom door reading and rereading Colette because I thought there were lessons to be learned there. I wanted to be someplace where there was no chance of meeting B. and his new wife. Above all, I wanted to be someplace where nobody knew me and I could use my voice again.

But why were my ears so sharp on that particular June afternoon? Because I was listening to a woman named Lillian.

# Two

---

THE FIRST TIME I met Lillian Roxon, it was to hire her to write *Mademoiselle*'s (I was its managing editor) sex column. "Forgive the lounging pajamas," she said to me in her wild Australian nasal when we entered Cheval Blanc, a French restaurant not far from the Graybar Building and, at that time, one of countless just like it. They all served chilly pâtés, sole meunière, crème caramel, and featured mean-looking middle-aged women at the cash register. "The exterminator came this morning, and the bug bombs stank up everything else."

"Everything else" was a collection of strange floating robes home-dyed in colors like puce and mustard and fuchsia, and patched, wherever a seam had split, with Mickey Mouse fabric transfers. The cortisone Lillian took for asthma had made her buoyant as a waterbed, and, embarrassed by her fat, she had turned herself into a billboard that was fun to read and, since one was amused on seeing her, unpitiable. There was only one public place where she would bare her body, a rundown rooftop solarium at either Coney Island or Brighton Beach, where old Jewish women went to strip and sun. Here there was no reason for self-consciousness, no reason to hide what had happened to a body that had not yet touched forty.

Most of Lillian's friends, many of whom were rock stars and their groupies, were younger than she, and she was to them as she was to Snow White, a Rabelaisian sort of mother. Lillian sent my daughter funny notes in envelopes she'd watercolored and stuck with gilt stars. She gave her records—one of them of the singing squirrels and all of them "guaranteed to drive your mother up a wall"—and a lavender-painted strongbox because "every young girl should have one to lock up letters and diaries." When she came to call she always went to Snow White's room first, and I could hear them giggling behind the closed door. "I think I ought to tell you, Mary, just to set your mind at ease," she told me once. "If your daughter ever runs away from home—and don't tell her I told you this—don't worry. I made her promise to run away to me."

Mother to her friends, mother to my daughter, Lillian was, ironically, my child. She liked the order of my house—her apartment was as messy as a child's closet—and the way that meals appeared on time and rituals like Christmas and birthdays were faithfully observed. "You're so ladylike, so discreet, my dear," she teased. Sometimes she was too, or tried to be. She looked beautiful the night that, wearing pearls and a 1920s chiffon dress, she was hostess of an evening at the theater for an Australian playwright, and stood in the lobby greeting the guests and waving them in like a small and pretty Texas Guinan. Soon after I went into the auditorium, however, she slugged a woman who was crashing. After the play there was a party, and everyone congratulated Lillian on her right hook, but the evening had been ruined for her. She had dressed up, she had been a grand lady even, but a flick of her fist had turned her, in the eyes of the guests and of her disappointed self, into funny old Lillian again.

Some people leave their ghosts in rooms where they've been, so whenever my mind's eye sees Number 83, it also sees Lillian, sitting round as a Buddha on an angular twig chair or on the small rug next to the loveseat, gesturing with her glass of diet soda. She is talking about the woman she had slugged ("I had to, Mary. That little bitch had it in for me") and what she should wear to cover Tricia Nixon's wedding for the Australian news agency for which she worked ("I thought I'd go very Middle America, so I bought this kind of polyester shift at Lamston's and a white plastic purse that snaps shut. Do you think it'll do?") and why David Bowie's wife bit her ("I suppose she wanted attention") and another

344 ◆    MARY CANTWELL

rocker's presumed genital measurements ("A lovely, lovely boy— bet you think that's naughty, Mary") and the day she'd get it together. "When I get it together, Mary, when I get it together, I'm going to Elizabeth Arden and I'm going to have a facial and a massage and a pedicure, the whole number." I loved her language and the way she spoke it, spun through the nose with a touch of Cockney. Mostly, though, I loved being able to have a friend who didn't have to pass B.'s taste test. Like most wives—most husbands too, I suppose—I had trotted out each new acquaintance as if it were a purchase sent on approval.

We were in the garden on this hot June afternoon because I had to go to Sydney. The magazine was involved in a promotion for Australian wool, and Lillian, who had lived there for most of her twenties, knew exactly whom I should see and whom I should avoid.

"If you're invited to meet ———, don't, I beg you, Mary, don't go. He'll come at you with those big teeth of his and he'll talk your ear off; and I know you, Mary. You'll be too polite to move away and you won't learn anything and you'll be covered with spit besides, because he sprays when he speaks.

"I'm only sorry you're going to miss G. Did I tell you her latest? She really wanted to fuck M" (Lillian named a famous American writer), "but he wasn't interested, so she picked up this cab driver. She had him around for about a week—he looked good you know; Italian—and she told everyone he was *muy macho*. But she told me he was a lousy lay. Then he split because he got bored, so she told everyone she'd had to dump him because he was so forceful she'd got vaginitis. My God, that woman's got a mouth. I felt like saying to her, 'But, G, how could he do that with a limp prick?' "

Lillian widened her eyes and covered her mouth when she saw I was blushing. "Oh, Mary, I keep forgetting I have to watch my language when I'm around you. Now to get to a cleaner subject, more your thing, Mary—there's a little antique shop, Kaleidoscope. And you must meet M.F. She's got a finger in every pie in Sydney. Not that Sydney's got that many pies, you understand."

I cannot remember saying goodbye any more than I can remember who took care of the children while I was gone. But I can picture the scene. My older daughter would have been stony-faced. The younger one would have been crying. I would have been poised at a midpoint between happiness and guilt, and promising to bring back souvenirs.

Sydney didn't provide much in the way of souvenirs, only kangaroo-fur change purses. Nor did it have many pies. Why else would I have been treated as the Messenger from the West, passed from hand to hand, usually by editors from Australian *Vogue*, as this week's novelty. "What's happening in New York?" I'd be asked. "What's happening in the theater?" "Have you ever been to Max's Kansas City?" On and on they went, endless questions from what seemed to me a coterie of displaced persons, uncertain of their place on this planet. When, desperate to maintain my un-earned status as a cultural Colossus, I mentioned a Hopper show at the Museum of Modern Art that I hadn't even seen, a fellow guest said, "At last! A spontaneous mention of Edward Hopper in Australia!"

Lillian's friend M.F. gave a cocktail party for me, culling the guests from an address book as big as an accountant's ledger. "I think you should meet an anthropologist, don't you? And a politi-cian, so I'll ask Gough Whitlam. I'll ask Barry Humphries, because he's got a big name here as a comic—does Edna Everage, you know. And, of course, you'll want an economist . . ." I was awed. Not even the mayor of New York could have summoned so fancy a group in so short a time, but, then, Australia was a very small pond, so small that its big frogs could be clustered on the pages of just one address book.

At the party, flashbulbs popped, the drinking and backbiting reminded me of Dublin, and one guest, flaunting what Australians called the cultural cringe, said grandly, "We're all copyists here." Soon everybody departed, my hostess included, and I was left in an empty house, looking for a phone to call a cab.

Out in the harbor the Opera House seemed to scud before the wind, like a schooner under full sail, but most of the buildings, my hotel included, and many of the shop signs evoked the England of Lilibet and Princess Margaret Rose. So did the women in their sen-sible shoes and practical coats and glazed gray hair, and the five-and-tens that at intervals announced a sale on counter six or counter eight and sent their customers scurrying through the aisles. I had always been infatuated with what I had read and seen of the 1930s—mostly in movies starring Fred Astaire and Ginger Rogers or James Cagney and Ruby Keeler—and now I was living in that decade, suddenly transformed into my own mother.

The Rocks, where the first convict ships docked, hadn't yet become a cross between Williamburg and Boston's Quincy Market, and the nearby streets through which I wandered, looking for antique shops, seemed sinister and Dickensian. Kings Cross, Sydney's version of Times Square, was thronged with fresh-faced hookers just in from the country, and every inner suburb—sections, still, of Sydney but with names of their own—had a High Street, lined with greengrocers and butchers. All that was missing to remind me of London were red double-decker buses brandishing signs for Ty-Phoo tea. Then night came and, with it, stars that were in the wrong places and the realization that I had never been on soil so foreign. My ancestors' bones were scattered all over Great Britain and Europe, maybe even Asia and Africa and the Americas. But not here, not on this curious continent. Home seemed impossibly distant; the miles between this world and mine incalculable. Some people long for lovers; those people who are said to be the missing halves of their psyches. The missing half of my psyche was not a lover but two daughters, three cats, an obstreperous dog, and the six o'clock smell of lambchops broiling on a rack. In truth, it still is.

THE PROMOTION for Australian wool meant that, in the great fashion magazine tradition of rolling over and playing dead for potential advertisers, we were to devote several pages to a sheep ranch. So, with a photographer, a fashion editor, and a young New Zealander we saw in a park and who, with his fair hair and toothy grin, seemed to us as essential a photographic prop as an emu or a koala, I flew south to an airport so small that it was open only if you called ahead and asked them to turn on the runway lights.

The ranch was miles from the airport, at the end of an empty road that arrowed through rust-colored earth and hard blue hills furred with dense green trees. It was like driving through a void, but for the occasional interruption of thick heavy birds that swooped, lumbered really, in front of the car, stands of tall, thin ragged trees, and sudden clumps of ugly, boxy buildings freighted with the elaborate ironwork called Sydney lace. The light was unearthly, filtered through pewter-colored clouds to sit on tiny towns that resembled sets for a movie about the American frontier.

The ranch house was enormous, Victorian, a Nob Hill monstrosity set in tangled grass and ringed with thousands of sheep. Its owner and sole occupant was a young woman who, when I asked if she was ever lonely, said, "Not when I see this land, this space . . ." and flicked a hand toward emptiness. My eyes followed her hand—she was pointing, it seemed, at infinity—and at that moment I fell in love with Australia. It was alien and yet it was not—when she said, "We think nothing of driving one hundred miles to a ball," I thought of Jane Austen—and, like the Wild West of my Saturday afternoons at the movies, it promised the impossible.

"You conquered your interior," a man at the cocktail party had said, "but ours defeated us." "For God's sakes," another warned, "don't let yourself be talked into a flight across the outback. The only diversion is spotting brush-fires." But I had forgotten all that. I was besotted with the air and the clarity and a silence that soothed like aloes.

The young woman and I talked all day, wrapped in the peculiar intimacy of people who will never see each other again, and walked among the small, silly sheep and the shearing sheds and men who looked like cigarette ads. At night we dined in a room as formal, as glossed with silver and slicked with china, as any Spreckels mansion, and the young New Zealander couldn't get over the pink linen napkins. "Pretty posh," he said, and watched to see how we settled ours on our laps.

The space. I had never been in such space. It should have made me feel small. It didn't. I felt magnified, and magnified even further by an image left me by a man whose letters I kept in the top drawer of my bureau. He had traveled through the outback, he said, and had met an aborigine carrying a didgeridoo, a wind instrument. He tuned his guitar to the didgeridoo, and they played together. It may have been a fiction—most of his stories were—but I didn't know that yet. Even so, I was suspicious. It was too good, too pat: civilized and primitive man meeting in a fugue. No matter. The image, combined with what I had seen myself, lifted me into the air, so high I was like the all-seeing eye on a dollar bill, scanning Australia, all Australia, all at once.

Then I came home and found Rose Red sad because I had missed her ninth birthday by one day. I doubt she has ever forgiven me, and I know I have never forgiven myself. There was nothing I could have done about it. The airline I was on, *had* to be on, because again, in the great tradition of fashion magazines, the flight was a freebie—had only three or four flights a week to the United States. Still, I kept telling myself, I should have been there. I should have baked the cake. I should not have left her to be wet-eyed on the day she turned nine.

THE LETTERS in the top drawer of my bureau were from a writer whom I had asked to contribute a short piece to the magazine's book column. He did, and we embarked on a brief correspondence that grew, on his part, flirtatious. Maybe he liked the way I turned a phrase. More likely he thought that the former wife of a former acquaintance of his, a man who had punctured his ego by declining to work any longer with someone whose mendacity outweighed his considerable talents (B. held no brief for the term "artistic license," no matter how craftily employed), might add a few imprecations to his own.

Eventually he wrote that he was going to be in New York for the weekend and could I have dinner. If I had heard unsavory things about him, and later I remembered I had, I disregarded them, so eager was I to talk about books and poetry. When I went to meet him one cold November night, an anthology of his work was hidden in my shoulder bag. If he was friendly, if he seemed nice, I was going to ask him to sign it for me.

There was a cab strike that week, and I'd had a long walk from the bus stop. The chilly air pinked my cheeks, made me prettier than usual, I suspect, because I saw his face light up when he saw me waiting by the house phones. My first sight of my husband—dark, wearing a raincoat, standing in the living room of my college dormitory—is etched on my mind. So is my first sight of this man, the famous writer: big, fair, balding (his back hair, which he'd let grow long, had been swept up on one side and brushed across his bare pate), in a bright blue suit whose paisley lining matched his tie.

I walked to meet him, extended my hand; he mumbled something and steered me to the dining room. Just as we were sliding into the banquette, he said, "Mary, you evah been screwed till ya screamed?"

Before I could reply (just as well, because I couldn't have), he said, turning to face me, "Ah'm a womanizer. Ah just love them tight-assed little girls."

He described a few: assorted college sophomores ("They don't know nothin' "), a waitress in Lubbock, Texas ("Said ah was the finest man she evah knew"), a movie actress ("flat-chested but a good-time gal").

Perhaps I should have stopped my solitary (he was too busy talking to extend a helping hand) struggle with my coat. Perhaps I should have pulled it back onto my shoulders and flounced out the door. But I was titillated. Besides, I was carefully weaving a tale for the gang at the office. "Talk about feet of clay," I was going to tell them. "His clay feet went right up to his hips!" Too, as I had with the man who dared me to drink a full glass of Scotch, I wanted to prove to myself that I was tough, that I could take it, that nobody and nothing could faze me. So I chattered, I glissaded, skittish as a hog on ice.

"We don't need all this food," he said, pointing to my steak tartare. (In all the years we dined together I always ordered steak tartare because I was too nervous to chew.) "Come up to mah room. I've got a couple of six-packs on the windowsill." A loud laugh. "I call it the Pigeon Bar."

I dodged, and mentioned the magazine I worked for and how proud we were to have published him. "Ah love ladies' magazines," he said. "Mah wife's a fashion freak and she buys them all. And ah love them Zonite ads."

("Mary," a friend said the next day. "You didn't find him just a bit of an oaf?"

"No," I said defensively. "It's just that he says what everyone else is thinking.")

"You know what these are?" He reached into his pocket and dropped two pieces of metal on the table.

I picked them up. "Guitar picks?"

He was surprised. "You know anything about guitar?"

"A little," I said. "I have a lot of Doc Watson records and . . ." I dropped the small talk. "But what I really love is fado. Have you ever heard fado?"

I was off, forgetting to whom I was speaking, forgetting what he'd been suggesting, intent only on describing the music.

"Fado is a Portuguese word for, I guess, fate. And it describes a certain kind of song, a kind of wail. And the women who sing them are called *fadistas.* They sing about *saudade,* which is sorrow, but that's too narrow a definition. It means longing and loss and regret for what you haven't had and cannot even name, as well as for what you had that's gone.

"B. and I used to hear fado in Lisbon. We went to Portugal twice and stayed in a little fishing village called Cascais—it's rather fancy now—and drove into the city almost every night to park our car near the Ritz Hotel. Then we'd take a cab downtown to the Alfama—that's a rabbit warren of narrow streets, the oldest part of Lisbon—for fado. We'd sit in a little room with benches and tables, and a man with a guitar would come out and perch on a stool. Then the *fadista* would appear and put a black shawl over her head and shoulders—they always put on a black shawl—and sing. It's like keening, Irish keening. You must get an Amalia Rodrigues record. She's the greatest *fadista* in Portugal."

On I went, my hands sketching the room and the night and the shawl dropping over the shoulders, out of New York and into Lisbon with my husband, excited and happy.

"Keep it up, mah Mary," he said. "You're lookin' good."

He quieted then. Maybe the bourbon he'd been drinking before he came down to the lobby—I didn't know he was a heavy drinker—had worn off. Maybe, though, what happened to him was what I saw happen many times later. He had run down. He was overexcited when he got to the city, overexcited when he saw a new face, overanxious to stamp himself on a person or a room so that she, even it, would know she had met someone.

He had performed so constantly, had so consciously constructed a public image, that he had erased his self. Maybe he had no self. Maybe to live he had to kill it. Maybe, too, his best work was behind him, so his next work, the one that would keep him busy for the rest of his life, was to create the legend he wanted to leave after himself.

For all his weight and height and boasts and booming voice, and the way he V'd his thin, pale eyebrows over his round blue eyes and drew back his lips over his tall, narrow teeth when he feigned anger, he was as insubstantial as the jack o'lantern he sometimes resembled. There was only one time when he was real, at least to me, and that time began when, after my description of the *fadistas,* we began capping one another's quotations. I was—we were? How can I speak for him?—as giddy as I had been on my first date with my first boyfriend when we discovered we both liked lemon Cokes.

"Dover Beach" turned out to be one of our favorite poems. We recited it, or tried to—neither of us had a good memory for verse—in alternating lines. We talked about Gerard Manley Hopkins, and I told him of how, when my younger daughter said she wanted to be "young in her youth," I thought of "Margaret, are you grieving/Over Goldengrove unleaving."

"There's a rather peculiar English woman I like, too," I said.

"I know. I know," he crowed. " 'I was much too far out all my life . . .' "

" 'And,' " I finished, " 'Not waving, but drowning.' "

"Mah Mary," he said, putting his hand over mine, "I'll bet we're the only two people in New York who know that poem. You know what I like about you? You're mah equal. Mary Cantwell, we're gonna be one long thing."

It was late, and I had to walk to Ninth Avenue to find a bus, so I got up to leave. On our way through the lobby he said, "It's just as well you didn't come upstairs. I wouldn't have been much good to you."

"That wouldn't have mattered. I think I'd have been happy just to sleep beside you." Then, stunned by what I had said, I put my arms around his neck and kissed him.

The next day, when I told a friend about my dinner with this writer I had idolized, she laughed, as I hoped she would, especially when I aped the way our natural accents exaggerated themselves as we spoke to each other, his getting more Southern, mine more New England. Then—flushed, flustered, a little teary—I confessed how much his saying I was his equal meant to me.

In a month or so he called and said someday he'd take down my panty hose and give me a good spanking. My marriage had been to me analogous to entering a convent—I never strayed outside the grounds—so my response, silence, was as innocent as that of a child who, despite a thorough warning, was about to take candy from a stranger. Yet I was cautious enough not to use the ticket he sent me for a panel discussion he was chairing in New York. I wouldn't risk going alone. When I called him at his hotel and said I was sorry I couldn't be there and wished him luck, he said, "Mah Mary, you're always running away from what you really want." And when I told Dr. Franklin, the psychiatrist at whose office I had so often wept during the wake I was holding for B., about the writer's phone calls and the vulgarity that had me as mesmerized as a mongoose faced by a snake, he said, "Don't you go near that man."

But one day I did, because I thought he was life.

# *Three*

———◆———

$\mathcal{D}$URING THE LONG STRETCH between separation and divorce, I had read a lot. I had read about how much better it was for the children if an end was brought to an unhappy marriage. I had read that staying together for their sake was practically a crime against nature. I had made an appointment with B.'s psychiatrist, who seemed surprised when I said that two people who had brought children into the world had a responsibility toward them that surmounted their own petty concerns. "You're a real Christian!" he said, amazed. More likely, in the world in which B. and I had lived for seventeen years, I was a real anomaly.

The house quiet but for the children's soft breathing and the occasional clunk from the radiator, I would steal from my bed and, sitting in the dark, humiliate myself with midnight phone calls. "Please," I would beg, "I can change. I can be anything you want me to be." Then, as usual, work saved me from being someone of whom my father would have been ashamed. (How he would feel about my self-abasement was ever on my mind and kept me poker-faced in public.)

*Mademoiselle*'s guest editors, winners of a contest that would enable them to edit the August College Issue (most of which had been completed before they arrived), had as part of their prize a week in a foreign country. I had semi-chaperoned a previous group in Israel. I was escorting the new group to Ireland.

Most of my charges didn't like Ireland—the g.e.'s, as we called them, tended to judge countries by their shopping potential—and I was glad to be shot of them soon after we got to Dublin. The editor-in-chief called to say the magazine had got some unexpected advertising from Yugoslavia, and, lacking a quid pro quo, she wanted me to make a rush trip for a rush article. It was June, the children were out of school and in good hands, and I would have one more week away from a city in which I saw the ghosts of my husband and myself on every corner. I arrived in Yugoslavia armed with the entire *Forsyte Saga*, and soon found myself immersed in a London that seemed far more real than the cities and countryside about which I was assiduously making notes.

Still, I recall sitting on the ramparts that surround Dubrovnik and thinking that if I just leaned backward a bit, I would fall to a death that everyone would think accidental. At the same time I was uncomfortably aware of the small stones that were pocking my backside. "As long as your butt is counting pebbles, mah Mary," the balding man said when I told him of that momentary hover between feeling and oblivion, "I'm not gonna worry about you."

I recall, too, an old woman watching me from the window of a building bordering the restaurant terrace on which I was eating an early dinner, and that I raised my glass to her. And another woman, in white, with a pyramidal straw hat and the kind of honeyed skin and hair and slanty brown eyes I always associate with Hungarians, standing in a rose-choked fourteenth-century cloister. "Dubrovnik," she said. "There is nothing more beautiful, is there?" When I mentioned her charm to my guide, he shrugged. "I have seen her before," he told me. "She is mad."

I remember Belgrade, and how brown and sluggish the beautiful blue Danube was as it slouched past my hotel window, and an evening sitting with people from the tourist commission while all around us the other diners sang the Yugoslav equivalent of "You Are My Sunshine." I was wearing my wedding ring, still, as I saw it, under my husband's protection. I spoke of him, too, as if he were home waiting for me. Instead, he was to me as dead as Virginia Woolf's brother Thoby was truly dead all the time she was writing her friend Violet Dickinson about his temperature, his moods, his crossness with his nurses because they wouldn't give him mutton

chops and beer. Even during the midnight phone calls that preceded my final letting go, I had recognized the man I was talking to
as B.'s simulacrum. This man, who one night hissed, "Cocksucker!" into my ear, could not be my husband.

I saw Germans, always recognizable because their shorts never
quite covered their rumps, and coveys of Russians, the women all
wearing the same kind of shoddy, low-heeled beige shoes, and elderly American women unconquered by their varicose veins and
elastic bandages. I dined one afternoon on roast kid (I thought it
was baby lamb), in what I was told was Tito's favorite restaurant,
and one evening with a young man who idolized Albert Szent-
Györgyi. When I spoke of Szent-Györgyi's having said that the
world was a small cave we could not afford to litter, the boy looked
at me with warm brown eyes and said, "You sound like a Yugoslav
student."

Talking. I was talking all the time, because there was no
Yugoslav who didn't want to practice his English and because I
have the gift, if gift it is, of instant intimacy. Add up those moments
when you and a stranger connect, I thought to myself, and you can
turn them into a life for yourself.

The longest talk was with a middle-aged woman who was
working for a new hotel on the Adriatic. The old town, settled by
Bosnian Turks, was nearby, and we walked through threads of
streets and the smell of sardines to a restaurant on the water, where
she spoke of her two brothers and a sister-in-law who had been executed during World War II. She couldn't forget them, she said, but
she had forgotten to hate. "We spend so much time looking inside
ourselves that all we see is darkness. But if we look out—there is so
much that is beautiful."

Ah, this is one of the good times, I said silently, this coming together with someone I would never see again, and both of us
looked toward the sky, hunting the Big Bear and the Little Bear. But
as we did I realized that my children, having grown up under a sky
in which the only star one could rely upon was Venus, had never
seen either, and I was sick with longing. No, this was not a life, this
little accumulation of epiphanies, not a life for me.

Before I left Yugoslavia, however, there was another good time,
in Split, which I liked because walking through it was like touring

fifteen or so centuries at the same time. Bits and pieces of at least a thousand years of construction had been jumbled together into the architectural equivalent of a magpie's nest. Rome is also a magpie's nest, of course, but Rome is too big for me to swallow. Split was just my size.

I was wandering through a small church, mostly Byzantine, I think, and asking more questions than the guide, a girl no more than twenty, could answer. "Oh, this isn't fair to you," she said, and ran off to get the head guide, a tall thin man in his fifties, dressed all in white but for the black beret tilted over his thick gray hair. He was enormously well informed, and polished to a degree that Americans (sometimes I feel a part not only of a recently evolved country but of a recently evolved race) never attain, but I suspect he was also poor. Why else would a university professor, which he was, spend his summers trying to educate tourists like me into some quickly forgotten semblance of scholarship?

Was he married, I wondered, or a bachelor? Did he have a house, an apartment, or one small room? Did he find what he was doing demeaning? I wanted to burrow my way into his head, because I wanted to burrow my way into his life. I didn't know how to live mine; I didn't even know how to sit still. That was the real reason I traveled. It was a way to quiet the ants that were forever crawling under my skin. But I asked him nothing except the period of this fresco, the provenance of those curious columns, thanked him politely, tipped him nicely, and returned to Soames and Irene and London's damp chill.

It was the same when I got back to New York. I needed books so that I could live their characters' lives, not mine, and I needed rooms beyond the virginal white bedroom in which I sat, propped against pillows, a glass of slivovitz (my only souvenir of Yugoslavia) in my left hand and a book, any book, in my right. I was listening, to Virginia Woolf, to Jean Rhys, and, mostly, to Colette, whom I believed to be the font of all wisdom, not realizing that she, who wrote so movingly about solitude, scarcely had a solitary moment in her life.

Beyond my bedroom door was a windowless inner room good for nothing but a library, and here it was that I had imagined my children doing their homework when they were old enough for it, at the big center table under the green-shaded hanging lamp. But when the time came, Rose Red did her homework wherever I was, and Snow White did no homework at all.

Their rooms were on the other side of the library, Snow White's strewn with strange caches of dirty glasses and gum wrappers and notes passed at school, letters from people barely met, and Janis Joplin records. Already, she had a passion for the doomed and the dramatic and would put on a long pink dress and tie a homemade black velvet choker around her neck on Sunday nights to watch the *Masterpiece Theatre* shows about Henry VIII, Elizabeth I, and their courts. Above all, she was obsessed with Anne Frank, whose diary she read over and over again. She identified with Anne Frank, she said. Anne Frank was her best friend.

Rose Red's room was neat, with a dollhouse, stuffed animals on the bed, birthday cards taped to the wall, and a small electric organ and miniature bottles and a soap collection and a candle collection and stacks of Archie comics. When the girls were small, I had sat in the room with bunny wallpaper and told them stories and sung "Rock-a-Bye, Baby." Now, with the streetlight shining in my window and the garden dark beneath theirs, we stayed apart too many nights, Snow White with Anne Frank and Rose Red with her Archies and I with my books, my wonderful books, which all my life had arisen and engulfed me in a reality more powerful than my own. When I was a child, immersion in a book deafened me to calls to come to the dinner table, help dry the dishes, get ready for bed. Now, at night, books deafened me to soundlessness—a phone that didn't ring, a door that would never open again to bring my husband home. But I *could* hear Daisy Buchanan weeping over Jay Gatsby's shirts, and Lord Peter Wimsey wooing Harriet Vane with John Donne.

Rose Red, determined to be "young in her youth," was also determined that I provide her with a childhood. If I came home from work tired and thinking about sandwiches, she would say, "It's a mother's responsibility to give her child hot meals," and send me, my exhaustion suddenly erased by her demands for order, to the kitchen. Out they would come, the linguine with clam sauce and the salad, and there my daughters would sit, the one lazily forking her pasta and the other grinning triumphantly.

We worked on her dollhouse together—one summer weekend when my mother was visiting, she and I had wall-papered all its rooms—and sometimes Rose Red and I spent long hours after supper with intricately detailed coloring books and colored pencils, each of us busily and quietly turning out fantastically ornate Elizabethan court dresses. The day she talked me into washing the clothes of her Meg, Jo, Beth, and Amy dolls and painstakingly ironing them, she watched from my bed, blissful because her mother was doing what a mother was supposed to do. As a baby she never tried to climb out of her playpen the way Snow White did, and, later, she never sat on a chair without first testing its strength with a timorous hand. Her ear was finely tuned to the moment of ripeness, and not until she heard it would she move on.

I was, and remain, grateful for her bossiness. In guarding her childhood, she was also guarding my motherhood. Too, she had my grandmother's earthiness—my grandmother, whom I once saw carry a live water rat by its tail to the backyard incinerator, and who inevitably uttered, "The old goat!" when a widower went courting. One evening Rose Red and I were cooling ourselves at my bedroom window when a car stopped directly under the streetlight. The passenger—male or female I do not know, because the nearby meat market was thick with transvestite prostitutes—promptly unzipped the driver's fly, then buried her head in his lap. Rose Red ran from the room, in shock I assumed, to come back a minute or so later with her bird-watching binoculars. After carefully adjusting the sights, she trained them on the couple and howled, "Mom, they're corrupting me!"

Snow White, though, didn't want to be young. Snow White wanted to grow up very fast, because adulthood—sixteen years old, anyway—meant emancipation. I had cried over B. and now I cried over her, wondering what made my husband and now my daughter want to run away from me. That it may have been something in them and not something in me never entered my mind, so convinced was I of my power to destroy.

Even so, there were moments, like the evening the two of us went to the theater and Snow White, wearing her best gingham dress, asked why people didn't dress up for great occasions like this one. I commiserated; I agreed; we were partners in condescension.

There was another evening when someone had given me house seats for the Royal Ballet and we sat next to an old woman draped in diamonds, whom I recognized as the mother of a famous murderee, and her escort, the usual young man in the usual tasseled Gucci loafers. Snow White couldn't see the stage for the diamonds, and finally asked the old woman if they were real. "Oh, yes," the woman said, and held out her braceleted arm for inspection. We were happy that night, she a child again and I a mother with a foolish, apologetic grin. She let me tuck her in for the first time in months when we got home—Rose Red was already asleep—and I thought of Sylvia Plath's poem about the dead woman who has folded her dead children "back into her body as petals / Of a rose close when the garden / Stiffens . . ." I would never wish my children dead, as I often did myself, but I knew all about wanting to fold them back into my body, where I could keep them safe and warm forever.

"MAH MARY," the balding man said, angry because his rare evening in New York was being ruined by the pain in my head, "you'd better do something about those headaches."

But I had. After their onset, when I was twenty-three, I had sat for years in a psychiatrist's office, because a doctor had told me therapy would cure migraine. It didn't. It doesn't.

The headaches came without warning; they were unavoidable, because I couldn't analyze their cause, and they usually left me crying and helpless for three days. More destructive than the pain, however, was the contempt I—and B., too—felt for me. I had read that personality was responsible for migraine, that it was the punishment accorded perfectionists and the high-strung, people who could not take criticism or confrontation. Once again I was proving myself impossible, and I could hear B.'s impatience in the balding man's voice. Perhaps a Bronx hospital's headache unit that I had just heard of might be helpful. Perhaps the doctor who had said I had migraine and sent me to a psychiatrist had made a misdiagnosis. Perhaps, I thought, hopeful because I didn't realize the seriousness of the alternative with which I was presenting myself, I had a brain lesion.

Week after week I took a long subway trip and a long walk to the hospital, to sit in a waiting room crammed with people who had whatever it was I had. There were small children there, and middle-aged men, and people who were dressed nicely, and people who were dressed poorly. Rather than the isolated neurotic I'd believed myself to be, it appeared I was part of a community of sufferers, and that knowledge was more useful than any of the countless ergotamine tablets I had swallowed over the years.

The tests, none of which I had had before, seemed endless. At the end of them the doctor, a young Filipino whose hair was as black and as stiff as the bristles on a clothes brush, said, "You have common migraine."

"Oh, God," I said to myself, "he's going to send me to another psychiatrist." I could see them all beginning again: the tears when I spoke of my father, who had betrayed me by dying, the tears when I spoke of B., who had betrayed me by loving someone else, the endless circling between my childhood and the present, and no exit from the pain in my head.

"You probably inherited it," he added.

A set of swollen arteries, as inevitable to a Cantwell as a prognathous jaw to a Hapsburg, had been handed down from generation to generation. For the pain in my head I'd been declared "not guilty."

"Your personality didn't create the pain. The pain created your personality," the doctor said. I should have been joyous. Instead, I was enraged. But for that cluster of aberrant arteries (not my fault, not my fault), I was normal. Yet for years, several doctors, countless magazine articles, my husband, and myself had told me that, in one respect at least, I was not.

To be normal. I became infatuated with normality, asked doggedly that it be defined, and measured myself against the definition. When a doctor told me that my blood chemistry fit "the textbook definition of normal," I bragged. My blood pressure, a steady 120 over 80, enchanted me. If I could have, I would have papered a room with the results of my Pap smears. All said, "No abnormal cells." It was not so much that I feared cancer as that I loved having a cervix that was lined with innocence. Others were enthusiastic about their abnormalities; I, about my normalities. I was crazy about my cholesterol count.

Heterosexuality, however, defeated me. I could not construct a norm. B. was the first naked man I had ever seen, and when I did, I thought of Jesus in His drooping loincloth. Surrounded by an iconography that showed God as a man, my sexual associations were religious, and what I wanted from sex, when finally I did want something from it besides babies, was Communion. Is that normal? History, psychology, and a millennium or two of literature say no.


IT IS OCTOBER. I love October. It makes me think I am in school and that I have homework and that my father and I are going to tune in *Inner Sanctum* and turn out the lights so that he can scare my sister and me with odd whistles and tappings. We still exchange memories of him, very different memories, because I knew one man and she knew another. The father I knew was pleased that I shared his bookishness and the joy he took in language, and he smiled whenever he heard me intoning, as he so often did, "Had I the heaven's embroider'd cloths . . ." Diana's father was enchanted by the eagerness with which she embraced swimming and softball and basketball, and he once had high-topped sneakers—she had weak ankles—made just for her. But whenever we speak of Papa, the identical smile lights our faces.

It is October, and I am on my way to a cocktail party with the balding man. He doesn't want to go, but I have promised—it is the first time the hostess has entertained since her husband died—so he is sitting half-drunk in a corner of the cab and he is sniping at me.

"You've got a mean, intelligent face."

I am silent.

"Mary Cantwell, the clock is running out on you."

"That depends on what clock you're watching," I say calmly. I have the resilience of a roach.

We get to the party and he stalks through it like an angry bear. He isn't rude, but he's showing off, and he's feeding so visibly on the adulation of his fans that he's swelling like the corpse in the Ionesco story who gradually swallowed up the room.

The hostess and a friend from the office take me aside. "Mary, stay here with us," she says. "You can't leave with that man," he says. "They'll be picking you up in bits and pieces all over Riverside Drive tomorrow."

"I have to go," I say, because I have made up my mind. I cannot bear any more dreams about B., and half-waking with my arms half-open. If this man is the sexual giant he has claimed to be during the year since we met, he is going to blast me right out of those nightmares. The children are away for the weekend, and I have put my best sheets on the bed.

I take his arm and we go to a dinner party, where none of the guests speak to him because he is drunk and because they dislike him.

"Mah Mary," he says, "please don't let me drink. I don't want to make a fool of myself."

So I don't, happy to be needed, happy to mother, and he goes off, to sit in a corner like a schoolboy with a dunce cap and sober up. The moderator of the panel on which the males of this distinguished group, all of whom have written for the screen, are to speak later, leans over and says, "Don't you go in for the Madonna Dolorosa. You've got the face for it."

I laugh. This is the light, skinny chatter I enjoy at dinner parties, and he and I sparkle right through dessert.

While the other panelists are drinking coffee, the balding man and I walk around the block. He is sober now, and he is unhappy.

"Mah Mary," he says, "last night I was in Chicago, at a forum, and they offered me a woman. And I didn't want her, I didn't want her, but I took her because she was *offered* me. I feel dirty."

If he had been B., the confession would have made me heartsick. But B. was real, whereas the balding man is an actor. An autumn night in New York, an empty street, a pretty, rather innocent listener, and, in a few minutes, an audience of at least a thousand: how resist the chance to speak such compelling lines? But if he is an actor, so too am I. Playing the Madonna Dolorosa suits me very well.

At the theater, where the panelists are to speak after a movie screening, I sit in what I immediately christen Mistresses' Row. Each and every one of these pretty women who had been guests at the dinner, each of whom clearly has a camel's hair coat and the Yale Bowl in her past, is sleeping with one of these men, some of whom are married, up there on stage. I do not like this. I have been a wife too long to like being lumped with girlfriends.

Actually, I don't like anything about the evening, because the panelists, eager to prove why they had earned a place on a stage, are speaking mostly to their peers and hardly ever to the audience. True, one of them announces he has a good Sam Peckinpah story. But he forgets to tell it.

An hour or so later, after the panel breaks up, the balding man and I are leaving the theater when a young man steps out of a shadowed doorway and says, "I've been waiting here, sir, to tell you how much I admire your work."

I look across Lincoln Center, which by this hour is empty, at the fountain, still sending sprays of water into the midnight air, and at the young man hurrying off into the darkness. Awed by fame and, in this great plaza, its perfect setting, I ask, "Doesn't that make up for everything?"

"No," he says, and I marvel at the despair that too many years of reading biographies of Hemingway and Fitzgerald have convinced me attends genius. Anyone emerging from a shadowed doorway to say he had admired, say, my piece on Yugoslavia would have had me soaring.

We are in my living room now, and he, used to hotel rooms and probably afraid his wife will call and catch him out, says, "This isn't right, my bein' in your house."

"If it isn't right in my house, it isn't right anywhere," I say, and lead him upstairs. Propped on pillows, wearing my best nightgown, quiet, self-possessed, watching him fold his clothes on an old rocker, extending my arms when he turns and says, "Well, this is me," no one would ever guess that he is only the second man I have ever slept with.

"You don't feel any shame at all, do you?" he asks the next morning.

"No," I answer, "only joy," and I think he is disappointed. He has written about the magic of guilt, but guilt is magic only to the amateur. I think myself my husband's killer, and in indulging the balding man and his sad semblance of lust, I am not committing another crime but doing penance for the first.

When we part in front of his hotel and, restless, I walk through Bloomingdale's, I am too dazed to shop, and go home to slide between the sheets he's just vacated. I feel as though I've given birth to him, and that the umbilical cord still connects us. Dr. Franklin says, reluctantly, "I guess you won't feel so alone anymore." And I don't, not for years.

# Four

---

*T*HE LAST TIME I saw the Snow White I had known from the day she was born was on a Christmas morning. We had opened the presents, and in a few minutes her father was to ring the bell—he never entered the house and I never entered the hallway to greet him—and take the children to the country for the holidays.

Actually, it is not the sight of her that I remember as well as I do the sharpness of her thin thighs. She was sitting on my lap, crying, because going away meant Christmas afternoon would be no turkey stuffed with chestnuts, no guests applauding when I came out with the plum pudding, no sitting past bedtime under the tree while I marveled at the stool she had made for me in shop and the handkerchief on which Rose Red had, in running stitch, embroidered my name. Perhaps what she was going to would be more fun, more filled with family, because her stepmother had many relatives, and we were only three. But one thing, perhaps the only thing, I know about children is that they are as wedded to ritual as old priests are to the Latin Mass.

The doorbell rang. Rose Red, dry-eyed, lips set, already the mother I was not sure how to be, took Snow White's hand and walked her to the door. I never saw my elder child again. Her semblance, yes, but never that same little girl. People are fond of saying that babies change from week to week. Go away for a few days and you come back to a whole other person. But it is not only infants that mutate. So do children, and while I was not watching, Snow White turned into someone I had not met before. Her younger self is present now only in old albums, in photographs where she stares at the world with wide wondering eyes, often with a flower—she loved to smell flowers—clutched in her small, short-fingered hand.

After the car drove off, I moved away from the curtains, around which I'd been peering, and allowed myself to cry. But not for long. I had to take down the tree, lug it to the gutter, and put away the ornaments for another, better year. Then I had to pack.

A few weeks earlier I had been in my office, working late. In truth, I didn't really need to work late. But I knew the nice young woman from Dominica who came in every afternoon so as to be there when the children came home from school—I could no longer afford a housekeeper—would stay until I got home, and here, in this office, was peace and order. Here I knew what to do, to move papers from In boxes to Out boxes, to sign my name to requisitions, to scribble in the margins of manuscripts that this paragraph here, that sentence there, needed more work. At Number 83, I did not. Perhaps I might say something to offend my daughters. Even worse, during our rare phone conversations, I might say something to offend B., whose contempt had a razor's edge.

I thought I was alone, so was surprised when the travel editor poked her head in my door. She had just got a promise of advertising from three different countries, but here it was, the Christmas season, and who on earth could she find to write the articles that would be the quid pro quo? I asked which countries, and when she mentioned Turkey, I said, "I'll go."

I would have gone anywhere, really, to escape a house that would be empty by Christmas afternoon and a Christmas tree that by the evening would be lying naked in a gutter. Going to Turkey meant fleeing absences—the smell of a roasting bird, the rustle of tissue paper—to embrace new presences. When I left, in the early evening, to deposit Fred at a friend's apartment until she could take him to a kennel the next morning, I felt as if I were closing the door on a tomb.

To enter my friend's apartment was to be surrounded by safety, because she was a woman who never took a risk. She hadn't risked marriage; she hadn't risked job-hopping; she hadn't even risked falling in love unless the man was a homosexual—closeted, of course. It was the era of the bachelor, the man-about-town, the always reliable escort to the Junior League Ball, and never did I, nor she, associate such a cadre with what we knew, for sure, were "fairies" or "the boys." We thought they were simply bachelors, in the sense that my grandfather's somewhat eccentric brothers had been bachelors, and assumed that somewhere out there were the someones who could catch them someday.

Oh, but it was so cozy in her apartment, she with her after-dinner framboise and her escort of the moment with his. The living room was strewn, but artfully, with discarded wrap and ribbons; a fire burned in the fireplace; Christmas ornaments—little birds, all of them—glinted on the mantelpiece. I didn't want to leave this pleasant room, these pleasant people, and Fred, who, scenting departure, tried to get in my lap and who, when at last I walked toward the door, hurled himself against my legs. But once in a cab, free of his howls and slicing through Queens, my calves were as tensed as a sprinter's before the pistol shot. Takeoff, and I wished I were lashed to the plane's nose like the figurehead on a ship, and soaring.

THE SMELL OF COAL SMOKE: that's what woke me every morning in Istanbul, that and the sound of boats hooting on the Bosporus. The hotel was old fashioned, an Edwardian relic, and my room so dimly lit that the only place I could read was the bathroom. At night I lined the tub with a blanket, put some pillows at one end, and climbed in quite happily, surrounded by a space as bright and white as an operating theater. This time I wasn't traveling with Galsworthy. This time it was Edmund Wilson.

Because the hotel was well off the American tourist route, its guests were the few Turks who traveled, families mostly, European businessmen whose expense accounts did not permit first-class accommodations, and a lone middle-aged woman who, one night in the dining room, started talking in I do not know what language and left the table in tears.

It was the kind of dining room that encouraged tears, because its good days, had there ever been any, were long ago and its revelers were long since dead. The room was cavernous, as big as the dining salon of an ocean liner, and a pianist played old show tunes—"I'm Gonna Wash That Man Right out of My Hair," "People Will Say We're in Love"—in a skinny forest of potted palms down by the kitchen door. Unless some member of the Tourist Board had been appointed to show me Istanbul by night, I dined there every evening, drinking my white wine and eating my lemon sole and thinking myself a woman of the world, no longer myself but a character out of Graham Greene. When I slept, there were no more nightmares. The silence was like a sable brush that someone had stroked me with from head to foot, and in the morning, when I left my bed, I was as sealed as an egg.

Most of the hotels were in the new city, but most of what I wanted to see was in the old city, so every morning, through the fog, I would cross the Galata Bridge, through a clutter of cars and buses and horse-drawn carts, to a spider's web of streets. In retrospect, I don't know how I got there, because I was too shy to hail a *dolmus,* a kind of cab with assigned stops, and certainly I didn't dare the city buses, so I suppose I walked. In strange cities I have always walked, everywhere, with more trust in my feet and a map than in any car or driver. Too, my lack of languages (French, my only other, I mispronounce and misuse) makes me feel as if I have a rubber plug in my mouth, the kind that stops up sinks. So, lost more often than not, I have walked and walked, my mouth closed over my useless tongue, and never have I failed to get where I was going.

I walked to Sancta Sophia, where a fragment—only the heads are whole—of a mosaic of Saint John and Mary pleading with Jesus for the world's sinners induced a kind of melting, like a wound draining. I walked to the Blue Mosque, paved with a faience so blue, it stabbed the eye, and, shoeless on demand, I wondered at the equality that prevails when you and everyone around you are padding around in stocking feet. There was another mosque, the Quarye, whose mosaics evoked Yeats's "Sailing to Byzantium" as surely as if he were whispering it in my ear. I had loved Yeats in college, even used him as a kind of sex manual. "For love has pitched its mansion in the place of excrement," I would murmur over and over, trying to turn the awkward college couplings in B.'s car—my back pinioned by the steering wheel and my legs splayed—into something resembling passion, ardor, romance.

"My God, we've sent a claustrophobe to the Grand Bazaar," the executive editor called out to *Mademoiselle*'s editor-in-chief when I phoned to report on the horror of walking through acres of embroidered robes and rugs, stacks of brass trays, and thousands of gold bangles, all of them illumined by fluorescent lights so bright they hurt my eyes. It was good to be able to speak English, even better to think of the gang back at the office fielding hyperboles and getting breathless over Anne Klein. If I was serious about doing my work well, I was wholly unserious about the work itself. It made me laugh too hard.

"*Buona sera*" and "*Quelle belle femme*," the dusty-looking young men would mutter as I walked by. (I suppose they would have muttered something in German had I been fair.) The American young men—one could tell them by their jeans and their godawful sandals—never said anything. They were too busy looking for hashish. "They seem to have an idea about the city," said a young girl the Tourist Board had made my luncheon companion as we were dining in a restaurant on top of the Galata Tower. It was wonderful talking again—about her university, her rent, and the one thing about the United States she really wanted to know. "What do you think of Jackie Kennedy now that she's married that Greek?"

Mostly, though, I was alone. I was alone the morning I took a crowded ferry across the Bosporus to Uskudar to see nineteenth-century houses that looked like weathered matchsticks, and an old Moslem cemetery pinned with cypresses and thick with tall tombstones that tottered drunkenly and seemed to leer at passersby. They seemed human, those tombstones, because their finials told me whether those beneath them had been men or women. "I am in Asia," I said to myself, awed that my own two feet had taken me so far. Perhaps I too could be a Freya Stark, wandering the Middle East, spying the past beneath the present.

But of course I could not be a Freya Stark, and not because I had two children and a tongue that could not twist itself around

the unfamiliar. I could not be a Freya Stark because that night, dining at the best restaurant in Istanbul with people from the Tourist
Board, I realized that this world, where tablecloths were spanking
white and waiters dipped their trays to one's left, was truly my
world. When we stopped on the long drive back to my hotel to buy
huge circles of flat, crackly pastry from an old woman in a little
lighted stand, alone in miles of dark, I shuddered at her isolation,
imagining myself into her role as easily as I had imagined myself
into that of a divorced housewife looking for lust at that roadhouse
near the Long Island Expressway. At the same time, though, I reveled in my own solitude, because for once I was free of the baggage
I'd been toting since, fresh out of school, I married a young man
who once kept a copy of *Orlando* in his trenchcoat pocket. A
stranger to the country, a stranger to the people who carted me
about, I was to the Turks only a woman with brown eyes, a big
shoulder bag, and an almost unimaginable life thousands of miles
away. To me, I was only myself, an integer again.

"No, no," the Turkish tourist office in New York had said when
I offered a rough idea of my itinerary after Istanbul. "You musn't
be in Ankara on New Year's Eve. Ankara is a city of civil servants.
It will be deserted, and you will be lonely."

B and I had celebrated New Year's Eve only twice that I can remember, and I'd never done so in childhood. At home, my parents
out for the evening, I would think deep thoughts and inscribe them
in my diary, one of the several little spiral-bound notebooks I
would buy during the year, write in for a month or two, then forget about. So New Year's Eve in an empty Ankara, me reading in
bed and turning out the light before midnight, would be no different from all my New Year's Eves. But no, the nice tourist people
said. "You must go to Izmir for the celebration. You will be happy
there."

My escort, from the Tourist Board, was a plump, curly-haired
man in his thirties who called me "Mees Mary" and ended his sentences with "et cetera, et cetera, et cetera," like the king in *The
King and I*. As oily and ingratiating as a seal, he was also anti-
Semitic. "What can you expect? They're Jews," he said when the

noise from an adjoining table drowned our conversation. I bit my tongue, knowing that I of all people—the ex-wife of a Jew, the mother of two half-Jewish children—should snap back at him. But courtesy, as always, made a coward of me, courtesy and the one habit, apart from liking to polish silver, that I had inherited from my mother. We were too much given to making excuses for others, too willing to overlook the unspeakable. I outgrew the habit. She, however, has been a "lady" all her long life.

We ate fresh sturgeon on skewers, snatched, he said, "from under the noses of the Greeks," then went to the "number one deluxe nightclub," which was on top of the hotel. I doubt he could have afforded such a place if he hadn't had to take me about, so I imagine he may have thrilled to the belly dancer, the four female violinists sizzling through "Play, Gypsy, Dance, Gypsy," the four male Paraguayans singing Italian standards, and the black-satined blonde breathing "Mammy Blue." But maybe not. Maybe he would have liked to be at home with his wife and children, assuming he had any, drinking *raki* and munching on pistachios. Or maybe he would have liked to be one of those men out on the dance floor, lean men with faces like hawks, dancing with women as plump and lush as overblown peonies. When the women, presumably their wives, returned to their tables, the men danced together, as I had seen Jewish men dance the hora, and it was then that I saw joy, only then that I saw love.

From Izmir on I traveled with a young Turkish woman just out of university and reluctant to marry, because she worried about her freedom. As we drove toward a coastal resort named Marmaris, I would look from her, dressed in imitation Pucci and teetering in high-heeled pumps, to the women I saw in yashmaks, layers of sweaters, and billowy pantaloons, bent double under bundles of branches or the fat, shawled children they were piggybacking (the men meanwhile were sitting in tilted-back chairs in every café doorway, under every tree), and wonder which of us she was more like.

I found out the afternoon we stopped at a camel fight we'd seen from the road. Past the veiled women standing on the walls surrounding the field we marched—she a monument to emancipation—straight to a pair of folding chairs some grinning men had set up for us in the front row. The camels were dressed to their long teeth in trappings shining with sequins, pearls, and gold embroidery, and blew bubbles through their fat pink lips. Their rear legs splayed, their stubby tails swinging, they seemed a peaceful lot until their keepers goaded them into halfhearted combat. Suddenly, one broke loose from its leading strings and chased me, the guide, and fifteen or twenty small boys from the field. Once, when I had longed for the Europe that Hemingway had known in the 1920s and whose footsteps B., like every junior-year-abroad student of the 1950s, had retraced, I thought that running the bulls at Pamplona would be *it*. I never had, and now I would never have to. Running a camel was terrifying, and, better yet, I didn't know anyone else who had done it.

We were terrified that night, too, in a hotel where we were the only guests. A man had knocked at the guide's door, saying he was the bellboy, and asked whether she had received her luggage. Since the hotel was empty, there was no possibility of confusion about the luggage, so she, unnerved, called the desk, only to get the same voice on the phone. This time, however, he said he was the night clerk.

We were two miles from town, the man was prowling about outside her room, and she, crying, wanted to sleep in mine. I pushed a big chair against the door, got out my Swiss Army knife, decided I could, if necessary, shinny down the balcony—we were on the second floor—and go for help.

For weeks, I, who had been a Cerberus to my children, had been responsible for no one but myself, for whom I was never brave (except at work) about mounting a defense. But now, with someone to protect, I was ready, even eager to test my guts. I sat up all night, my hands poised for violence, courageous because I was needed. Then morning came, and with it a covey of cleaning women, and we moved on.

There was more horror to come, in a toilet in the town of Mugla, from which we both emerged pale and gasping. It was on the second floor of a restaurant—a man was posted at the foot of the stairs to hand out paper napkins—and served both men and women, though not, I prefer to think, together. The toilet was a big room with a slanted floor that had been segmented into narrow alleys down which water flowed. One squatted at the head of an alley to evacuate, then watched while whatever emerged floated to the foot, where presumably it dropped into some kind of sewer. Several turds in the adjoining alleys had been becalmed along the way, however, and the smell and sight were well beyond what I recalled from Girl Scout latrines. "How are we to have tourism if nothing is done about the toilets?" the guide moaned once we were outside, dousing ourselves from the bottle of lavender water she kept in the glove compartment of her car. We laughed; then, friends who had been in peril of prowlers, runaway camels, and marooned turds, and today I cannot remember her name or her face.

SOMETIMES, HOWEVER, I must have traveled alone, though never without a driver. With him, most of the time, I sat in silence, because I cannot remember anyone being with me in a small hotel in Bodrum except the five shawled women I used to sit with every night in the tiny lobby. It had a coal stove, on which a pot of marmalade was forever simmering, and we crowded around it—me reading, they knitting and chatting. We could not speak, but we smiled at one another often, free to do so because we were all female. I would never have smiled at a strange man in Turkey, and any upward curve of a Turkish woman's lips was hidden outdoors by her yashmak. But in this tiny lobby, with its smell of coal and oranges, we shared a shelter that was less a matter of bricks and mortar or wood and nails than of mutual femininity. But no. Femininity is not the right word. Femaleness. We were creatures of our bodies in a way that men can never be, equally fearful of infertility, equally fearful of childbirth, equally fearful of the lump in the breast or the bloody flux. We knew one another without ever having to open our mouths.

I was also alone when I went to Priene, a Greek ruin not far from Ephesus, set on a plateau above the Menderes River. The climb to the ruin, along a steep path, was lung-cracking, but not as difficult as Freya Stark's route. In her time—I think it was the 1920s—there was no path to Priene, and one had to cross the Menderes and climb that side of the hill which faced it. Heavy rains had swelled the river, so she spent several days on the low-roofed second floor of a fisherman's cottage before she could cross, speaking to no one, eating whatever the fisherman's wife set before her. Purgatory and silence before Priene: I was envious.

It was very quiet on the plateau, and, but for the quick green of licorice plants, the only color—of the sky, the grasses, the ruins— was a pale cool gray. I hopped from toppled stone to toppled stone, watching for the snakes I had been told lived among them, and listening to the dull thunk of a sheep's bell in the distance. The stillness was crystalline, and I fantasized coming here again someday and sharing it with the balding man. So I picked up a small marble shard, assured myself that it was of no archaeological value whatever, and decided to bring it home to him. Now I should love to be able to run my fingers over that worn vestige of egg-and-dart molding, but at the time I could think only of how much more complete I would feel if I could once more give a present—apart from the necktie I chose every Christmas for my brother-in-law—to a man. For years I had pondered over what to give B. for his birthday and Christmas, Valentine's Day even, and his shirt size—16 1/2-34— was written on my heart. But divorce meant an end to Brooks Brothers, an end to secondhand bookstores for old Joseph Mitchells and Berton Rouechés, an end to leaning toward a salesman as I would toward a priest in a confessional and saying, "My husband wears pajamas, but I was thinking a nightshirt might be fun."

Ephesus was near Priene, acres of white marble splintered by the light and, unlike most archaeological digs, accessible to the amateur's eye. One could walk past the library, the temples, the priest's house, the sailor's brothel, the theater, with its two thousand-year-old seats, and actually *see* them. Paul, upon whom I was prone to pile half my problems with Catholicism and with sex, preached here; Saint John is buried here, under a sixth-century basilica; and not far away, it is claimed, is Mary.

Mary's house, or at least the foundations of somebody's first-century shelter, was a little Lourdes, full of discarded crutches and framed prayers of thanks. Desperate as always to sniff the odor of sanctity, I breathed deeply of the room, waiting—as I had ever since the days when I knelt in the attic in Bristol praying to my Aunt Margaret, who, since she had died at eleven, I believed must be a saint—to sense a presence. None came, any more than an answer came after I had scribbled a plea that my husband not go away and stuck the paper in Jerusalem's Wailing Wall. So once more I lost my faith in prayer at the same time as, remembering a phallus-shaped stone in Bodrum and a nearby tree from which fluttered rags symbolizing cries to Allah from barren women, I retained my belief in magic.

It was that faith in magic which had me photographing Mary's house with my Brownie Starmite and eventually giving the pictures to the deeply religious Polish woman who often babysat for the children. She was very old, and tears came easily to her, so she cried when I gave them to her. "You make me so happy," she said, her tongue thickened by her accent and her sobs. "Now I know I work in a good Catholic home."

I AM, AS I HAVE SAID, proud of my memory, which lays tenacious monkey fingers on much I would rather forget. Still, it has the occasional hole out of which I can pull nothing, not even the slightest wisp of a meeting or a journey. So all I know of Ankara is waiting, with a mustachioed Kurdish driver, outside an apartment house that looked like mud huts set upon mud huts. From it emerged my interpreter, a young man immaculately suited and tied and faintly ashamed of my having seen where he lived.

We drove east, toward the Valley of the Göreme, skirting a big salt lake to enter a landscape that was all beige and gray, occasionally spiked with black. A few more hours through naked, wrinkled hills, and we were in Nevşehir, a town of a desolation so complete, I was forever finding a reason to wander its scabbed streets. Dust flew up in our faces and hung in the air. The girls in the town brothel, the young man told me, made seventy cents a customer.

We were in Nevşehir because it had the only hotel near the valley that was open in winter, and we were the only guests, apart from some prospective guides who were there for training.

At sunset the air chilled, my radiator, a cheap English plug-in, didn't work, and the manager, realizing that I was freezing in my room and longing for the moment when I could sit in the dining room beside the flaming spits, set in the wall, for *doner kebab,* would invite me to his stuffy, overheated office for a drink. We had pistachios and a bottle of Johnny Walker and listened to Turkish 45s played on a small portable, and, although I couldn't speak to him, his wife, his three harum-scarum children, and the covey of guides, each of us falling over one another's feet, it didn't matter, because when you're eating and drinking and listening to music, talk becomes redundant. Later, after dinner, I would crawl into one of my room's twin beds, heap it with the blankets from the other, position the lamp with its forty-watt bulb on a pile of books, and open Edmund Wilson's *Classics and Commercials*. Outside, dogs racketed in the desert. Inside, my toes wriggled ever deeper into the blankets and I thought of how seldom I was lonely in the country. There was nothing here but me and the dogs and the dust, all of us the same thing.

My usual excuse for touring Nevşehir as to look at and maybe buy a couple of prayer rugs and some kilims, and here my interpreter, surely fifteen years my junior, took over and treated me like a toddler. While I sipped cup after cup of Turkish coffee, he haggled with the owner of whatever shop we were in until he got what he thought was a good price. Then he nodded, and off we would trot, my purchase rolled up and tied with twine. I liked the routine in a way, this giving myself over to a Big Daddy, but I was furious when he firmly forbade me to accept a dinner invitation for the two of us from the mayor of Nevşehir. I didn't have the right clothes (I had packed only corduroy pants and heavy sweaters); I would disgrace him. There was no way I could convince him that the mayor would forgive me my wardrobe, no way I could budge his stubborn Turkish stance. That evening, in an effort to make up for the toddler's disappointment, he took me to the weekly movie, where we sat on wooden benches and saw a double bill: a Turkish version of *The Wizard of Oz* and a costume drama, whose hero, he told me, was in jail more or less for life for possession of hashish. Every man, women, child, and infant in Nevşehir was at the movies that night, and when the voluptuous star of the costume drama, draped in roughly ten pounds of veiling, did a belly dance, the cheers were wild.

I liked him again then, liked him especially the next day, when we went through one of the underground cities, built perhaps by the Hittites, in a place called Kaymakli. Sometimes the ceilings were high enough for us to walk upright; more often we slid along on our bellies; in each instance our misery was mutual.

We emerged into a dusty, golden afternoon and the sight of a fat, bespectacled woman in a yashmak calling me to her house, the only one for miles and set in a sea of mud. Her name was Fatima; she had a son who was restringing a Moslem rosary and a husband kneeling on a prayer rug and facing Mecca. Neither acknowledged me while we sipped tea and talked in a language known only to women. True, we had no words but we had motherhood—she pointed to her son; I brought out a photograph of my daughters—and we had housekeeping. Her home had one room, whitewashed, carpeted with old pieces of linoleum, and lined with rug-covered banquettes, so there was little to tour but the walls. Pictures of Atatürk and Menderes, an executed premier, were pinned there, and postcards from tourists who, like me, had answered her wave. Somehow I made it clear that I had pictures on my wall, too, and together we mourned the difficulties of keeping a place clean and of raising children, and I don't know how we did this, but we did. Later, she pulled me outdoors, swathed me in a yashmak, pulled my arm around her shoulder, and the interpreter, who, bored by all this woman talk, had been waiting outside, photographed us with my Brownie Starmite. Because we were both veiled to our eyes, the only way one can tell which of us is the Turk and which is not is by my sweater. It came from the Aran Islands.

A few days later we drove to Konya, Turkey's holiest city, to the Mevlana Medresi, a museum and shrine to the thirteenth-century founder of the dervishes. Shoeless, I walked through kneeling, praying Moslems to see Mevlana's clothes and prayer rugs and Korans, the beard of the Prophet in an elaborate coffer, and Mevlana's tomb, hung with golden trappings. Then I, whose only God has been my father and, after his death, my husband, read what Mevlana said about being consumed with love for the God I could not find outside humanity. "I was raw," he wrote. "I am now cooked and burnt."

One of the small rugs I bought in Nevşehir disintegrated at the dry cleaners, and the other is stored in the basement. The kilims, I had made into pillows, and they are stored in a closet. A door knocker shaped like the hand of Fatima is stuck in the brick of my living room wall, and my blue worry beads disappeared a long time ago. So did a necklace with tiny blue stones and the presents I bought for the children. All but one. For Snow White I had bought a ring with the same tiny blue stones as were in my necklace, and it showed up not long ago, twisted now and tarnished. No matter how glorious one's children are in adulthood, it is painful to look at reminders of their childhood. The children who drank from those silver baby cups and carried those Flintstones lunchboxes will never again love as cleanly and as purely as they did then. Time will have darkened them.

"But what," you may ask, "happened to Snow White while you were in Turkey and she was at her father's country house?" I do not know. I suppose she went sledding and saw movies and, because she was getting interested in clothes, took to hanging around the area's quaint little shops. At night she probably popped popcorn and watched television, and, once put to bed, spent hours under the blankets reading by flashlight.

I do not know, however, what was going on in her head, or what it was that turned her into someone I had never before met. "Adolescents," a social worker told me once, "are walking time bombs."

I don't think I was. Neither was my sister. Or maybe we were and lacked only the fuse to set us off. But there were no fuses in a house in which two grandparents, two parents, and a maiden aunt built for us an armature that would last us all our lives. Perhaps those two weeks in the country marked the time that nature—can I call it nature?—stripped Snow White of those protections (I think of them as the immunities passed along in mother's milk) afforded by innocence. Oh, God, I am only speculating, fruitlessly as usual. Because if I, and all those parents who have seen their children turn into strangers overnight, knew the answers, we would no longer be asking ourselves—as we are always asking ourselves—"But what did I *do?*"

# *Five*

———◆———

$\mathscr{N}$UMBER 83 was beginning to fill up. The Turkish rugs spilled color onto the bare floors, and two brown velvet couches arrived in the living room. "But Daddy's just bought the same couches!" the children said when the furniture was delivered. Having formed our tastes together, B. and I, all unknowing, were constructing parallel universes. If they differed in any respect, it was probably in what we hung on our respective walls. During our marriage I had never entered an art gallery without him. Now I was hanging around Fifty-seventh Street, making choices that I knew would not have been his. Finally, I had broken with B.'s esthetic, and all it took was opening my mouth to say, "I'd like that collage, please," and a $25 deposit. The gallery owner would then root around in the coat closet for an old shopping bag, and off I would go to the bus, feeling like a Medici and clutching a purchase that, short of clothing, was the first in many years that was truly mine.

People started arriving, too. It was unnatural for someone who had once lugged copper pots and pans from Paris and cherished her few lessons with Julia Child's partners, Mmes. Bertholle and Beck, not to be feeding crowds, so I started inviting people for dinner and never gave a thought as to whether there was a man seated at the foot of the table, even though friends said an extra man made a useful bartender. I was proud of being able to handle anything short of a Manhattan—which nobody drank anyway, the only mixed drink I have ever known a New Yorker to like being a martini—and ran from ice cube tray to glass closet to the old wine carriers that held liquor bottles, feeling a power I had never known in marriage. Ceres I was, the great goddess, dispensing stuffed bass and a modest Sancerre as if I were reaping and sharing the fruits of the earth.

I was proud of everything I did on those evenings, rejecting the guests' offers to clear the table, bring out the dessert, make the coffee. Pride forbade my asking for help, pride and the fact, slowly dawning upon me, that I didn't need any. Perhaps I looked silly sometimes, hostessing, bartending, cooking, serving, and clearing simultaneously, but I never felt silly. Rather, I felt—as the guests murmured, "You did it again, Mary," and "Loved that chocolate mousse!"—the fabulous exhaustion of the long-distance runner. I had crossed the line. I had made it home.

I am a good cook and was turning into a pretty good talker, but I doubt that is why people came to the house. I think it was the house itself. Everyone wants to crawl into a cave once in a while, and although I have never had a place I thought big enough (wherever I have lived I have had the same dream, that of finding a previously unnoticed door and beyond it another room), I am a digger of caves. At night I would loose the living room curtains of their ties and pull them shut, turn on a few low lights and a little Lee Wylie, and then I, and everyone with me, was safe. Only in the rear, where there were no curtains at the big dining room window, did the house seem dangerous. If we were alone, the children and I ate our suppers as quickly as we could, fearful less of the intruder than of the impenetrable black out of which he might arrive.

Most of the neighbors had lived on the block for years. On summer nights they sat on their stoops, weaving tales out of the inconsequential, which are perhaps my favorite kind, because I can summon a profound interest in the possible reasons behind a favorite delivery boy's defection from one supermarket to another, or why the lights were on so late in So-and-So's apartment. It is the gift of growing up in a small town, I believe, this tendency to magnify the ordinary into the extraordinary. "Now tell me everything that happened," I still say to friends returned from holidays, "starting with when you got on the plane."

Once the weather became too cool for stoop-sitting, the neighbors disappeared indoors and issued last-minute invitations to come over for drinks. The women invariably wore long skirts, and one of the men invariably put on his sequin-striped party sweater, and all would greet one another with glad cries, even though they may have met at the supermarket a few hours earlier. I liked that; I like it when people put a sheen on their days. But I seldom sat on the stoops in summer, and I seldom went to the cocktail parties, because, a newcomer and diffident, I did not belong to the inner circle. "Mom," my younger daughter said sadly, as she watched people exchanging gossip from their respective front steps, "I don't think you're really a member of Jane Street society." She was right, but it didn't matter. What did matter was that on this odd, isolated block, I had an identity: the rather pretty woman at Number 83 who had two young daughters and a dog who was forever pulling frantically at his leash.

I also had an occupation distinct from my daily stint, one that imposed order on weekends which, *sans* church attendance, *sans* a husband carving the roast at Sunday dinner, *sans* afternoon treats with Daddy while Mommy takes her nap, might otherwise have been made up of listless perusals of section after section of the endless Sunday *Times*. A few years earlier the then managing editor of *Mademoiselle*, friend of the famous and giver of cocktail parties featuring skinny women and paunchy men who were always just back from or en route to Mount Desert or Hobe Sound, and who elbowed their way to the bartender with the ruthlessness of basketball players elbowing their way to the hoop, was looking for a food writer. When she listed the potential candidates, an editor whom I had fed often said, "I don't know why you're going outside for someone. You won't find anyone better than Mary."

For years I had wanted a chance to write something besides "a mere slip of a dress" or "damask carved like ivory," but I was too timid to ask, too much in awe of what I thought of as "real writers" and "real writing." Handed a modest food column, I was ecstatic, so much so that I never asked about money, which was just

as well, because the managing editor wasn't planning to pay me
any. So one Sunday every month, after having spent the previous
weekends getting recipes from friends or little-known French magazines and testing them on the children, I would sit at my desk
and lose myself in happy amateurism. The columns are, but for my
adolescent occasional effusions, the closest thing I have to a diary,
and among my favorite reading.

> *I do not like the view from my window today. It is a chilly*
> *Sunday and the air is gray, and for a week Con Ed has been*
> *tearing up the cobblestones so that the road in front of our*
> *house is one long trench railed with orange ropes. The few*
> *who walk by seem concussed, but no more so than our*
> *dog, Fred, who is asleep on the rug—flat on his back, paws*
> *dangling, and looking like a dead beetle. The three cats and*
> *my younger daughter are staring mournfully at this dismal*
> *landscape and I am staring mournfully at a picture of*
> *myself taken when I was six. I have changed for the*
> *worse . . .*

As I read that, the past sweeps over me, and my recall of the
pain that twisted my ribs whenever I thought of B. dissolves into
images of the cats capering on my bed, of Rose Red, wearing what
she called her pancake hat, making Sunday breakfast, of Snow
White, in love with Elizabeth I, confiding stories of the Tudor court
as if only she were privy to them. If it weren't for those columns,
pasted in a school-child's three-subject notebook, I would have forgotten—so powerful, maybe even preferable, is the memory of misery—that there were many days at Number 83 when I was joyous.
When the balding man called to say he was coming to town, I was
excited, because now I was going to have the kind of evening that
society, by which I mean friends, psychiatrists, and assorted magazines, said a woman of my age and hormonal perfection should be
having. Still, my feet dragged when, babysitter installed, I left that
paradise of children, pets, and dinner on the stove to go uptown
and pray that the other people on the hotel elevator hadn't guessed
that the woman accompanying the man to his room on the twelfth
floor was not his wife.

AGE—HE WAS ABOUT ten years older than I—and alcohol had taken its toll of the balding man, and although he was never impotent, he was demanding. Neither the athlete his publicity claimed nor the sexual Goliath his reputation promised, he was more myth than male. That may not have been true when he was young. "The first time I ever had a girl, mah Mary, I couldn't wait and neither could she. So I took her on the kitchen table, only a room away from where her parents were sitting. Oh, mah Mary, I wish you'd known me then." But by the time we met he needed fantasy. I was Scheherazade.

Unless having read *The Story of O* counts, I had only a nodding acquaintance with pornography. Once, a friend who was an incurable scavenger had picked up a pile of paperbacks from the floor of the office elevator ("The guys in the mailroom," she said darkly) and carted them to her apartment on a night we were dining together. While she was in the kitchen, cooking, I was in the living room, reading about a woman who preferred stallions, so hypnotized that I forgot my cigarette and it burned a small hole in her couch.

For the balding man, though, I became a teller of tales of Great Danes and girls' reform schools and female warders and whippings and frightened virgins on all fours, urged onward by his murmured, "That's good, mah Mary, that's real good." Once I would have felt myself degraded by my nasty, nimble tongue, but not now. Telling stories to him so that he could make love didn't seem all that different from telling stories to my children so that they could sleep. "You don't need fantasy, do you?" he asked. "No," I said, "you're the fantasy," and snuggled along his magic back and slept.

Years later, marooned in someone's summer house, I picked up a copy of *The Pearl* and laughed to see that I had the mind, and the limitations, of a Victorian pornographer.

MARRIED, DISHONEST, drunk as often as he was sober, the balding man nonetheless added cubits to my stature when he came to the office. A certain contrived madness ran through its corridors;

we hugged our craziness—"Women! We *are* a silly race," the editor-in-chief was fond of saying—to our Rudi Gernreiched bosoms. That I had to send my secretary out for a bottle of bourbon when he came in for a photo session, and that he once wrestled with a sturdy, knee-socked woman in the personnel department when she asked for identification from this unexpected caller, only added to my glory. True, I had not lost an entire skiffload of clothes while photographing on the Charles River, as had a fashion editor, nor did I keep a quart of Scotch in my bottom drawer, as was the custom with production editors. But I had a famous admirer, and so what if he sometimes seemed a sot? Wasn't that the price of genius? Wasn't I lucky to be partaking of it? My compliance—collusion, really—was predictable. I was, after all, the daughter of a man who believed that to be involved with books was to live at the heart of light, and the former wife of a man who shared his faith. Papa, however, had never met an honest-to-God writer, and B., who knew acres of them, was shrewd enough to separate the dancer from the dance. I was not.

WHEN I SEMI-CHAPERONED *Mademoiselle*'s guest editors on their trips abroad, it was usually because they were going to a country the editor-in-chief didn't want to see. Who could blame her? Sad, raggedy Ireland suited me right down to the ground, but en route to Israel I nearly wept when we flew over the presumed glories that were Greece. I balked at Russia, too, despite knowing that I would never have such a chance again. But reluctant as I was to leave for Moscow, I was more reluctant to leave a house that was acting on me as an oyster does on grit. I knew what would happen, though, because it had happened before. I would be miserable for the first few days and ask myself, "Why did I do this?" Then, because travel was the only true cure I had for loneliness, I would sever all connections with my world and rock myself into the swing of a new one. I seldom sent postcards, and in Russia I didn't have the choice.

I remember little of Moscow, because I saw little of Moscow. Instead, I stood for hours at the Intourist desk in the hotel lobby watching while women thumbed through ledgers reminiscent of

Bob Cratchit's, trying to confirm my travel plans. When I did go out, I was forever on the edge of the law, sitting down where I wasn't supposed to, suffering the warning whistles of policemen whose eyes were as opaque as pennies. The evening I finally left the city, I saw a box of matches on the airport floor, bent to pick it up (I was running out), then stiffened quickly, afraid of yet another shrill *nyet!* No matter. The g.e.'s were well behind me, on their way back to New York, and I, armed only with a little Russian-English dictionary, was going to Uzbekistan and Siberia alone.

If you travel great distances in Russia, you are always flying at night and sliding in and out of time zones. All airport and official clocks were on Moscow time, maybe still are, so neither my watch, which I was doing my damnedest to set correctly, nor my body was ever in sync with the official hour. It would be an exaggeration to say that I hallucinated, but after a while time and space started shifting. I was there but I was not there. The sun was at this point but it was not. Conversations were sudden and absurd. Flying to Tashkent, I was so swathed in heat, I took off all the clothes possible as well as my shoes, and was sitting directly opposite an elderly, well-dressed American and his wife, both of whom were also barefoot. They were courteous people, and we exchanged a few courteous words about the godawfulness of Russian food before they fell asleep. A few hours later the man woke, smiled, looked down at my feet, which were planted a modest inch or two from his, and said, "I've always thought I could win any beautiful feet contest I entered, but I think you'd beat me." He dozed, and neither of us ever spoke to each other again.

Tashkent was where I shook to another whistle, because, exhausted from waiting eight hours in a torrid airport, I put my rope-soled espadrilles on a battered old coffee table, thus scarifying Soviet property. But it was also the place where, sick of the seedy lunchroom to which all foreigners were herded, I stubbornly stood in line at a rooftop Uzbek restaurant until a worn-down waitress finally sat me at a table full of Russian soldiers.

They gave me vodka, I gave them my American cigarettes, and together we talked and laughed about what, I cannot imagine, because we were communicating by semaphore and my little dictionary. But what a good time we had, and how well-companioned I was. My shishkebab was skewered horsemeat, and the champagne that came later, along with indecipherable toasts, was sickly sweet, but no matter. I was in the group, part of the party, not one of whose boisterous participants would have dreamed of daring me to down a glass of Scotch.

I hadn't danced for a long time, but now I was queen of the hotel's dollar bar, where I usually went after dinner for a coffee. Young Russians hung around there, in lieu of anywhere else to go, and all asked me to dance, thinking that I, an American, would know the new steps. I didn't, so I made them up, my shimmies and wiggles and windmill arms followed silently and intently by boys half my age. Then I would go up to my bed and pray for deliverance from a city where the temperature never dropped to bearable and the only cultural institution was a museum filled with photostats and replicas of Lenin's boyhood furniture. "Oh, God," I whimpered, "once I am out of here I promise I will never leave my children again."

Samarkand was different. It was just as hot, but here I could drag my mattress to the tiny balcony outside my room and listen all night to drums and clapping and the whine of Uzbek music. In the morning I rode the trolley out to the market, where all the fish were interred in one big block of dirty ice, climbed the hill on which the sextant of Ulugh Beg, a fifteen-century astronomer, had been excavated, and wandered through a park that was full of—is this possible? Is my memory accurate?—Ping-Pong tables. In the afternoon I invariably visited the Shakh-y-Zinda, a complex of mosques, and the tomb of Tamerlane because they were close to the cherry-juice dispenser and the ice cream stand.

I never spoke unless it was to name my destination, except in the evening, when I shared my dinner table with a Canadian woman, a big-boned blonde with a raucous laugh, and an old Anglican minister from Bristol, England. When I told him I had grown up in Bristol, Rhode Island, he exclaimed, "Did you know Canon Parshley? Saint Michael's Church was so good to us during the war."

"He was one of my father's closest friends," I said excitedly, suddenly out of Samarkand, out of New York, too, and returned to what I persisted in calling "home." "My sister was a bridesmaid at his daughter Marjorie's wedding and . . ." There was no stopping my speech, not simply because once again I could use English, but because I could talk about a time before B., before children, before loss.

I had assumed the Canadian woman was much younger than I, since she giggled a lot about Russian officers met in the parks, and had glorious hangovers. Something of a snob, I had her figured for a secretary out on what my parents would have called "a toot," until the afternoon we were strolling along a street of mud houses and she started talking about herself.

She had never worked, never had to, only taken a course in flower-arranging at a famous London florist's. Like me, she had been married and divorced, but had given custody of her children, who were the same age as mine, to her husband. How could she be smiling and laughing and having such a good time when the end of her trip meant an empty house? I couldn't imagine living without my children, and panicked every time I thought they might be taken away. That fear was why I was so secretive about the balding man; why I lived a life so steeled with propriety.

After the Canadian woman left, the hotel dining room seemed very quiet, and the minister and I spoke often of her gaiety. "But I don't see," I said, "how she could have given up her children."

"I admire her courage," he said. "She believed her husband could give them a better home."

Disapproval had edged my voice when I spoke of the woman, and his charity shamed me. I had never thought about whether B. or I could have given Snow White and Rose Red a better home. I thought only that I would die without them. Friends said I gave too much of my life to my daughters. The truth is that I would have had no life to give anyone were it not for them. What courage I had was for their sake: I had turned into a tiger the day Snow White was born. But without her and her sister to give me a reason for being, I might have been as flaccid, and as shapeless, as a jellyfish.

The minister's name is gone from my mind and he is probably gone from this earth, but I can still hear him telling me about his church's jumble sales and about the years he had saved money for this journey, so wild was he about Islamic architecture, and how sad he was that he couldn't have saved enough for his wife to see it as well. I remember the nights he didn't come to the table, because, low on funds, he was eating alone in his room out of cans he'd brought from home. And I remember the morning when, soggy with tiredness, I met him at breakfast and he told me a ghost story.

"One night," he said, "I was home alone—my wife was visiting our daughter—and had gone to bed when I heard a knock at the kitchen door. I went downstairs, and there was a friend I hadn't seen in years.

"I let him in and led him to the kitchen. He was very hungry, so I fixed him a bowl of cereal and a cup of tea. He was also very tired—he said he'd had a long trip—so I showed him his room and went back to bed. The next morning he was gone, and I would have thought it a dream except that the cereal bowl and cup and saucer were still on the kitchen table. That night my wife called and said she'd heard he'd died two days earlier. Now Mary—may I call you Mary?—Mary, that is really true."

We were silent, I wondering if it had indeed been a dream, and hoping, because I longed for belief, that it had not been.

ON THE FLIGHT to Eastern Siberia the big string bag an old man had labored to bring on board the plane burst and sent dozens of oranges rolling down the aisles. The stewardesses had no interest in whether or not seatbelts were fastened at takeoff and landing, and passenger luggage was stowed in what seemed like hammocks over our heads. But by now I was used to Aeroflot; I was used to Russia; I was used to talking to myself. In Irkutsk, however, an Intourist guide (I had had none in Samarkand) suddenly appeared and took me to the churchyard where the Decembrists were buried ("This is a working church," I was assured) and on a hydrofoil across Lake Baikal and through street after street of elaborate wooden houses. "Why do you wish to photograph these?" she chided me. "They are old, no good."

She took me to a daycare center where all the children used their potties at the same time, and a woman gave me dolls for my own children. One evening I shared a restaurant table with a German engineer who, having asked me to write in my magazine about how much his countrymen wanted peace, made me feel like a Messenger to the World. Another day I was taken to tea with some middle-aged women who, laughing and excited, fussed with their hair and tugged at their girdles when I asked to take their picture. They gave me the best tea—oranges and sweet preserves to be eaten with little spoons—that Irkutsk could provide, and the hostess said, "I can hardly wait to tell my husband I had an American in my apartment." Suddenly I envied her the tiny bedroom with its brass bed, the tiny living room on whose couch her son slept, the tiny balcony on which she had placed pots of gloxinia. A husband came home at night and kept her warm, whereas I, resident of the land of the free and the home of the brave, and looking, though I was not, a generation younger than she and her friends, could not come in from the cold.

At night I lay in bed muttering my usual prayer—"Get me out of here and I will never leave my children again"—but when the time came, I was reluctant to leave Irkutsk. I had fallen in love with the old churchyard and the old Cossack houses and the little dachas out at Lake Baikal, and thought how fine it would be to stay here and write the town's history. A year or two ago I wanted the peace of the grave, and now I wanted the peace of the carrel and a burial in books. But I was kidding myself, I knew, not only because I had no Russian and had lost the habit of scholarship but because I had too little of what an Austrian friend called *sitzfleisch*, "sitting flesh." "You have no serenity," B. had said more than once, and I didn't, not even when I slept. Out of waking life I would enter dreaming life, and emerge exhausted.

So I left on schedule, depending on my usual trick—following the people whose boarding cards were the same color as mine—to get me on the right plane. This time, though, there were no colors and I had to ask the members of an American tour group, pair after pair of Darby and Joans, if I was at the right gate. Without exception they drew back, averted their eyes, answered with nods, fearful of getting stuck with a woman traveling alone.

A FEW WEEKS BEFORE, on my first morning in Moscow, the three Russian men with whom I shared a breakast table offered me a drink from their carafe. I assumed it was mineral water, Instead, it was vodka, and they laughed, but not unkindly, at the look on my face when I took my first sip. Hearing I was from New York—they too had Russian-English dictionaries—they were dumbstruck. Had I seen the Empire State Building? Had I ever been to Radio City Music Hall?

The morning after my flight from Irkutsk I shared a breakfast table again, this time with an American salesman. "Why don't you stay for another day?" he suggested. "We could have some fun." Then he winked. So, in the morning sun, did his wedding ring.

To the Russians, male and female both, I had been a visitor from an almost unimaginable outside, treated with the kind of innocent curiosity that reminded me of the questions—"Perhaps you have met my niece who is a waitress in a restaurant called Schrafft's in New York?"—that country people had asked me on my first trip to Ireland a long time ago. But to the Americans in the tour group, I was that dangerous thing, a woman nearing middle age and on the loose. To the American salesman, I was that easy thing, a woman nearing middle age and on the loose.

A few hours later, taking a last walk through this city I had never really seen, I strolled down a street lined with linden trees just like those which had lined the sidewalk in front of my high school. Their scent was, as always, heartbreaking, and, just as the minister's mention of Canon Parshley had, brought me back "home." Then I realized at last that all journeys—the final one, too, for all we know—are circular.

# Six

*I*T WAS A WARM AUTUMN NIGHT in New York, a few months after Moscow, too warm to sit in the hotel lobby waiting for the balding man. So I crossed the street and sat in Central Park, breathing in the green from the trees that were still hanging on to their leaves and the blue from gasoline fumes, glorying in being dressed up and about to meet a man who, however ineligible, was someone I could boast of knowing. I never did boast of knowing him, though. I was afraid of B.'s hiring a private eye to find me an unfit mother. "You ever see any guys in felt fedoras hanging around?" my sister asked before my divorce. She, who had liked him, and I, who had loved him, knew how I enraged B. simply by being myself. But, then, isn't that always the case with husbands and wives, even when their marriages endure?

I looked east and there he was, my secret suitor, my secret Santa maybe, coming up the street, carrying two big Doubleday shopping bags. Wearing a leather jacket, his face shadowed by a broad-brimmed hat, his shoulders bent forward by the weight of the bags, he looked like an aging cowboy. Had he seen me first, he'd have raised his head and started to strut, trying to belie the years that were written on his face and in the way his stomach had started to slide over his belt. But he didn't, so for once I saw him before he had a chance to put on his armor: slowed down by bags that had a weight he wouldn't have felt twenty years ago, and walking with an old man's flat-footed caution.

Usually we ate in his hotel dining room, but this night we went to a nearby restaurant. It was crowded, so we had to wait at the bar, and although people made room for us, no one looked at him.

"It's hard bein' a middle-aged man, mah Mary. If I sat on one side of a good-lookin' girl and some young truck-driver sat on the other, it wouldn't be me she'd turn to and smile at."

"Would that matter a lot?"

"Oh, yeah, it'd matter."

"You mean you want the applause of strangers?"

"Thass right." He laughed. "I like the way you put that. I want the applause of strangers. They're not out to get me, like my enemies are. But now Lowell is in the madhouse, and I am King of the Cats!"

"MAH MARY," he said later as he put down the telephone on which he had been talking to his wife, lying about his day and the way he was spending the evening, "I want you to understand exactly *who you are*. You are the other woman."

Bull, I am one of many other women and I know it. I say nothing, and he continues the performance.

"Now mah wife's a good woman, a good country gal, but . . ." I turn and look out the window, not because what he is saying hurts, but because he is pouring another bourbon, and the liquor, as they say, will start talking.

"Fat! She's got the sex appeal of a walrus. And squeamish! So *nice* with that douche bag. She's always got a hose hangin' out of her."

I feel sick. I cannot bear the way he talks about his wife, but I sit silent because I am taking my punishment.

He is raging now and I am about to pick up my shoulder bag and leave, because God is telling me that my listening constitutes participation, that I am sinning again, when he shifts—he is always shifting—and says, "You want to hear a little guitar, mah Mary?"

He showed me her picture one day: she is dark and pretty with a nice straight nose. I think he loved her once, but even more incapable of surviving deep feeling than I, he had severed the nerve so that love was like a dead tooth in his head.

She telephoned me one New Year's Eve, his wife, when I was at a next-door neighbor's drinking eggnog. When I came home, Snow White, suspicion written all over her face, told me that while I was out a Mrs.—— had called. Surprised that his wife even knew of my existence, I waited all night for her to call again, fearing she would, fearing she would not. Because if she had asked me not to see her husband again, I would have said yes and meant it. I could not stop myself from seeing him. I wanted her to stop me.

Still, he sustained me for several years. I used to say good night to him, to the air, when I went to sleep, and I would always note the temperature in the city in which he lived when they gave it on the *Today* show. I laughed through all our phone calls, while he played a harmonica and told shaggy-dog stories or we got excited about a book we were both reading. When he was in New York I sang to his guitar and capped his limericks, and we told each other stories about ourselves and our childhoods.

He was like an old shoe I couldn't slip off, and I was . . . I don't know. One day he said, "Mah Mary, I think we're kinder to each other than either of us has ever been to anyone else."

He was lying supine and I was on top of him, as comfortable as if floating on a raft. My arms were folded across my chest and over his and I kept nuzzling his lips open with my mouth and kissing his tall, narrow teeth.

We always lay like that early in the morning, following a familiar litany.

"You've got long teeth."

"My brother always said I should have got a dollar from the tooth fairy when I lost one."

"You've got small ears. My grandmother says small ears indicate stinginess or madness."

"Madness, mah Mary."

"Now that I see them in this light, I think your eyes are more gray than blue."

"I always thought they were green."

"Never! Do you suppose you're a genius?"

"I suppose I am."

"But can I call you by your first name?"

"Sure."

"What'd you say your first name *was*, honey?"

He'd whoop and roll me off his chest, sit up, catch me across his lap, and pretend to spank me. I'd wriggle, never quite sure he wouldn't, and once, when I was twisting around, I saw his face. It was puzzled. I think he was in love.

Who knows? Certainly not he. Was I in love? I've never figured it out. All I am sure about is that I was grateful to him for liking me. My husband did not. "I don't think he could stand my silences" was the only answer I had when he asked why B. had left.

"Mah Mary!" he crowed. "Ah *love* your silences."

Oh, I was grateful, all right, maybe even more grateful for the haven that was the hotel room. Because once I left it, I had to go home, and I couldn't bear what was going on at Number 83.

LILLIAN WAS DEAD. Early one morning I was sitting in my office, drinking coffee and reading the paper, when the phone rang. It was a friend. "Lillian died yesterday during an asthma attack, and someone found her late last night."

She had been alone, in her crazy-closet of an apartment, probably dressed in one of her trailing garments, the kind with the Mickey Mouse transfers, and maybe—I am imagining this part—grabbing desperately for her inhaler when she dropped. Snow White mustn't hear this, I thought, except from me, so I ran from the office and out into the street for a cab. When I am faced with death, my self-control deserts me, and Snow White, seeing my red eyes when I got home, knew something terrible had happened. I had no words but the simplest—"Lillian died yesterday"—and, looking hunted, Snow White turned and started to run up the stairs to her room.

I tried to hold her, but touch couldn't bring her back from the place where she was going. I begged her to come to church with me, but church meant little to her or her sister. I had been sloppy about Sunday school and religious instructions and lazy about Mass and resentful of every priest who had ever told me what to do even while I was silently begging to be told what to do. That Snow

White couldn't have the consolation even of lighting a candle and saying a prayer for Lillian's soul—"Free her from purgatory," she could have said, "and bring her into heaven"—was my fault.

But I had that consolation. Nearby, on Fourteenth Street, was a church built to hold a thousand or more parishioners and, now that the old Eighth Ward's old Irish had died out, empty most of the time. Tall and drafty and silent, smelling of floor wax and last Sunday's incense, it was just like the church I had known in childhood. I was that child again, shoving a dime in the slot, reaching for a spill, dipping it into a votive cup, and hoping against hope that my prayers were not just words lost in space. Then I came home, poured myself a stiff vodka, and sat crying in a corner of the living room.

The telephone kept ringing, friends of Lillian whom I had never met, and I spoke over and over again of getting her out of the morgue so that she could be buried from my house. The kind of funeral I was familiar with was preceded by a wake, and that was what I wanted for Lillian. I think she would have wanted it, too. But nothing could be done, so I cried some more and drank some more until Rose Red came home from school, determined as always to have a family like the one in *Little Women*, and frightened by my grief.

Still, there had been comfort in the lighting of the candle and the prayers, the merciful vodka and the tears I shared with those gulping strangers on the phone. Snow White, however, stayed in her room alone, without solace, and a long time later I found written on her wall, in green ink, "Lillian, why did you leave me?"

I took her to Dr. Franklin, and when I mentioned Lillian, I cried again. But Snow White was stony-faced and wouldn't talk about her. There was a second doctor to whom she went alone, but I heard from her father, whose suggestion he had been, that she wouldn't talk to him either. I think, though, that he was the doctor who suggested an institute that specialized in family therapy. When I told the man who was its head that the institute-supervised family weekend he recommended was a bad idea, he said, coldly, "Don't you want to help your child?"

Shamed into an alternative, I assembled, in the institute's formal living room, Snow White, her father and stepmother, Rose

Red, who wept bitterly at her cruel distance from the life lived by Marmee, Meg, Jo, Beth, and Amy, and myself. This time I was the one who wouldn't talk. Instead, I reverted to the fearful child I had so often been with B. and shrank in my chair. By now our marriage was something dimly remembered, or misremembered, but B. had remained the only adult in the world whose approval I wanted.

Because the psychiatrist who presided over this torturous hour realized that family therapy was out of the question, she decided to see Snow White alone. During their hours together she fed her tea and cookies, and as long as Snow White was with her I could breathe again. But when, having made an appointment for myself, I asked what I could do, praying for guidelines and lists and modes of behavior, anything that would help me help my Snow White, the doctor said, "Just try being her mother."

As if I weren't trying! Snow White was living in a place I could not enter, no matter what my efforts, and I doubt that the doctor, smugly encased in credentials and self-confidence as she was, ever entered it either. But Lillian could. Somehow she could walk into Snow White's world and in it find ways to keep her moored to the middle class and its mores. Without Lillian and the giggles and jokes and whispers they shared, my daughter was beyond my reach or anyone else's.

One night, very late, when I was dozing I heard a knock at the door downstairs. The landlord had found one of the cats meowing in the front hall. I took the cat, went back to bed, and was slipping into sleep again when I remembered, with the kind of terror that keeps one mute in nightmares, that, hours earlier, when I had put the night lock on the front door, all the cats were inside. There was no way for one of them to have got out unless someone else had gone out.

I ran to Snow White's room. It was empty. Her bag was on the library table. She never went anywhere without her bag and its jumble of letters, diaries, and an address book of names only she would recognize, although many of their owners might not recognize her. They were people met in passing and perhaps never seen again. That she knew their names, however, made them, if only in her imagination, her friends.

I dialed B., so frightened that I could hardly talk. "You'd better search the cellar," he said.

Fred, the semi-Schnauzer, trailed me to the basement, and we searched together, the flashlight poking around the worn wing chair and tattered posters, and into the dark and dusty side rooms with their cargoes of paperbacks and 45s. But it was not them I was seeing. Instead, I saw all of Snow White's life, from the time she was a baby so beautiful I was afraid to hold and crush her, to the slouching mutiny she was now, eyes sliding, always sliding, walking with her pelvis thrust forward, more in threat than in invitation. I also saw all the times in between. Snow White slipping into sleep after the nightly reading of *Eloise*. The day when, her finger broken, she asked my permission before yelling "Shit!" as the doctor set it. The afternoon in Bristol when we sat on the rocks under the Mount Hope Bridge, trying to catch crabs with mussels tied on a string.

With the flashlight darting over the basement walls, I saw a hanging figure, sneakered feet projecting from a corner, a flaccid hand crowded with the silver rings she'd learned to make in a course at the YMCA. She and her father had the same small, short-fingered hands, hands that made me tender because my own are so long and fierce. I saw the figure clearly, and then not at all. Fear had distorted my eyesight, made me see what wasn't there.

I came upstairs—it was two or three o'clock by now—and was dialing B. again when I heard a key turn in the lock. I rebuked her; I told her she had frightened me, I told her it was dangerous out there. But mine was the impotent squawk of one who can no longer find words or voice or even passion. There was no way any longer to keep her off the dark streets and in the light of the house, so in the fall she went away to a boarding school in the Berkshires that B. had heard of, for decades a kind of therapeutic *salon des refusés* for the children of the literati, and now also a place to which the state of Massachusetts sent the occasional delinquent in lieu of juvenile hall. She kissed Fred and her sister goodbye, nodded to me, and left.

On Saturday nights when I walked up a nearby street toward the newsstand and the Sunday *Times*, past a wire-fenced cement playground and its complement of teenagers giggling and groping in the dark, and, once, past a man in the doorway of a warehouse who, on seeing me, exposed himself, I would think of my elder daughter. She was safe now, in the country, and somebody else's responsibility. She was not out wandering through the city, in and out of a life about which I knew nothing, and I was not sitting up in bed waiting for the click of the lock downstairs, unable to look at her when she came in.

People say, "No matter what your pain, remember the child's pain is worse." I'm not sure. One is willing to die for one's child, and the hardest trial is that one is not allowed to do so. Dying is often easier than worrying, especially when the greatest worry is that one will stop worrying. Then one will die anyway, but of guilt, which murders slowly.

Parenthood, I realized, was a life sentence. My children could run away from home. I could not. My children were free to hate me. I was condemned to love them. When I was in the balding man's room, I was out on parole. With him, I was what I had been before I became barnacled with a husband, house, and children: a student, bookish, with a terrible crush on her teacher. I don't know what, during those dark strolls to the newsstand, I missed the most: the student, her teacher, or the room. No. I am lying to myself. I missed the man.

THE WINTER SNOW WHITE was away, Rose Red's godmother died. We had met as college freshmen and as adults lived on adjoining streets. For many years we baked our Christmas fruitcakes together, she, a better baker than I, working the dough with her strong freckled hands while I greased the pans. The week before she died we were planning to have tea, but chemotherapy had tired her, and she forgot. A few days before Christmas, her house cleaned, her baking done, the presents wrapped, and the tree trimmed, she got into bed and went to sleep.

At her memorial service I sat far to the rear of the church, because I knew myself and my tears. I had tried hard to emulate my family's granitic stoicism, the calm and graceful faces they turned to the world when they were sick with sorrow, but the attempts were useless. When I got home the phone was ringing. It was the balding man, and he had no patience with my nose-blowing and my stuttering monologue. "What must be, must be," he kept saying. "You cannot fall apart like that."

But I can. When friends or family die, I leave a space for them, and not until that space closes of itself can I move on. If I try to rush the process with crowds and busyness, I am laying a thin sidewalk over a crevasse, and someday I will tumble in again.

A few days after the service I dreamed Rose Red's godmother came to the house, and together we went for a walk around the Village. As we walked she grew frailer and frailer and leaned into me so that I was half-supporting her, but we kept moving until two men arrived and picked her up, the size of a small child now, and carried her away on a silver tray. "It is funny," I wrote in a letter to Snow White, "but sometimes we say goodbye to people more finally in dreams than ever in real life."

"That dream you had," she said the next time I saw her, "that's the way I felt about Lillian."


"I WISH YOU COULD SEE BRISTOL," I say to the balding man, who is sitting on the red couch at Number 83. It is the only time he has been here since the night we first slept together, four years earlier. Snow White is home from school for the weekend and is wary of him. But Rose Red, who would rather love than not, ran into his arms when he held them out to her.

Like a little girl who's brought home a new playmate, I am showing him all my treasures. We have been to my favorite Italian restaurant and he has liked his lunch, and since he is not an eater I am as pleased as a mother whose finicky baby has just finished every scrap. We have one of our favorite books, *The Journal of a Disappointed Man*, with us and I read aloud to him while we eat. The rest of the restaurant's customers are staring at us, but I am so used to his flamboyance and to concentrating on him, never mind what people think, that I have at last lost the self-consciousness that made me miserable in public places.

We have reached the stage where, because we have been together so seldom over the years, we keep bringing out and brushing up the times we have been so that we can say, "Remember when we were at the movies and you . . ." and "Remember the night it rained and we were going . . ." thus creating the illusion of a shared past. He has met the neighbors, about whom I had written him so much, and now we are listening to "Dill Pickle Rag" on the stereo. We had been in the garden, he picking burrs out of Fred's surprised eyebrows, I watching and wishing it would last forever: the man and woman in the garden, the man playing with the woman's dog, and a spring night coming down. He felt chilly, however—he felt the cold more than I did—and we had moved indoors.

We have been together for the last three days. As usual, he has wanted me to believe that he is having nightmares about World War II, and as usual I have put my arms around him and said, "No, no, you're here with me now. Go to sleep." It is a little game he plays, but he doesn't know I play it, too.

As usual, we have had breakfast at the delicatessen near his hotel, and as usual the owner, the man with the concentration camp number tattooed on his arm, has said, "Still taking care of your girl, I see, Mr.——." And he has said, "Still takin' care."

We have sat at opposite ends of the big hotel bathtub, unconscious of our nakedness, reading. First, though, I have run the tub for him and shampooed his hair with a bar of Ivory soap. He won't rinse the soap out—he says it makes his hair look thicker—and later, immaculate, hair battened with Ivory, he has gone to sit on a platform with a lot of distinguished people while I sit in the front row wondering if, at the end of the speeches, I can leave by the family exit, the designated exit for the first three rows, since I am not family.

Behind me are assorted literati, all of them talking about grants and fellowships and applications to artists' colonies like Yaddo and MacDowell. Listening hard, I decide there is no angle they don't know how to work. Finally, as the ceremonial begins, they hush—all but the wife of a very famous writer, who is talking loudly to herself. Up on the stage Agnes Neel, who has just received a medal, is gesturing to the audience to applaud more! more! more! We laugh. An elderly critic, whose name is now more often in textbooks than in the newspapers, makes a speech about the Fugitive poets and sets everyone to yawning. A few more people get medals, and at last it is over. Daring the family exit, I walk outdoors and into a garden party, where the distinguished guests are attempting to mingle, although mingling does not appear to be among their talents. I think I am on Parnassus, and they know they are.

The balding man introduces me to a lot of people, and I am proud that I can introduce him to a lot of people. On the long cab ride back to his hotel, however, it happens, what I have seen happen so many times before. He is running down and, cold sober but exhausted, has put his head in my lap. I stroke the high, rounded forehead and the soap-stiffened hair and think to myself that if I die on the spot I'll be going out happy.

Tonight we are going to a dinner party, and I, tired of pretending to the children to be staying with a friend, have told them that I will not be home because I will be with him. Snow White is not surprised; she guessed long ago. At thirteen, however, Rose Red cannot bear to think of her mother being with a man. But I have told her that he makes me very happy and that I hope she can be happy for me. Too, Lucille, the babysitter who has kept us bemused for many years (once, when my daughters were ten and eight, she took them to a speech at City Hall, heckled the speaker, and landed the three of them at a police station), has told her, "Your mother is not an ordinary woman and you can't expect her to lead an ordinary life." I know I am a very ordinary woman, but Rose Red likes definitions and sliding things into their proper slots. Lucille has provided her with one for me. Also, she is an old-fashioned child, and, quite simply, she likes having a man around the house, if only for a short time. It makes her house more like other people's houses.

We go to the dinner party and in walks a woman with whom the balding man had had an affair. I think she is nice, and since the East Coast, not to mention the West Coast, is littered with his one-night stands, and I don't know much about his activities in the Midwest but assume he has maintained the same high standards, I am friendly and we chat. Later, though, she giggles and slides her eyes at him when we hear on the radio a song he always sings to me during my morning tub, one I thought was ours alone. Suddenly I am sixteen again, and my boyfriend has just stuck a knife in my ribs.

The balding man has started the evening booming and boisterous, but again he is running down. He is tired, too tired to eat, and if I don't leave with him right now, he hisses, embarrassing two guests who can hear him and not caring because he has a child's disregard of his tantrums, he is leaving with her, because "she always delivers." We leave.

He is quiet and I am angry, knowing that he is both a four-year-old who has had too much cake, ice cream, and excitement at the party and a grown man who has spoiled my golden day. I don't know which to speak to, so after he has crawled into bed I sit on the floor, leaning against the footboard, smoking and talking aloud to myself. "I don't know why you had to do that. I did nothing to provoke that attack. It was cruel. But what's worse is that I don't know why I left with you, why I'm here now."

He is quiet throughout the monologue, the cigarette, my later, stubborn silence. I move to the window embrasure and sit there, watching the headlights of cars driving through and past Central Park, turning to look around the room, at my clothes piled on the slipper chair, and the long mound on the bed. There is no air in this room—the windows cannot be opened—and I want very much to be out of it, out on the street, smelling the late spring that is wafting over the wall from Central Park and mixing with the curious meld of gasoline fumes and low-tide decay that is peculiarly Manhattan's. I love that scent because it is my city's scent, just as I love my city's rump-sprung taxis and the familiar bounce when they hit a pothole.

Oh, God, how much I want to be back in my clothes and out of this room and hailing a cab to take me home. I want to feel complete unto myself again. But I am not complete unto myself anymore. Something like an umbilical cord is connecting me to a man whose favorite jest is, "Well, I'll be a nigger aviator," and who, after once praising B., had said, "But I don't see how you could have done it."

"Done what?"

"Marry a *Jew*."

I am ashamed not of his speech—it is, after all, his sin—but of my silence. That, my moral cowardice, is the greatest sin. "Through my fault, through my fault," I am saying silently to myself, "through my most grievous fault."

The only sound is of the traffic fourteen stories below the window, and I think he has passed out until I hear him say, "Maybe it's because you love me."

I get up then and slip into bed beside him. Both of us are speechless and stiff as effigies. "I feel so alone," I say at last. "So do I," he says. We turn to each other and he drifts into the serene sleep of those who can, and always will, get away with murder.

# Seven

———◆———

$\mathcal{O}$NCE, WHEN I WAS STILL MARRIED, I had a strep throat and, thinking it cured, stopped taking my penicillin. A day or two later I found nodes on my shinbones, was sent by a nervous dermatologist to a heart specialist, and was told I had something called erythema nodosum. I had never heard of it before, have never heard of it since, and perhaps I have the wrong words for it. All I know about the ailment is that it can indicate rheumatic fever, nephritis, or, as in my case, the foolishness of cutting back on one's penicillin.

For several weeks I stayed in bed, because walking was close to impossible, while Rose Red, too young for school, sat on the floor beside me and played her toy xylophone. She had also arranged what she called a "comfort table"—one of a stack of TV tables, draped with a dishtowel and equipped with a glass, a comb, and a book chosen at random because she couldn't read—and put it within easy reach. Despite the pain in my legs, I had never been so happy.

While our Jamaican nurse, Hoppy, fetched Snow White from nursery school, Rose Red napped on my chaise longue, and when her sister got home neither could bear to leave the bedroom because, for once, they had me to themselves. To this day, I am saddened by the speed of Rose Red's speech. Talking fast, she figured, was the only way she could cram what she wanted so much to tell me in the little time I had to listen.

But now, the office being out of the question, there was time to hear about what Snow White had cooked on the toy stove at nursery school and where Rose Red had gone on her morning walk with Hoppy. There was time to hear them chattering downstairs while Hoppy gave them their baths, time to listen to Lucy and Desi, although I was too far away to hear anything but Desi's occasional "Looo-cy!" Illness had sentenced me to a term as their mother and my husband's wife, and I loved my prison.

Early evenings were the only part of the day in which I was alone, and then I would put down my book and turn toward the bedroom window, to watch the dog in the window of a red brick building across the street. The dog was a small white poodle, and along about five o'clock, it would climb onto the sill, wriggle itself in front of the Venetian blind, and stare up the street toward Eighth Avenue. Twenty or so minutes later it would commence a barking that, of course, I couldn't hear, then wriggle past the blinds again to jump from the sill. A minute or two later a light would go on behind the blind; a woman whom I could see only in silhouette would raise it and vanish into what must have been the kitchen.

The kitchen was beyond my sight, but the table at which she sat was not. Every night I noticed the care with which she set it for her solitary meal and invariably lit a pair of candles. I admired that woman, whose face I never saw and whom I could not have recognized had I passed her on the street. Left to dine alone, I would probably live on ends of salami and sardines on crackers. But I didn't have to dine alone; I would never have to dine alone. B. would be with me, as he was about an hour later, sitting on the chaise longue and telling me about his day. Like the children, he too wallowed in my undivided attention. "I like to play with my mind," I had once told Dr. Franklin in explanation of the captiousness of my attention span. "No, Mees Cantwell," he said. (His Mitteleuropa accent was as adhesive as Krazy Glue.) "Your mind likes to play with you."

For years thereafter I was never again physically sick, although during the time between B.'s leaving and our divorce I prayed for pain, for an illness that would hurt so much that it would erase the illness in my head. It didn't come. Often I longed to faint, to be deaf and blind and unknowing. But the heart pumped, the blood traveled, the engine drove without a stutter. Eventually, I learned to love my body, the way my fingernails, drawn lightly across the skin, could erase an itch and the way the bone seemed to rise to meet the palm I laid on my cheek. My legs could cover miles of ground with the regularity of an automaton's; my hair grew without orders. How could anyone wish to transcend the body? Three score and ten was far too short a time to explore the cosmos bounded by my skin, and eternity a terrifying word. But one Saturday in June the engine finally faltered.

My head had ached for three days, but that was nothing new to a veteran of migraine. By Friday night, though, I had a fever that left me dry and burning one minute, cold and wet the next.

My sole doctor was my obstetrician, and he was away. So was Rose Red's pediatrician, the only other doctor we could think of. The doctor suggested by a neighbor was away, too. The children called Lucille, who knew everything, and she suggested a medical student who lived nearby and who might have reached a chapter in his studies that covered whatever I had, and a chiropractor who was a faith healer and who worked through the feet. Eventually Rose Red telephoned for a cab—the taxi services were just beginning to make house calls—but when the dispatcher heard the destination, St. Vincent's Hospital, he sent no one. Maybe he feared a birth in the back seat of the car or, worse, a demise.

At last I got out of bed, and, wearing a bra, underpants, a wrinkled green caftan, and Dr. Scholl health sandals, carrying a bag with a lipstick, a hairbrush, and my Blue Cross–Blue Shield card, I walked through the Village's steamy streets to St. Vincent's emergency room.

There I lay for a long time on a cot in a cubicle while my sweat soaked the mattress, listening to a young girl on the other side of the curtain who'd come in with a venereal disease. She had a sweet, soft voice and seemed shy, and she cried and moaned as a doctor, who spoke gently and kindly, cleaned out her vagina. And I, with little else to think of, thought of how the body declares a moratorium on sex, how the body itself proscribes promiscuity.

I lost track of time and didn't know that the children, teenagers now and nervous because I hadn't returned home, were sitting in the lobby outside the emergency room. A nurse pulled the green caftan over my head, pausing to ask, "Is this a Carol Horn?" referring to a designer of medium-priced sportswear, before tossing it into a garbage bag along with the underwear and the Dr. Scholls. Then she tied me into a hospital gown and called an orderly, who wheeled me out of the emergency room and through the lobby. Dripping wet, whiter than the sheets, a garbage bag holding my clothes and purse plopped by my right hand, I lacked only a tag on my big toe to proclaim me a corpse. Tired, I closed my eyes, and a moment later opened them to see a muddled, almost incredulous Snow White standing beside the gurney. "You can come and see your mother in a few minutes," the orderly said.

St. Vincent's is a Catholic hospital, and someone had left a piece of a Palm Sunday palm draped over the crucifix on the wall of my room. Seeing it, I released myself . . . to God or fate, I guess. They are the only words I have to describe that letting go of my self. Snow White was with me and so was that crucifix and I didn't need anything else, not even the priest who arrived a few minutes later. But I needed the nurse's aide—plump and black and glossy as a plum in her pink uniform—who threw herself across me while a doctor did a spinal tap. Without her sweet, solid flesh to pin me into place, I might have moved, and the needle, of which I was afraid, might have wandered. "Thank you, God," I breathed, thinking her an angel.

As the days passed and I realized that I must be very sick, I called a friend and said she'd better tell B. Everything and everyone else fell away. Always a conscientious housewife, I finally had my house in order. The bills were paid, my will was made, and my children were strong and straight. As for the balding man, I knew that I would take on more reality dead than fleshed. He had buried a lot of women, or so he claimed, and he had loved them all, more in death than in life. I would become one of his gallery of dearly beloveds. Besides, I would not really die, because every day those two mock-ups of myself—Rose Red stiff-backed and determinedly tearless, Snow White anxious to get on with her constant circling of the Village and its lures but there nonetheless—were standing on either side of my bed, not me, but me, and living. At last I had a free pass to the Father, by whom I really meant Papa, and I was going with a collection of venial sins but no mortal ones. My duty was done, and the last thing I would see with earth's eyes was my daughters, my descendants, growing like trees.

Rocky Mountain fever, or a version thereof (no one was ever really sure), was diagnosed. I was dosed with Tetracycline, and my world expanded to include the morning papers being pulled past my room on a little red wagon and the old woman in the next bed who, half-dead from emphysema, hid cigarettes in her Kleenex box and crept from the room, when the nurses weren't looking, to smoke on the fire escape. Our room was opposite the back door to the kitchen, and when at night I saw a few ambulatory patients lined up for leftovers, I told a nurse I was starving, and she sneaked me a slice of chocolate cake and, in lieu of a fork, a tongue depressor. A neighbor came over with my typewriter; a friend brought pounds of cherries into which my hand dipped with metronomic regularity.

Still, I missed those days in which I had floated, only my nose poking from the water, and those nights of thermometer-interrupted sleep. I missed cotton blankets that absorbed sweat and rubber gloves filled with ice cubes and laid along my groin while nurses whispered. One seldom gets to die before the final death, to have the final view and live to look again, to see what is extraneous and what is not. In the end I saw my children, and nothing else. Now it is hard to remember that, just as now it is hard to reconstruct pain or love, time being a kind of universal solvent, but I want to remember. Because I read *The Waste Land* during my first year in college, it has sunk into my skeleton, and whenever I think of "these fragments I have shored against my ruins," I think of what to me will always be "my girls."

ONE OF MY GIRLS, though, was leaving home again, not for the boarding school in the Berkshires this time but for a place on Eighth Street. From her former classmates, she had acquired the skills of a jailhouse lawyer and was now, she told me, a "self-emancipated minor." It was on a late November afternoon she left, carrying shopping bags crammed with clothes and the dented pots and pans she'd saved from trashcans for a kitchen of her own. Now there would be no mother to say, "Where have you been?"

and "Where are you going?" and no sister, busy with her home-work, begging her to turn down Janis Joplin. Now there would be another school, this one, too, stocked with misfits but not, thank God, with juvenile delinquents, and other friends whom probably I would never see or, if I did, learn to like.

The shopping bags were draped over her left arm, Tucked under her right was one of the Hallowe'en pumpkins I had carved for her and her sister. "You're still a child," I longed to say when I saw it. But she wouldn't have believed me, nor paused for a second in her dogged walk toward an adulthood she construed as freedom from all adults.

WHENEVER WE PARTED the balding man would say, "Mah Mary, let me lay this on you. If we ever *could* marry, and I'm not sayin' we ever could, would you marry me?" I always said yes. "I'd come to you in my shift," I would say, in love with the sentence, which I had read in a book or heard in a movie, and safe in saying it because I knew I would never be put to the test.

One morning, in bed with his arm around me, he said, "Oh, mah Mary, we're never going to be able to get married."

"I know that, but we have to believe we can."

"Think you could manage in an academic community?"

"Of course."

"Bet you're a good hostess."

"Yup."

"Can you run an adding machine? Mah wife can. You ought to see her fingers fly. I'm practically a conglomerate, y'know."

"No," I said, "but I can hire someone who can."

I was lying. I could run an adding machine. But there were lim-its beyond which I was not willing to take this conversation, and a possible career as an accountant was one of those limits.

He could be as blunt as a hammer, and as destructive. "The only person I'd marry if I didn't marry you would be some idealis-tic twenty-one-year-old I could train and teach and . . ." My eyes reddened, and the balding man added quickly, "Now, mah Mary, don't get upset about a rival you haven't even got."

I never thought of his wife as a rival. I never, away from him, fantasized a possible marriage. What he gave me, or, rather, what I took from him, was our shared passion for language, which may not seem like much compared to a marriage and children and the way B. had looked at me on our wedding night. But it was all I wanted, especially since it came from someone whose work I loved. Had he been a lesser writer, he would have been a lesser lover. No, I am lying. He would not have been my lover at all. I could overlook a lot of imperfections, but not a rotten prose style.

Sometimes I thanked Jesus for the balding man, believing that he represented absolution. If earning that absolution meant enduring indignities, it was the price I had to pay for having heaped indignities on B.—for not having been a good wife—and on my children—for my failure to make a home in which their father could be happy. Waiting, frightened, in a hotel room for a house detective to burst through the door and haul me away for prostitution, knowing that every lie I told my daughters about where I'd spent the night meant a black mark on the white paper that was my immortal soul, knowing the mark was even blacker when, by my silence, I conspired in the balding man's bigotry: these constituted my punishment.

Once, we fought, and when I accused him of lying to me, he said, "Yes, I lied. But what has truth to do with me? I'm an artist. I *make* the truth," and I, impatient with so artsy-fartsy a distinction, had gone home. As I walked in the door, the phone was ringing. It was he, and he was crying. "Mah Mary," he said, "we mustn't lose this."

I was crying, too. We'd come too close to severing the cord that connected us. Occasionally the cord had had to stretch five thousand miles or six months, but it never broke. I knew other men. One proposed and a second hinted, but I was already married, to him, and I would have been happy to stay married to him for the rest of my life. I suspect, too, he might have been happy to stay my make-believe husband for the rest of his. But reality got in the way.

Early one autumn morning he phoned and said his wife was dying. Would I marry him? At first I was stunned. I had never wished her dead. I had never wished anyone dead except, when the night's zero hour and mine coincided, myself. Then I remembered another morning, several years ago, when he, fond of drama and of playing wolf, had called to say that his wife was very possibly breathing her last. That time I had cried for hours, thinking myself—with the guilt-ridden's arrogant belief in her power—partly to blame. So this time, wary of his playacting and the pleasure he took in turning circumstance into crisis, I said something vague about how he should think only of her and not of any future we might have together, because I had always been with him and I always would be. That afternoon I told a friend he'd probably been on the phone all day proposing to everyone in his address book.

In a week she was indeed dead. A week after the funeral he called me. Two days later he came to New York.

A few nights before he arrived I was standing at the bedroom window looking out at the street, which was wet and empty. A woman appeared, walking toward the docks, drunk and waving an umbrella at nothing. There was a time when I would have felt sorry for her, poor soul with no roof over her head. This time I thought, "Maybe she likes it outside, and yelling." Maybe I did, too.

True, I had a roof over my head. I had raised it myself, and there is no pride like the pride that comes from being able to build a house for oneself. But for six years I had lived outside the world where the animals went into the ark two by two. It was a world I had lived in for a long time and since I was very young, and although I was ambivalent about moving back in, not marrying the balding man would have meant losing him. Or, to be more precise, losing the only strong connection I had ever made to any man besides my father and B.

We were to meet at the delicatessen where we always had breakfast. He was late, so I stood outside in the morning cold, my eyes fixed on Sixth Avenue and the corner around which he would appear. A woman I worked with came by, walking her dog, and asked what on earth I was doing fifty blocks from home at nine in the morning.

"I'm having breakfast with an old friend," I told her. "If you see my secretary, tell her I'll be in a little late." I spoke calmly, but my body was urging her to walk on so that I could be alone when I saw him. The dog pulled on its leash, she waved a casual goodbye, and moved toward Fifth Avenue just as he rounded the corner of Sixth, wearing his big hat, his hands stuck in the pockets of his bulky sheepskin jacket. I ran to him, slid my arms inside the jacket and around his waist, and laid my head on his chest for a moment. We walked slowly, my right arm still around his waist, to the delicatessen.

I carried my coffee to a table, and we sat facing each other.

"Thank you for that lovely letter, mah Mary," he said of my condolence note. "Of course I know you only wrote it because you want to marry me."

The floor opened and the walls slid away and I was dizzy. There was nothing to hold on to but that cup, so I wrapped both hands about it and stared. His eyes were those of a breeder at a horse auction.

"Tell me about your daughter. I've got to know everything about her if you're going to be mah wife."

I told him about Snow White, but not everything about Snow White. My child was entitled to her grief, her terror, and, above all, her privacy. "But she's got a good psychiatrist, whom she likes," I finished, "and she's coming out of it."

"Mah Mary," he said, "there's somethin' awful wrong here. A child who hates her mother. And I just don't think I can take on your financial responsibilities."

I was enraged. How dare he imply that I couldn't provide for my daughter, or that her father, that "Jew," would not?

"If you don't want to marry me, don't," I said. "But don't you dare use my children as an excuse."

He asked a few more questions. He did everything but check my wind.

"What is this?" I asked. "A job interview?"

"What do you think it is?"

"A job interview."

He walked me to the corner and I got in a cab. A glass bell had dropped, the bell that drops whenever air might crumble me, and I saw Fifth Avenue, and later my desk, my secretary, the magazine's "staffers" walking past my door, from the inside looking out. I didn't cry and I didn't faint. I was as sealed in, and as dead, as the stuffed canary under its dome on the library mantel. That night I went with an old friend to a party for the balding man. Together we watched the performance: the smiles, the hugs, the swelling of the corpse. "Are you sure you want that, Mary?" my friend asked as he took me home. He didn't say "him." "Him" had disappeared.


I HAD TRIED to keep my father from dying; I had tried to keep my husband from leaving; I was equally incapable of letting the balding man go. We had dinner the next evening. When he cried about his wife and about watering the plants himself, I cried, too, because I couldn't bear the image of him with a little brass watering can in his hand.

Sometimes, though, his martinis and the novelty of his new role dried his tears, and then he was as giddy as Pandora facing the box. "You wouldn't believe the number of women willin' to console the grievin' widower. You know——?" (He named a well-known novelist, someone who, because I was still too naïve to realize that a widower's phone starts ringing about ten minutes after his wife's interment, I thought beyond pursuing the bereaved.) "She called last week."

Then he spoke again of his wife, swinging as ever between love and anger, and I cried some more, for both of them. We soaked the restaurant's pink napkins with our tears, and when my handkerchief, which we'd been sharing, was soggy, we blew our noses on them. I don't know if anyone noticed us. My eyes were on him.

We went to his room. We were calmer now, and we started talking about a "decent interval" and an Irish writer we knew. He asked if I would like to go to Ireland again "with your husband."

"Oh, yes," I said. "We'll go to the Dingle Peninsula. Have you ever been there? We'll . . ."

I was sitting in a club chair, my hands open on my lap, my stocking feet crossed on the bed, feeling the familiar ease fall over me. He brought out his guitar. "Let's make up a blues," he said.

"She's a New York woman," he sang, "and she's got big brown eyes. She's a New York woman . . ."

"And she's tryin' me on for size."

He laughed and hugged me. "Mah Mary. We are *fated* to be man and wife."

He wanted me to spend the night.

"But I can't. I would have called a sitter to come and stay overnight, but you said you were leaving terribly early in the morning, so I didn't think . . ." I didn't add that, with his wife a few weeks dead, I thought he'd want to give her her space in his bed just a little longer.

"Your daughter is old enough to stay alone."

"No, she isn't," I said, thinking of New York and open windows and a figure sliding noiselessly under the sash. "She'd get scared."

"Mary, how can I marry a woman who can't manage her time?"

"That's not fair. I manage my time very well. I . . . come on. You get into bed and I'll read you to sleep."

He undressed and lay down, curled on his side. I pulled a sheet over him and sat in the crook of his body and read sections of one of his own books.

"Young man who wrote that's got a pretty big future," he said.

"He sure has," I said.

"Man who wrote that hasn't done *half* of what he's goin' to do."

"I know. Remember that time at Lincoln Center when that boy waited in the dark to tell you how much he admired you, and I said, 'Doesn't that make up for everything?' and you said 'No.' "

"I was lyin', mah Mary. It makes up for a lot."

We were silent for a moment, and I pulled myself higher on the headboard.

"Y'know. I was a good-lookin' boy in my youth."

"I know that, too. I can still see him."

"I keep thinkin', mah Mary"—and he rolled over on his back—"that if I get back into trainin', I could be an Olympic runner even now."

"I'm sure you could."

I wasn't humoring him. I had always believed he could do anything but love anyone very much.

"Mah Mary, thank you. You can't imagine what these last six weeks have been like. You've restored me."

He was sleepy now, so I got up and turned off the light.

"Mah Mary," he said in the dark, "I want you to make me a statement. *Do you love me?*"

"I love you very much."

"Would it hurt you a lot if we didn't marry?"

"Yes," I said, "it would hurt me a lot."

Four weeks later he married a student. "She restored me," he told the press.

I was saving the morning paper to read with breakfast, so I didn't know until someone called and read the little news item aloud. Speechless, I hung up the phone, left the kitchen, went into the bathroom, and turned on the shower. I was so cold my bones felt iced, so I stood for a long time in the stream of hot water, but they didn't melt.

I left the house and walked, I always try to walk off sadness, heading crosstown to a friend on Fifth Avenue. "Age," she said, "his age."

Punctilious as ever, I walked to a Christopher Street hairdresser's to keep my appointment. After my shampoo, while I was waiting for the haircut, I went to the pay phone on the wall and called the friend who had asked me if I was sure I wanted "that."

"Leo," I said, starting to cry, "he blew it."

"You had too much baggage," he said.

Dr. Franklin, whom I had not seen for a long time, found an hour for me that afternoon. He had seen me cry till my tears wet my skirt when B. left, and once again he was looking at me, bent over, trying to stanch my running nose.

"Mary," he said, for once breaking through the formality that had been our style for many years, "you have a tendency to fantasize."

"Did I fantasize those years? Those proposals? Last month?"

"No. You fantasized the man."

Soon after I got home, the doorbell rang. Two friends, a man and his wife, had driven in from Long Island when they saw the paper. By now my eyes were slits and my face was swollen. I couldn't cry enough. It was like the time many years ago when I had had food poisoning and vomited until I was heaving only air.

"I don't know why, but I keep remembering the afternoon my father died," I said as they came in. "His bed was in the bay window of the living room so that he could watch people going by, and we were all standing beside it when his breathing got heavy and he went into a coma.

"I said 'Papa!' and the nurse, a family friend, said, 'Mary Lee, don't. It makes it harder for them to leave if they hear somebody trying to call them back. Let him go.'

"When his breathing got even heavier, she ordered us into the dining room, because he had told her he didn't want any of us to see him die, not even my mother. We sat there until we heard the breathing stop.

"You know what? He's been dead so long now I can't even remember his face. But I keep looking at the door," and I pointed toward the hall, "because all I really want is for it to open and my father to walk in."

After they left, I splashed my face with cold water until it was scarlet and put cold tea bags on my eyes so that Snow White, who had been spending the Christmas holidays with us, and Rose Red wouldn't see that I'd been crying when they came home from calling on their father. The tree was still up, and I sat next to it, breathing in the balsam. Minutes passed, and as they did, something funny started happening to my back. It was as if a pack were sliding from my shoulders, leaving me lighter by ten pounds. I have paid the penance for failing my husband, I told myself. I have been absolved. I felt as I did on the Saturday afternoons of my childhood when, my soul as clean as unmarked paper, I left the confessional and walked as if on zephyrs across Bristol Common toward home.

# Eight

O<small>N MY WAY TO</small> A<small>USTRALIA</small> five years earlier, I had stopped overnight in Honolulu. As I got off the plane, a fat woman in a muumuu draped a lei over my head and handed me a bottle of a local firm's suntan lotion. The fashion editor, the photographer, the enormous box, always called "the coffin," in which were packed the clothes to be photographed, and I were then driven to a hotel on a highway that might as well have been the New Jersey Turnpike. At sunset a series of drumbeats, on tape, was played over the lobby's public address system while torches were lighted around the hotel swimming pool.

I had a drink served in a coconut shell under the thatched hut that was the outdoor bar, and drove with the editor and the photographer, *sans* coffin, to a fern-thicketed restaurant, where we ate tinned shrimp in a gelatinous sauce over instant rice.

The next morning I looked for the Pacific. Wearing a swimsuit and carrying the suntan lotion, I picked my way along the edges of countless swimming pools until I found a gritty track that led to a lagoon. It was not quite the Pacific; it was as tepid as a tub drawn and forgotten. But it was the best I could do.

Now, a few years later, I was back in Hawaii, on an island called Lanai, just a hop and cheap ticket away from the small northern California town where I had been describing the life, times, and makeup mistakes of a group of young women who had written *Mademoiselle* asking to be "made over."

We—a beauty editor, a hairdresser, and a makeup expert—stayed in an old hotel outside of which was a plaque screwed to a rock celebrating the generous ladies who, during the Silver Rush, had made the days and (mostly) the nights bearable for prospectors and lumberjacks. The bar across the street had customers by seven in the morning, the sidewalks were wooden, and the air was pure as Eden's. By day, while I took notes, the traveling troupe cut hair, brushed on blush, and introduced the novitiates to the miracle that was the eyelash curler. At night, we all dined together, so linked in comradeship and our sense of a superior esthetic— "Did you see the one with the purple eyeshadow and the awful shag?"—that we strangers seemed old friends and this town, our town, Once the job was over, however, we were over, too. Everyone went back to his or her real life, all but me, who was grateful for the hiatus that would delay the return to mine.

Lanai, which was tiny, produced pineapples but no palms, had a tall lava shelf but no cliffs, a string of sand but no sweep of beach. I've been twice to Hawaii, but since I've never seen any of its geographic wonders, never even been to a luau or watched a hula, one could say I've never been there at all.

Running, of course. I ran to a man. I have done that more often than I have acknowledged to myself. But I do not see men as amalgams of muscles, penises, and hair in places in which I have none. Rather, they are enormous easy chairs in which I like to sit a while. Frederick Exley, though, was nobody's idea of an easy chair. It was just that over the years during which he had visited Lanai, staying with his childhood friend Jo and Jo's wife, Phyllis, once a nightclub singer in the Philippines, he had handed out invitations thick and fast, serene in the conviction that nobody was ever going to show up. I fooled him.

Lanai was mostly flat, with a bony spine called the Ridge running through its center, and was notable mostly because it was *not* flat and was home to some rare insects. Seldom has a developer had less to work with, but the island has since become chic, thus fulfilling Fred's worst fears. Money did it, of course, and Fred, while deriding the rich, would have liked a stab at being one of them. But not as much as he would have liked to walk down Fifth Avenue and hear people murmur, "That's Frederick Exley, the famous novelist."

"Other men," Fred wrote of himself, "might inherit from their fathers a head for figures, a gold pocket watch all encrusted with the oxidized green of age, or an eternally astonished expression; from mine I acquired this need to have my name whispered in reverential tones." Because of that need, I have eschewed my customary discretion (memoirs, after all, are never the whole truth, only that portion their authors choose to discuss) and revealed his name. Were he still on this earth, he would have killed me if I hadn't—not by the sword but by a torrent of speech, which, when Fred was in full form, could fell an ox.

I treasured Fred's first book, *A Fan's Notes*, and never argued when he claimed his second, *Pages from a Cold Island*, was better. It is hard for a writer who longed, as he put it, to produce "a shelf" to admit that he may have done his best work on his first time out. The two novels that followed, and a few occasional pieces, were postscripts.

A stocky, bearded man in his late forties, Exley had considerably more gut than when I first saw him, a few years previously. He wasn't writing much on Lanai. He was "circling," he said. In the evening, when he put on his seersucker pajamas ("Like my 'jammies, Mary?") and his big straw hat, slathered a plate with Pecan Dandy ice cream, climbed on the couch, arranged an afghan over his feet, slid his vokda bottle, which lacked only a nipple, within easy reach of his right hand, and talked back to the television set, he was our child. Jo and Phyllis's children by their former marriages were grown and far away, and I am a mother before I am anything else, so we all needed a baby.

Fred and I met when I went to upstate New York, to Alexandria Bay, where he had a small, pin-neat apartment in a gangling Victorian house. *Mademoiselle*, like every other magazine that year, was celebrating the two-hundredth anniversary of the Spirit of '76, and I, who thought him the quintessential male American writer, wanted him in the issue. Fred, though, didn't know or care why I'd flown upstate in a little plane that at one point seemed to brush the treetops. All he wanted was his picture in the papers.

We shook hands shyly and got into the car he'd borrowed from a "buddy"—all Fred's friends were "buddies," and I doubt he'd ever had enough money for a car of his own. Before I had settled myself in the seat, he said, "All I know about you is that you're B.'s ex-wife."

"Do you know him?"

"No. But when I finished my first novel somebody said I should have an agent. So I sent it to him. He kept it for what seemed a verry long time, and when I called him about it, he said he didn't want to handle the book, then added some verry gra-too-i-tous ree-marks. When it won all those awards, I felt like calling him again and saying, 'Fuck you, B.' "

"Dear Lord," I thought, "what a start for an interview."

I needn't have worried. Fred liked to talk. It wasn't long before he forgot my ex-wifehood, and only a little longer before he forgot my sex. He was describing how, when in college and penniless, he was persuaded by a friend to service a homosexual who paid well.

"But, Cantwell, I just couldn't do it. You know how it is when you've been swimming and you come out of the water and your prick is cold and limp?"

"No," I said.

His ears blocked by the sound of his own voice, he didn't even laugh.

Interviewing creates a spurious intimacy. If one is a good interviewer and the interviewee is a willing talker, the two of you become, for several hours, each other's best friend. When the interview is over, so is the friendship.

Fred was an exception. A lonely man, he was not comfortable face to face with most women—he preferred them groin to groin and gone before breakfast—so the phone became an intermediary. His vocabulary was that of the best man at a prenuptial smoker, and he never failed to make me laugh.

"Cantwell," he would growl over long distance, "there's this cunt up here . . . oh, I forgot . . . you don't like that word. There's this douche bag up here who's giving me trouble."

I would murmur a weak "Oh, Fred" (I felt I should), and he was off on one more long story of boats missed and islands lost and women left wailing on the dock.

He called the office. Galleys were left unread, meetings postponed, secretaries stood waving in the doorway, while I, feet propped on an open desk drawer, listened, laughed, and tried to figure out what on earth he was talking about. He became a local legend, like the editor of my youth who thought her possibly forgotten cigarettes would incinerate us all, and would have her assistant scour her office for an hour after she herself had left for home, looking for insufficiently snuffed-out stubs. "Frederick Exley is on the phone," my secretary would whisper to the supplicants, and my absences were forgiven.

He called me at home, sometimes yanking me out of bed at three in the morning. He had seen an old girlfriend, a twenty-two-year-old with skin like satin and hair like cornsilk and legs like inverted bowling pins. They had had a *contretemps*. Did I understand it?

"Fred," I would answer, "I cannot spend the night dissecting the thought processes of ex-cheerleaders."

The doctor of one of his former wives had made a pass at her. What should he do?

"Nothing," I'd say. "It's not your problem."

His publisher has done this; his agent has done that; and Alfred Kazin is a fuck. "Yes," I say. An admirer of Kazin's, I am lying. But lying is preferable to listening to an exegesis on Alfred Kazin's fuckhood.

Letters arrived, too, a folderful of letters, in one of which he told me that if I wanted to bring my daughters for a holiday to Alex Bay, he would vacate his pad and we could have it for free and we would love it. We would love it because the St. Lawrence River flows through his backyard, there is a cinder-block fireplace on which we can barbecue, as well as a picnic table and benches. I was about to dab my eyes, moved by this middle-American scenario, when I read the next sentence. He had caught yet one more dose of the clap in Florida, but the drip seemed to be drying. I put the handkerchief away and laughed helplessly. Fred was my bouncing baby boy, and I loved him.

To listen to Fred was to go down the rabbit hole. His world, which was wholly bounded by his skull, was a world in which everything was tilted, and nothing was as it appeared, not even pain. Walk into it, and you looked at your life through windows that had the bubbles and distortions of eighteenth-century glass. I didn't want to see my life plain. Clarity seemed a curse. Too, I was captivated by obscenity, because I never used it myself. (When, in the course of one day, Fred managed to anger his agent, his editor, and me, the agent, a woman, yelled, "Fuck you!" His editor shrieked, "Cocksucker!" I said, "That was damn rude, Fred.")

Fred's language was in Technicolor. My own was in black and white. And he attracted friends for much the same reason a burning building attracts spectators. We were mesmerized by the flames and falling rafters and buckling walls, we who kept our houses under a thin film of ice. But Fred's house was never totally consumed, and I, who was always frozen, had become used to warming my hands at its heat.

When I stepped from the tiny plane in Lanai, he handed me a necklace, a plastic dolphin on a chain—"in lieu of a lei"—grumbled when he heard the airline had lost my luggage ("You would, Cantwell, you would"), led me to the portable bar that was the jeep, introduced me to Jo and Phyllis, and deposited me at the island's one store. The airline had said I could charge up to $25.

There were no nightgowns, so I bought a T-shirt, extra large, that said LANAI '76. Toothpaste, but forgot to ask for a toothbrush. No makeup. They didn't have any. Shampoo. Underpants of a style I had assumed was discontinued around 1958. The bill was $12.76, and Fred and Jo berated me for not having had the wit to expend the remaining $12.24 on a stack of sixpacks.

One doesn't wear shoes in Hawaiian houses, and the floors were chilly, so Fred gave me his socks. The nights are cool, so he gave me his basketball jacket. Walking through the small living room, seeing me ensconced on his couch with a wineglass in my hand and my eyes on a televised basketball game, he shouted,

"Fifteen fuckin' minutes in this fuckin' house and you've absconded with my fuckin' whole damn wardrobe."

I think he was glad to see me.

THE HOUSE WAS ON A DIRT ROAD lined with others like it: close together, backyard vegetable gardens, the sounds of cocks crowing and hens clucking and of television sets in every living room. Sometimes, before dinner, I took a walk, afraid to wander too far, because there were no streetlights and night came thick and fast. Even the stars, stars I had never seen so close and dense, couldn't penetrate the darkness.

Imagine us at dinner, at the kitchen table, which we seldom left before bedtime. "Fred," Phyllis says, "tell Mary about the time the telephone company detective came to your house." Fred, tapdance for the lady.

"Well, I was off the booze and out jogging, trying to get some of this fuckin' fat off. I came home and was standing in the kitchen in my little sweatsuit pouring some fuckin' Seven-Up in a fuckin' clean glass when the doorbell rings and this guy in a blue suit and wingtips tells me he's a detective and would like to ask a few questions.

"The FBI was always doing employment checks on my former students, so I let him in and poured him some fuckin Seven-Up in a fuckin' clean glass. I even gave him some fuckin' ice cubes.

"He says, 'We've had some complaints about your making obscene phone calls, Mr. Exley.'

"I was scared shitless. I've done some time on the funny farm, y'know, and I thought, 'Jeezus! I've flipped out again and I don't even know if I've been calling old ladies' "—he crossed his eyes and dangled his tongue—" 'and going huh-huh-huh into the phone.' Then I remember my mother's asleep in the next room and she's going to come out, rubbing her eyes, just in time to see her son, Fat Freddie E, being led off in a straitjacket.

"I finally get the balls to say, 'But I haven't been making any obscene phone calls,' and he says, 'But the girls have reported . . .'

" 'Wait a minute. Who do you work for?'

" 'The telephone company.' "

" 'The phone company? You mean the operators . . . *those* dumb bunnies?' All the time I thought he was the FBI! And here I'd given him my fuckin' Seven-Up. In a fuckin' clean glass. With fuckin' ice cubes! *My* Seven-Up!

"The way I see it, Cantwell, the operators are there to work. But what the hell do they do? I was trying to call the mainland last week and the operator said"—he lifted his voice a few notes— " 'Sir, that number can be dialed direct.' And I said, 'Please, ma'am. I've got this paralyzed right arm and I can't . . .' And she said, 'Sir, that number can be dialed direct.'

" 'My left arm is paralyzed, too.' 'Sir, I told you, that number *can be dialed direct.*' 'Lady,' I say, 'the truth is I'm paralyzed from head to foot and I've been sitting here five minutes trying to get an erection so I can dial.' "

Fred's words fly, like ascending columns of birds, up, up, up, until finally they are out the window and into space, where we can't follow them. "Disagree with him, Mary," Phyllis nudges me, as still another diatribe against the armed forces, the entertainment industry, the communications industry, the fuckin' New York literati, takes flight and whizzes past us.

"I can't," I answer. "I never disagree with Fred."

Sometimes, though, I am frightened for him when I realize how slippery is the edge on which he lives. One time I am sad for him, when, in the midst of a harangue about women and the way they drive—they *force* men to violence—he says, "If only I could love somebody," and I see the terrible roots of misogyny.

Still, he is a lover, even of women, provided he can forget their sex. He is loyal to his buddies and as generous as a fool, and he has arranged for me to stay in the local doctor's guesthouse, where I read all day and dispense beer and dry-roasted peanuts to him and Jo and Phyllis and the doctor and his pregnant wife from four o'clock on. Once I try to provide dinner, but when I go to the island store, I find nothing, but for a pig's head staring at me from the freezer, that I recognize.

"You're Fred's friend from the mainland," the proprietor says. (I must be. There are only eight Caucasians on this island, the eighth being me.) "We have some Chab-liss you could try." So I buy two bottles, along with a Maui onion and some ground beef so that I can do burgers.

"Jeez!" Fred says when everybody arrives. "And you claim to be a cook!"

I wear his dolphin for luck and, although my luggage has shown up, his socks for security. When he mentions the balding man, who he knows was my friend but does not know was my lover, and I start to cry and stop, embarrassed and blaming my tears on overwork and overtiredness and maybe a kind of craziness, he says, "Don't worry, Mary. My views on craziness are a little different from other people's. You're not crazy. Just aim for a selective memory, like mine."

But I will never have a selective memory. Mine is out of control. It provides me either with everything or with nothing, and is triggered by my senses, which are far keener and far more intractable than my brain.

There is an evening when we are around the kitchen table and I say . . . what, I don't remember now, but it evokes from Jo: "We've got another crazy Irishman on our hands."

"Who's the first?" I ask.

"Fred."

"Fred!" I am surprised, because his surname is as English as, say, Windsor.

"Don't let my last name—I love my last name—fool you. How I've hated being Irish! I'm always trying to disguise it. Phyllis, remember all those clothes I ordered from the Abercrombie and Fitch catalogue? But, Jesus, am I Irish!"

I look at him very hard, past the thick beard and the thatch of gray hair, and see a pair of familiar-seeming, flat brown eyes staring back at me.

"Fred!" I start to laugh. "The beard fooled me. You look like my Uncle Bill. I've run five thousand miles and found my Uncle Bill."

But he was not my Uncle Bill, because my Uncle Bill was not the son of a telephone lineman and a woman who stood behind the steam table in the high school cafeteria. My Uncle Bill didn't have to have a friend pretend that he, not Fred, was So-and-So's date for the prom because the girl's parents wouldn't have wanted her seen with him. My Uncle Bill knew nothing of the rage that had Fred screwing in adulthood the wives of the boys who had snubbed him in childhood. My Uncle Bill was an executive in a rubber company, not an open wound that could be bandaged only with words. All the time Fred had me laughing and gasping and throwing up my hands, I was wondering why a man who was so drunk was also so curiously clearheaded. That he often struck me as mad was another thing entirely.

I WAS LIVING in the suspended time that follows grief, when the nervous system shuts down and only the heart and lungs and muscles are working, those and the part of the head that permits dailiness. Except for the moment when Fred mentioned the balding man and a nerve jumped and made me cry, I was insulated. The insulation was not willed. Rather, my body had taken over for my brain and was giving it a few weeks' peace.

Thrice I was jolted into happiness. The first night on Lanai, before I could move into the guesthouse, Fred gave me his bedroom—iron bed, creaky bedsprings, shabby deal bureau, typewriter on a table, a varnished bookcase jammed with paperbacks, no curtains—but I couldn't sleep. I was too infatuated with the susurration of banana leaves against the window screens and, at dawn, the roosters' wakeup calls. I was happy, too, on the afternoon I first dispensed beer and peanuts to the group and thought, "What nice people." Both times I was also thinking, "And I got here *all by myself.*"

The third time was the night we had dinner at the young doctor's house and I sat on the floor eating sukiyaki and drinking warm sake. Beside me sat Phyllis's father, a barefoot nut-brown man who spoke only Tagalog. He laughed when I laughed, looked sober when I looked sober, showed his appreciation for the food with deep, rumbling burps, and wound me in the peace that comes when there is no possibility of talk. I was, I am, so tired of talking.

Then the newspaperman arrived.

He had been covering what Fred called the year's major sporting events—the Superbowl, a prizefight in Las Vegas, and Gary

Gilmore's execution—and had called from Los Angeles, sobbing and exhausted. "Come to Lanai," Fred said. "Leave that fuckin' job. Take some fuckin' time off."

"Poor guy," he told Jo, Phyllis, and me, "those fuckin' bastards are squeezing him to death."

I didn't like the newspaperman. Perhaps it is simply that I was prepared to resent anyone who pierced that small circle in which I was seeking deafness and blindness, and turned it into what Fred called Payne Whitney West. Or perhaps it is the malice bred from consciousness of one's self-control that makes me say I wish he had just hung a sign reading I AM A TORTURED PERSON around his neck and let up on the theatrics.

We were in the guesthouse living room when he started telling us about the newsmen near the prison, the television cameras, and, finally, the procession into the execution shed and past the execution chair, led by a tour guide who counted out the five bullet holes. One bullet had been a blank so that the riflemen were all able to participate in one of their fellows' accidental innocence. The newspaperman acted it out, repeated the dialogue, and paced the living room, pretending to be a television announcer, a guard, the tour guide.

It was ironic. I had run as far as I could from memories of the balding man but was reminded of him time and time again by Fred, who spoke often of famous writers he had known or brushed against, because it made him feel a member of their church. And, horrified that murder was legal again, I had run from all the brouhaha that preceded Gilmore's death, because it meant that once more I, who had been told by an uncle in childhood that execution meant that someone set your hair on fire, would once again dream of my head bursting into flames. But both had followed me to Lanai.

How could I not hate the messenger with the bad news? Execution was in the room, and with it the photographs I remembered blazoned on the front pages of the tabloids on my first few weeks in New York. The Rosenbergs were to die, and I, just out of college, apolitical, and soon to marry a boy who, though almost as apolitical as I, was Jewish and thus possibly scarred with the mark of Cain, was about to be caught and fried for crimes unimagined as well as uncommitted. I wasn't crazy. Truly. It was just that young, missing my father, torn (willingly) from the WASPS and laid-back Catholics who had constituted the bastion that was my childhood, I had traveled too far from home.

Fred slept on the guesthouse couch that night; the news-paperman had his bed in Jo and Phyllis's cottage. Actually, Fred didn't sleep—he seldom slept—and I heard the pop of beer cans opening and the soft padding of his bare feet as he walked between the couch and the television set.

I was frightened. I had toppled off the edge of the world. I kept seeing the last walk, that last mile, and I was the walker. I remem-bered lying along the balding man's magic back, how he moored me as a piling does a skiff. He had said, "Mah Mary, make me a statement. *Do you love me?*" Was it possible I hadn't answered? Or had I, and spoken too softly? What else had I done wrong? Was it because I went to *Einstein on the Beach* on the night he had said he would arrive in New York since I knew him to be unreliable and *Einstein* was rumored to be unmissable? But he did arrive when promised, and found me, not planted by the phone, as I was sup-posed to be, but out. Or was it because I hadn't understood that leaving him in an empty bed was like leaving him in a desert?

I wished I could go into the living room and ask Fred to get into bed with me, to be a stuffed animal I could hold until I slept. But I had never asked that of anyone. Besides, Fred had said once, "I never ball anyone I like," and might have felt compelled to say no. He might have thought I wanted more than a teddy bear.

When the dark faded to gray, I heard the screen door slam. I got up, dressed, and went back to my work, my old companion. I did that almost every day on Lanai, sitting at a card table with notes and a pile of typing paper. I was sifting through memories— of the way snow hitting the hot air at the bottom of the air shaft outside our first apartment bounced up again, say, and of B. rub-bing my back when I was in labor with Snow White—thinking that if I wrote them down, they would form a shape, make sense. I was looking for cause and effect, not knowing then that often there are no links, only happenstance.

At five o'clock every day Fred would arrive in the jeep to fetch me for dinner, restless and anxious to get back to Jo and Phyllis and the kitchen table, where he was safe. I was a nuisance but a diversion, too, and once when Jo said, "Mary, why don't you move to one of the bigger islands—you can do your editing from there—and take this old goat with you?" I saw a little flicker in Fred's dead eyes. The promise of normality, of a well-regulated life, always lured him, though only for a second.

With the newspaperman's arrival the balance of power had shifted. We were no longer four friends at a kitchen table, but three boys sitting in a tarpaper clubhouse and two girls they wouldn't let in the door. Not that their conversation fascinated Phyllis and me. I doubt it fascinated them.

"What kind of an expense account you got? . . . Yeah? Must be rough out there on the road . . . Yeah? Must be a lot of boozin' . . . Suppose you have to bury the liquor bills somewhere, huh? . . . Yeah? The fucks!"

Sometimes Jo looked down the table at Phyllis and me. I could tell he wanted to hear what we were saying, maybe even join us, but that would have meant breaking a club rule, so he didn't.

Fred had taken a walk alone every night before dinner, but no more. After he'd been gone for ten minutes, the newspaperman would say, "Guess I'll go look for Fred," and go out, to reappear with him about half an hour later. He was like a sheepdog working a flock, only he was working Fred out, not in. Perhaps if the newspaperman's wife had been there we would have achieved détente. The girls could have done the dishes while the boys talked. Alone with Phyllis and me, the newspaperman never spoke. I guess he felt we had no common denominator.

I take that back. Once he spoke to me. We were in the back of Jo's jeep, and he said, "I read your article about Fred. Enjoyed it."

"Thank you. I'd like to read the one you did on him for——," and I named his newspaper.

We turned and looked at our mutual subject, the Pulitzer Prize nominee. He was standing twenty feet away, legs spraddled, urinating against a tree. The newspaperman's face was expressionless. I was trying not to laugh.

Later, returned to New York, I embroidered a dinner party with my anger at the newspaperman—how, working out his formidable *angst*, he, equipped with a snorkel, had made a Byronic run toward the Pacific and settled instead for a racing dive into a tide pool; how, gypping me of my longed-for place in the fishing boat, he had set out to snare a marlin while stoked on Dramamine.

"Maybe you felt you were half of a couple before he arrived," a friend said.

I thought about that statement. I think about what anyone says of me with the concentration of a watch repairer looking for a faulty cog. No, she wasn't right. I was angry because the newspaperman had pushed me into the cold. He was an intruder who hogged the fire around which we were all keeping warm. I was jealous, too, because he and Fred excluded me, jealous the way Jo was the night he ordered Phyllis to bed because he found the two of us speaking low. I think we were talking about children. It didn't matter. Jo thought we were telling our secrets, and maybe, in a sense, we were.

But the anger evaporated; my anger always does, because I am distracted by small pleasures, as easily charmed as a cranky baby responding to a well-placed tickle. One afternoon Phyllis and I walked along the little beach and across the black rocks to a cliff, down which we climbed to a semicircle of sand called Shark Cove. We didn't have much in common besides life, I suppose, but sometimes that can be enough. While we waded, the waves curling like cream around our footprints, I told her about the balding man, and Phyllis told me about her first husband and a lover she once had. We scaled the cliff to rejoin the gentlemen and never spoke of those men again. Strangers on a train we were, getting off at our different stops with a little less luggage than when we had boarded.

I don't know how long I was on Lanai—a week or ten days, maybe—but it was long enough to slip into its spin. I loved shopping in the one store and trying to construct fettucini Alfredo out of Japanese noodles and processed cheese, and most of all I liked nodding to people who were beginning to recognize me as I trundled down the aisles with my cart. When the young doctor's wife came back from one of the big islands with her sonograms, she shared the photographs of the little blob in her uterus with Phyllis and me. Was it a boy? A girl? I often wonder. Did the rich American woman, an anomaly on Lanai, ever get her longed-for hot tub? Are Jo and Phyllis still there? Are the roads still rutted? Is dawn still a matter of crows and hens and the stirrings of banana leaves? Never mind. It will be until my brain shuts down.

My last night on Lanai the newspaperman, dizzied by alcohol and Dramamine, passed out in Fred's room. Jo, drunk, had gone to bed. Fred had fallen asleep on the living room couch. There was no one to drive the jeep through the dark to the little guesthouse, so Phyllis pulled an air mattress onto the living room floor and gave me a muumuu, which, since she had an Asian's small bones, I shimmied into like a snake retrieving a shed skin.

Then she, too, went to bed, and I lay on the floor thinking about returning to the mainland—there was no choice nor did I really want one, because all islands are, in the end, too small—and listening to a cacophony of snores.

Fred's I could endure—they were deep and rhythmic—but the newspaperman gurgled between snorts. I crawled across the room on my hands and knees, V'd my index and middle fingers around the knob, and slowly pulled his door shut.

I was making my way back to the air mattress when I suddenly thought of the sight I must make: sausaged into a muumuu and creeping. I looked around at this latest place to which my feet had brought me. To my left, a small, feisty man and his Filipino wife were snoring in their bedroom. Behind me, the tortured newspaperman was snoring in Fred's bedroom. To my right was Fred himself, snoring on the couch.

I was, at that moment, literally on my knees. But I was moving. I was laughing, too. "Mary," I said to this woman I had lived with so long, "I've enjoyed knowing you."

# *Nine*

———◆———

NOT LONG AGO I was standing on the corner of Second Avenue and Fourteenth Street, waiting for a crosstown bus, when the smell of some kind of spicy food curled, almost like a veil, around my nose. It came from one of the nearby restaurants, though I knew neither which one nor which country's cuisine was on its menu. But I had been in that country, I knew, because the aroma brought me back to twilight and the end of a day's sightseeing and narrow streets thronged with people on their way home. It was always, I remember, "the hour between the dog and the wolf," the hour in which I, no matter how pleasant the circumstances, longed for a roof between me and the sky. And for a few minutes, sniffing that spicy scent—a kind of curry, it may have been—I knew again the loneliness I had known so well.

But it was my neighborhood in which I was waiting, my bus I was soon to board, my people, however different their blood and their pasts were from mine, with whom I was sharing complaints about five o'clock traffic and buses in happy herds camping out by the East River. I was going home to my place and my table. I would shut the door on the dark and sink into a cave of my own making. That's what all houses are really, caves. Of course one reads about houses with big windows and big sliding doors, those houses designed to "bring nature indoors." But how much do you want to bet that, once the sun goes down, the blinds will be drawn and the curtains closed on those monuments to glass and T-beams? It is pleasant to lie in bed, as I do, with the shutters parted and the moon riding between them. But to sit in a curtainless living room and feel the night pressing in is to realize that the dark can be much stronger than bricks and mortar. Better not to look.

The bus, finally separated from its herd, arrived, and I got on to sit next to the window, because I can never get enough of looking at New York City. No matter how often I travel crosstown, for instance, the people are people I have never seen before, the building that was naked on Tuesday is tracked with scaffolding and swathed in orange netting on Thursday. An old sign is scarcely down before a new sign goes up. The seafood place is now a tapas bar, the secondhand bookstore is suddenly a health food emporium. The notion that there are bucks to be made, if one can only find the right angle, the right goods, never goes out of style in New York.

Getting off at Ninth Avenue, I took a short cut to my apartment, past the impossibly long-legged transvestite hookers, who, after the occasional police sweep, invariably migrate back to the meat market district. Because it was chilly, a few fires had already been started in the rusted metal barrels, and I started one myself, in my fireplace, when I got home. Of all the cities in the world, New York is the most sensual. No mangoes or papayas grow here, and oranges are not for stripping from the trees. Summer breezes are humid and laced with the stink of asphalt, low tide, and, if you're near a subway entrance or a boarded vacant lot, urine. But my senses are enlivened here as they are nowhere else in the world.

The sensuality emerges from disparity. There is a vast distance between the fire in the fireplace and the one in the trash barrel, a million miles between the "ching-ching-chong" (or so it sounds to me) of Chinatown mothers chattering to the babies strapped to their chests and the subdued purr of Upper East Side nannies pushing baby buggies as big and as soundless as Rolls-Royces. A stretch limo, analogous to the motor car in *Mrs. Dalloway*, in which passersby had "just time to see a face of the very greatest importance against the dove-gray upholstery," slips down Fifth Avenue. This time, too, mystery—who is it? could it have been . . . ?— brushes the passersby with her wing. One block west, on Sixth

Avenue, a woman naked from the waist up sprawls in a doorway, picking lice off her breasts.

"I've got to get away," I say to myself when I see that part of the city and its life, which make me want to curl into a creature as blind and deaf and unfeeling as an earthworm. "I've *got* to get away." But when I watch the sun dropping into the Hudson like a polished penny slipping through a slot, or a neighbor stubbornly planting pansies at the foot of a street tree, I am turned into Lot's wife. The pansies won't last; nothing lasts here. But nothing ever changes either. There will always be the sun setting into the Hudson and a New Yorker fighting cement with pansies, and as long as I am able, I will be trying desperately to take it all in. "Your eyes are too big for your belly," my grandmother warned me over and over again. I heard her and remember the warning, but what should I do? Shut them to the pleasures and torments of this place? They are, after all, what drew me here. What keeps me here, too.

I don't travel now, at least not the way I used to, although I still talk, albeit more casually these days, to strangers. But before I left the magazine for a newspaper at which I sat day after day making endless phone calls, asking endless questions, and drawing endless conclusions (the job was, I used to tell friends, rather like being a brain on a plate), I went on a few press junkets. One was to France, to celebrate Perrier, but once in Paris I hardly ever left my room at the Crillon because I couldn't bear to part with walls covered with apricot-colored silk and a tub encased in mahogany. Another time I was in France again, but in the Cognac region. I don't remember much about it except that the weather was cold and the trees skeletal, and I ate three different fresh foie gras, each slab brandishing a little flag. The best junket was to Spain, where, the ticket having an open return, I eventually stayed with friends on the Costa del Sol. But first I had to endure a week of education about the growing, harvesting, and packing of olives. Part of the procedure involved someone's standing for hours on a wooden block, scraping seeds off pimientos. Another took sitting at what looked like an old-fashioned school desk and crooking one's arm over a little jar so as to, with tongs, arrange the olives in pretty tiers. Whenever, rarely, I drink a martini, I am reminded of torture. "If you only knew," I am half-disposed to say to my fellow drinkers, "what went into getting that stuffed olive into your glass!" Then I console myself by thinking (I have, despite considerable evidence to the contrary, great faith in the mind of man) that there must now be a technological solution to seeding pimientos and inserting olives into jars.

I loved those junkets, the camaraderie imposed by drowsy day trips to Source Perrier and barrel-making factories and olive fields, and, in the evening, the afterdinner giggles over which unattached male company executive was after which pretty young editor. Actually, the males were never unattached, but their wives, out of sight, were also out of mind.

I loved the sharing of eyeshadow and tips about lip liner, and the way one or another of us was always called upon to order the teeth on the inevitable spine-tracking zipper on somebody's long evening dress. All the junkets ended in elaborate dinner parties, and even though we knew the speeches would be boring and the entertainment second-rate, we were as enveloped in bath powder and perfume and expectation as if this night was prom night. After a certain age—thirty-five seems about right—one cannot count on ever again knowing the girlishness that comes of a flirtation. But feeling silk against your skin or the way your hair is falling—*just right*—along your cheek never fails.

Now I go to Australia, the country I assumed I would never see again.

Snow White and Rose Red had inherited a little money. The latter, predictably, spent hers on graduate school. The former, also predictably, headed straight to Newark Airport, where she waited three days for a flight to London on an airline whose finances were so precarious that it never took off until all the seats were sold.

Once in a while I would lose track of her, but never for long, because she often made midnight calls from pay phones in the middle of nowhere. When, as was frequent, she ran out of change, she would hurriedly give me the number and I'd ring back. Sometimes I didn't know which European city I was dialing. But she was well, she was happy, and if I have never received precise descriptions of the towns in which she stayed and the streets along which she walked, it is not because she didn't want to tell me. It is because Snow White is such an assiduous keeper of journals that all her words go into them. Little is real to her unless she writes it down.

If I were to ask her, for instance, what hiking through the Scottish Highlands is like, she would have to consult one of her journals to find out.

Then one day she came home with a young Australian met in a Dublin bus station (their hands touched as they reached for the same street map), and suddenly I had a son. He had red hair and blue eyes and a gap between his two front teeth, and when I baked bread he pulled a rocker into the kitchen to keep me company. When he wanted Snow White to go to Brisbane with him (he was bent on marriage), I said, "Go, because Australia is a wonderful country and, besides, his kind doesn't come twice."

So she went, but less because of him perhaps than because of Lillian. "She's still taking care of me," she said.

The marriage did not last, but Australia did, and Snow White is there, in Sydney, in a little house furnished mostly with furniture she has found on the street and with my mother's needlepoint pillows. My mother also paints tole trays and little boxes and sends them to her, along with watercolors of Bristol scenes she bought years ago from Bristol's old Women's Exchange. The Women's Exchange, which took consignments only from the certifiably genteel, is where a lot of Bristol matrons bought wedding presents when I was a child. It is strange. Just as I found a semblance of my Uncle Bill on Lanai, so I have found a semblance of Bristol on a continent thirteen thousand miles away. I see my mother with her needle, her canvas, and her skeins of yarn. I see her sitting at a kitchen table, which has been spread with newspapers, drawing a gold line on a black enamel tray with a brush as thin as a hair. When I look at the watercolors, I see Bristol Harbor as it was when I was young, before a factory was built on its south shore and spoiled the vista. I see a dimly recalled gazebo built on a small spit of land not far from our house. I see what Snow White has never seen but what, because she assures me she is psychic ("Lillian came to me the night she died and sat in the rocking chair in my bedroom, and said she would never leave me"), I am convinced she sees anyway.

In Australia I have also found a semblance of myself. It is in my elder daughter. Some children are the spit-and-image of their parents, but usually they are people we have never seen before. It takes only a minute or two to figure that out. But it may take years before we realize that sometimes our children are people unlike any we have ever known. For most of her life I searched for bits and pieces of myself in Snow White, thinking that if I found them we could connect, that we would be like two strips of Velcro finally uniting. But I never found any until she moved to Australia, and then I discovered that my child and I shared the same itchy feet, the same curiosity, the same willingness to wake every morning to a new vista. "You are," she told me a year or so ago, "my favorite traveling companion." Sleeping over pubs because we cannot find a hotel room, taking buses whose destinations we don't quite know, feeding loaves of bread to kangaroos, shivering at the terror that is a Tasmanian Devil and at the glory that is a cockatoo—we are, while in transit, one person.

Recently we were wandering through an amusement park in Melbourne, built in the 1930s and entered through a huge, laughing mouth. Around the perimeter was a roller coaster, its dips so gentle we thought it worth daring (neither of us looks for things that might frighten us, because we know too well that they are looking for us). But when we went up to the booth for tickets, we were told the roller coaster was temporarily out of order.

How I had wanted that ride on the roller coaster, not so much for the journey itself but because it would, in a sense, bring us full circle! Here we would be, my baby and I, side by side again and, as in the years when her life was bounded by a room with bunny wallpaper, a rundown park with rubber swings, and a mother who, whatever her faults, was always good for a bedtime story, looking in the same direction.

My disappointment was erased the next morning, though, when Snow White came to my hotel to pick me up for the ride to the airport. It was very early, so I was sitting in bed sipping coffee and reading the newspaper. She slid in next to me, picked up the section I had finished, and, the paper still in her hand, dozed off, with her head resting on my shoulder.

When she was born I cried, because until that moment I hadn't realized that in giving her life I was also giving her death. I wanted her back in my womb so that I could keep her safe and warm for as long as I lived. Now, her sleeping head against my shoulder, she was safe and warm again, and once more I was pregnant with my first-born.

It is easy to write about sorrow dry-eyed, but not about joy. When I remember that morning in Melbourne, my eyes get wet, but no more so than they do when I am watching Fred Astaire dancing. It is happiness that makes me cry, happiness and maybe some kind of as yet undiscovered gene that's handed down from Celt to Celt and sometimes makes weepers of us all. "Ah, Mary Lee," my father said when I was sobbing over my introduction to "Sailing to Byzantium," "you're a sentimental Irishman, just like your old man." Ah, Papa, you were right.

Rose Red I have met before, mostly in my grandmother. At her christening she was given my grandmother's name and, with it, her tenacity and self-discipline and impatience with what Rose Red calls the "artsy-fartsy" and what Ganny called "nonsense." In my childhood, Ganny cured my occasional sadness by taking me to play bingo and tour our town's five-and-ten. In my adulthood, Rose Red does it by dragging me to Bloomingdale's and Saks Fifth Avenue. "I think my mother could use a brighter blush," she says to the woman at the cosmetics counter, and I extend a docile cheek.

She loves books and movies, but, unlike me, she does not look to them for wisdom, only amusement. For instruction she goes directly to life itself, and it is life that she is forever steering me toward. There is something of my father in her, too. Like him, she expects a lot from me, courage mostly, and if I have ever been brave it is because she has forced me to be. Knowing her, I now believe that the greatest favor one can do people is to ask of them more than they think they can give.

The day she married I thought to find her nervous, frightened even, as I was on my wedding day. But the only nervous person walking down the aisle was I, coupled once more with her father. She had a swan's serenity. I, while we delivered her to her fiancé and the judge who performed the ceremony, was fighting tears until I sat down and reached for Snow White's hand.

Still, despite all that Rose Red has done to show me what matters and what does not, I remain confused. My head is so crowded with long-ago images and concluded conversations that I cannot shut the lid on myself. Some people marvel at my memory; others, novelists usually, distrust my ilk. They believe that those of us who write memoirs are, in truth, writing fiction. "How," they ask, "can these people *remember* so much?" But we can. In fact, we cannot always see the present until it is the past, which means that, although some part of our brain is observing and preserving the moment, we are not truly living it. Years later, though, it will be resurrected, more often than not without our willing it. "I write," I've told those who've cared to inquire, "because I have mud between my ears, and writing is my way of making things clear." But the statement is inaccurate. It is not mud but a logjam that is between my ears.

Twice the logjam exploded and set my mind to moving as smoothly as a river. The first time was when I had Rocky Mountain spotted fever and thought I might die. The second time was recently when, again, I thought I might die. My response to both scares was the same. "My duty was done," I have written of the fever, "and the last thing I would see with earth's eyes was my daughters, my descendants, growing like trees."

Even so, something was different about the second terror. There was no balding man to wonder whether or not to call. He was dead. Nor, although I would have liked to speak to him, did I think of calling B. He has always been very much on my mind, but I suspect I disappeared from his many years ago. What could we have possibly said to each other? Unlike those people with whom I had laughed and chatted and, yes, communed while I was roaming around the world, he was not a stranger. Ergo, communication, above all communion, was impossible. We knew each other too well.

Instead, I turned off the ringer on my phone, was cheerful for the sake of the few people I had told about my illness, and spent most of the time; day and night, staring out my hospital window. The room was high up, on the fourteenth floor, I think, and all I saw was a sky into which intruded the spires of several buildings and the occasional small plane. There were books I could have read and magazines scattered at the foot of my bed, but morphine had me slightly dozy, the way I am just before I settle down for sleep. So I drew out the long gray ribbon, the one with the brightly colored blocks with which I so often amuse myself. One of the blocks, one I had not examined for many years, was of the day soon after college graduation when I emerged from a train into Grand Central Terminal, a leather-cased Smith Corona portable in one hand and a suitcaseful of unsuitable—old Bermuda shorts, Brooks Brothers shirts, a gingham skirt, and a dress for after-football cocktail parties—clothes in the other. That was the day, I realized on the instant, that I embraced my true bridegroom. That was the day I married New York.

# FOR THE BEST IN PAPERBACKS, LOOK FOR THE

In every corner of the world, on every subject under the sun, Penguin represents quality and variety—the very best in publishing today.

For complete information about books available from Penguin—including Puffins, Penguin Classics, and Arkana—and how to order them, write to us at the appropriate address below. Please note that for copyright reasons the selection of books varies from country to country.

---

**In the United Kingdom:** Please write to *Dept. EP, Penguin Books Ltd, Bath Road, Harmondsworth, West Drayton, Middlesex UB7 0DA.*

**In the United States:** Please write to *Penguin Putnam Inc., P.O. Box 12289 Dept. B, Newark, New Jersey 07101-5289* or call 1-800-788-6262.

**In Canada:** Please write to *Penguin Books Canada Ltd, 10 Alcorn Avenue, Suite 300, Toronto, Ontario M4V 3B2.*

**In Australia:** Please write to *Penguin Books Australia Ltd, P.O. Box 257, Ringwood, Victoria 3134.*

**In New Zealand:** Please write to *Penguin Books (NZ) Ltd, Private Bag 102902, North Shore Mail Centre, Auckland 10.*

**In India:** Please write to *Penguin Books India Pvt Ltd, 11 Panchsheel Shopping Centre, Panchsheel Park, New Delhi 110 017.*

**In the Netherlands:** Please write to *Penguin Books Netherlands bv, Postbus 3507, NL-1001 AH Amsterdam.*

**In Germany:** Please write to *Penguin Books Deutschland GmbH, Metzlerstrasse 26, 60594 Frankfurt am Main.*

**In Spain:** Please write to *Penguin Books S. A., Bravo Murillo 19, 1° B, 28015 Madrid.*

**In Italy:** Please write to *Penguin Italia s.r.l., Via Benedetto Croce 2, 20094 Corsico, Milano.*

**In France:** Please write to *Penguin France, Le Carré Wilson, 62 rue Benjamin Baillaud, 31500 Toulouse.*

**In Japan:** Please write to *Penguin Books Japan Ltd, Kaneko Building, 2-3-25 Koraku, Bunkyo-Ku, Tokyo 112.*

**In South Africa:** Please write to *Penguin Books South Africa (Pty) Ltd, Private Bag X14, Parkview, 2122 Johannesburg.*